# MODEL: SIX

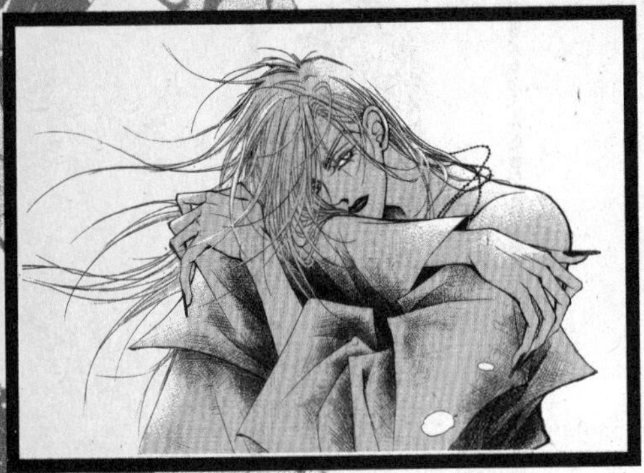

**MICHAEL**
A Vampire. He has agreed to model for Jae, but she'll pay for his beauty...with blood.

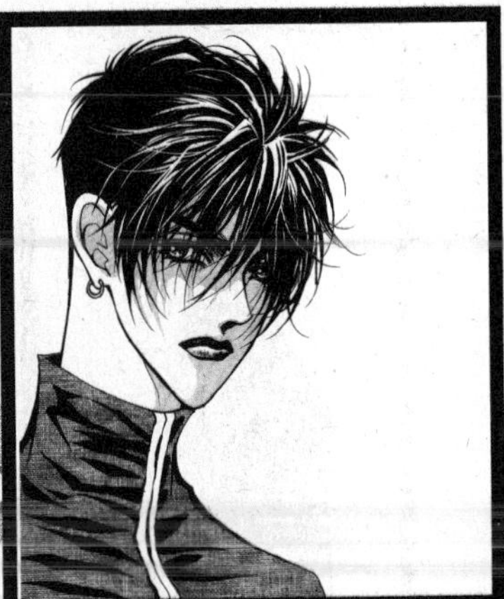

**KEN**
A Youth. A member of the household who may, or may not, be Michael's prodigal son.

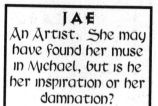

**JAE**
An Artist. She may have found her muse in Michael, but is he her inspiration or her damnation?

**EVA**
The Housekeeper. She serves only Michael. But she hasn't always called the Vampire "Master."

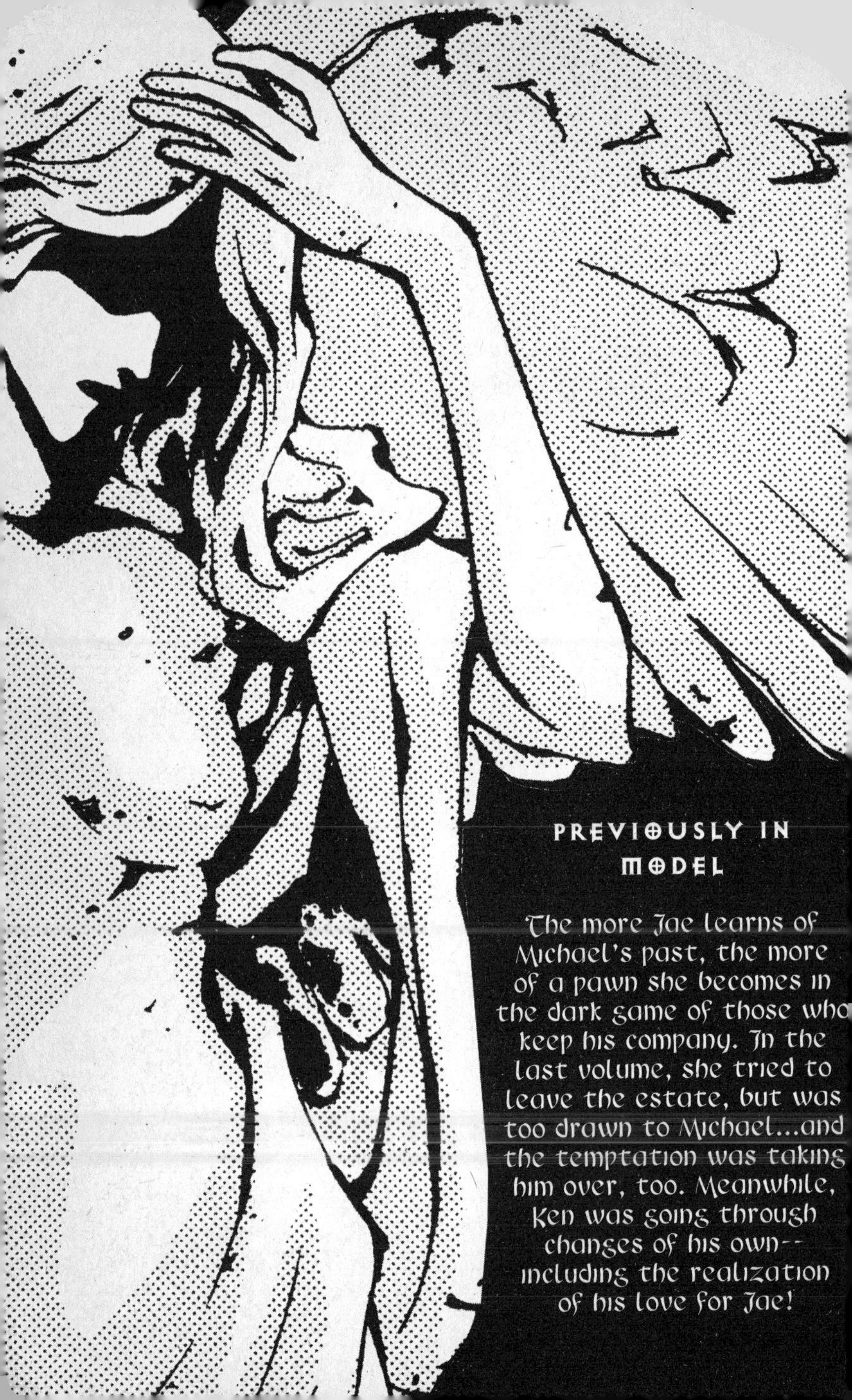

## PREVIOUSLY IN MODEL

The more Jae learns of Michael's past, the more of a pawn she becomes in the dark game of those who keep his company. In the last volume, she tried to leave the estate, but was too drawn to Michael...and the temptation was taking him over, too. Meanwhile, Ken was going through changes of his own--including the realization of his love for Jae!

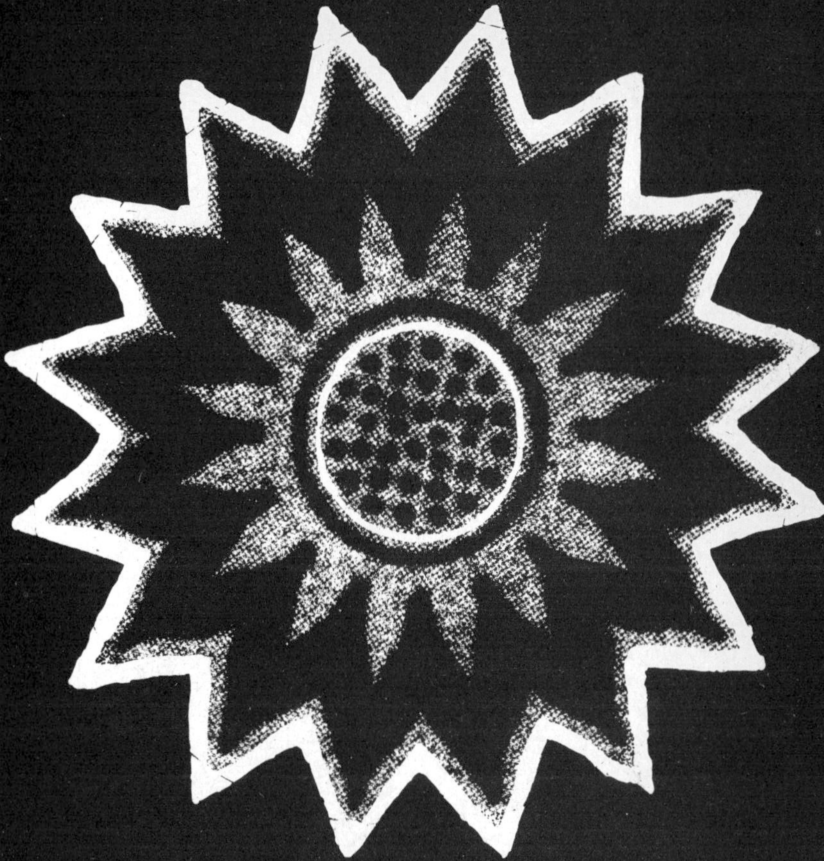

# MODEL

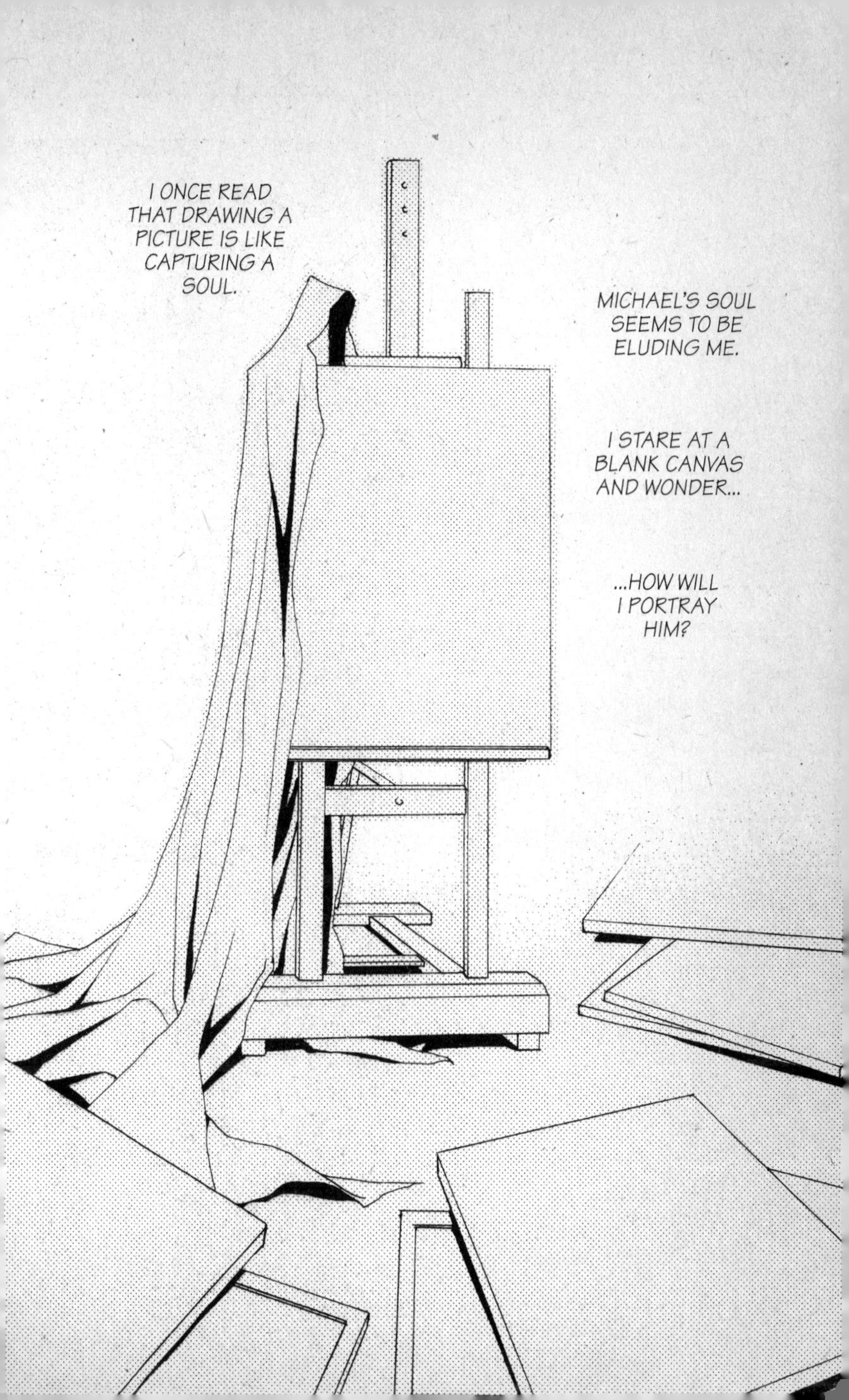
I ONCE READ THAT DRAWING A PICTURE IS LIKE CAPTURING A SOUL.
MICHAEL'S SOUL SEEMS TO BE ELUDING ME.
I STARE AT A BLANK CANVAS AND WONDER...
...HOW WILL I PORTRAY HIM?

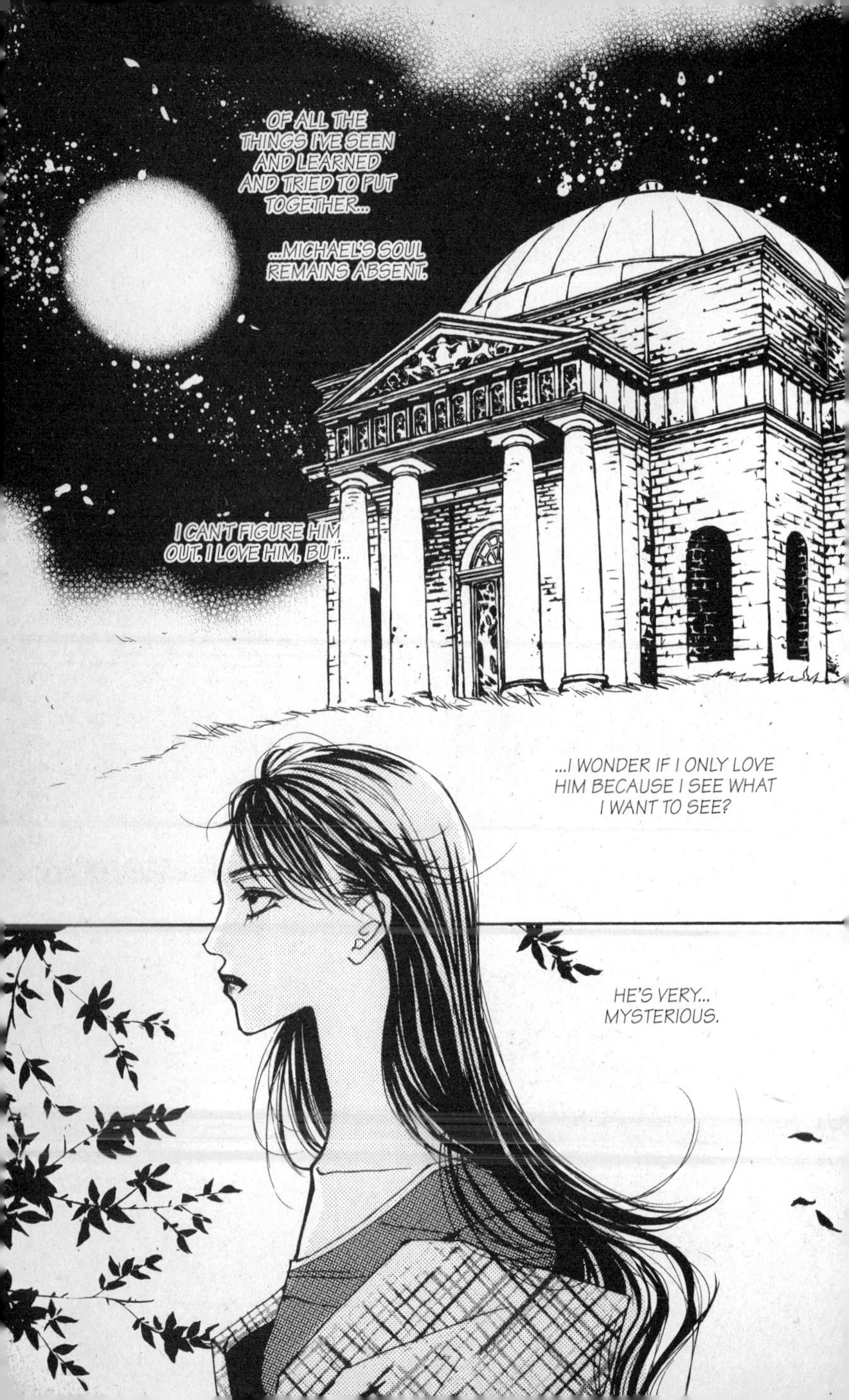
OF ALL THE THINGS I'VE SEEN AND LEARNED AND TRIED TO PUT TOGETHER...
...MICHAEL'S SOUL REMAINS ABSENT.
I CAN'T FIGURE HIM OUT. I LOVE HIM, BUT...
...I WONDER IF I ONLY LOVE HIM BECAUSE I SEE WHAT I WANT TO SEE?
HE'S VERY... MYSTERIOUS.

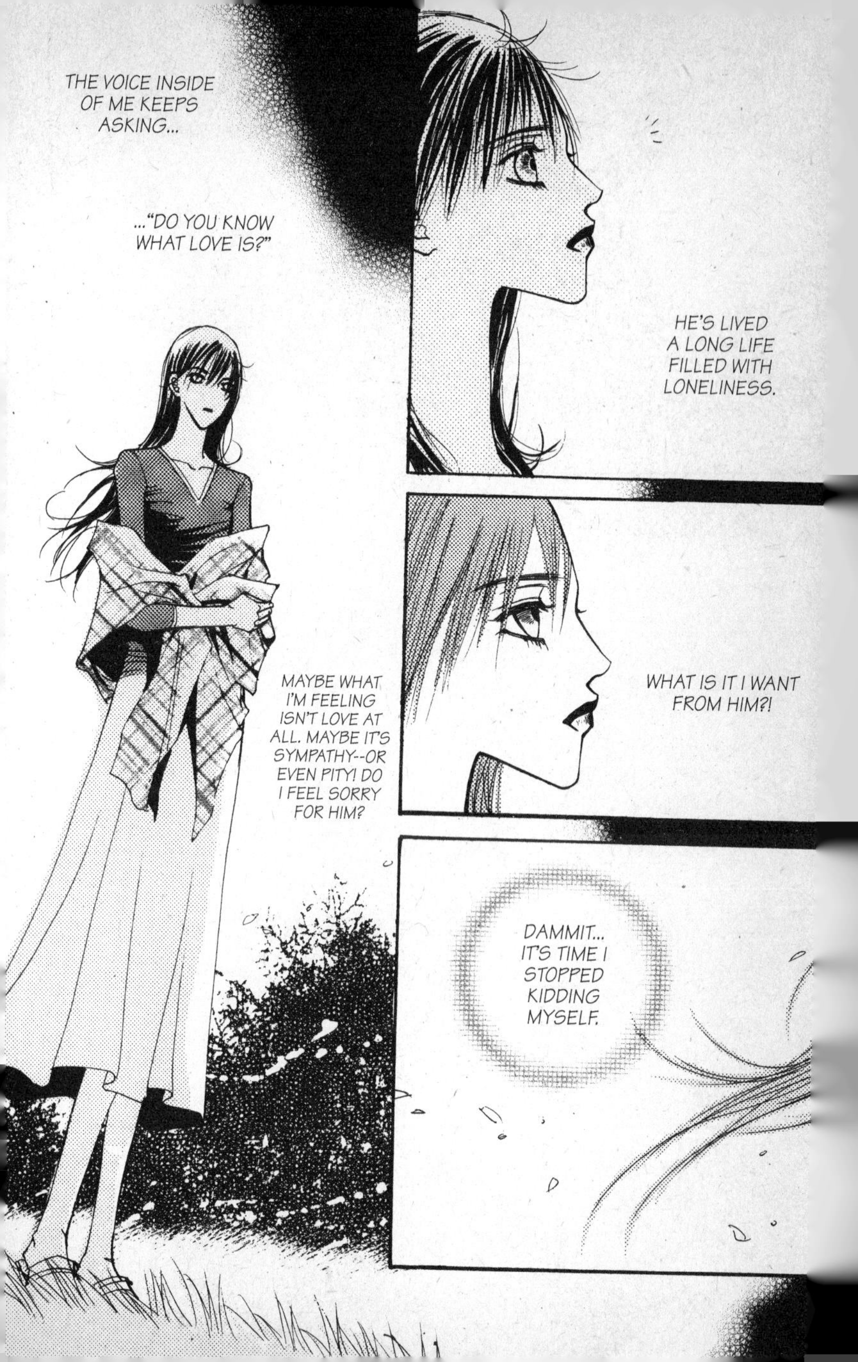
HE'S LIVED A LONG LIFE FILLED WITH LONELINESS.
WHAT IS IT I WANT FROM HIM?!
DAMMIT... IT'S TIME I STOPPED KIDDING MYSELF.
THE VOICE INSIDE OF ME KEEPS ASKING...
..."DO YOU KNOW WHAT LOVE IS?"
MAYBE WHAT I'M FEELING ISN'T LOVE AT ALL. MAYBE IT'S SYMPATHY--OR EVEN PITY! DO I FEEL SORRY FOR HIM?

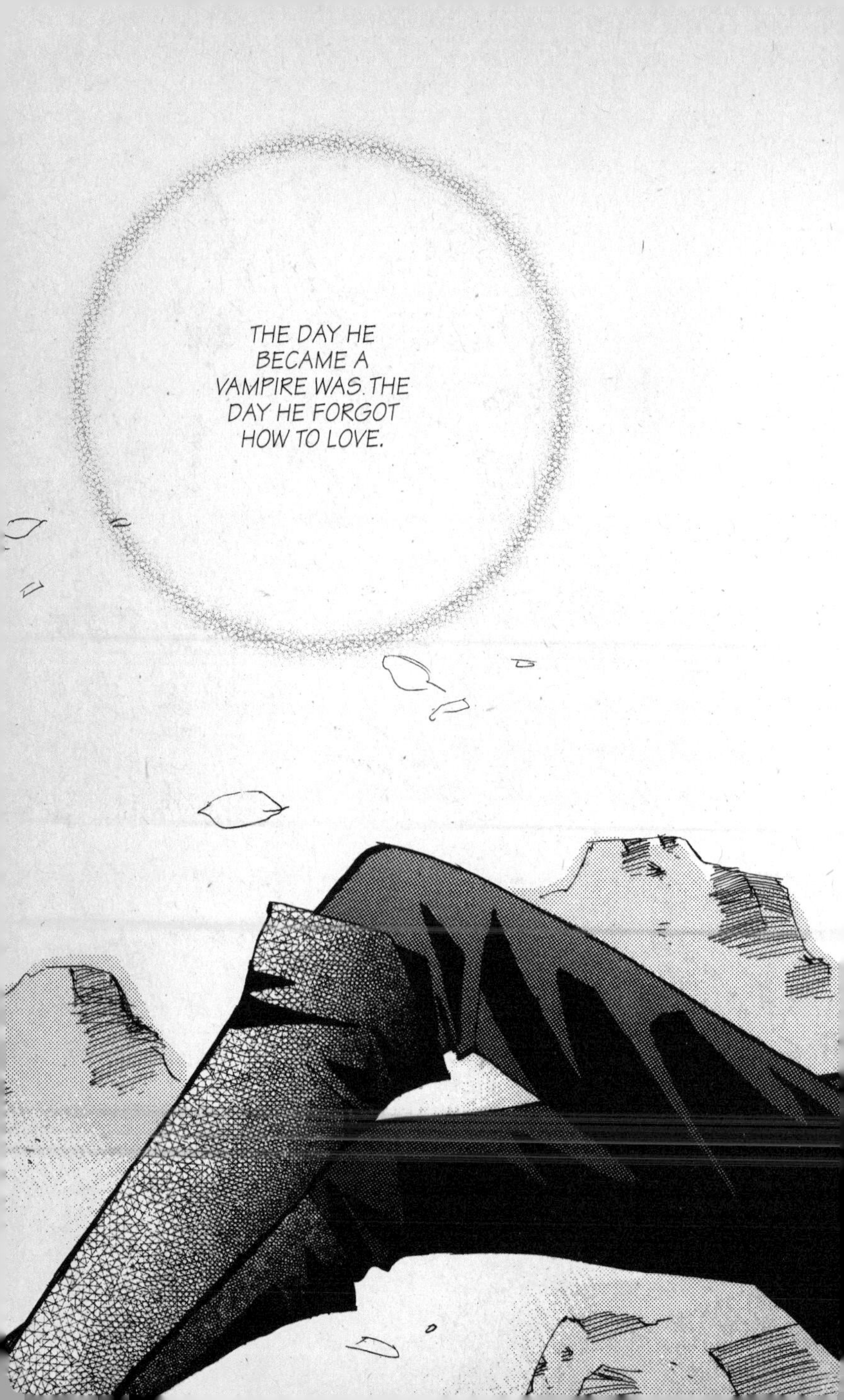
THE DAY HE BECAME A VAMPIRE WAS THE DAY HE FORGOT HOW TO LOVE.

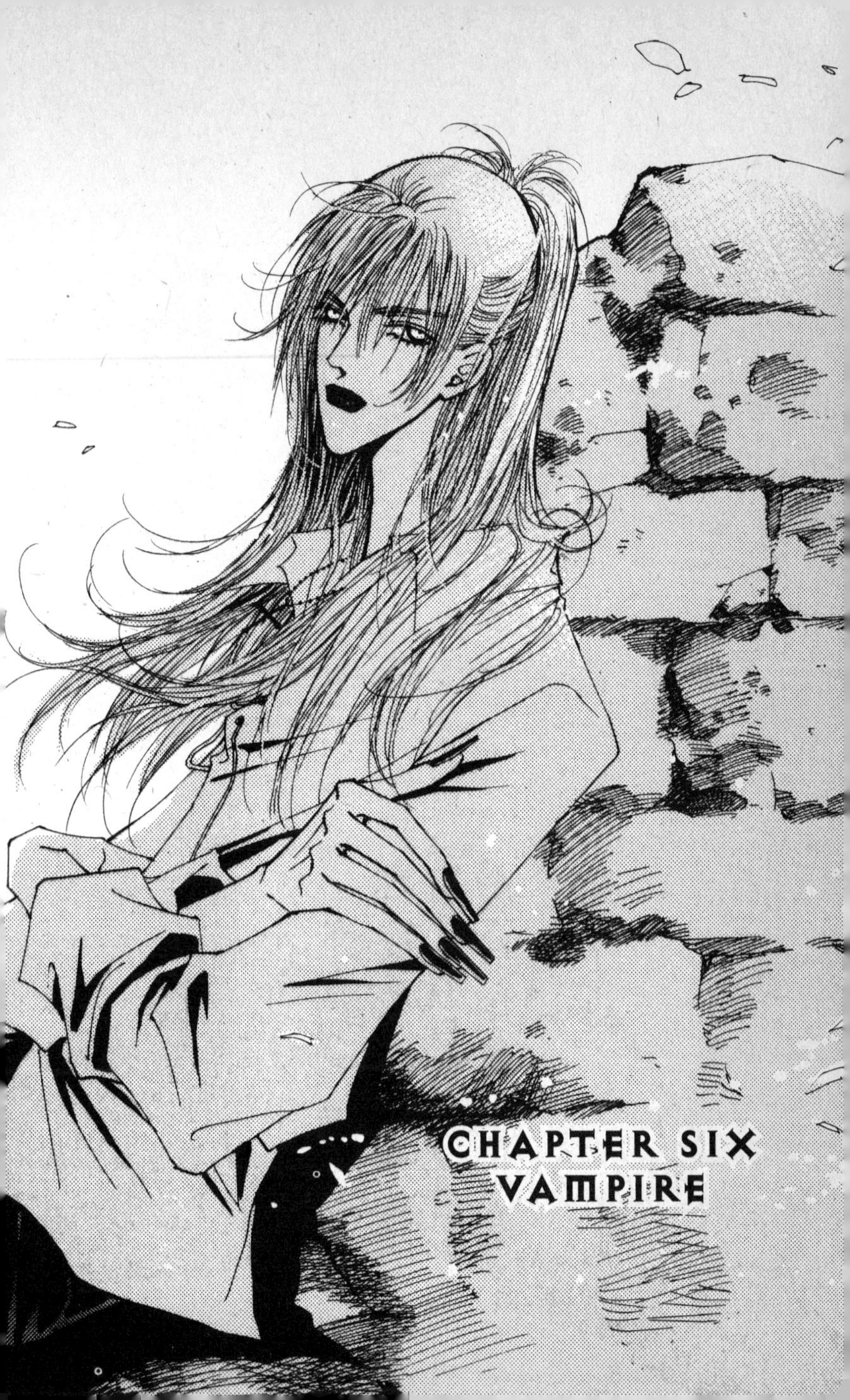
CHAPTER SIX
VAMPIRE

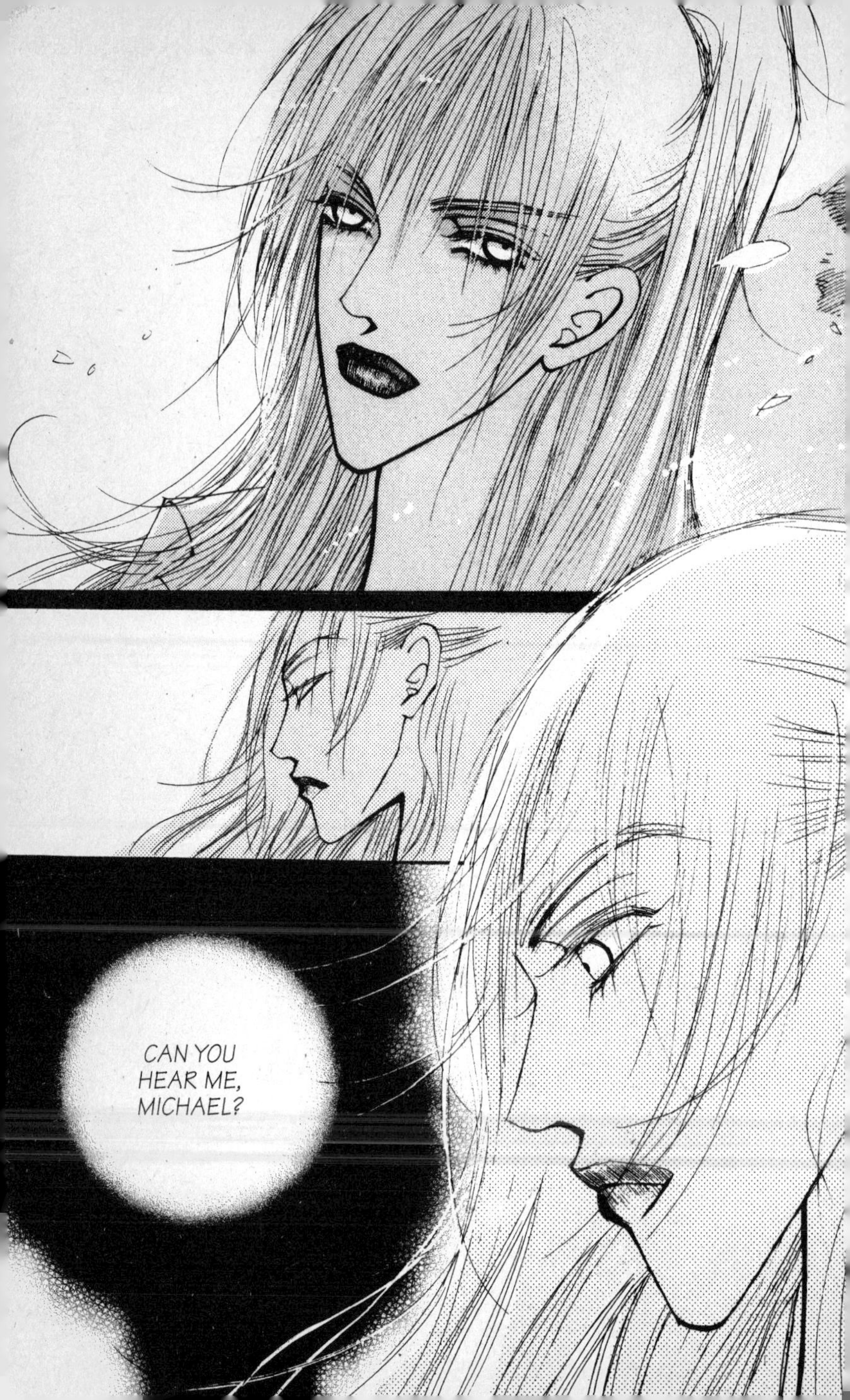
CAN YOU
HEAR ME,
MICHAEL?

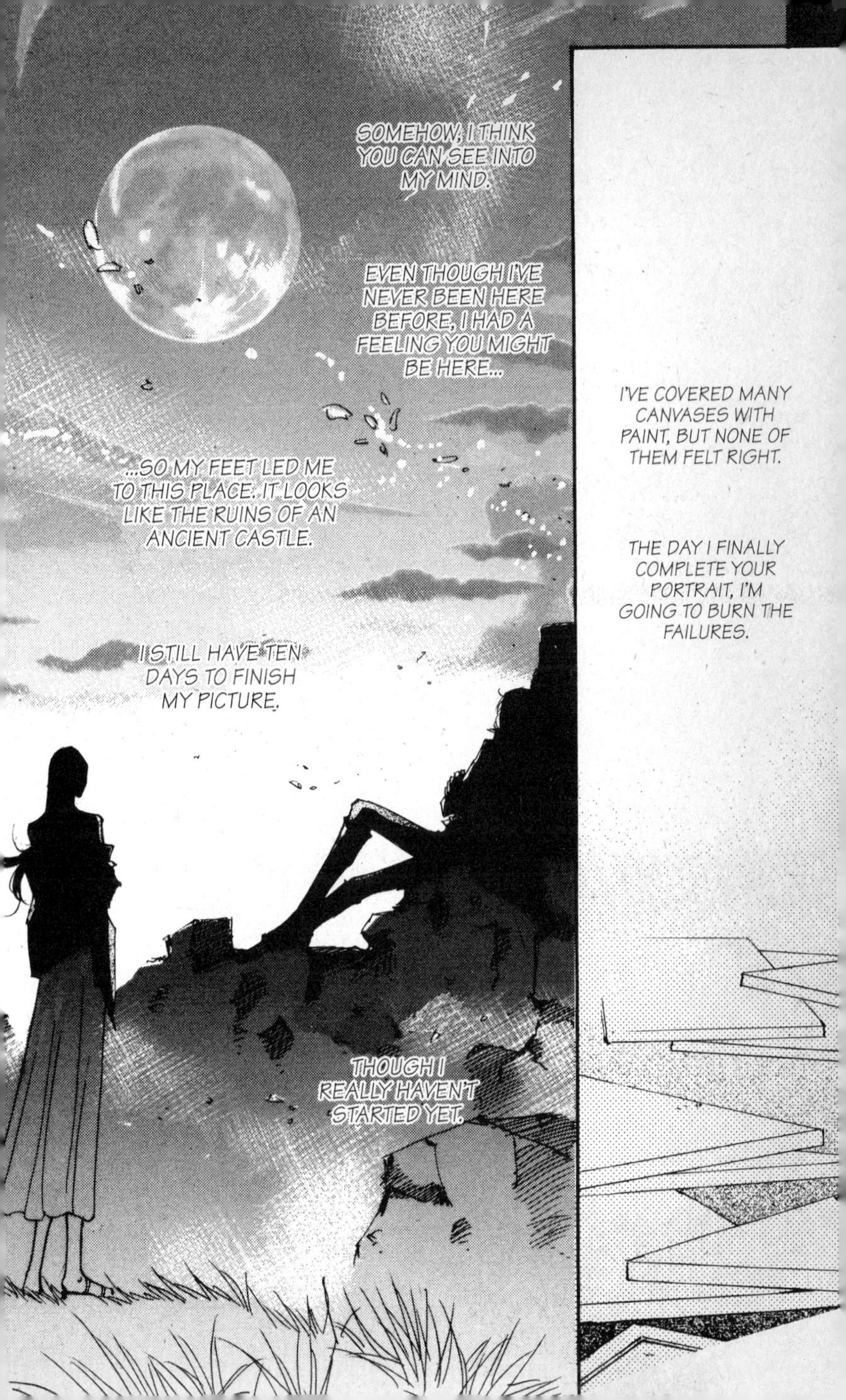
SOMEHOW, I THINK YOU CAN SEE INTO MY MIND.
EVEN THOUGH I'VE NEVER BEEN HERE BEFORE, I HAD A FEELING YOU MIGHT BE HERE...
...SO MY FEET LED ME TO THIS PLACE. IT LOOKS LIKE THE RUINS OF AN ANCIENT CASTLE.
I STILL HAVE TEN DAYS TO FINISH MY PICTURE.
THOUGH I REALLY HAVEN'T STARTED YET.
I'VE COVERED MANY CANVASES WITH PAINT, BUT NONE OF THEM FELT RIGHT.
THE DAY I FINALLY COMPLETE YOUR PORTRAIT, I'M GOING TO BURN THE FAILURES.

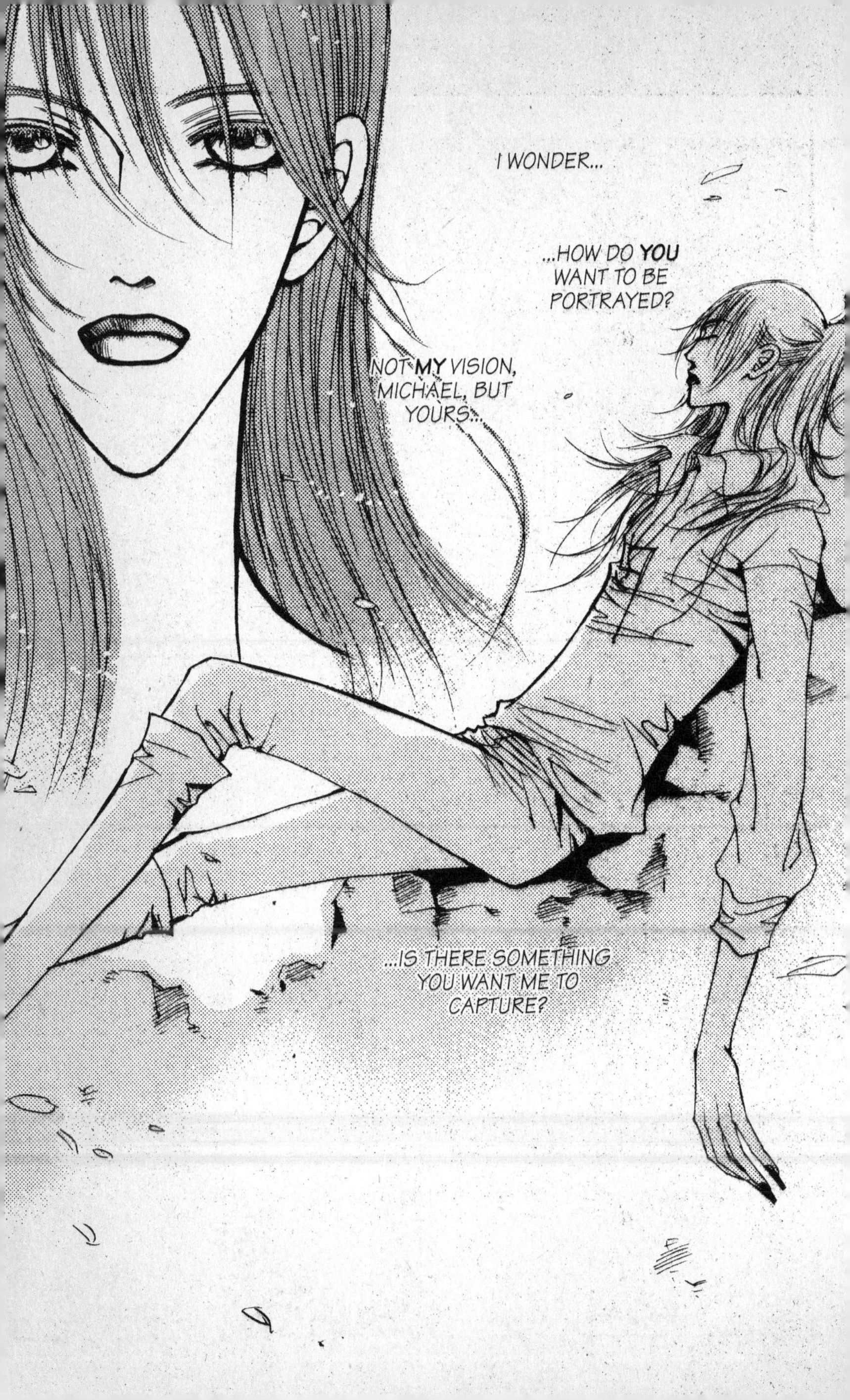
I WONDER...
...HOW DO YOU WANT TO BE PORTRAYED?
NOT MY VISION, MICHAEL, BUT YOURS...
...IS THERE SOMETHING YOU WANT ME TO CAPTURE?

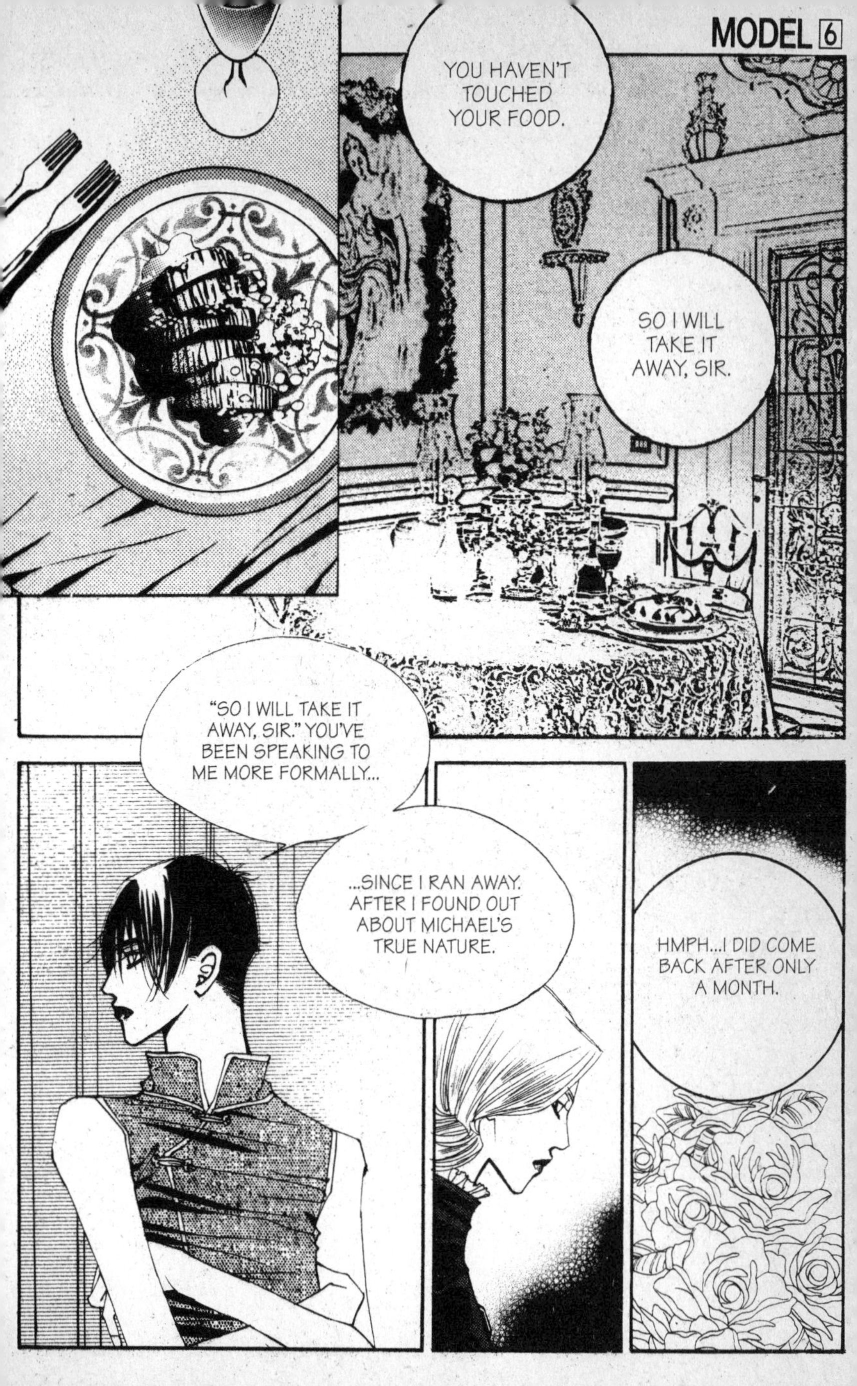
YOU HAVEN'T TOUCHED YOUR FOOD.
SO I WILL TAKE IT AWAY, SIR.
"SO I WILL TAKE IT AWAY, SIR." YOU'VE BEEN SPEAKING TO ME MORE FORMALLY...
...SINCE I RAN AWAY. AFTER I FOUND OUT ABOUT MICHAEL'S TRUE NATURE.
HMPH...I DID COME BACK AFTER ONLY A MONTH.

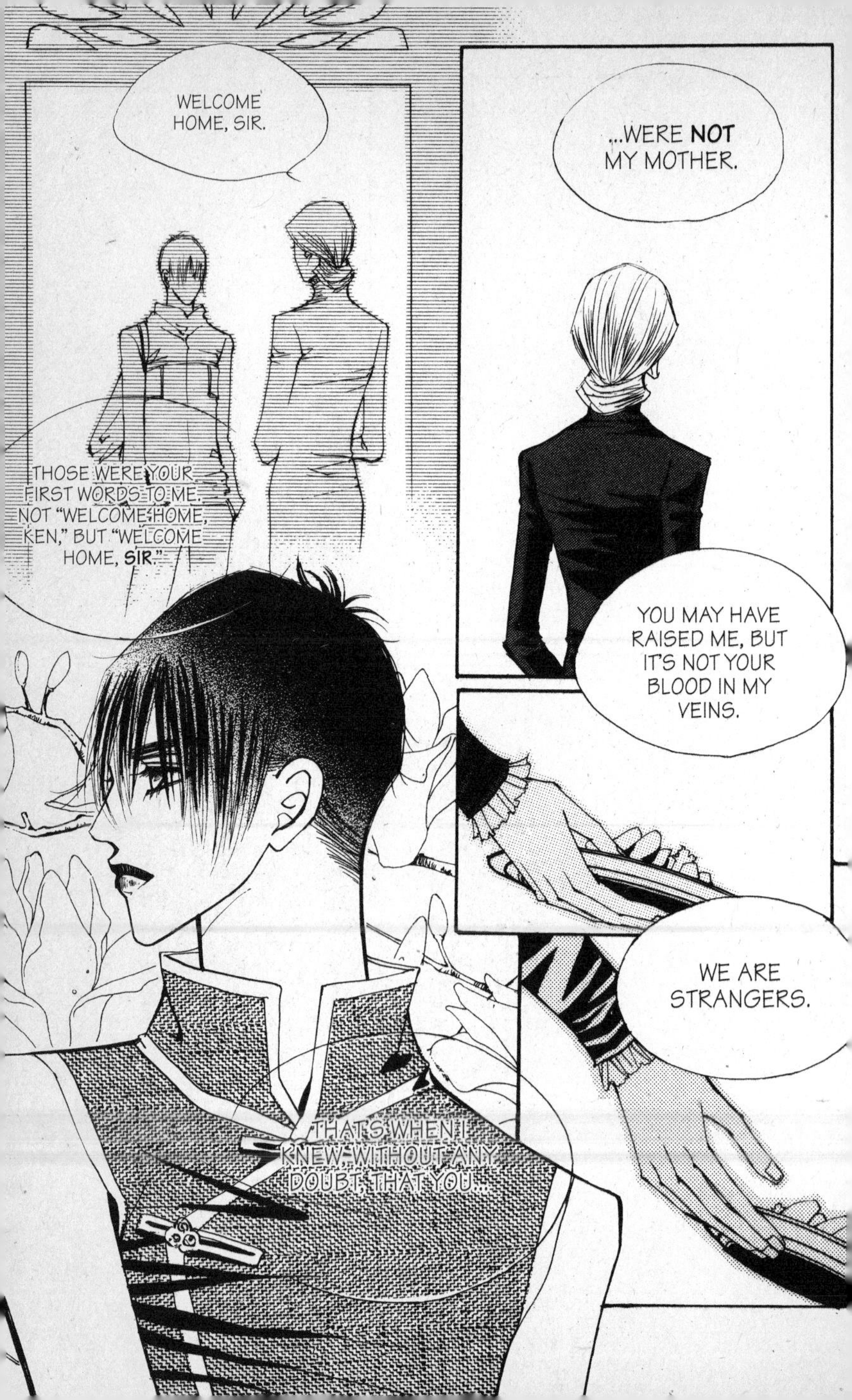
WELCOME HOME, SIR.
THOSE WERE YOUR FIRST WORDS TO ME. NOT "WELCOME HOME, KEN," BUT "WELCOME HOME, **SIR**."
THAT'S WHEN I KNEW, WITHOUT ANY DOUBT, THAT YOU...
...WERE **NOT** MY MOTHER.
YOU MAY HAVE RAISED ME, BUT IT'S NOT YOUR BLOOD IN MY VEINS.
WE ARE STRANGERS.

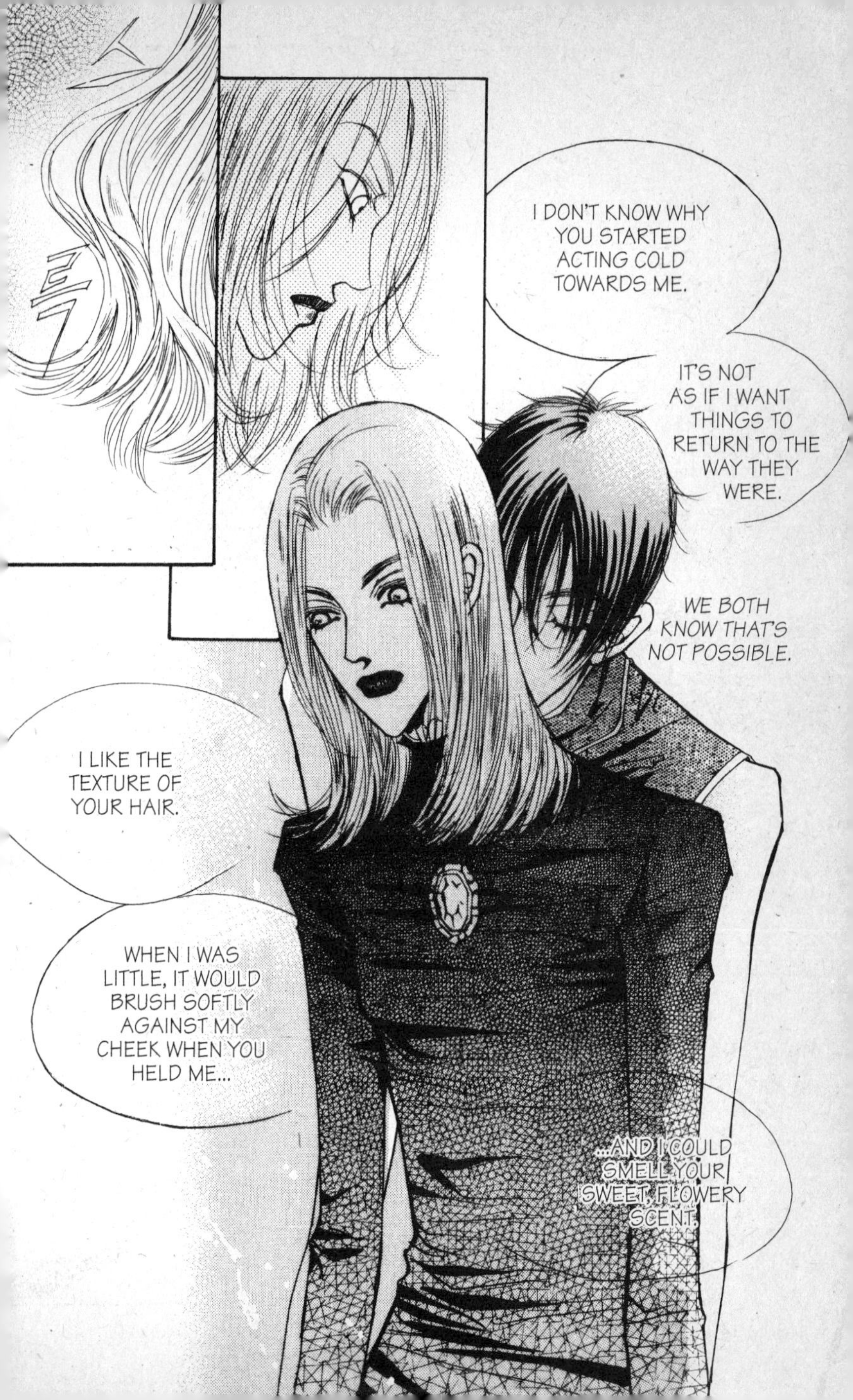
I DON'T KNOW WHY YOU STARTED ACTING COLD TOWARDS ME.
IT'S NOT AS IF I WANT THINGS TO RETURN TO THE WAY THEY WERE.
WE BOTH KNOW THAT'S NOT POSSIBLE.
I LIKE THE TEXTURE OF YOUR HAIR.
WHEN I WAS LITTLE, IT WOULD BRUSH SOFTLY AGAINST MY CHEEK WHEN YOU HELD ME...
...AND I COULD SMELL YOUR SWEET, FLOWERY SCENT.

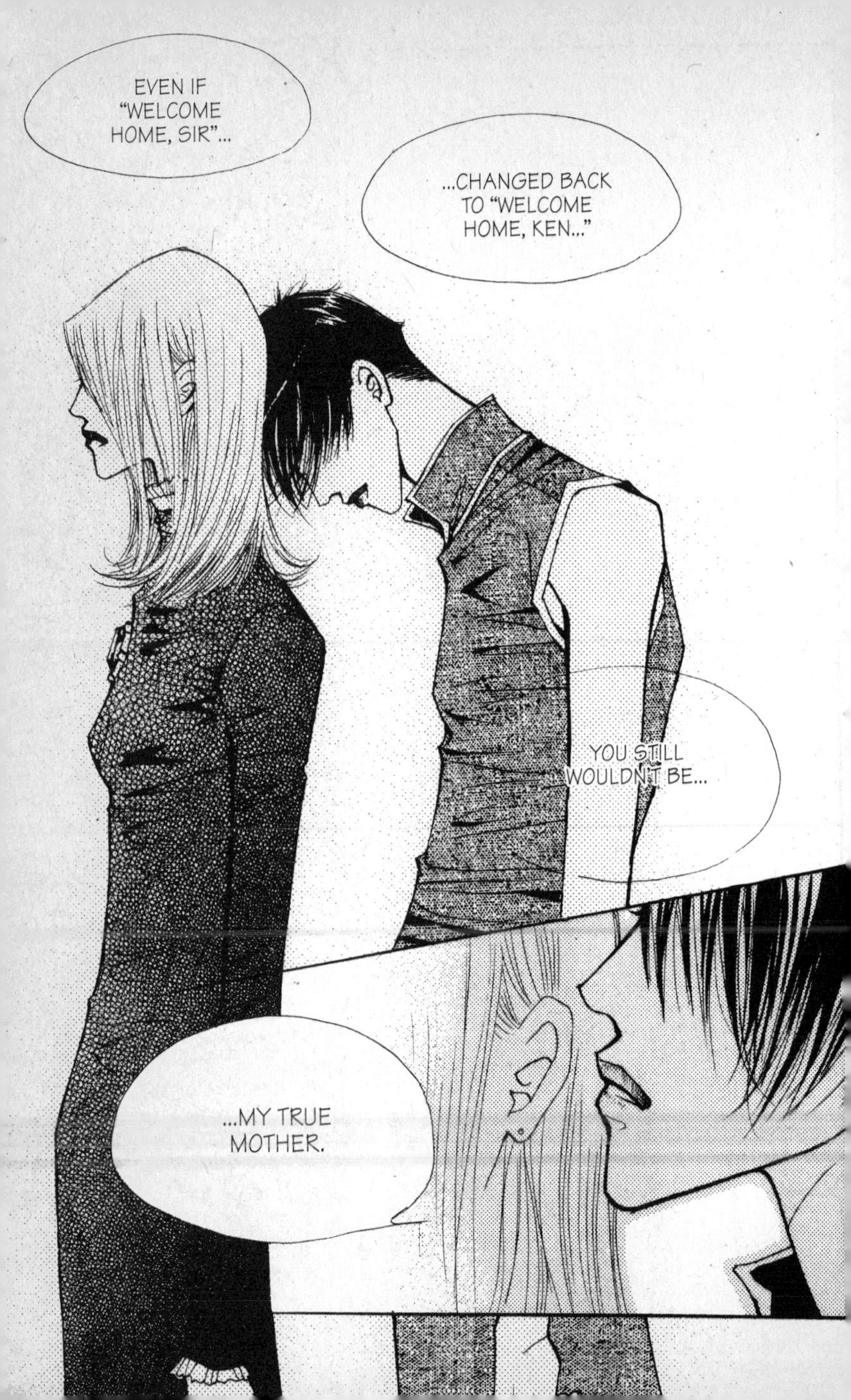
EVEN IF "WELCOME HOME, SIR"...
...CHANGED BACK TO "WELCOME HOME, KEN..."
YOU STILL WOULDN'T BE...
...MY TRUE MOTHER.

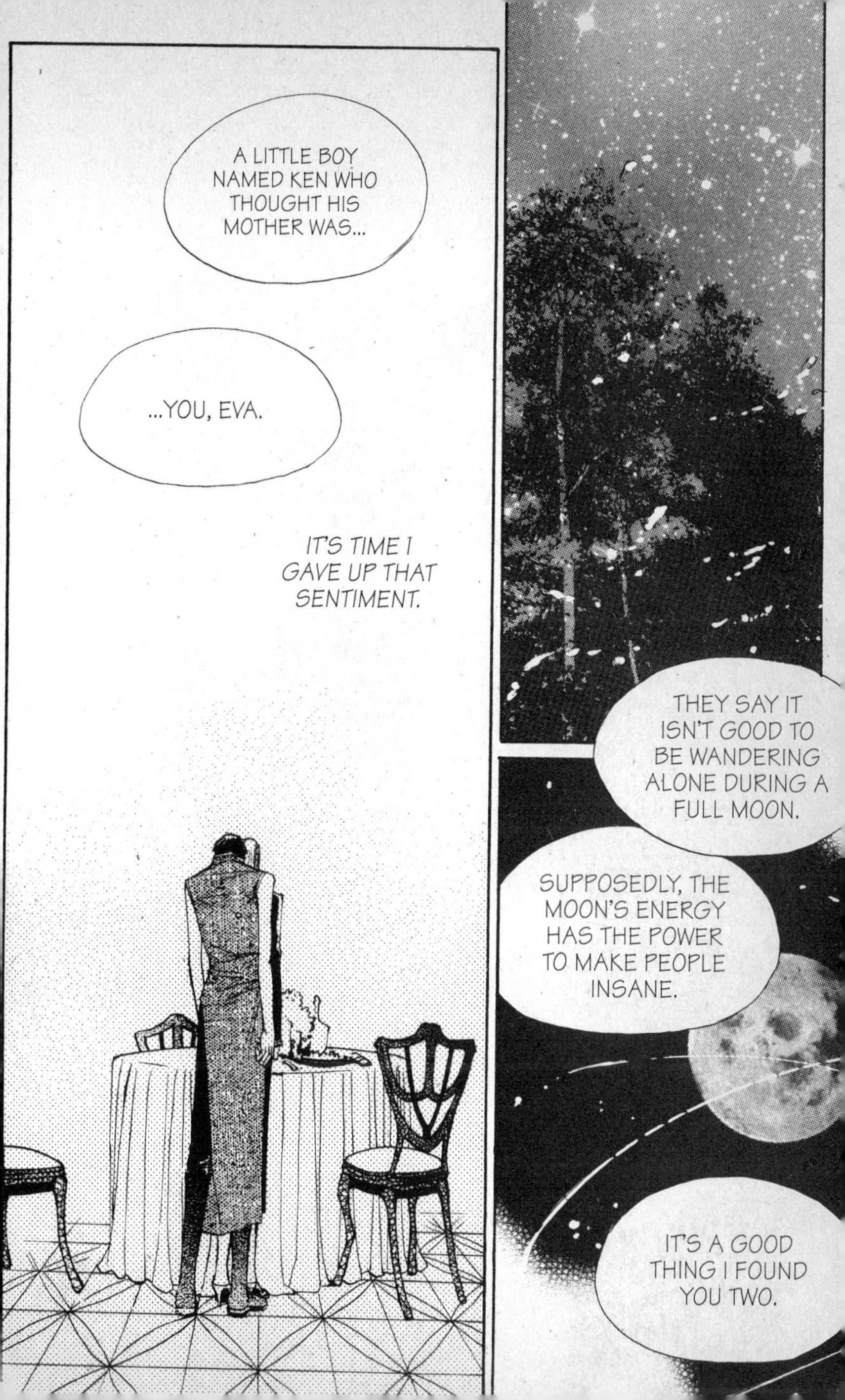
THEY SAY IT ISN'T GOOD TO BE WANDERING ALONE DURING A FULL MOON.
SUPPOSEDLY, THE MOON'S ENERGY HAS THE POWER TO MAKE PEOPLE INSANE.
IT'S A GOOD THING I FOUND YOU TWO.
A LITTLE BOY NAMED KEN WHO THOUGHT HIS MOTHER WAS...
...YOU, EVA.
IT'S TIME I GAVE UP THAT SENTIMENT.

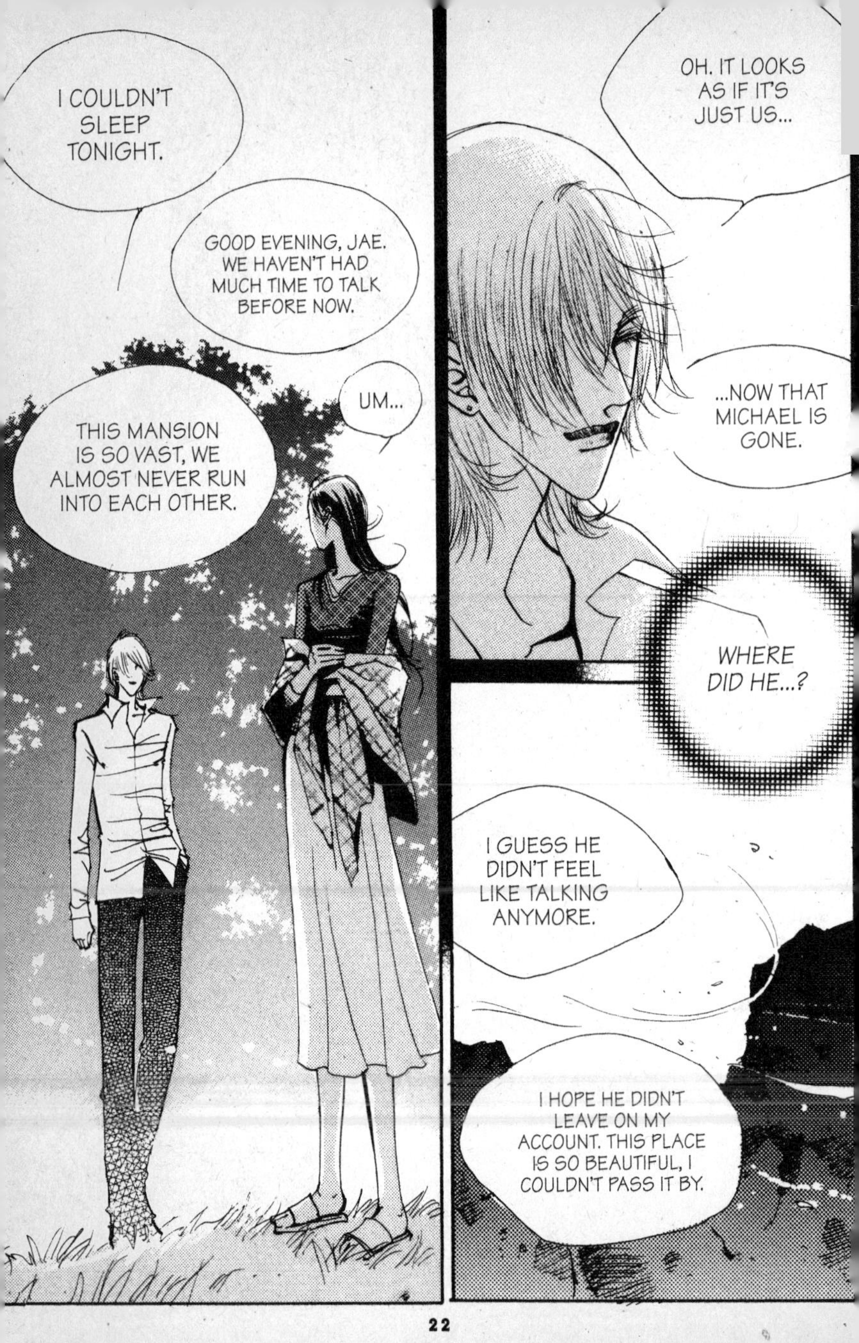
I COULDN'T SLEEP TONIGHT.
GOOD EVENING, JAE. WE HAVEN'T HAD MUCH TIME TO TALK BEFORE NOW.
UM...
THIS MANSION IS SO VAST, WE ALMOST NEVER RUN INTO EACH OTHER.
OH. IT LOOKS AS IF IT'S JUST US...
...NOW THAT MICHAEL IS GONE.
WHERE DID HE...?
I GUESS HE DIDN'T FEEL LIKE TALKING ANYMORE.
I HOPE HE DIDN'T LEAVE ON MY ACCOUNT. THIS PLACE IS SO BEAUTIFUL, I COULDN'T PASS IT BY.

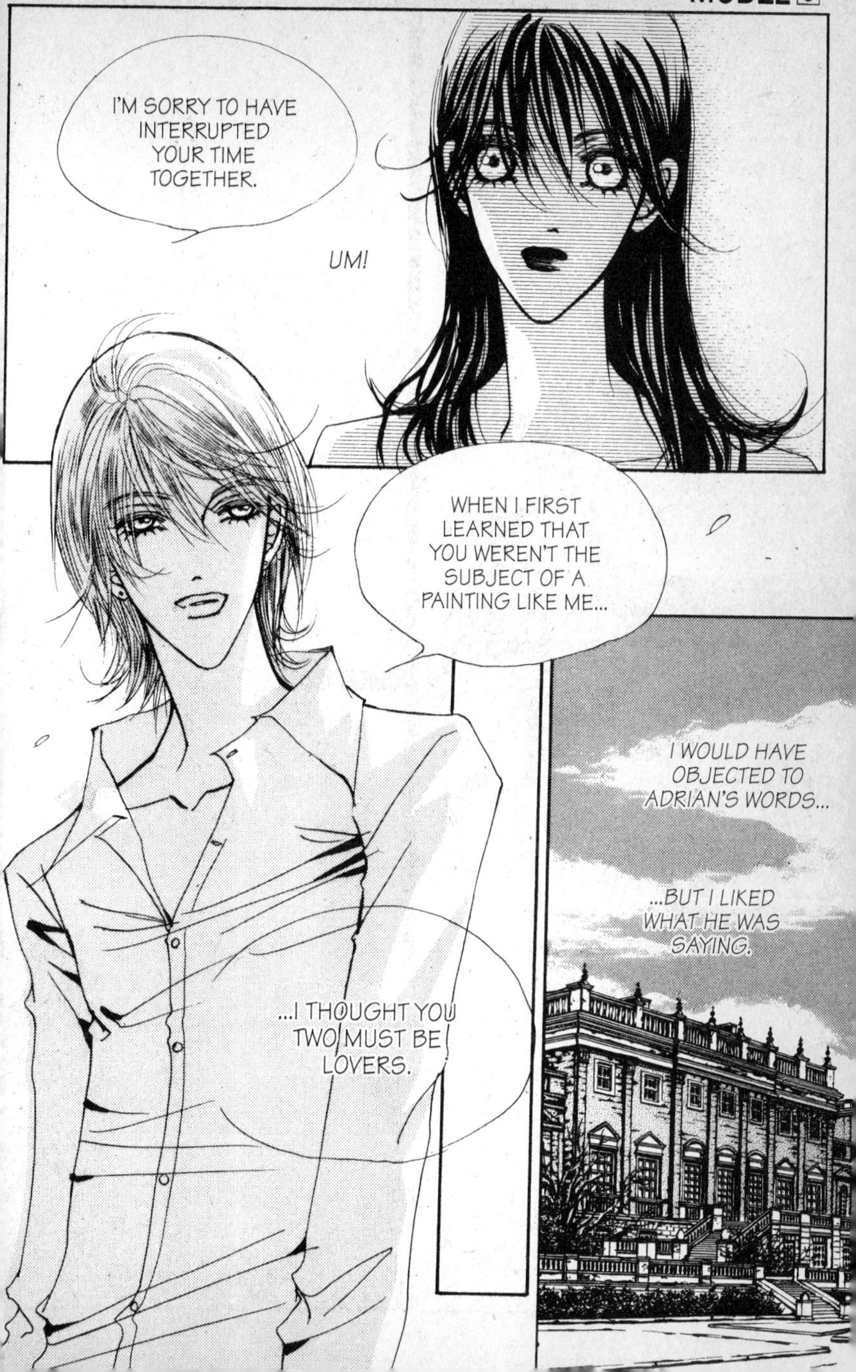
I'M SORRY TO HAVE INTERRUPTED YOUR TIME TOGETHER.
UM!
WHEN I FIRST LEARNED THAT YOU WEREN'T THE SUBJECT OF A PAINTING LIKE ME...
...I THOUGHT YOU TWO MUST BE LOVERS.
I WOULD HAVE OBJECTED TO ADRIAN'S WORDS...
...BUT I LIKED WHAT HE WAS SAYING.

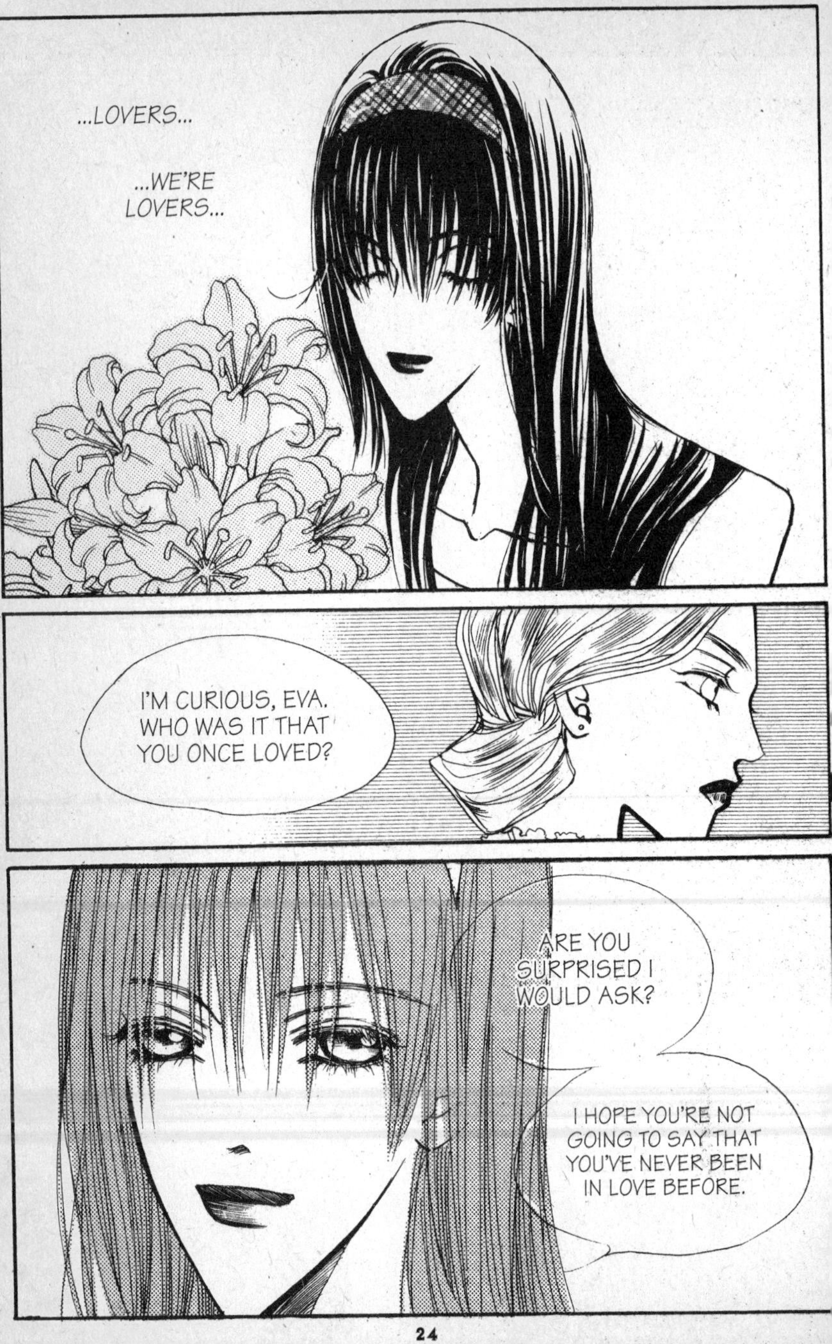
...LOVERS...
...WE'RE LOVERS...
I'M CURIOUS, EVA. WHO WAS IT THAT YOU ONCE LOVED?
ARE YOU SURPRISED I WOULD ASK?
I HOPE YOU'RE NOT GOING TO SAY THAT YOU'VE NEVER BEEN IN LOVE BEFORE.

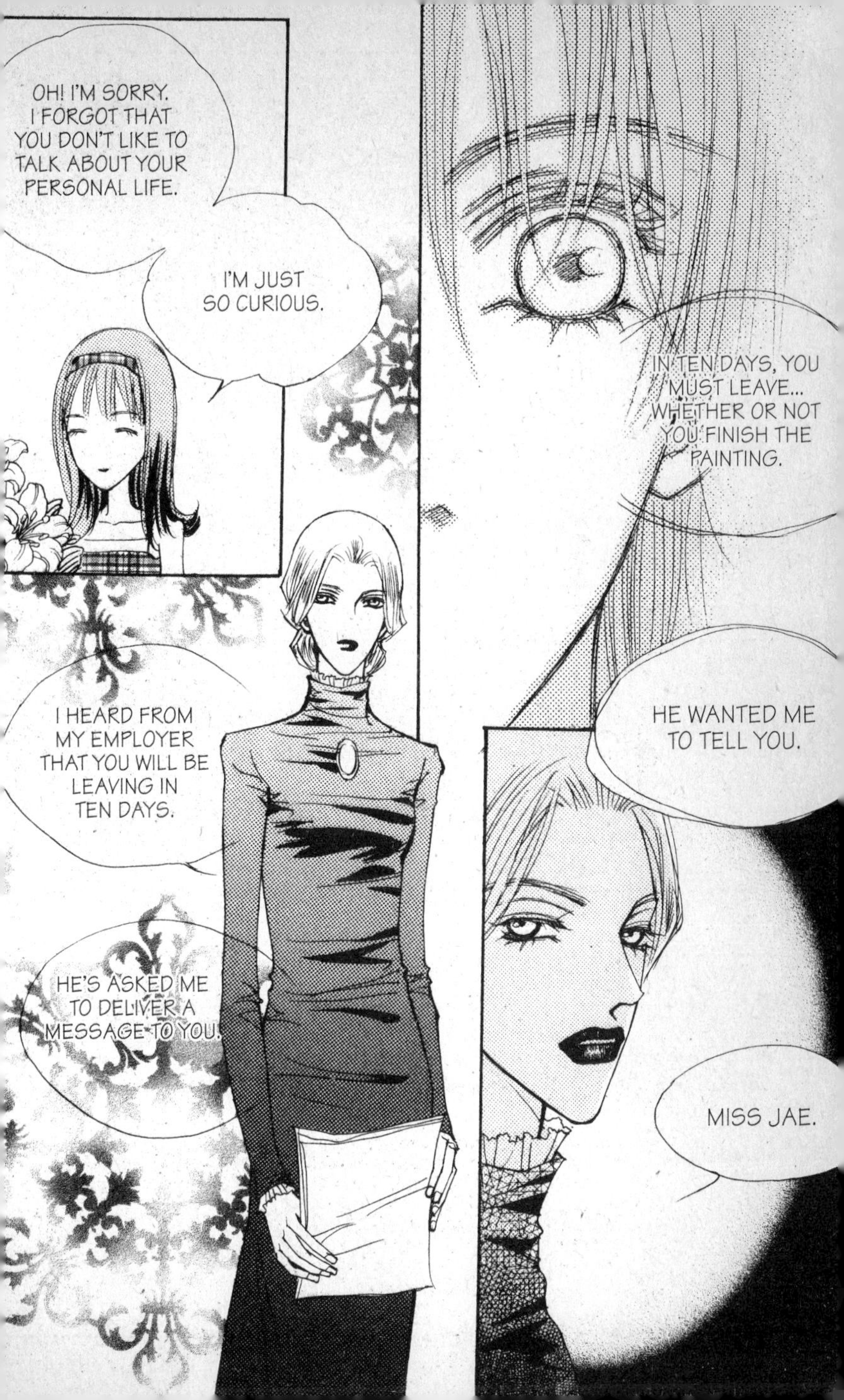
OH! I'M SORRY. I FORGOT THAT YOU DON'T LIKE TO TALK ABOUT YOUR PERSONAL LIFE.
I'M JUST SO CURIOUS.
I HEARD FROM MY EMPLOYER THAT YOU WILL BE LEAVING IN TEN DAYS.
HE'S ASKED ME TO DELIVER A MESSAGE TO YOU.
IN TEN DAYS, YOU MUST LEAVE... WHETHER OR NOT YOU FINISH THE PAINTING.
HE WANTED ME TO TELL YOU.
MISS JAE.

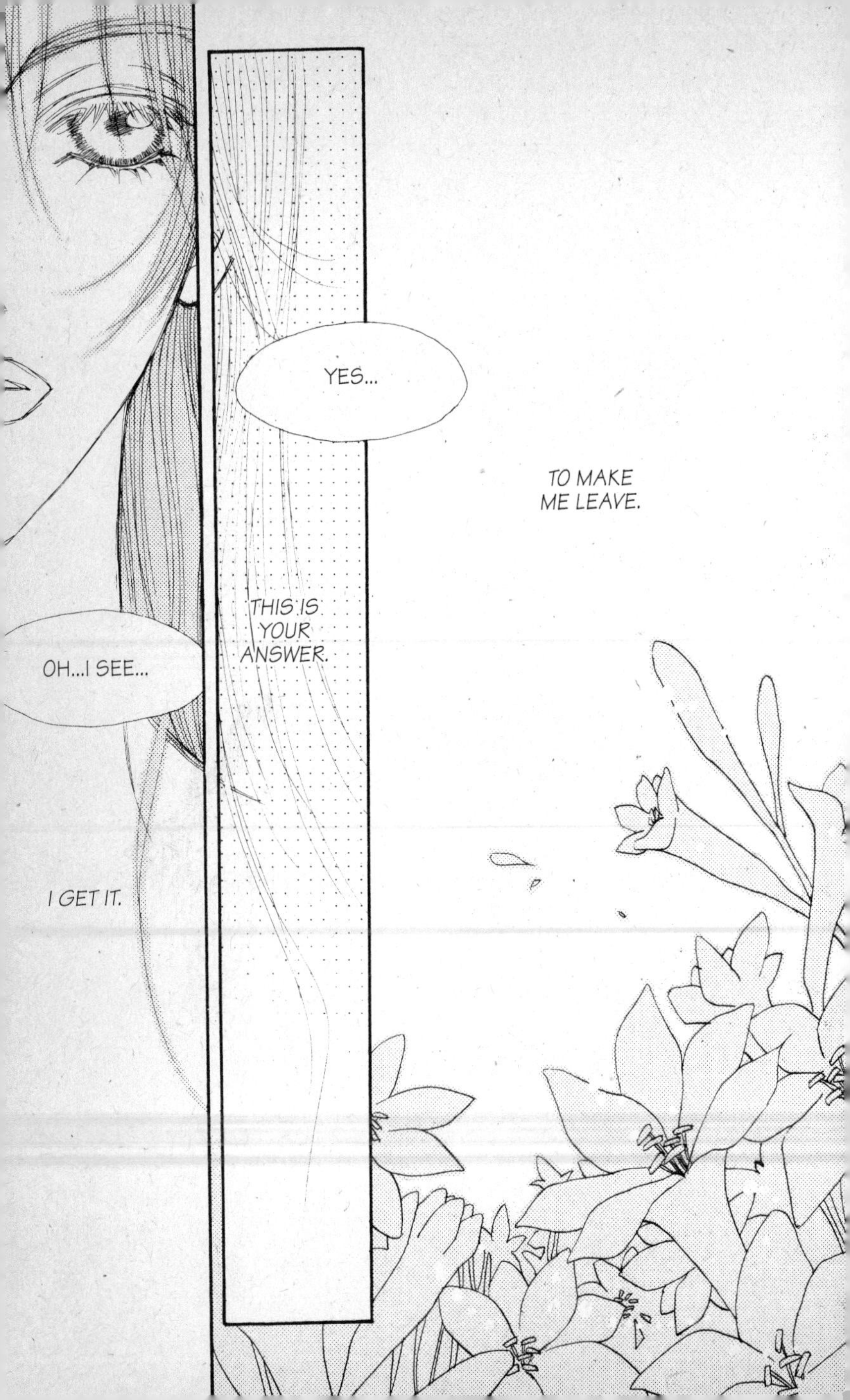
TO MAKE ME LEAVE.
YES...
THIS IS YOUR ANSWER.
OH...I SEE...
I GET IT.

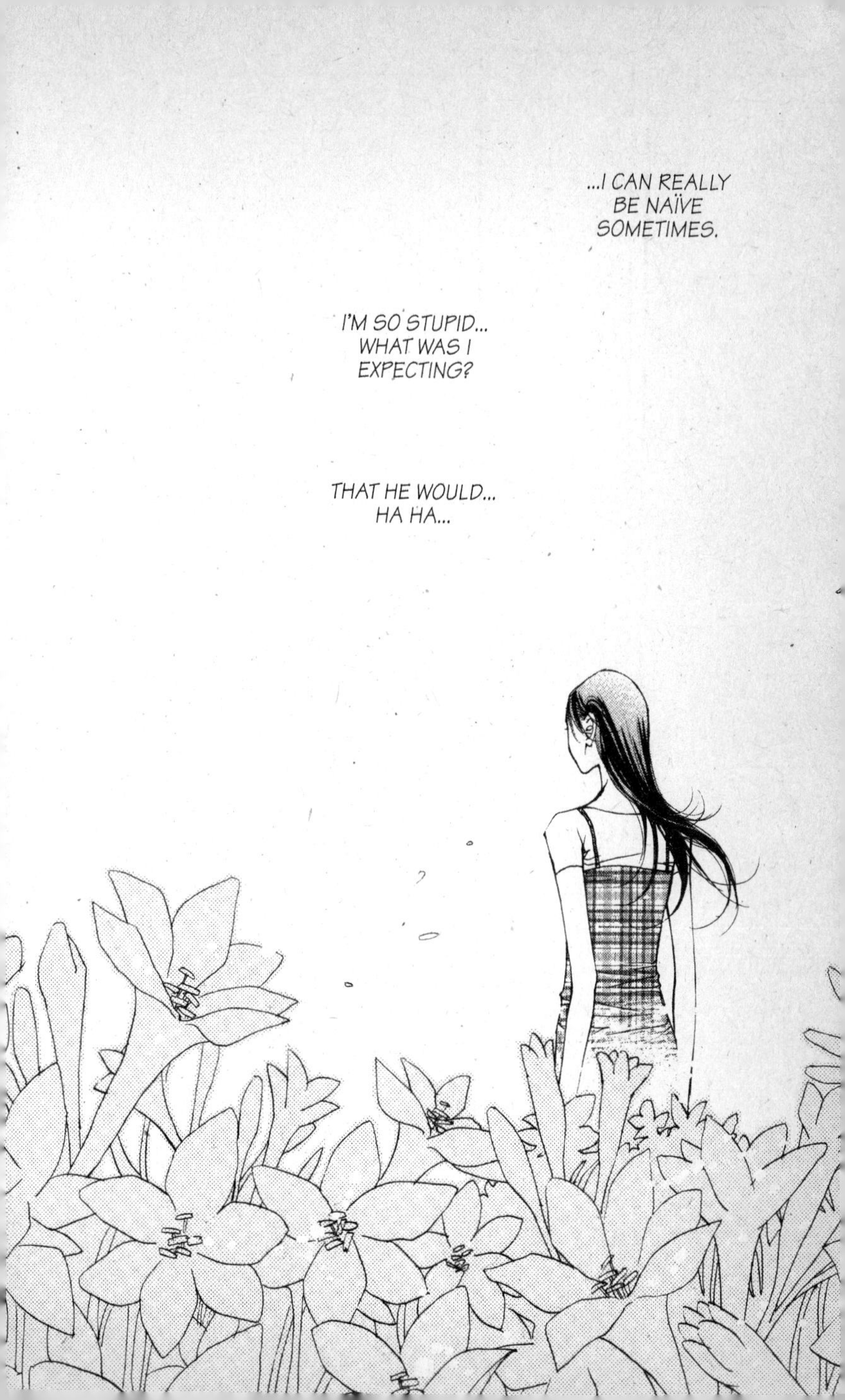
...I CAN REALLY BE NAÏVE SOMETIMES.
I'M SO STUPID... WHAT WAS I EXPECTING?
THAT HE WOULD... HA HA...

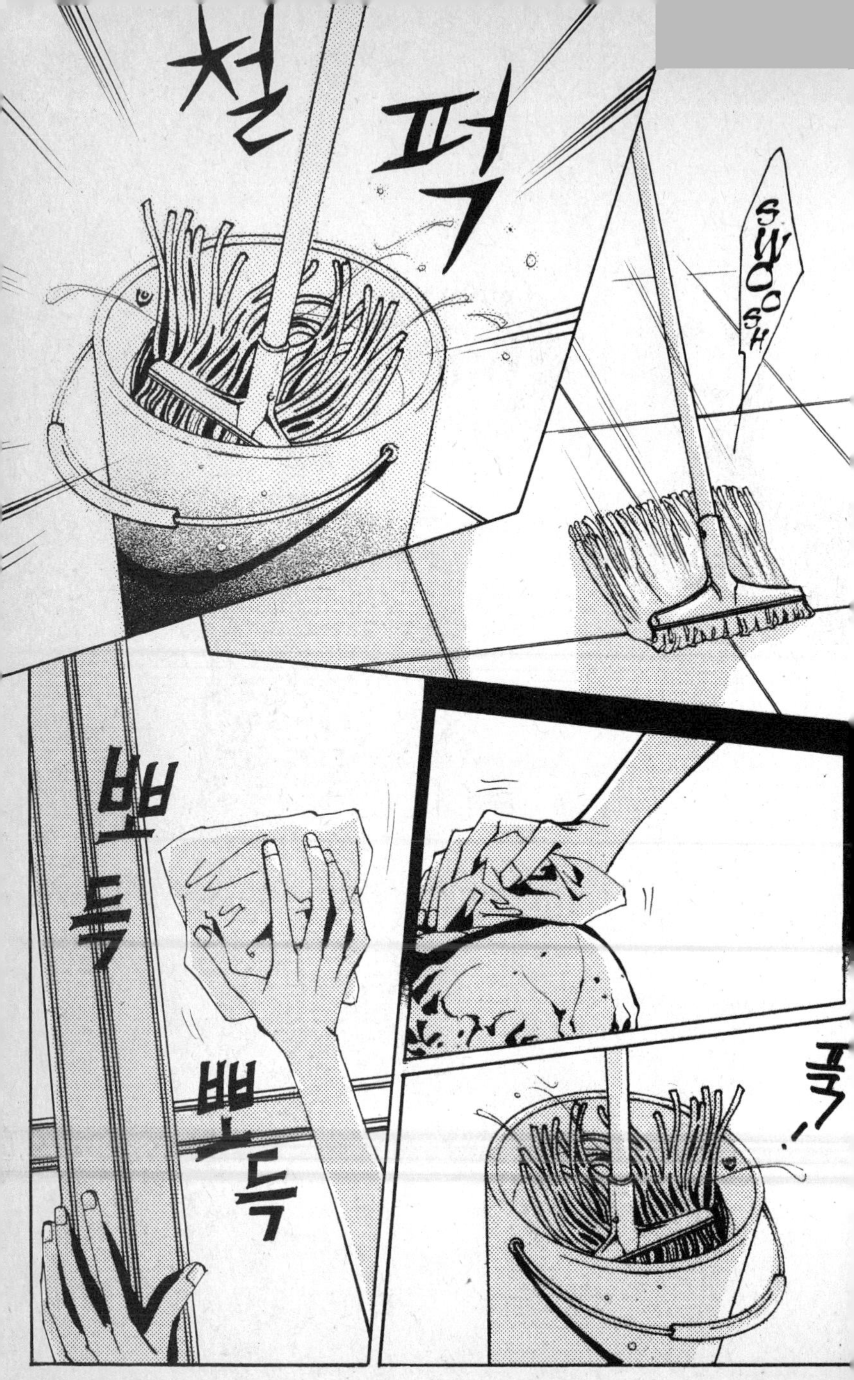
철퍽
SWOOSH
뽀득
뽀득
쿡!

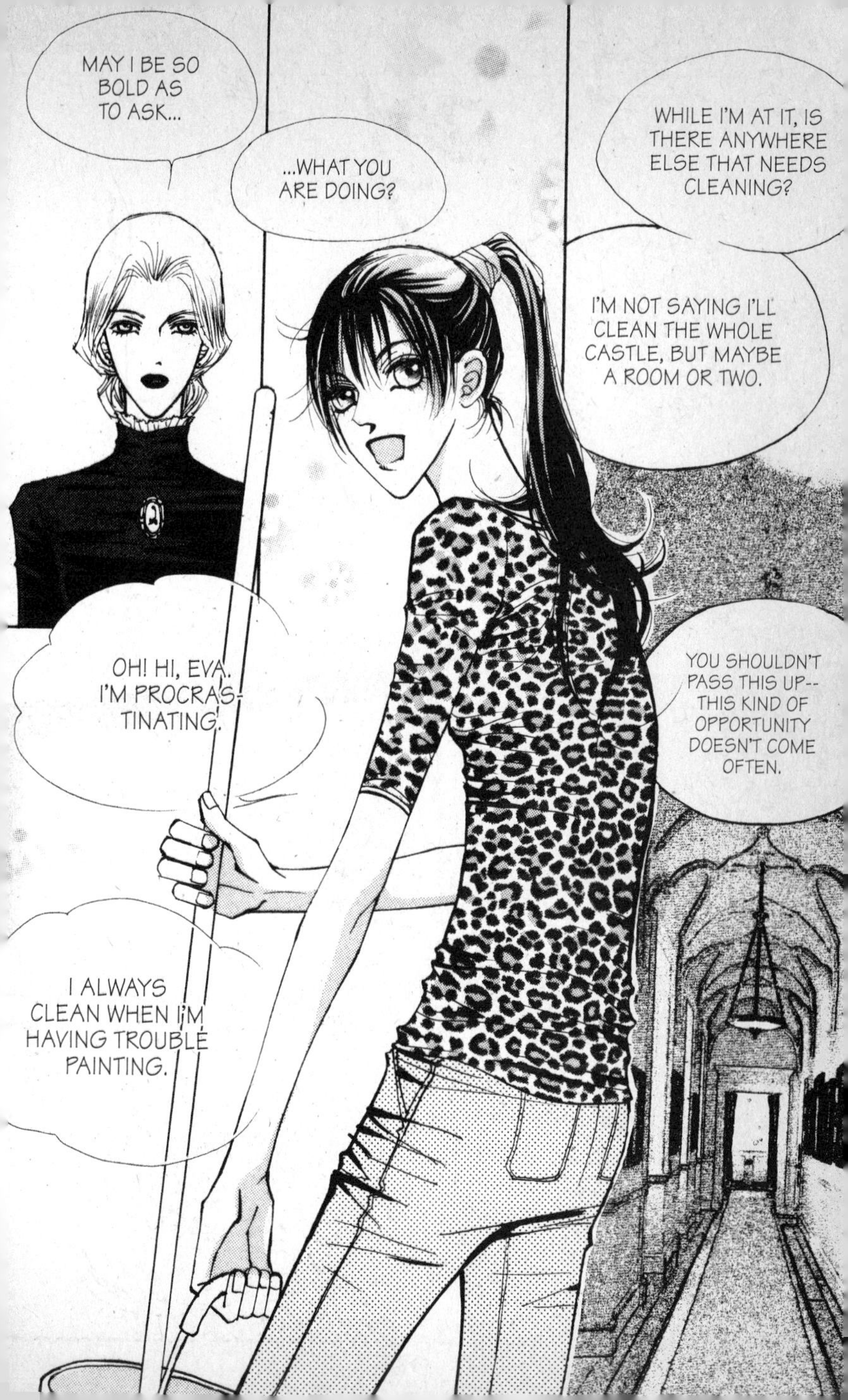
MAY I BE SO BOLD AS TO ASK...
...WHAT YOU ARE DOING?
OH! HI, EVA. I'M PROCRAS-TINATING.
I ALWAYS CLEAN WHEN I'M HAVING TROUBLE PAINTING.
WHILE I'M AT IT, IS THERE ANYWHERE ELSE THAT NEEDS CLEANING?
I'M NOT SAYING I'LL CLEAN THE WHOLE CASTLE, BUT MAYBE A ROOM OR TWO.
YOU SHOULDN'T PASS THIS UP-- THIS KIND OF OPPORTUNITY DOESN'T COME OFTEN.

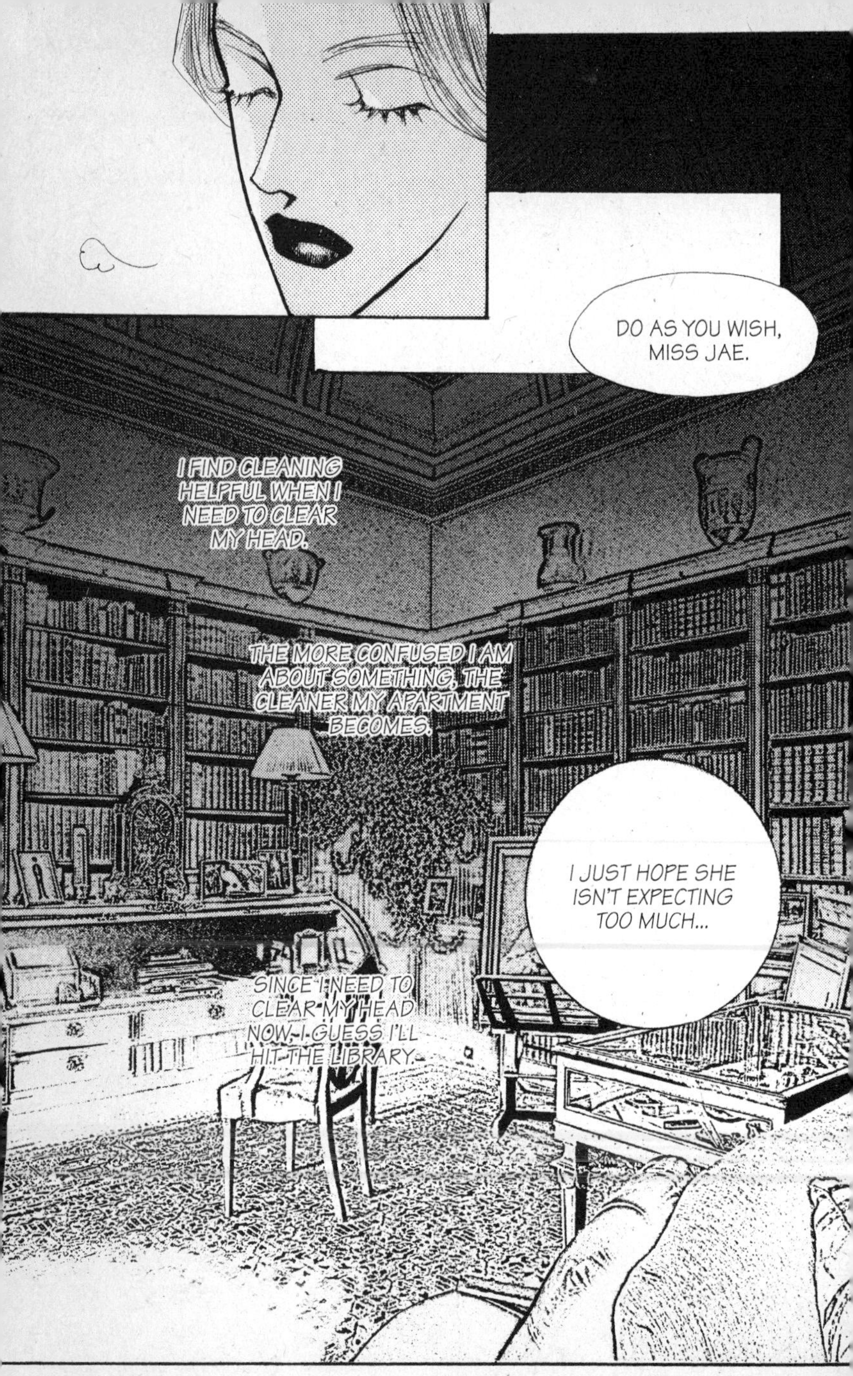
DO AS YOU WISH, MISS JAE.
I FIND CLEANING HELPFUL WHEN I NEED TO CLEAR MY HEAD.
THE MORE CONFUSED I AM ABOUT SOMETHING, THE CLEANER MY APARTMENT BECOMES.
SINCE I NEED TO CLEAR MY HEAD NOW, I GUESS I'LL HIT THE LIBRARY.
I JUST HOPE SHE ISN'T EXPECTING TOO MUCH...

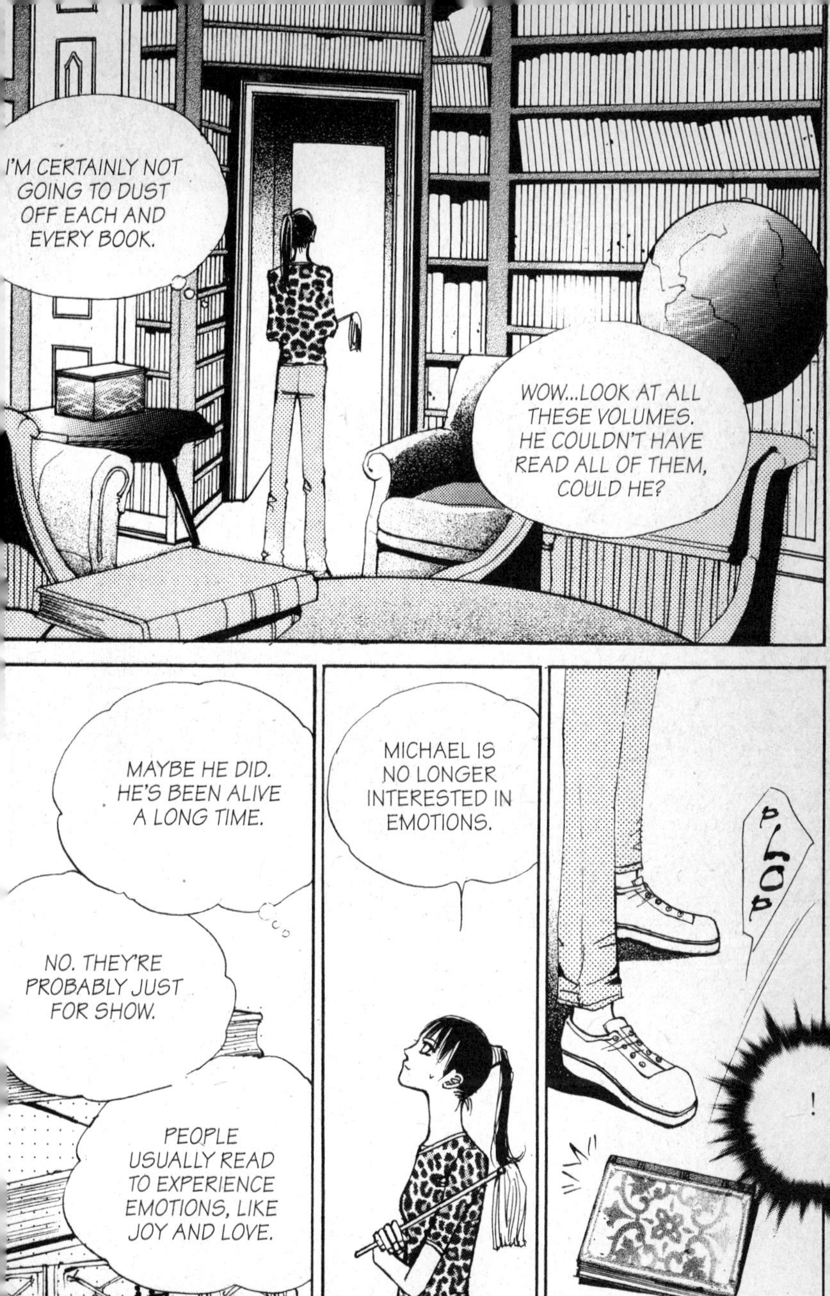
I'M CERTAINLY NOT GOING TO DUST OFF EACH AND EVERY BOOK.
WOW...LOOK AT ALL THESE VOLUMES. HE COULDN'T HAVE READ ALL OF THEM, COULD HE?
MAYBE HE DID. HE'S BEEN ALIVE A LONG TIME.
NO. THEY'RE PROBABLY JUST FOR SHOW.
PEOPLE USUALLY READ TO EXPERIENCE EMOTIONS, LIKE JOY AND LOVE.
MICHAEL IS NO LONGER INTERESTED IN EMOTIONS.
PLOP
!

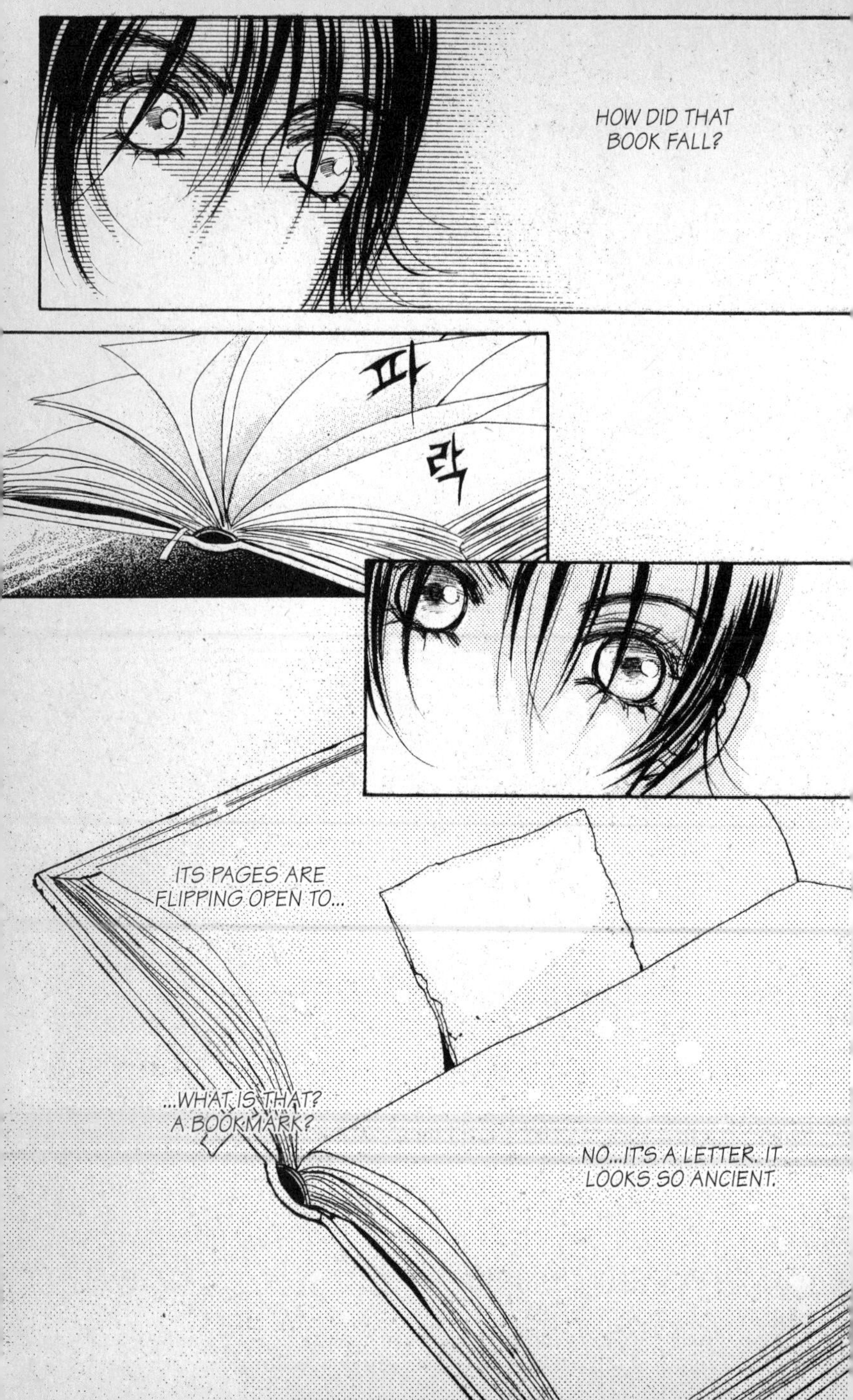
HOW DID THAT BOOK FALL?
파락
ITS PAGES ARE FLIPPING OPEN TO...
...WHAT IS THAT? A BOOKMARK?
NO...IT'S A LETTER. IT LOOKS SO ANCIENT.

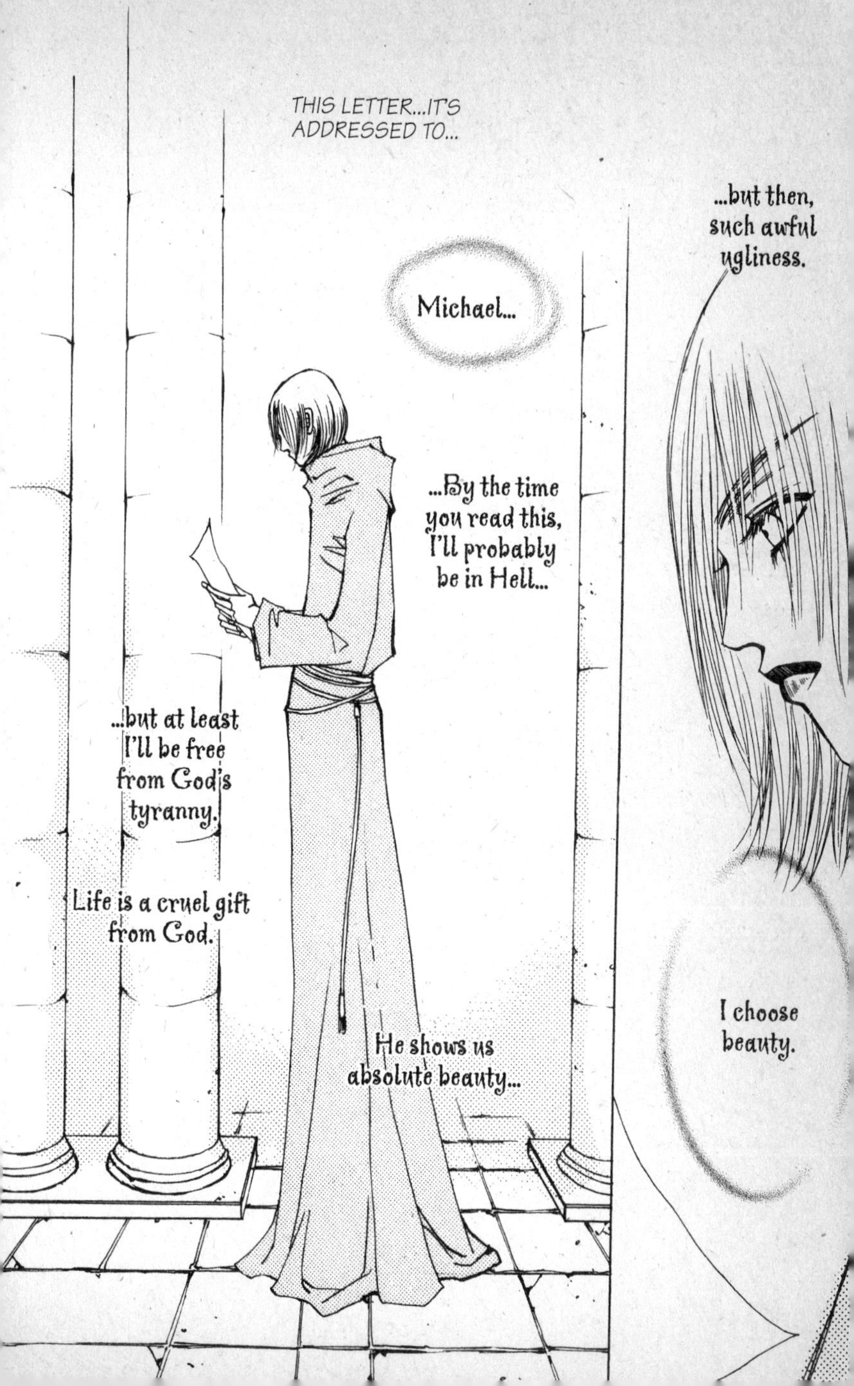
THIS LETTER...IT'S ADDRESSED TO...
Michael...
...By the time you read this, I'll probably be in Hell...
...but at least I'll be free from God's tyranny.
Life is a cruel gift from God.
He shows us absolute beauty...
...but then, such awful ugliness.
I choose beauty.

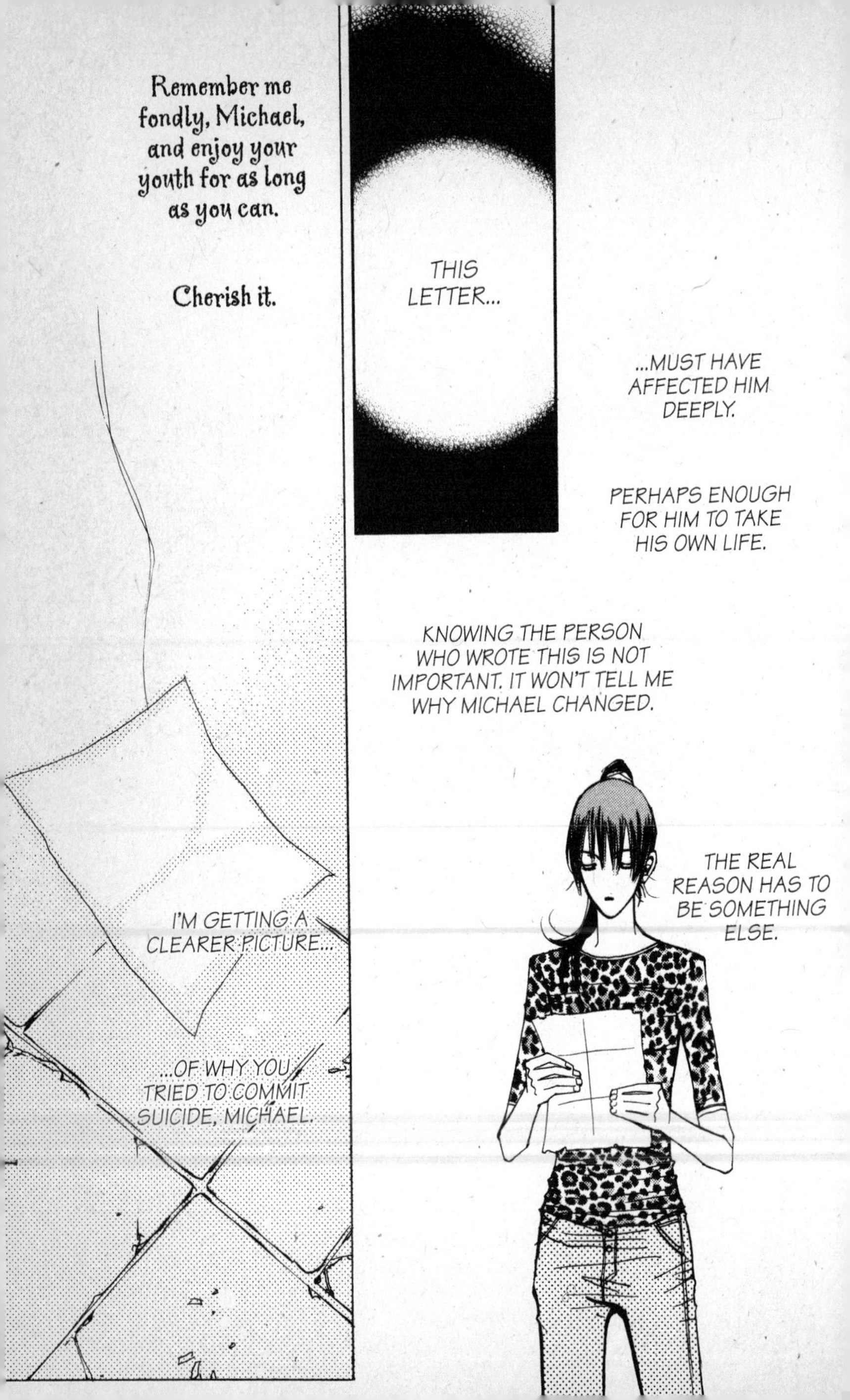
Remember me fondly, Michael, and enjoy your youth for as long as you can.
Cherish it.
I'M GETTING A CLEARER PICTURE...
...OF WHY YOU TRIED TO COMMIT SUICIDE, MICHAEL.
THIS LETTER...
...MUST HAVE AFFECTED HIM DEEPLY.
PERHAPS ENOUGH FOR HIM TO TAKE HIS OWN LIFE.
KNOWING THE PERSON WHO WROTE THIS IS NOT IMPORTANT. IT WON'T TELL ME WHY MICHAEL CHANGED.
THE REAL REASON HAS TO BE SOMETHING ELSE.

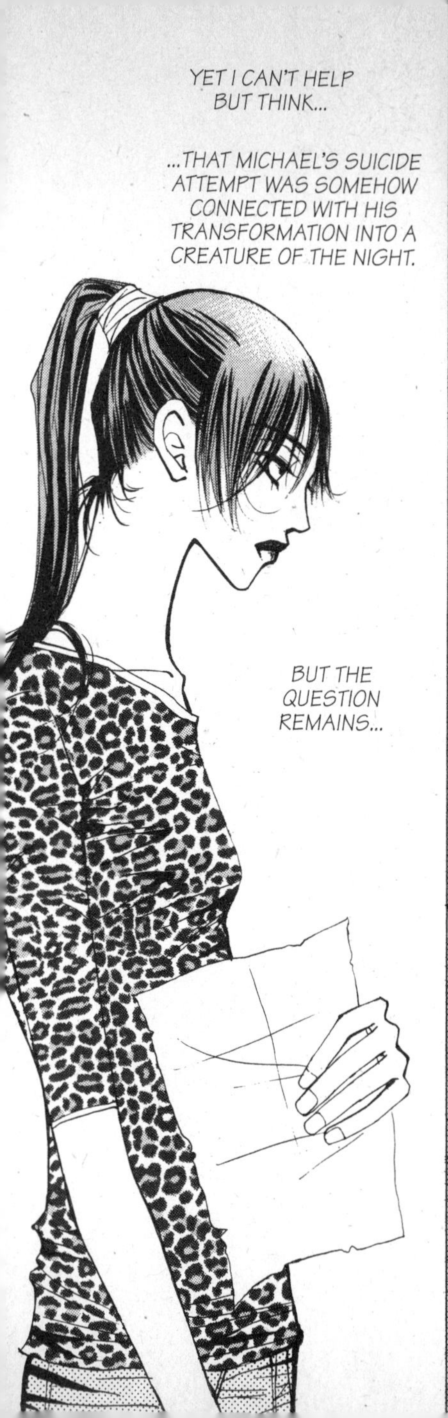
YET I CAN'T HELP BUT THINK...
...THAT MICHAEL'S SUICIDE ATTEMPT WAS SOMEHOW CONNECTED WITH HIS TRANSFORMATION INTO A CREATURE OF THE NIGHT.
BUT THE QUESTION REMAINS...
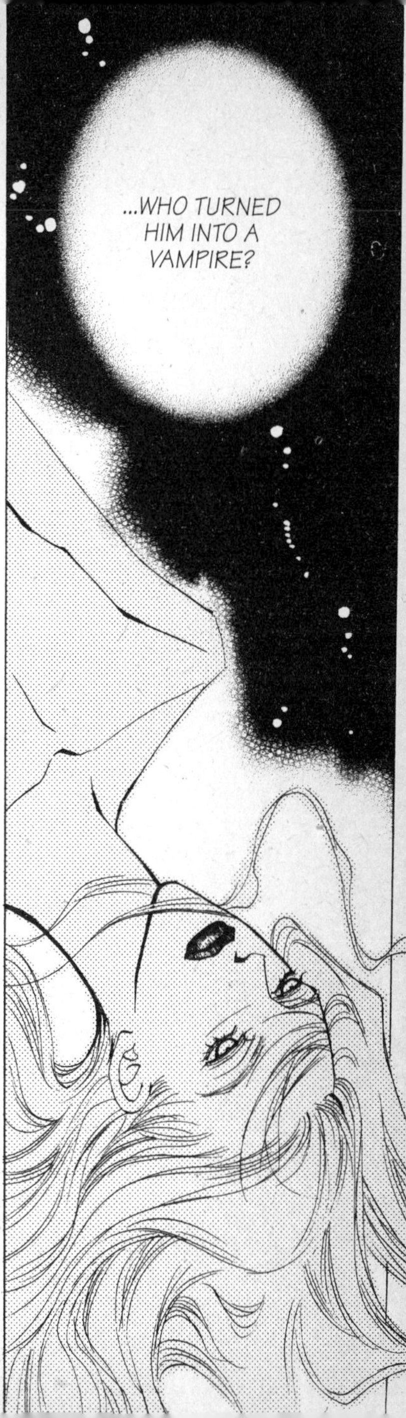
...WHO TURNED HIM INTO A VAMPIRE?

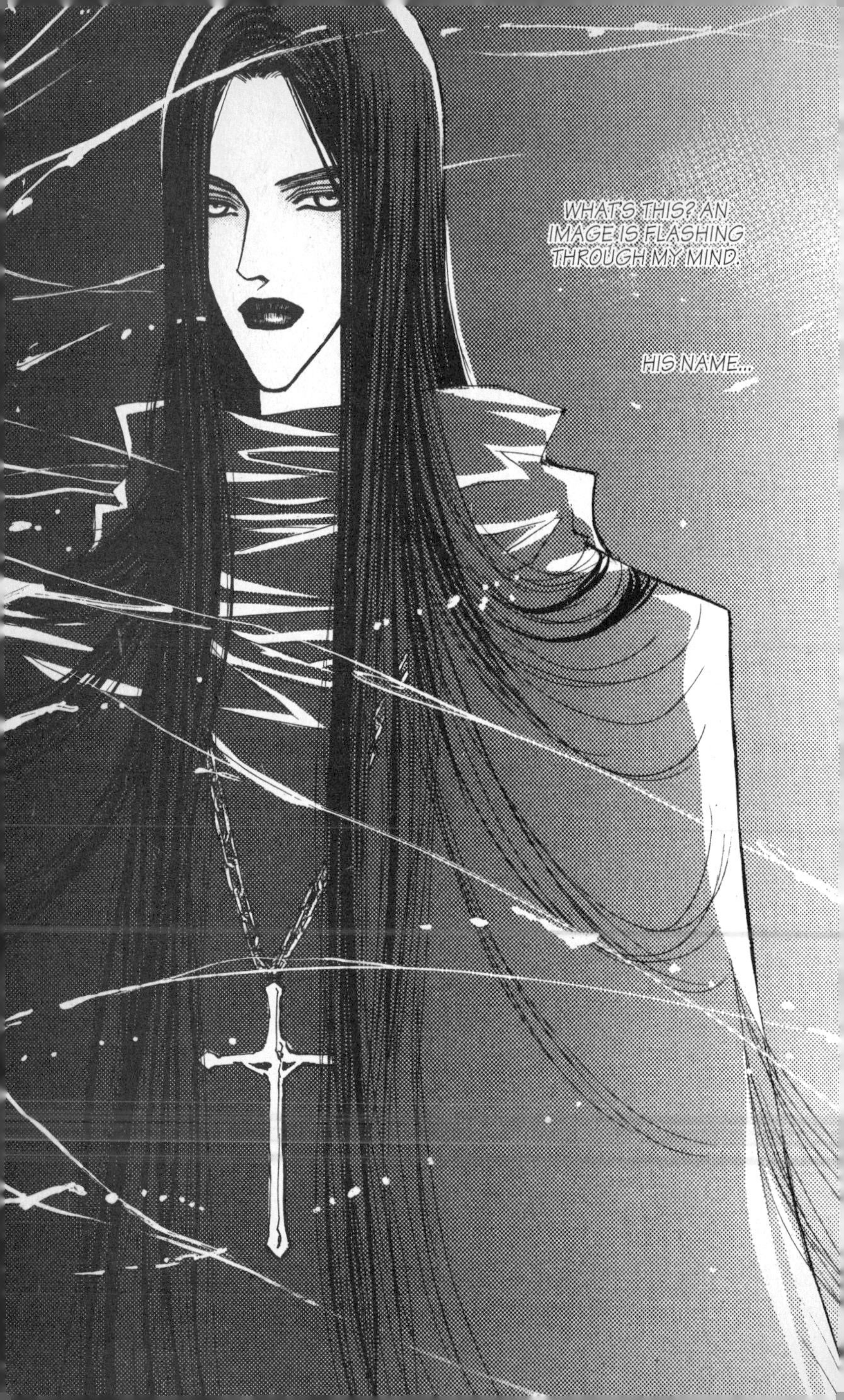
WHAT'S THIS? AN IMAGE IS FLASHING THROUGH MY MIND.
HIS NAME...

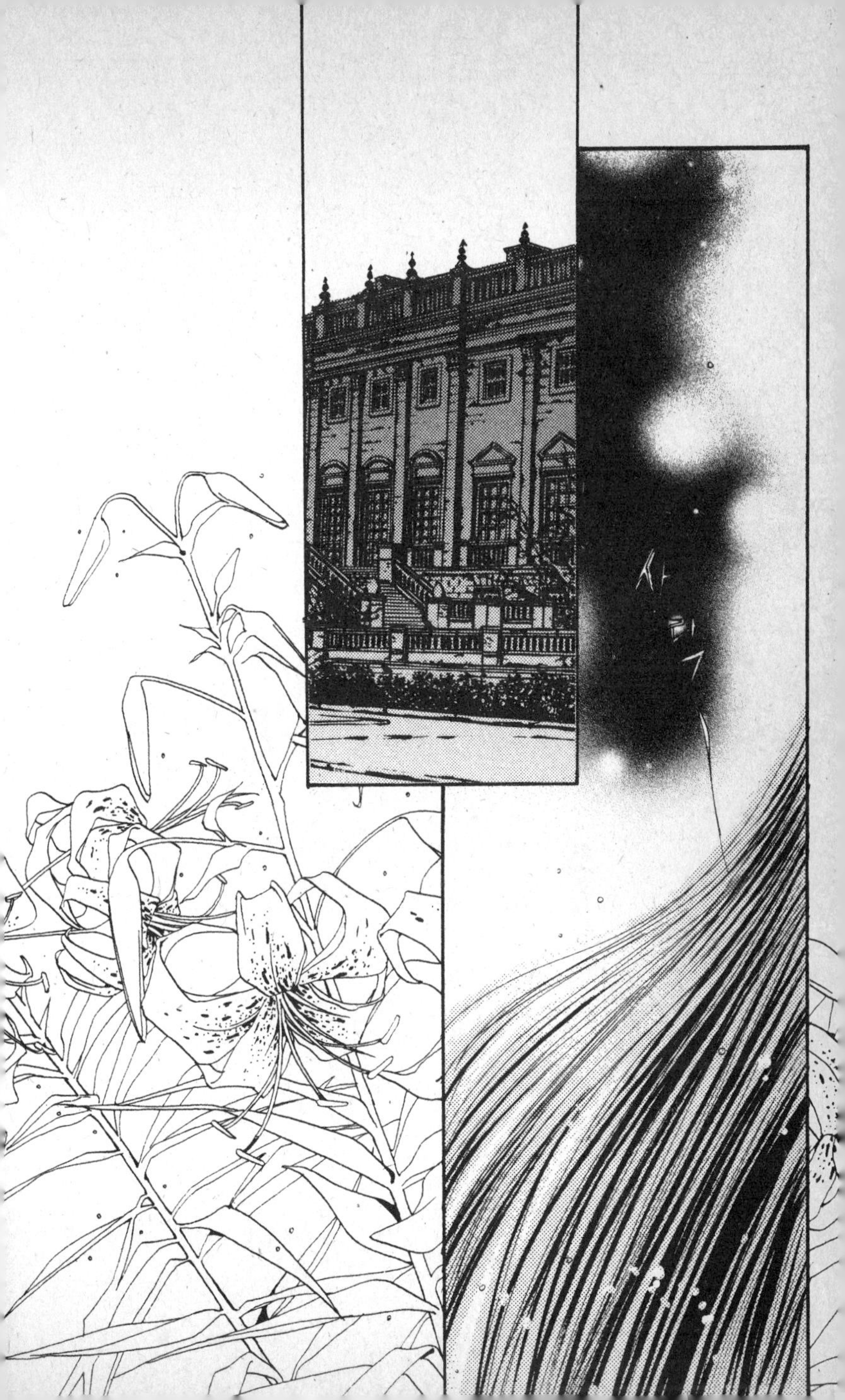

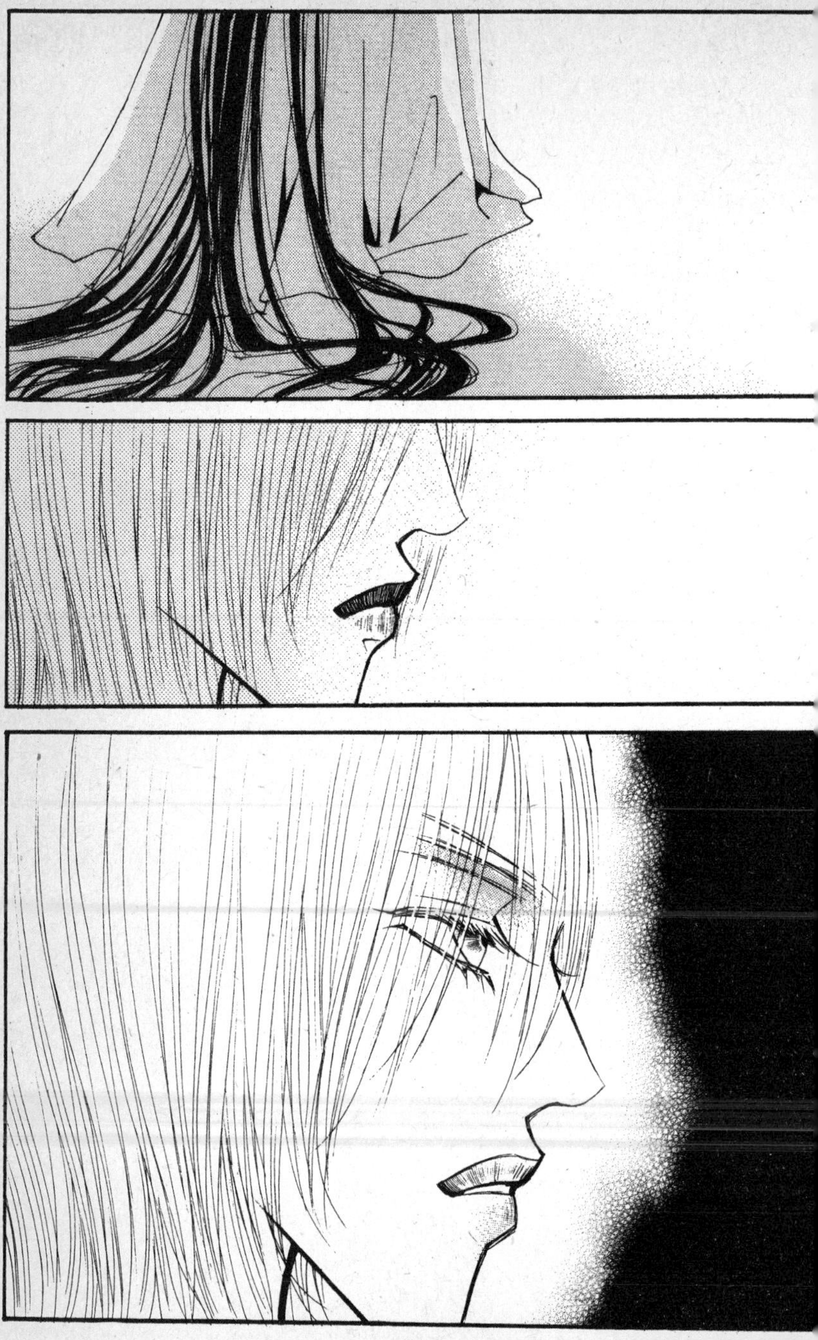

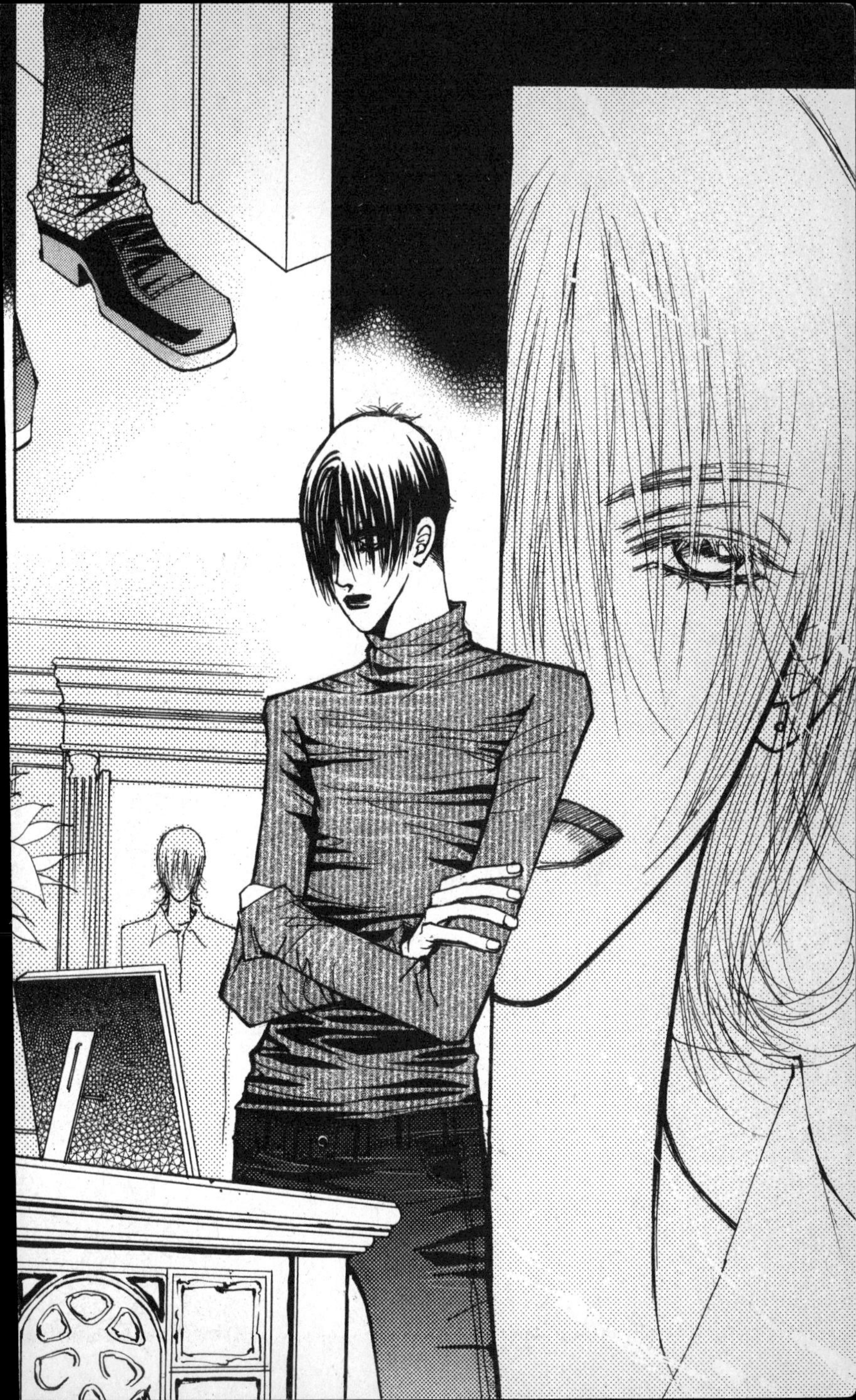

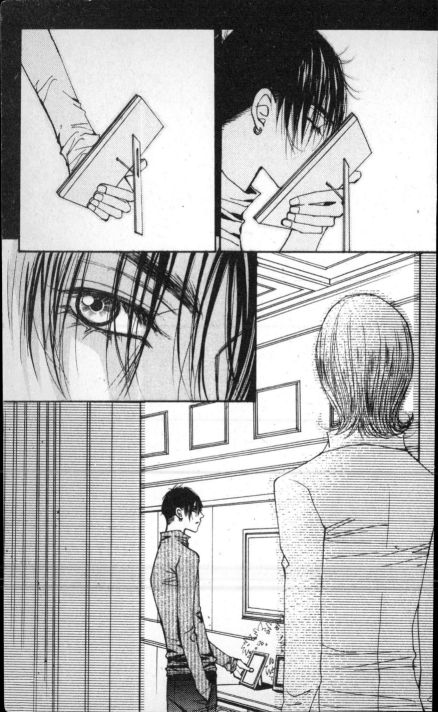

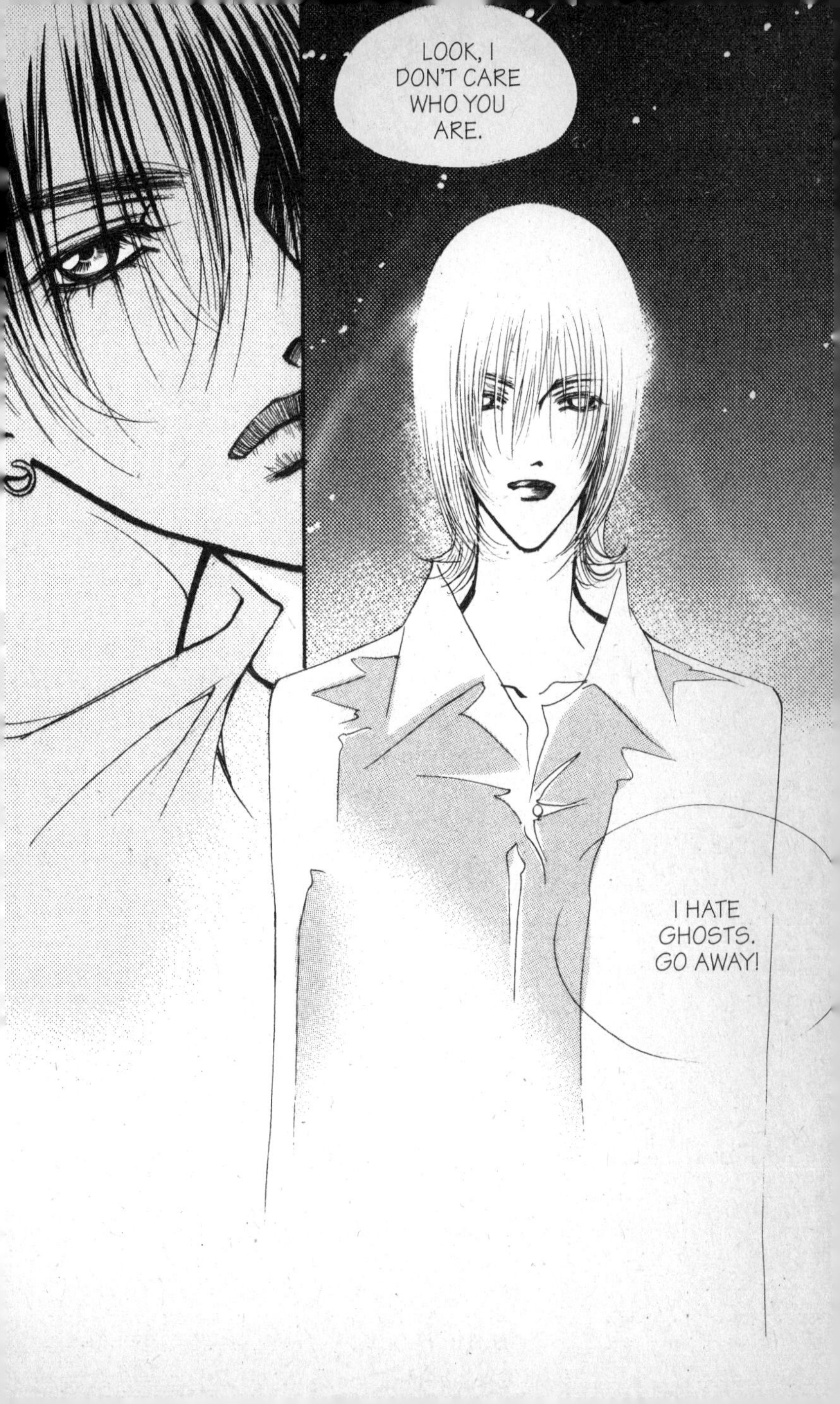
LOOK, I DON'T CARE WHO YOU ARE.
I HATE GHOSTS. GO AWAY!

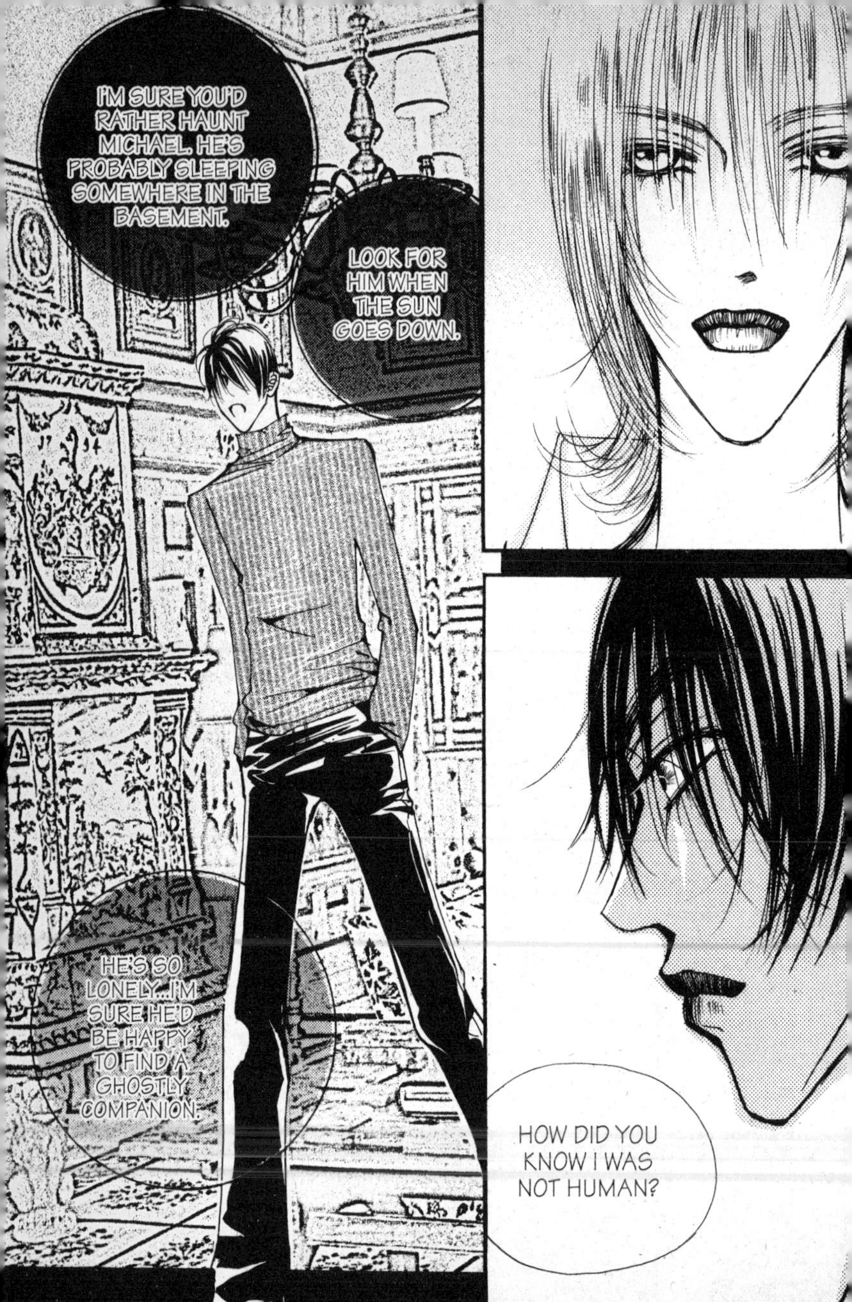
HOW DID YOU KNOW I WAS NOT HUMAN?
I'M SURE YOU'D RATHER HAUNT MICHAEL. HE'S PROBABLY SLEEPING SOMEWHERE IN THE BASEMENT.
LOOK FOR HIM WHEN THE SUN GOES DOWN.
HE'S SO LONELY... I'M SURE HE'D BE HAPPY TO FIND A GHOSTLY COMPANION.

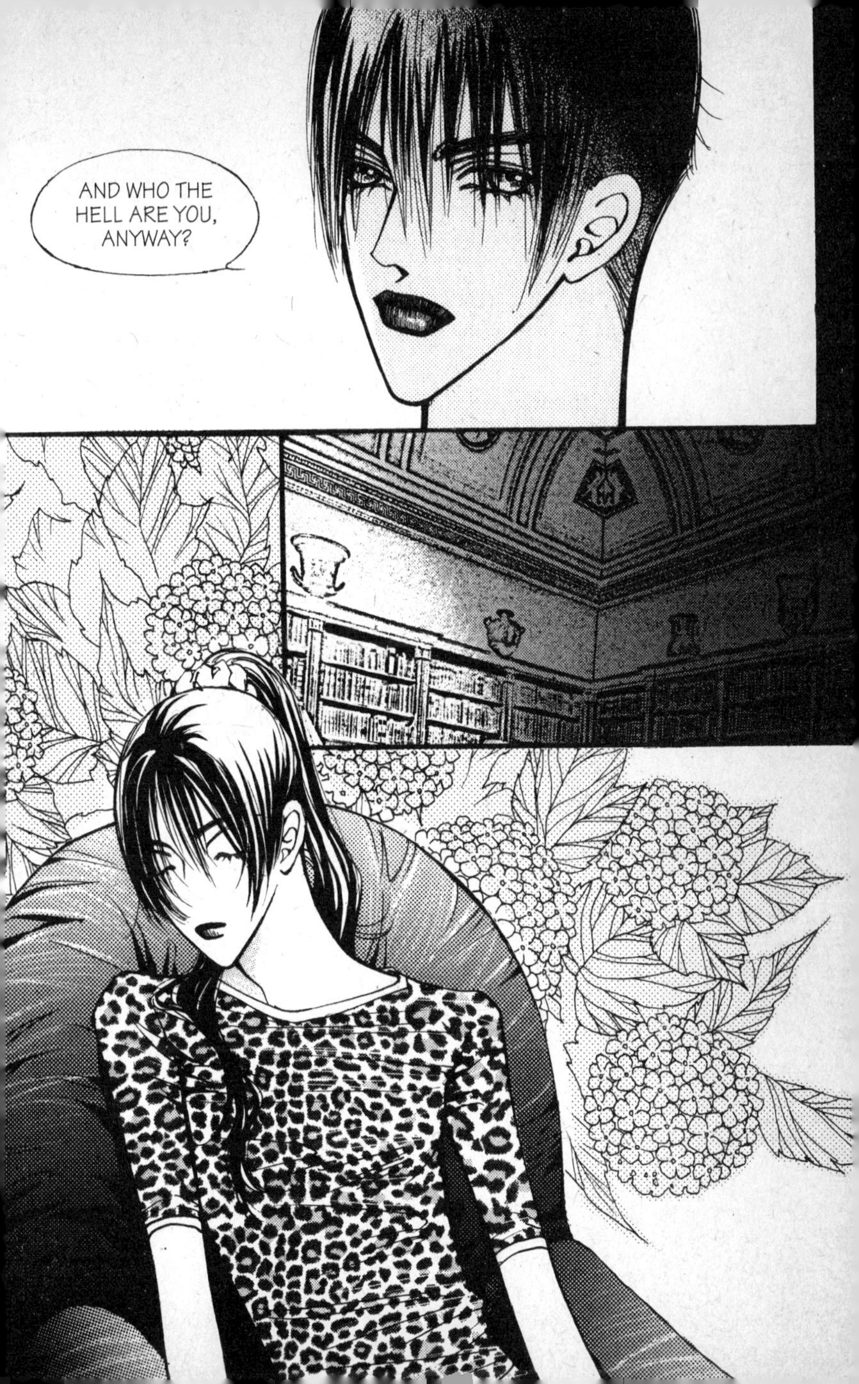
AND WHO THE HELL ARE YOU, ANYWAY?

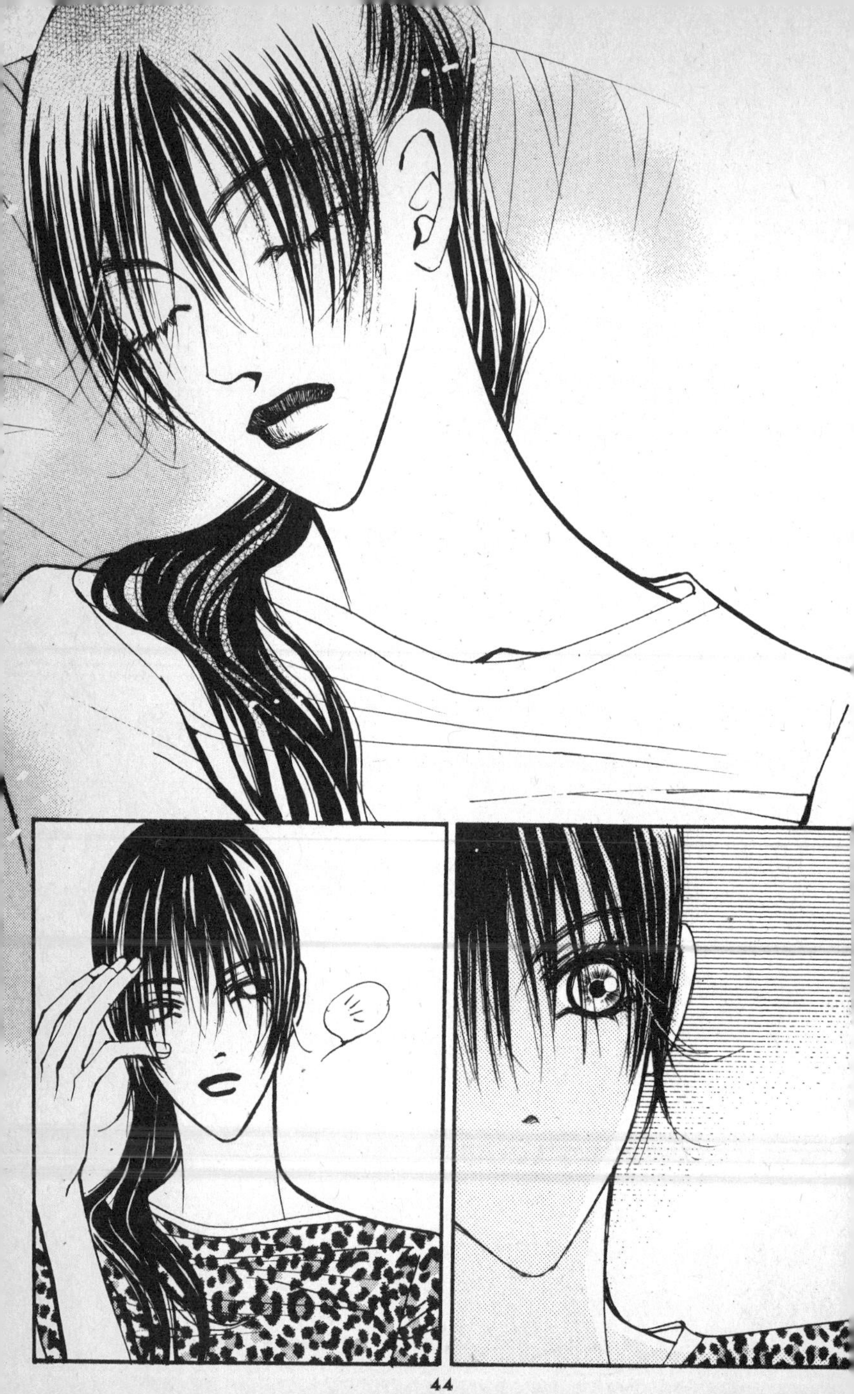

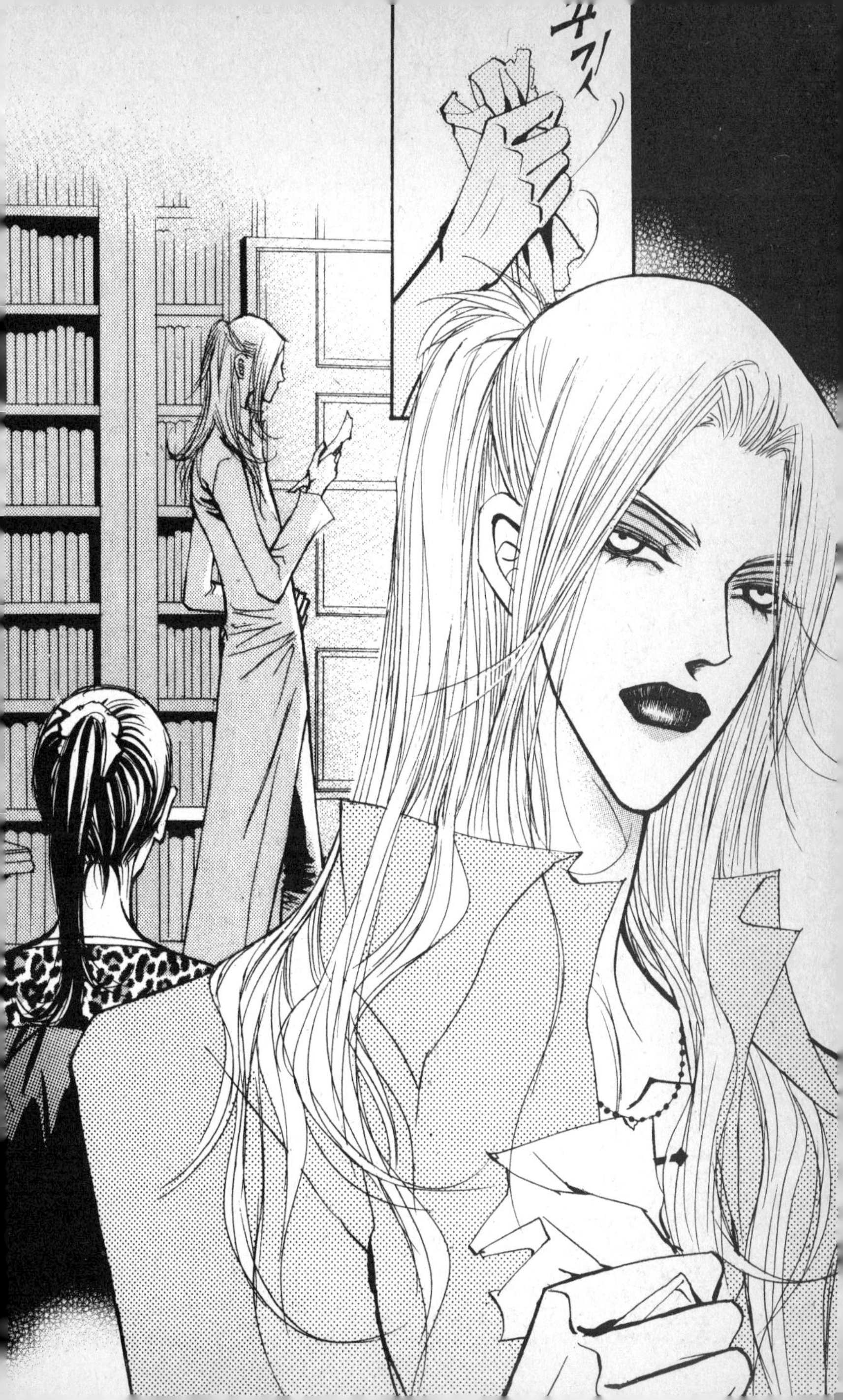

깃

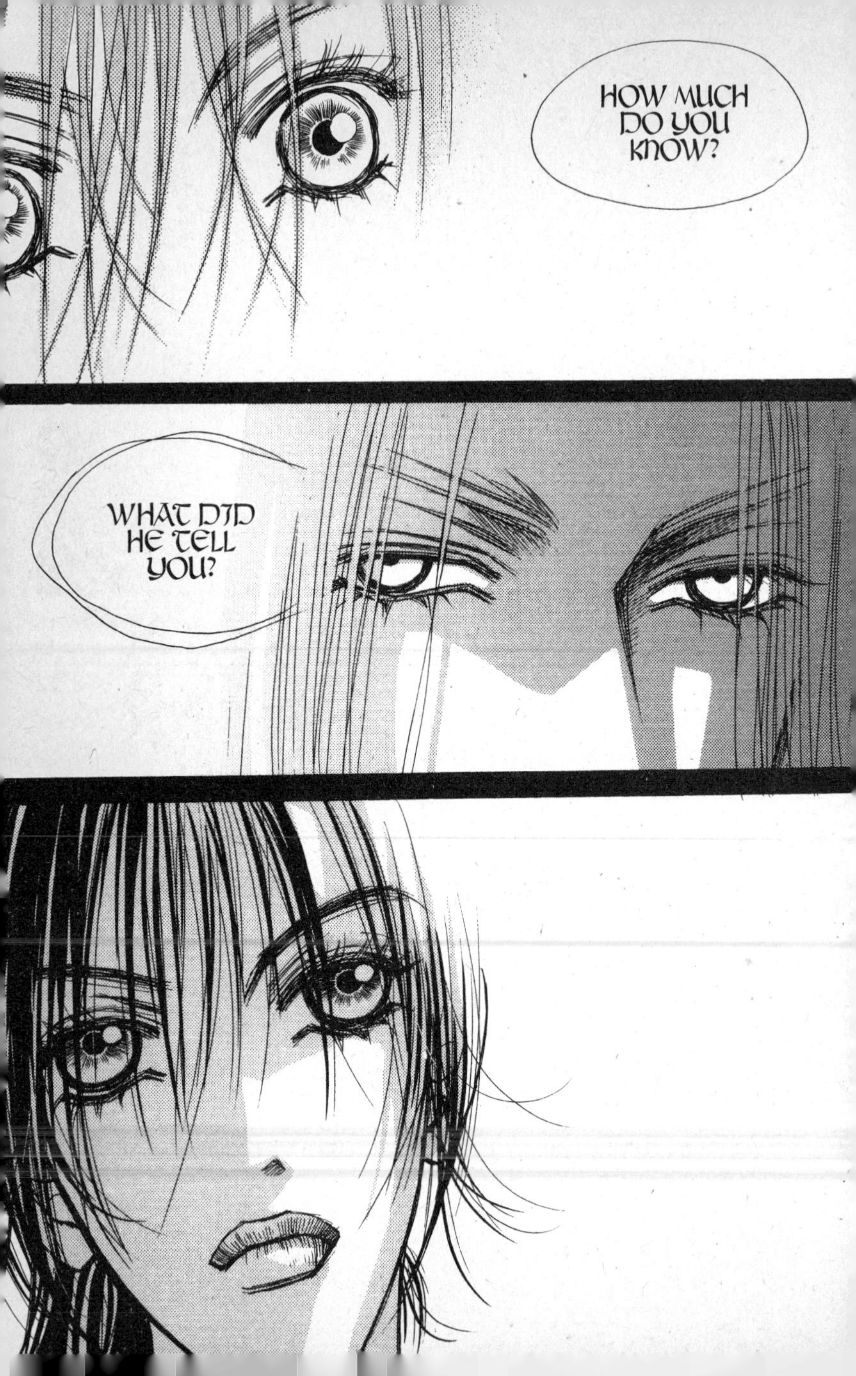
HOW MUCH DO YOU KNOW?
WHAT DID HE TELL YOU?

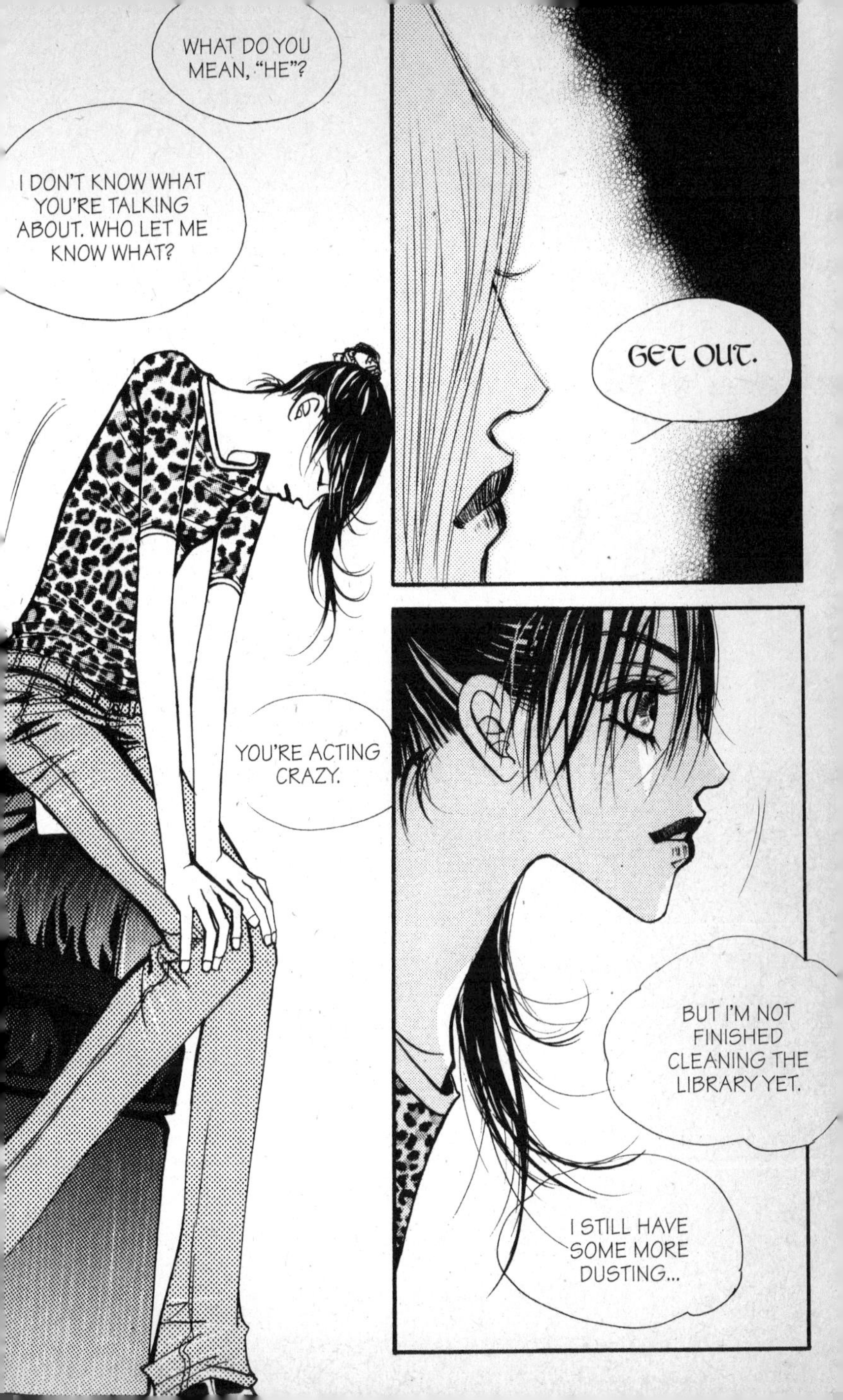
WHAT DO YOU MEAN, "HE"?
I DON'T KNOW WHAT YOU'RE TALKING ABOUT. WHO LET ME KNOW WHAT?
YOU'RE ACTING CRAZY.
GET OUT.
BUT I'M NOT FINISHED CLEANING THE LIBRARY YET.
I STILL HAVE SOME MORE DUSTING...

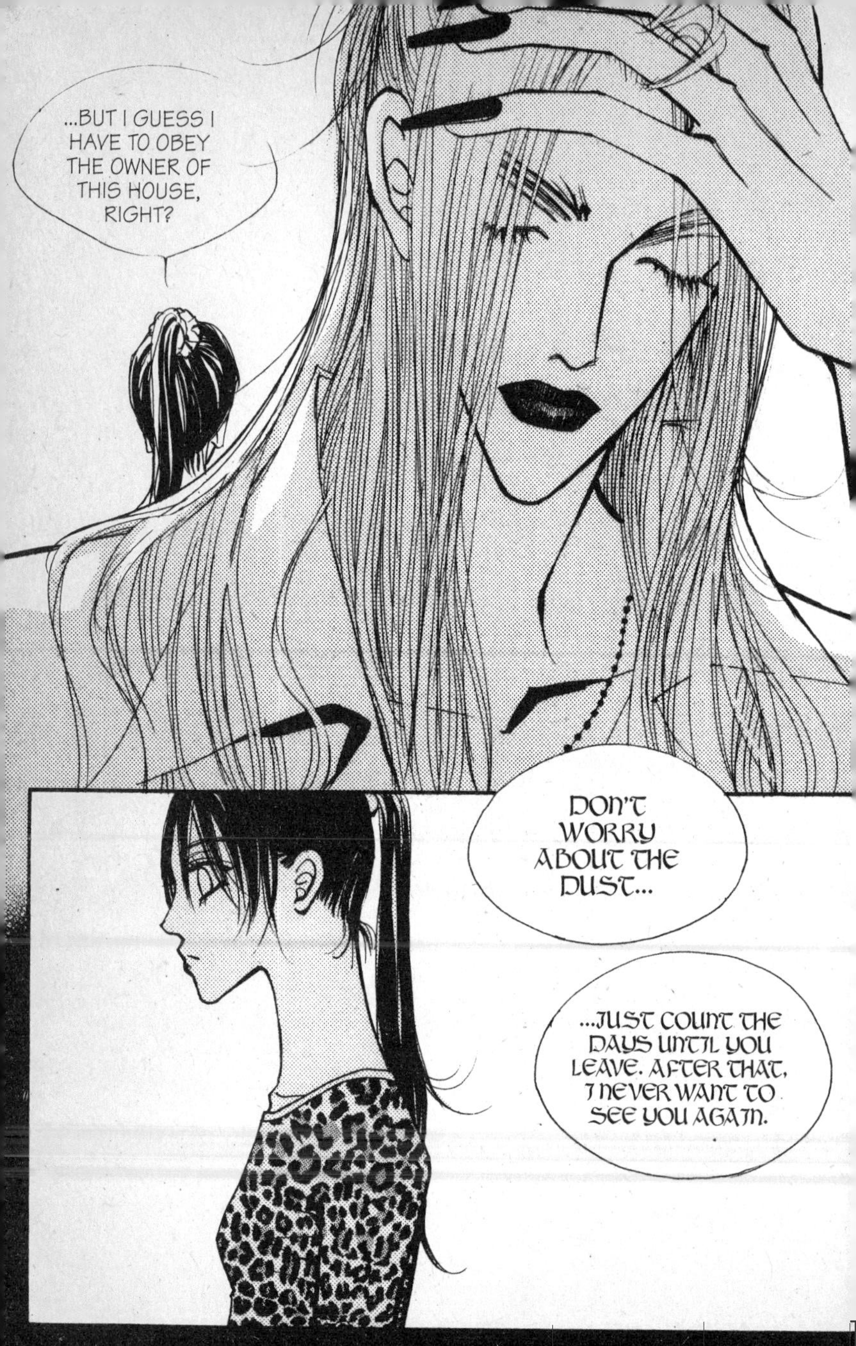
...BUT I GUESS I HAVE TO OBEY THE OWNER OF THIS HOUSE, RIGHT?
DON'T WORRY ABOUT THE DUST...
...JUST COUNT THE DAYS UNTIL YOU LEAVE. AFTER THAT, I NEVER WANT TO SEE YOU AGAIN.

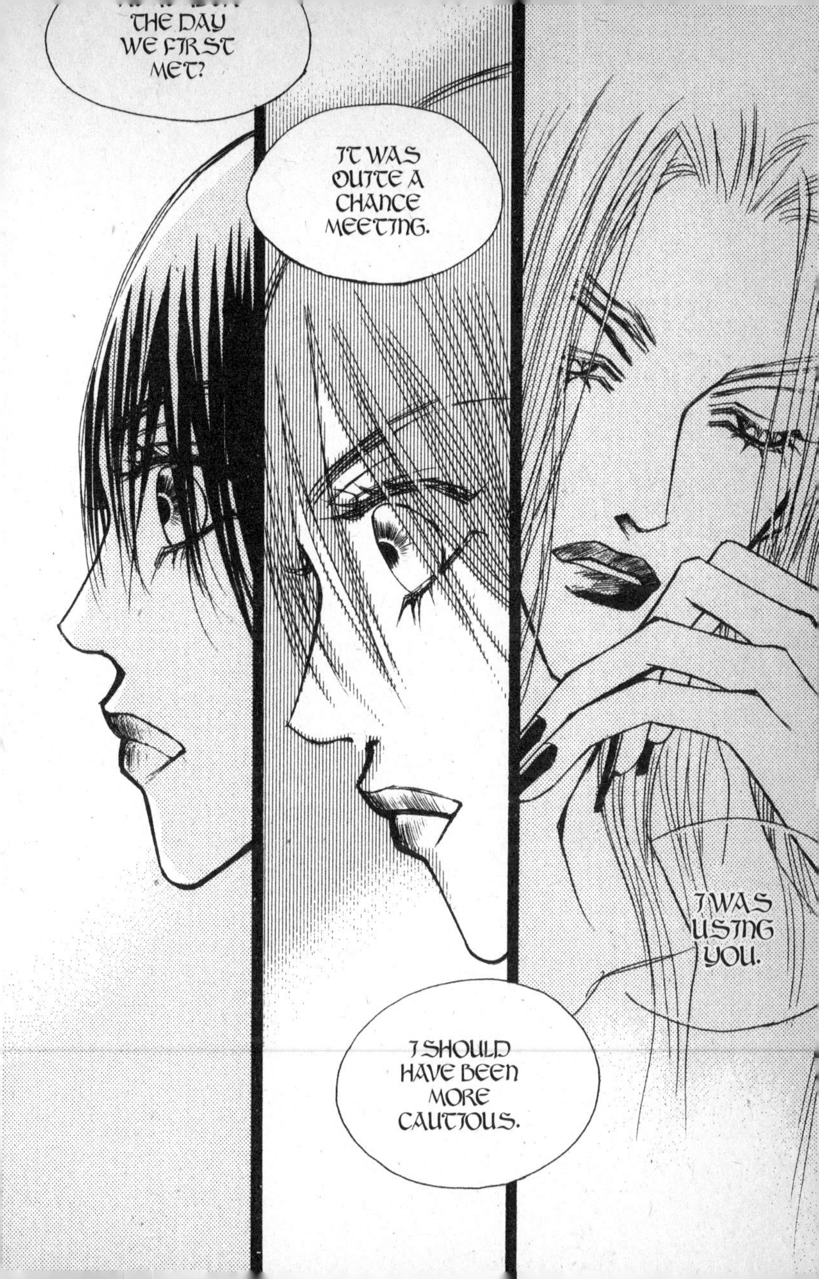
THE DAY WE FIRST MET?
IT WAS QUITE A CHANCE MEETING.
I SHOULD HAVE BEEN MORE CAUTIOUS.
I WAS USING YOU.

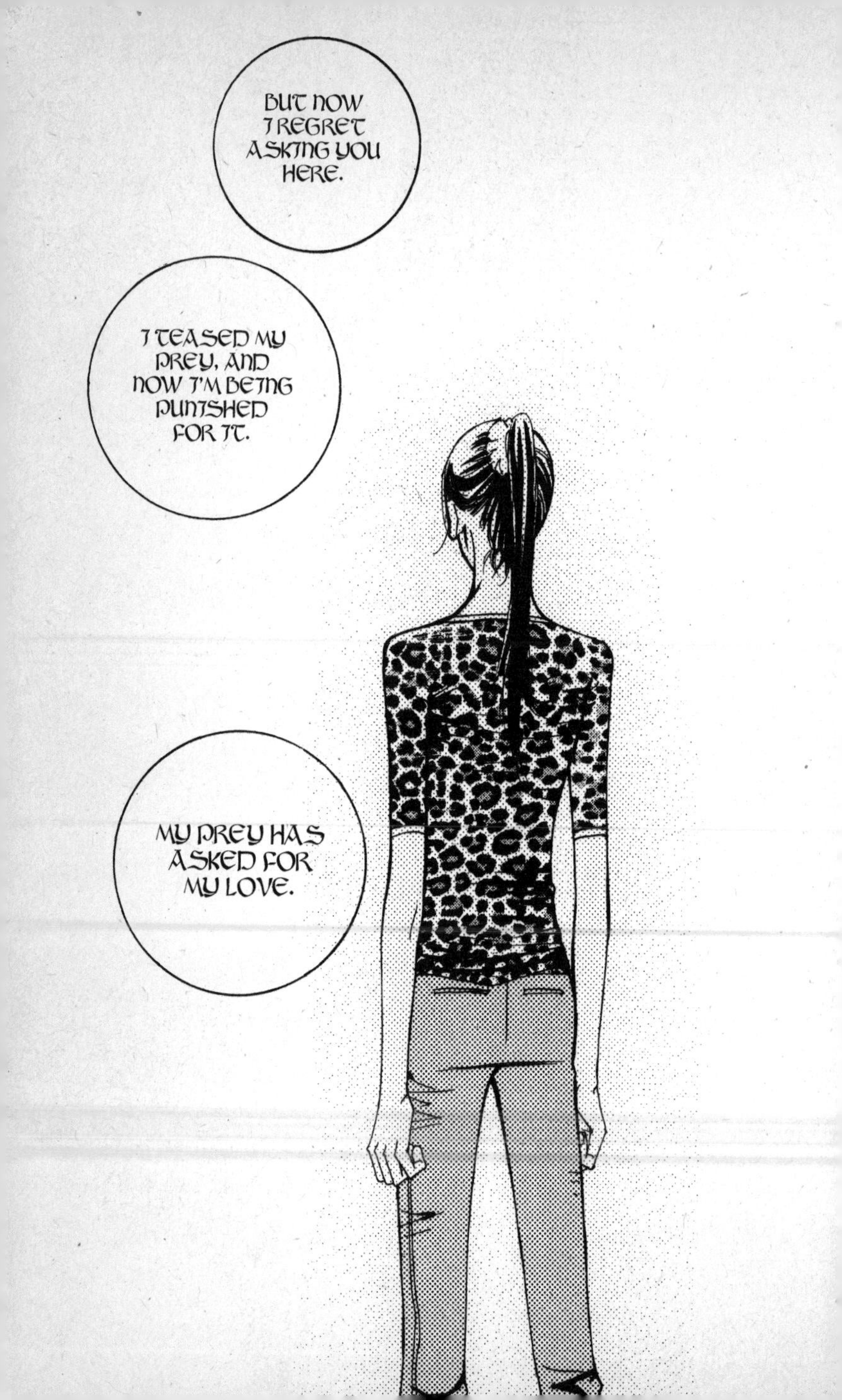
BUT NOW I REGRET ASKING YOU HERE.
I TEASED MY PREY, AND NOW I'M BEING PUNISHED FOR IT.
MY PREY HAS ASKED FOR MY LOVE.

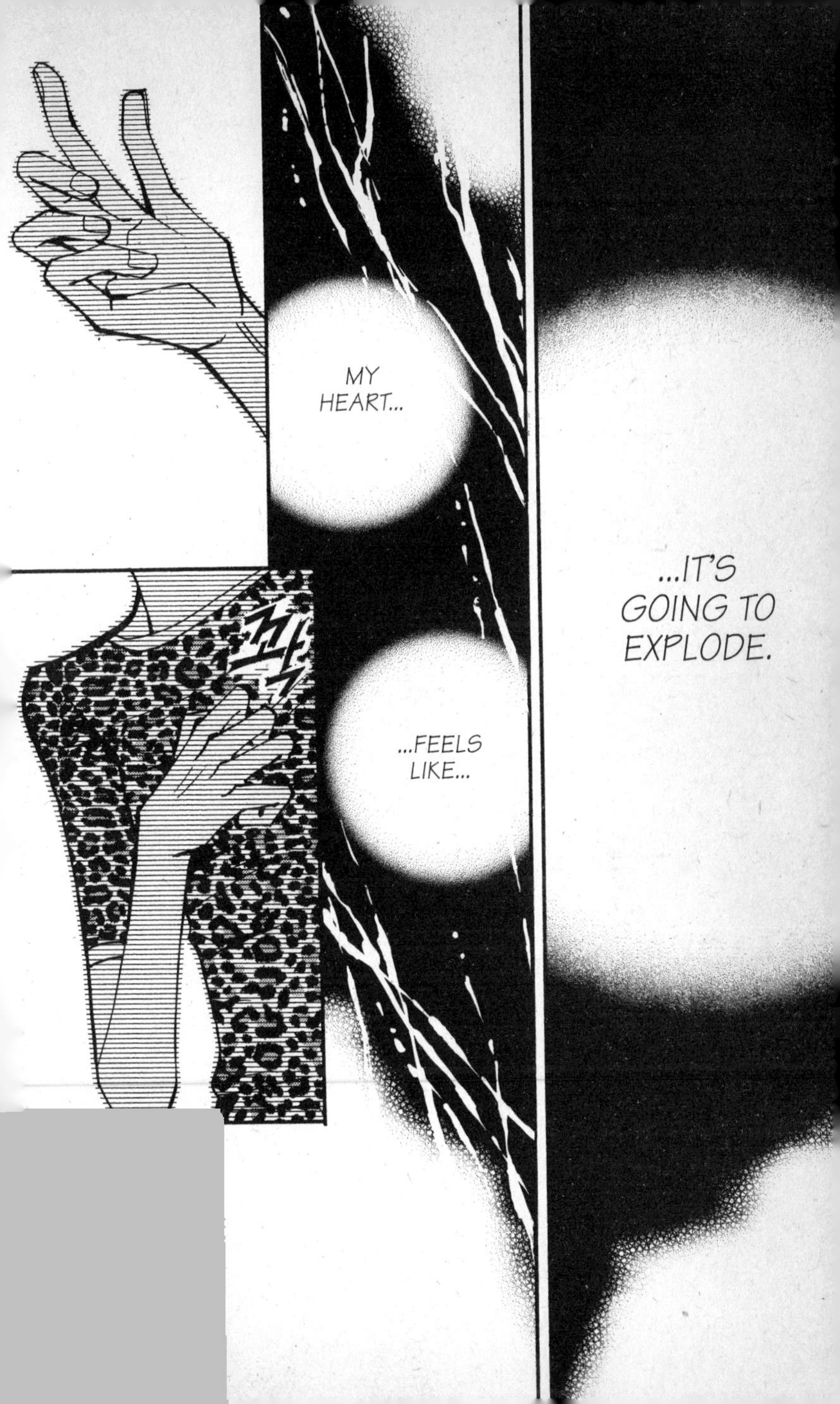
MY HEART...
...FEELS LIKE...
...IT'S GOING TO EXPLODE.

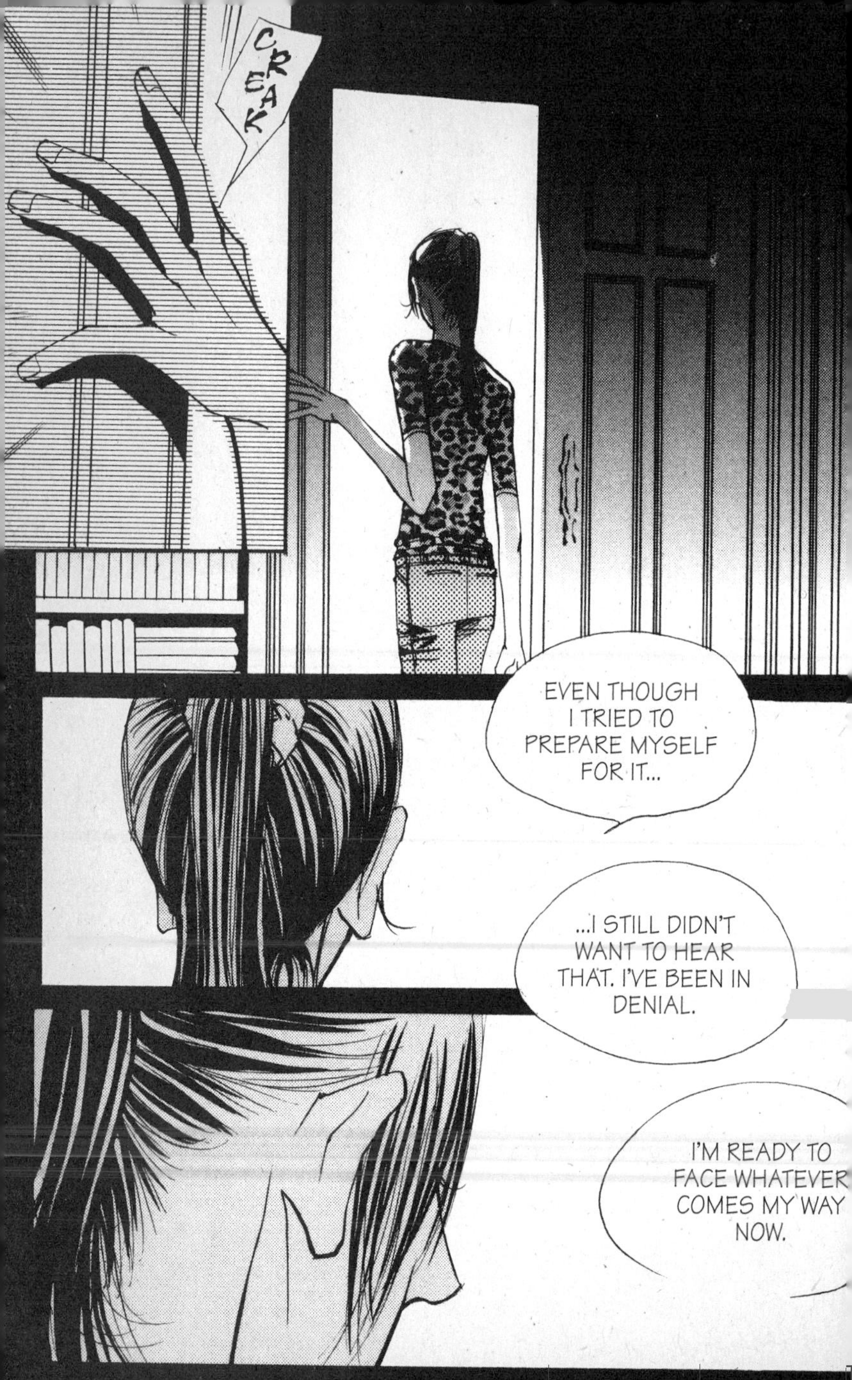
CREAK
EVEN THOUGH I TRIED TO PREPARE MYSELF FOR IT...
...I STILL DIDN'T WANT TO HEAR THAT. I'VE BEEN IN DENIAL.
I'M READY TO FACE WHATEVER COMES MY WAY NOW.

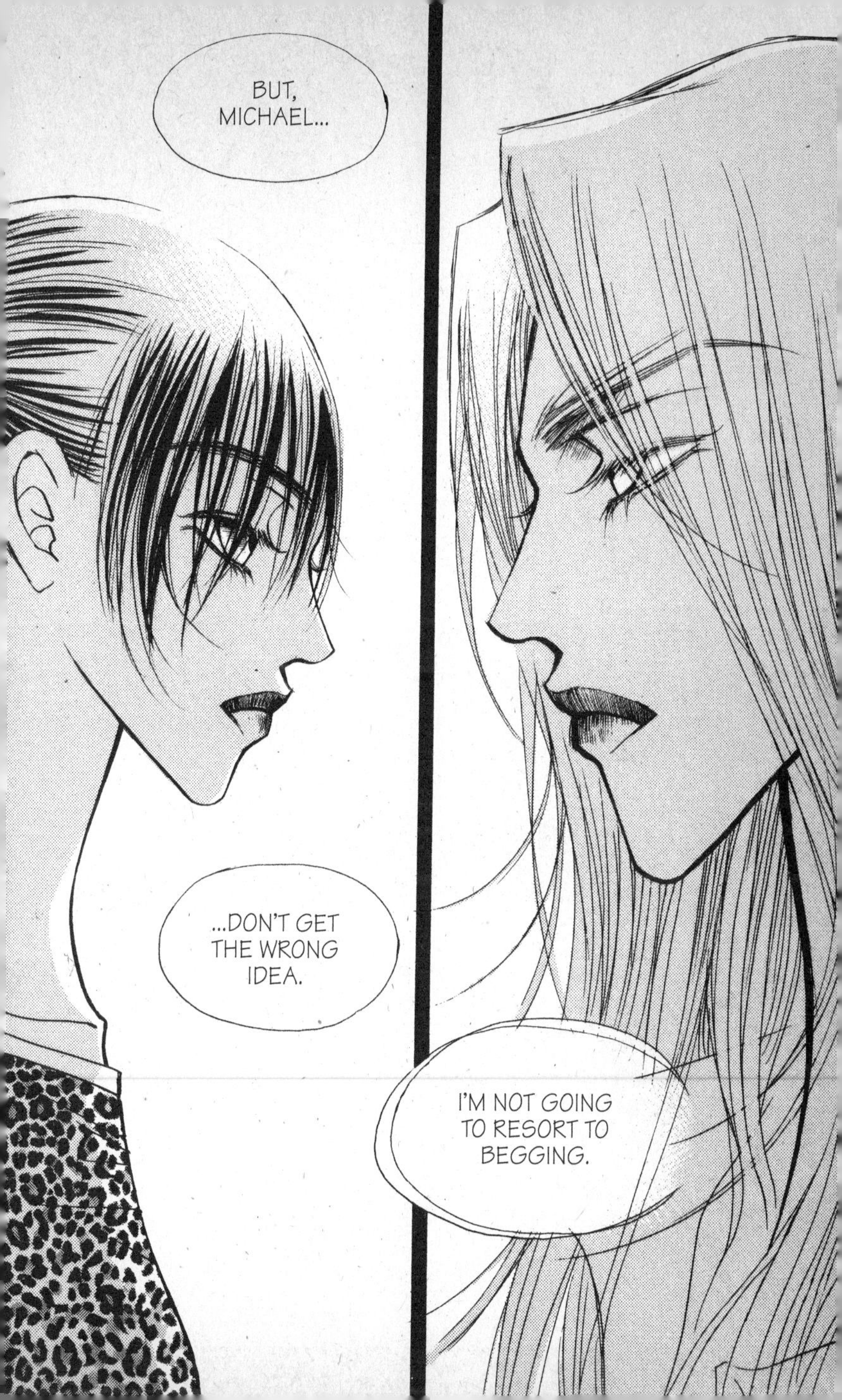
BUT, MICHAEL...
...DON'T GET THE WRONG IDEA.
I'M NOT GOING TO RESORT TO BEGGING.

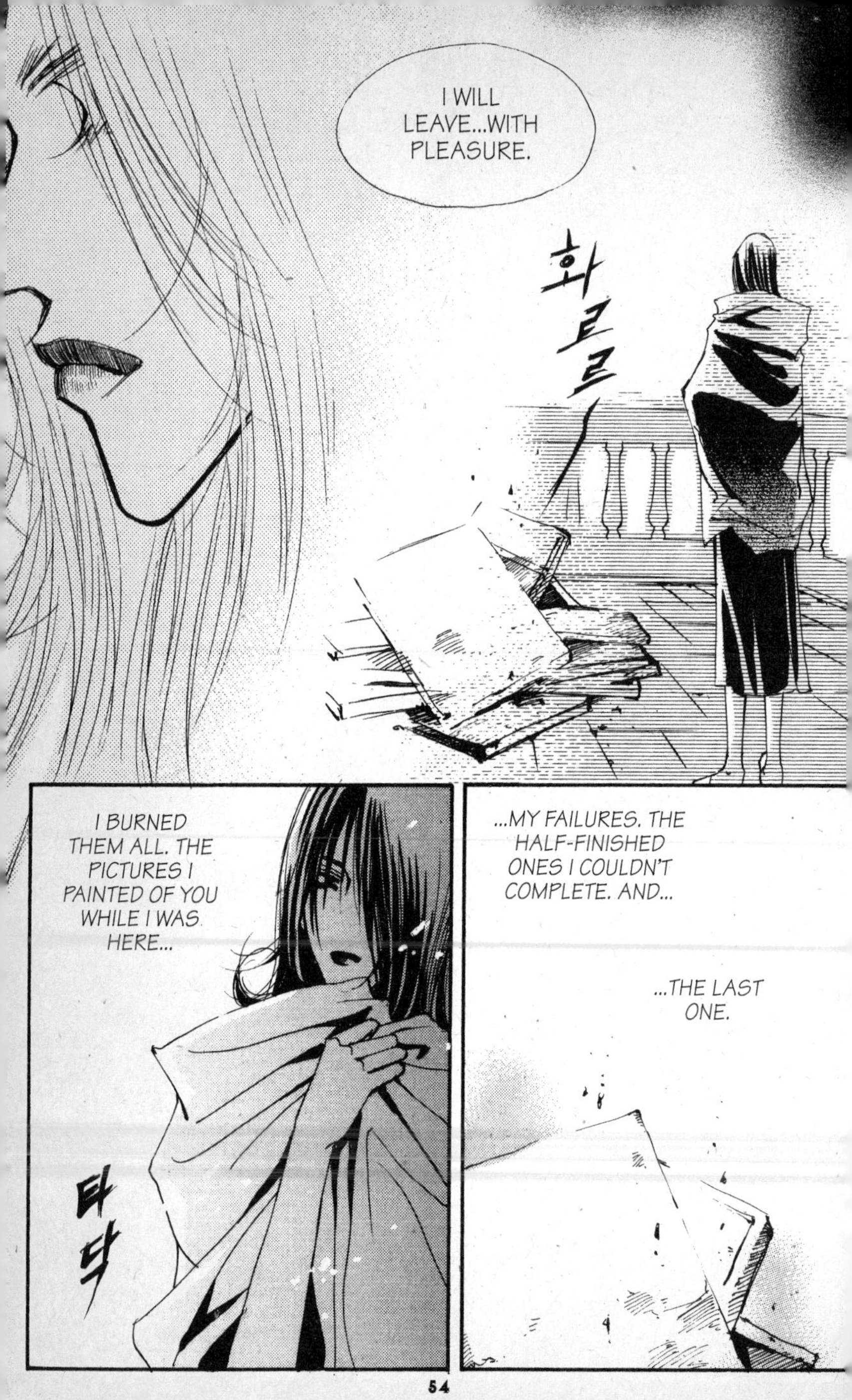
I WILL LEAVE...WITH PLEASURE.
화르르
I BURNED THEM ALL. THE PICTURES I PAINTED OF YOU WHILE I WAS HERE...
타닥
...MY FAILURES. THE HALF-FINISHED ONES I COULDN'T COMPLETE. AND...
...THE LAST ONE.

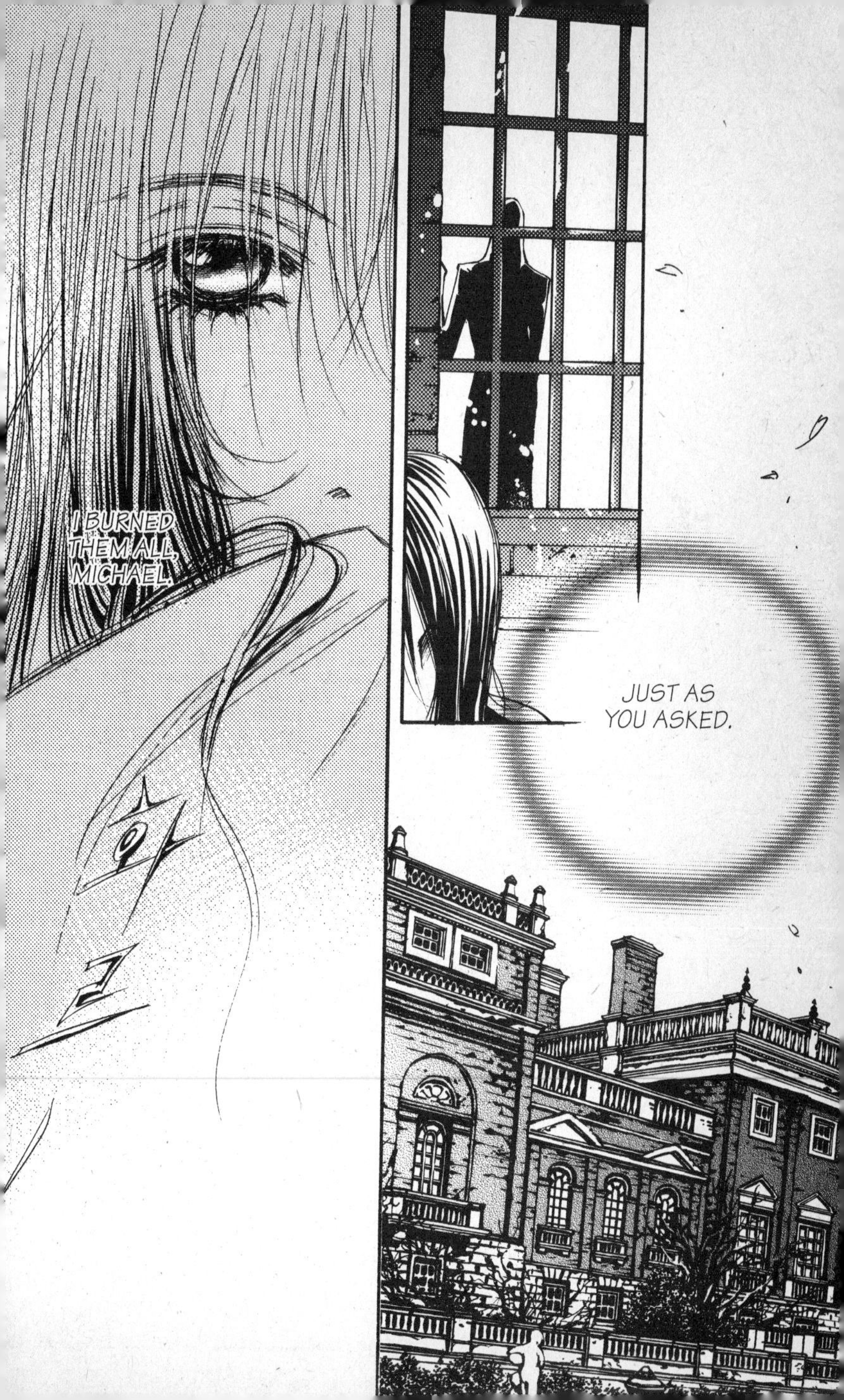
I BURNED THEM ALL, MICHAEL.
JUST AS YOU ASKED.

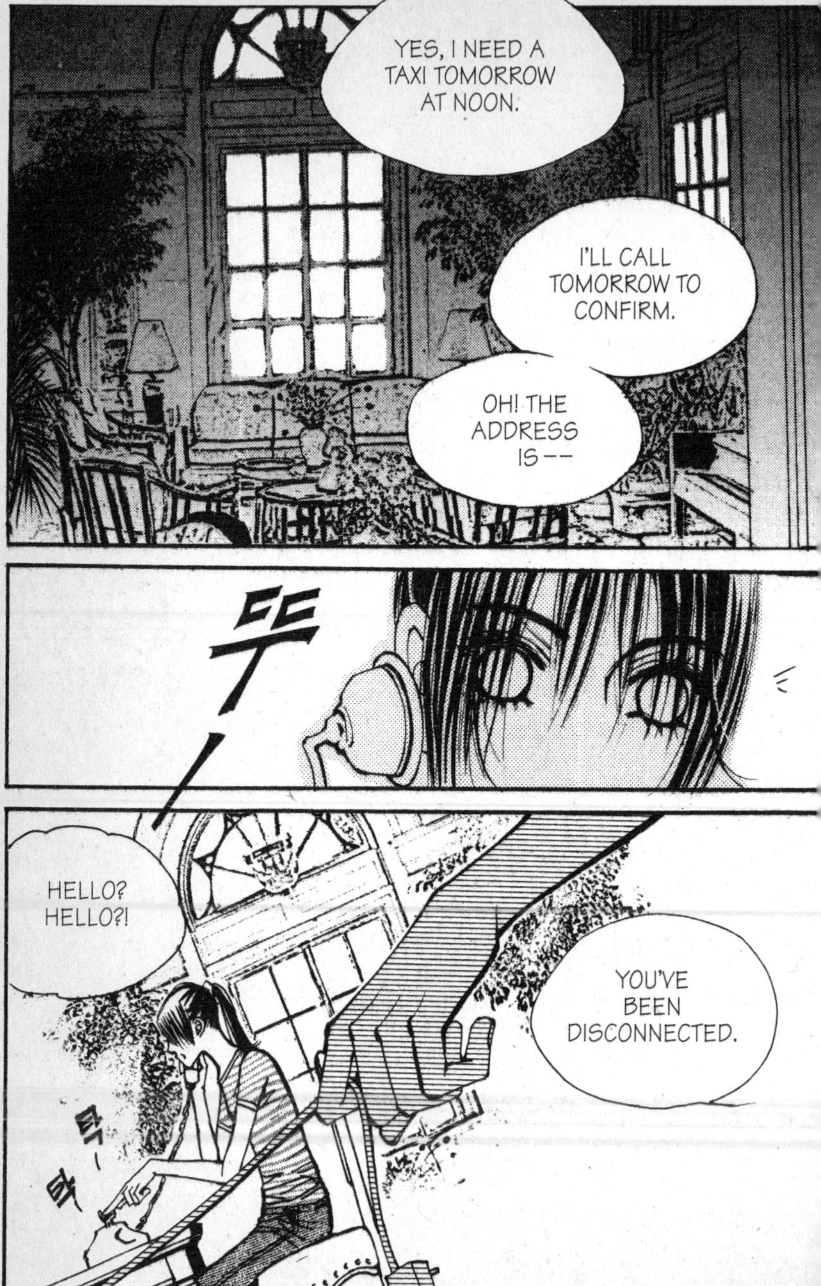
YES, I NEED A TAXI TOMORROW AT NOON.
I'LL CALL TOMORROW TO CONFIRM.
OH! THE ADDRESS IS--
HELLO? HELLO?!
YOU'VE BEEN DISCONNECTED.

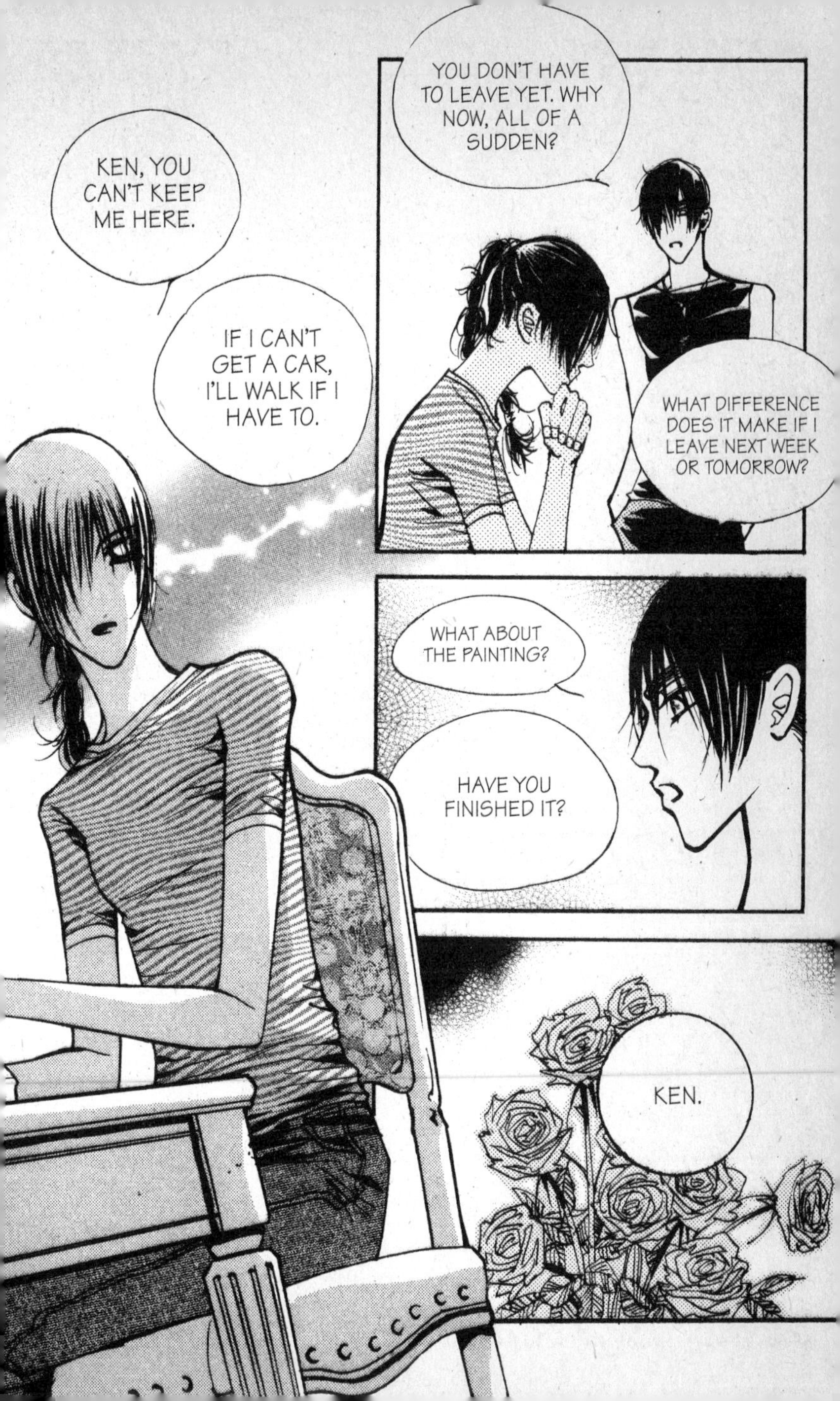
KEN, YOU CAN'T KEEP ME HERE.
IF I CAN'T GET A CAR, I'LL WALK IF I HAVE TO.
YOU DON'T HAVE TO LEAVE YET. WHY NOW, ALL OF A SUDDEN?
WHAT DIFFERENCE DOES IT MAKE IF I LEAVE NEXT WEEK OR TOMORROW?
WHAT ABOUT THE PAINTING?
HAVE YOU FINISHED IT?
KEN.

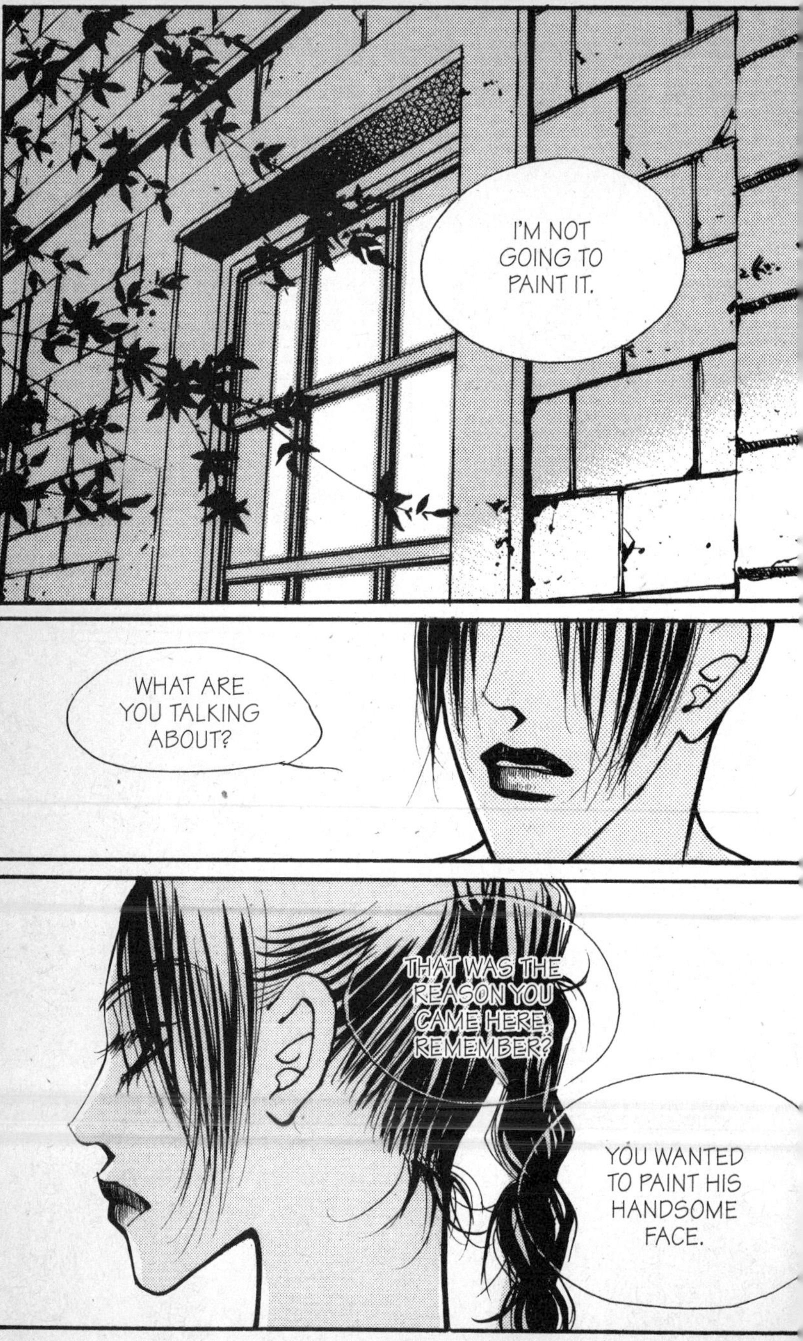
I'M NOT GOING TO PAINT IT.
WHAT ARE YOU TALKING ABOUT?
THAT WAS THE REASON YOU CAME HERE, REMEMBER?
YOU WANTED TO PAINT HIS HANDSOME FACE.

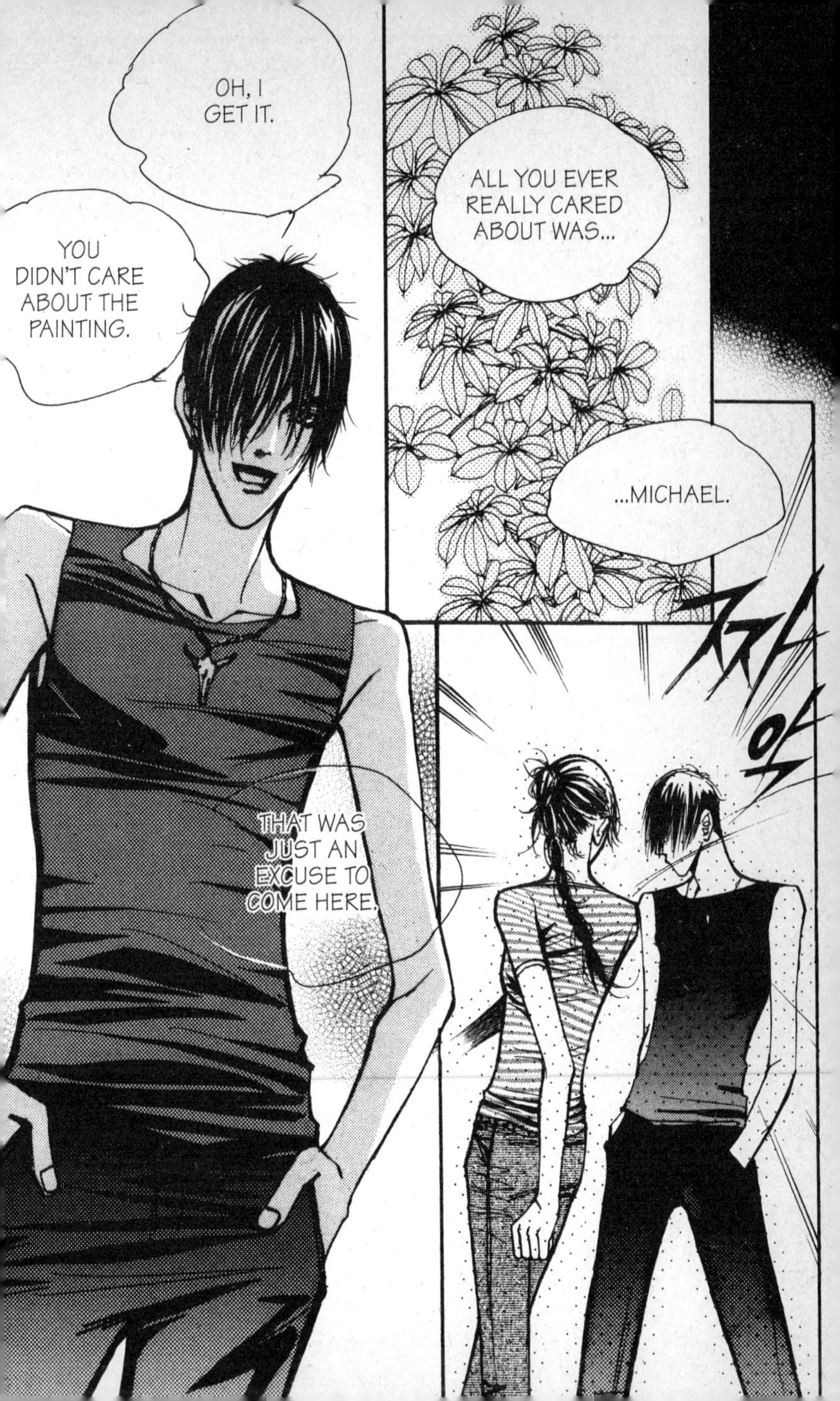
OH, I GET IT.
YOU DIDN'T CARE ABOUT THE PAINTING.
THAT WAS JUST AN EXCUSE TO COME HERE.
ALL YOU EVER REALLY CARED ABOUT WAS...
...MICHAEL.

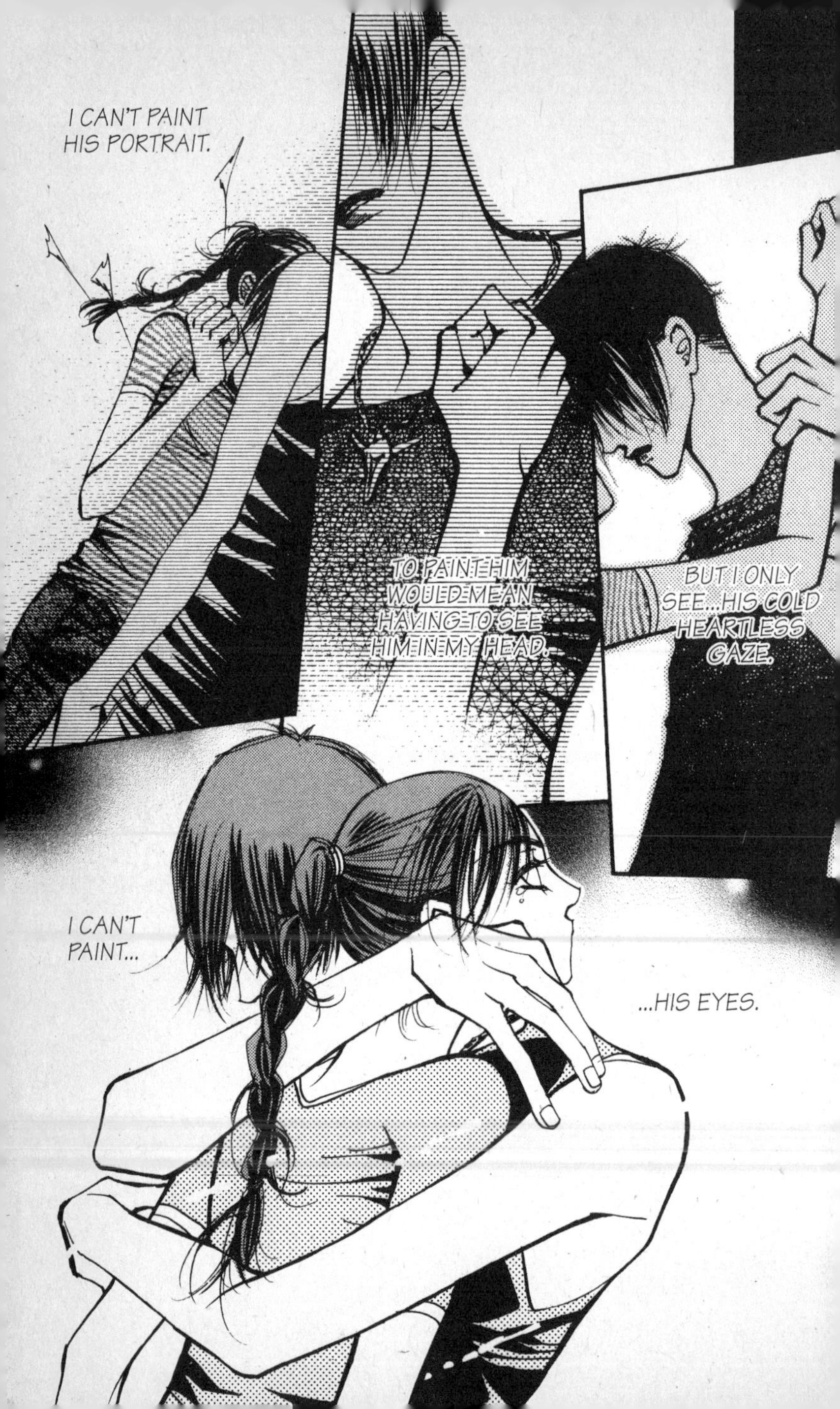

I CAN'T PAINT HIS PORTRAIT.
BUT I ONLY SEE...HIS COLD HEARTLESS GAZE.
TO PAINT HIM WOULD MEAN HAVING TO SEE HIM IN MY HEAD.
...HIS EYES.
I CAN'T PAINT...

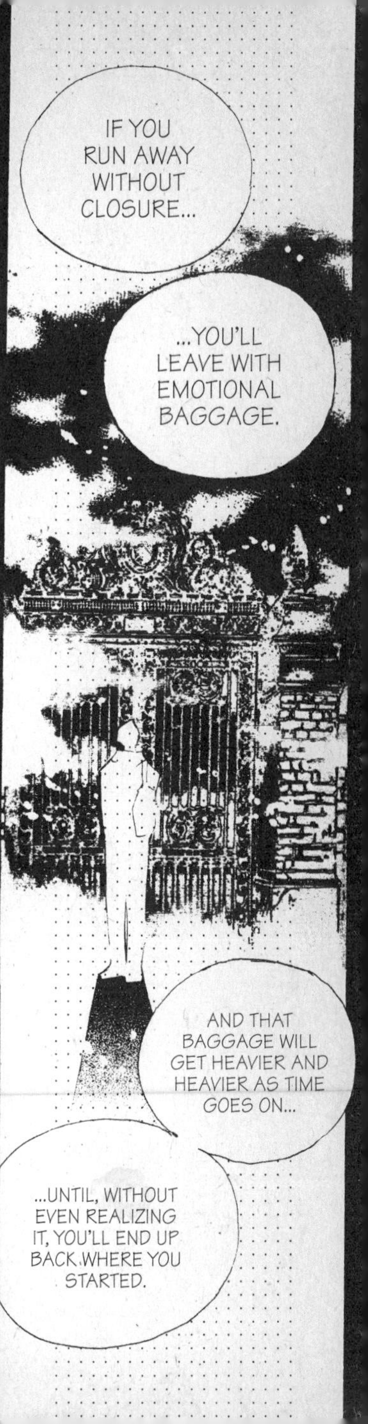
IF YOU RUN AWAY WITHOUT CLOSURE...
...YOU'LL LEAVE WITH EMOTIONAL BAGGAGE.
AND THAT BAGGAGE WILL GET HEAVIER AND HEAVIER AS TIME GOES ON...
...UNTIL, WITHOUT EVEN REALIZING IT, YOU'LL END UP BACK WHERE YOU STARTED.
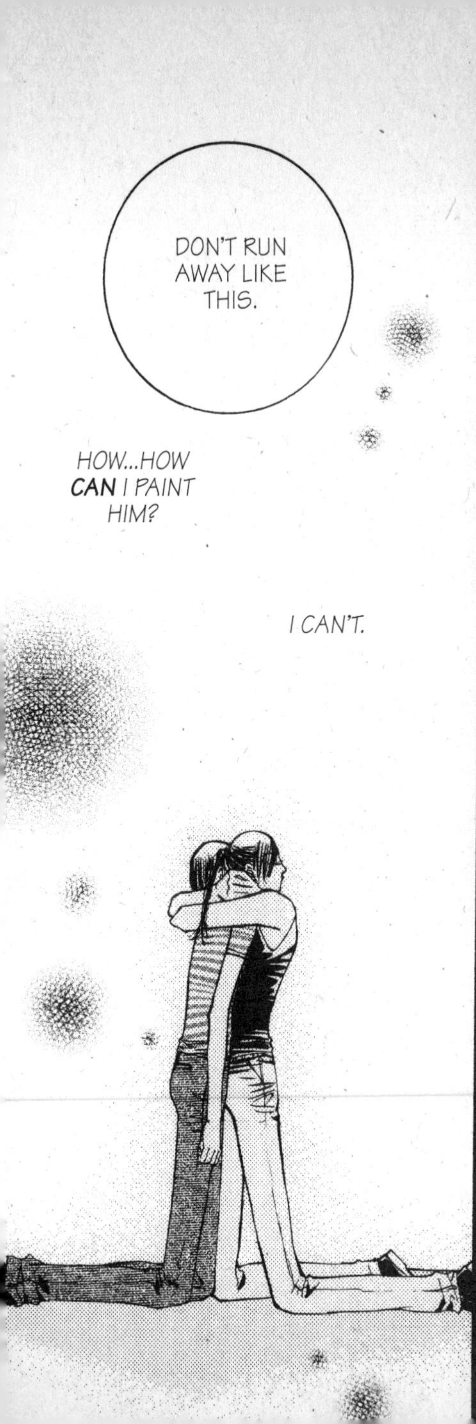
DON'T RUN AWAY LIKE THIS.
HOW...HOW CAN I PAINT HIM?
I CAN'T.

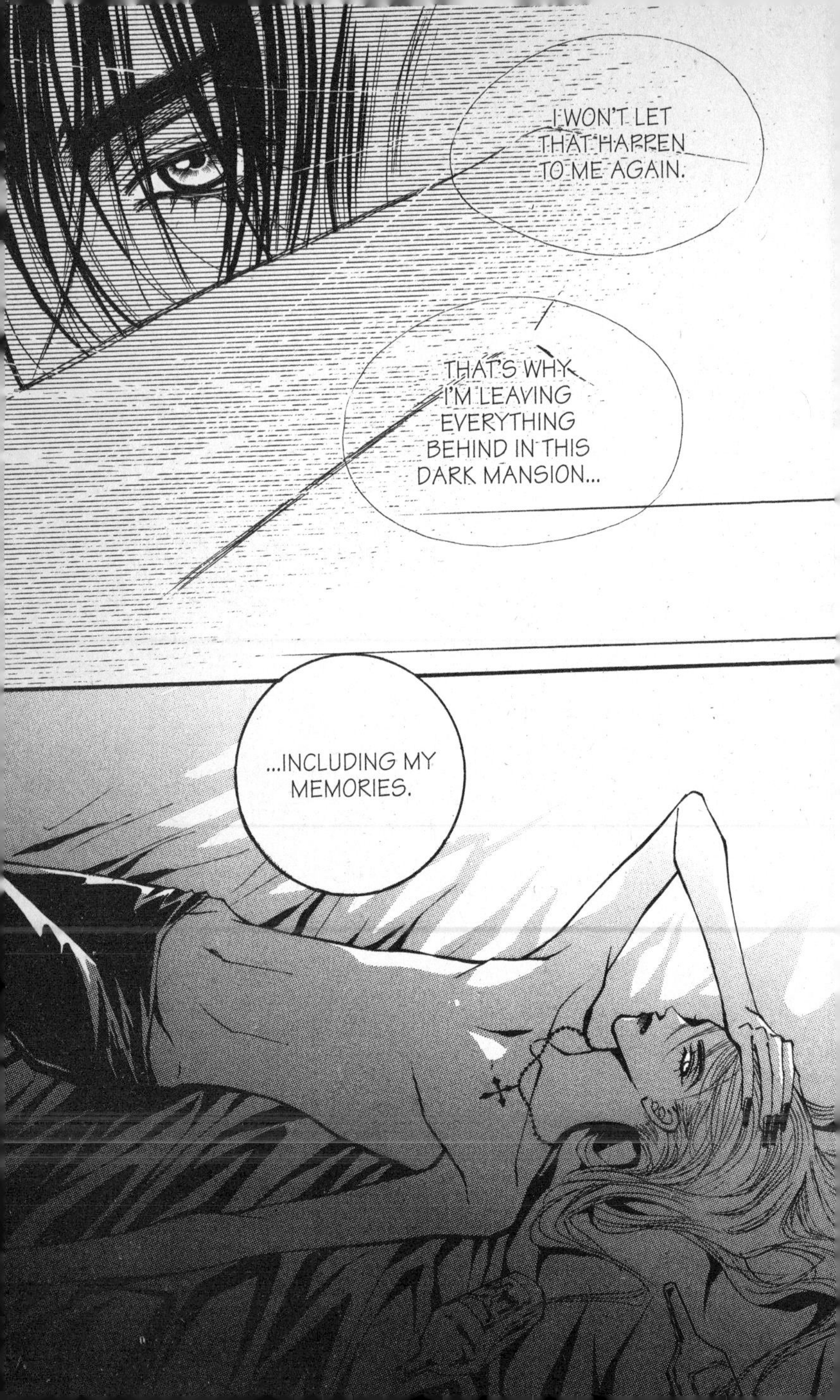
I WON'T LET THAT HAPPEN TO ME AGAIN.
THAT'S WHY I'M LEAVING EVERYTHING BEHIND IN THIS DARK MANSION...
...INCLUDING MY MEMORIES.

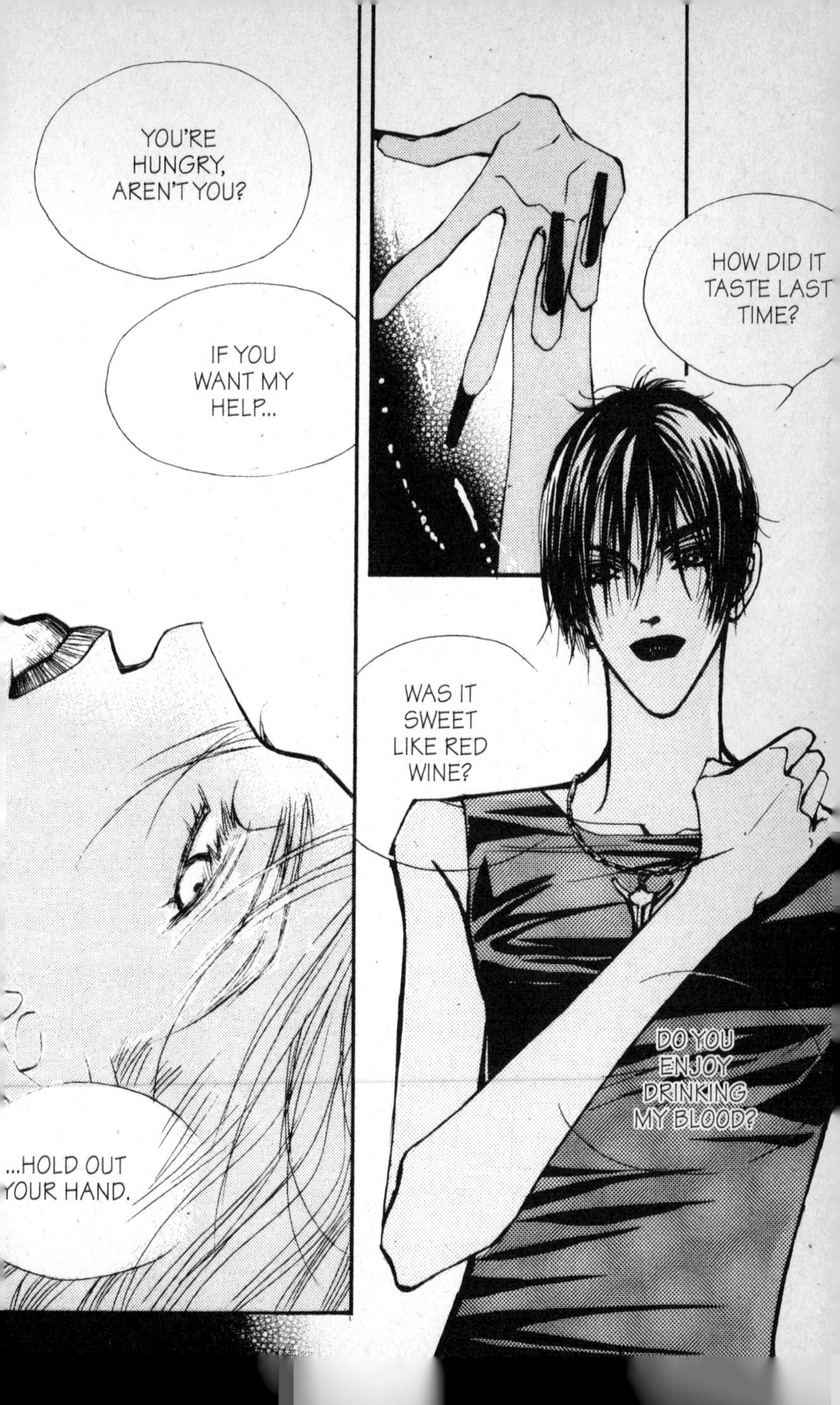
HOW DID IT TASTE LAST TIME?
WAS IT SWEET LIKE RED WINE?
DO YOU ENJOY DRINKING MY BLOOD?
YOU'RE HUNGRY, AREN'T YOU?
IF YOU WANT MY HELP...
...HOLD OUT YOUR HAND.

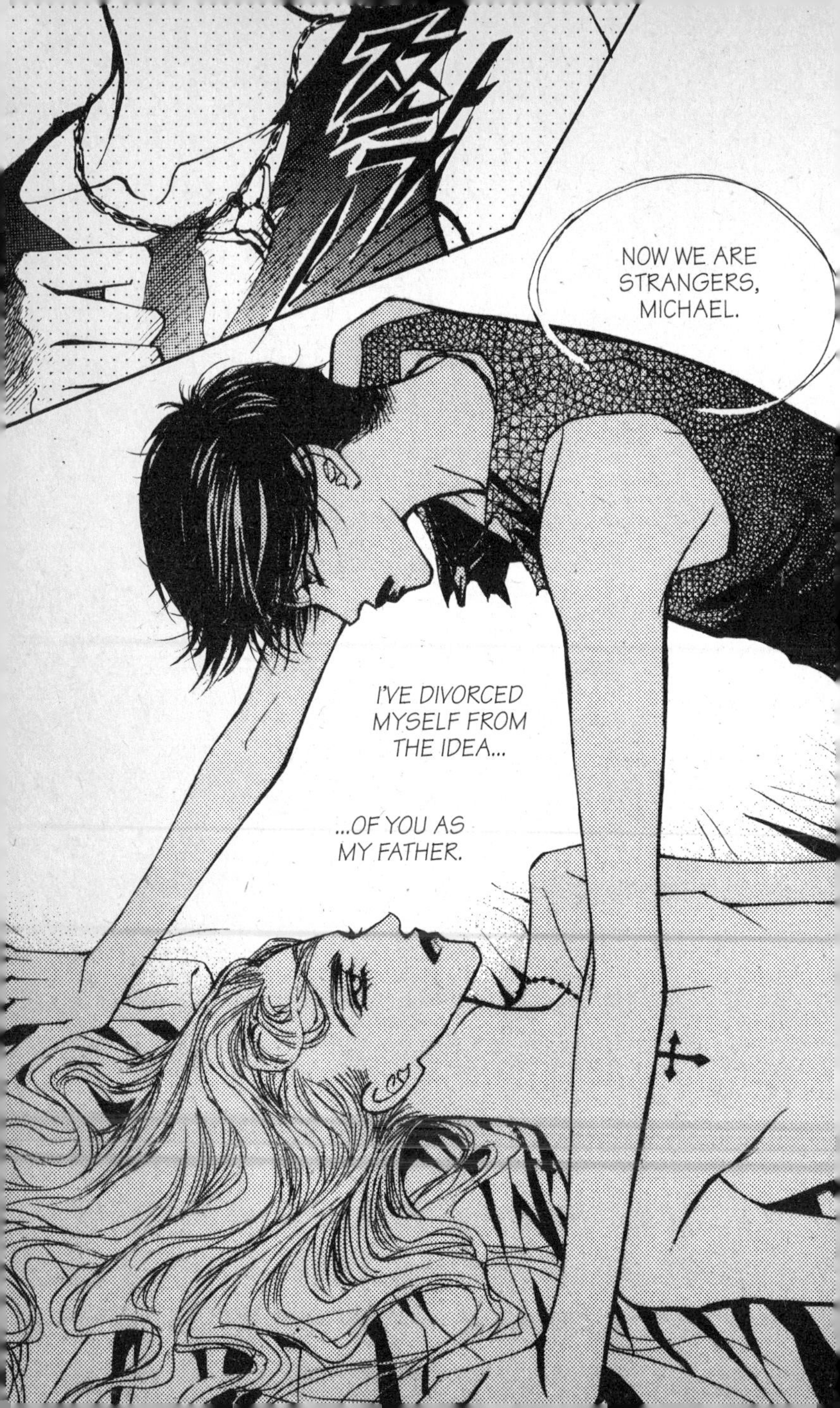
NOW WE ARE STRANGERS, MICHAEL.
I'VE DIVORCED MYSELF FROM THE IDEA...
...OF YOU AS MY FATHER.

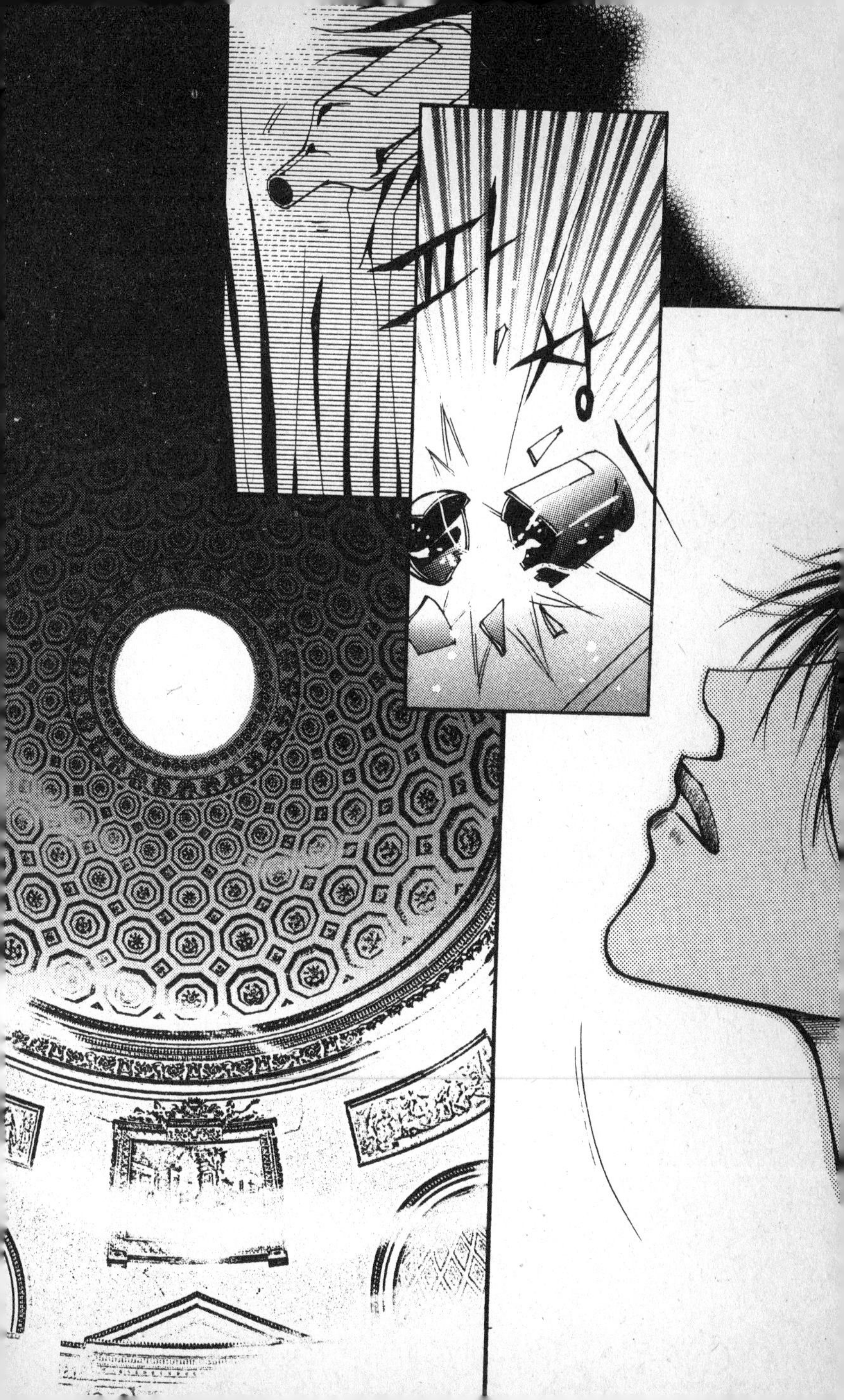

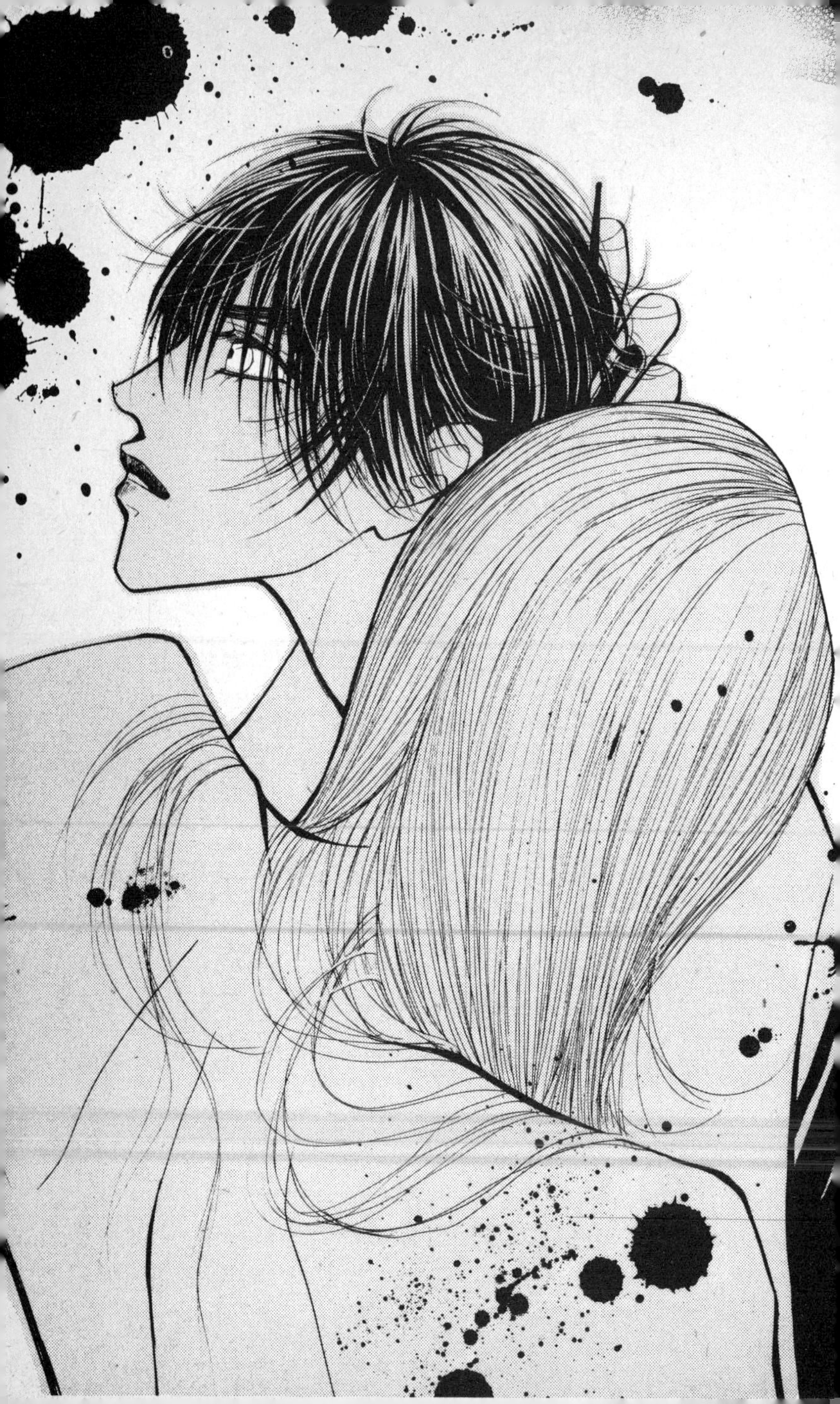

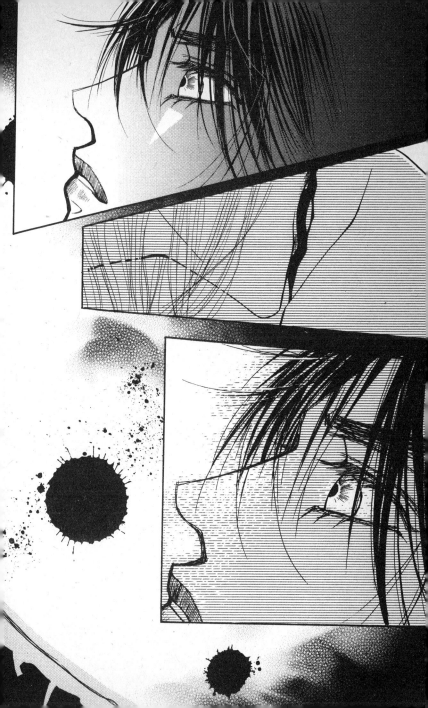

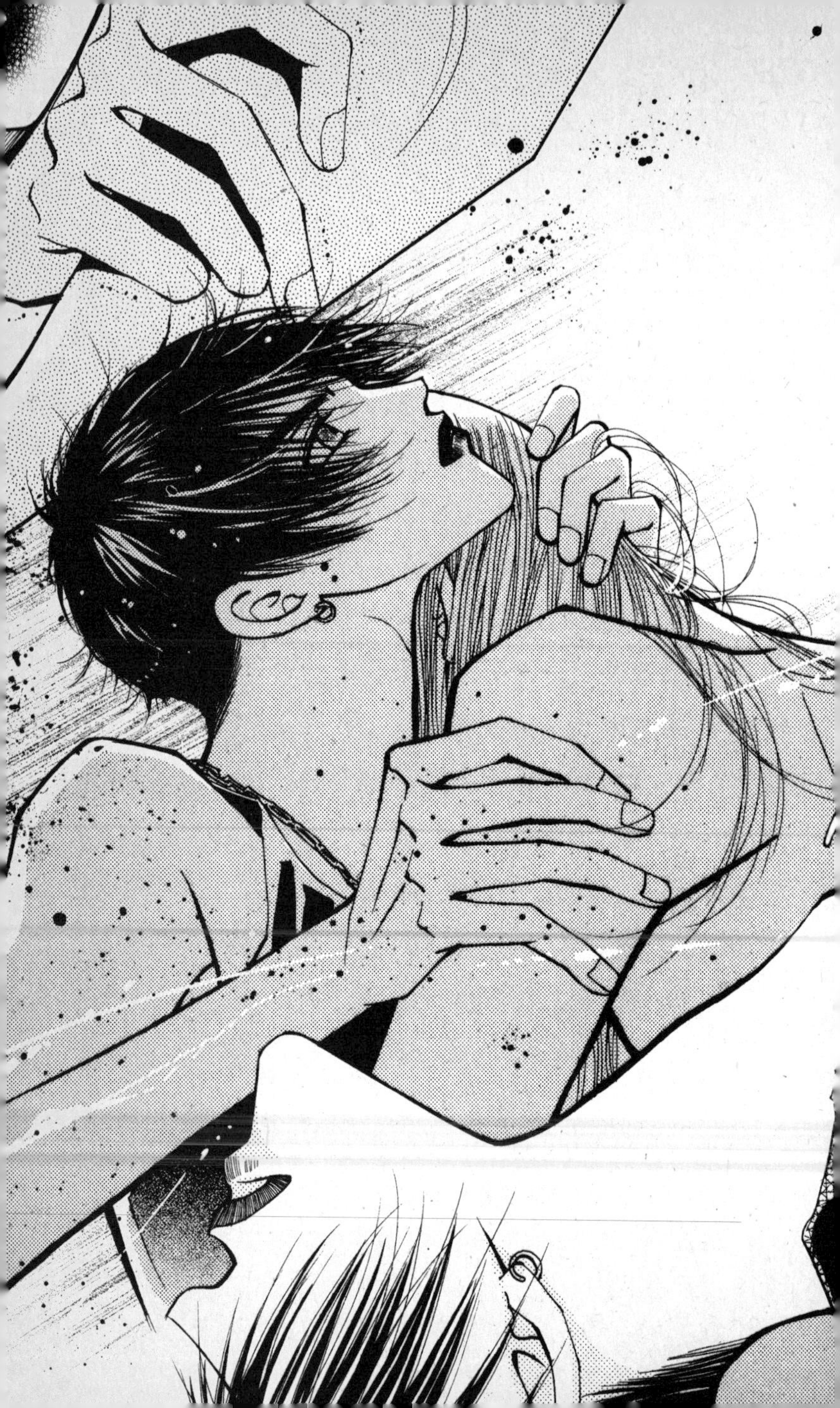

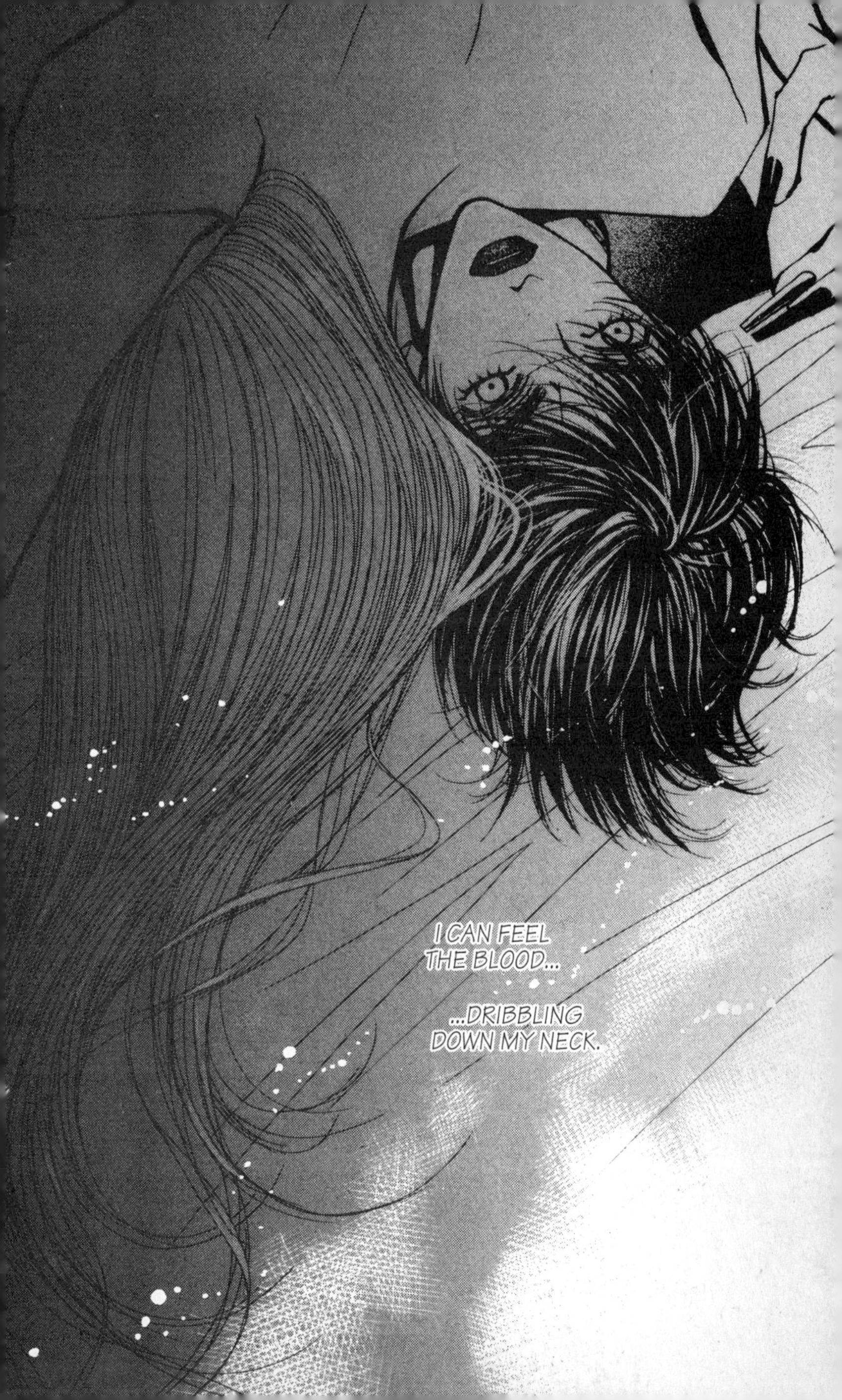
I CAN FEEL THE BLOOD...
...DRIBBLING DOWN MY NECK.

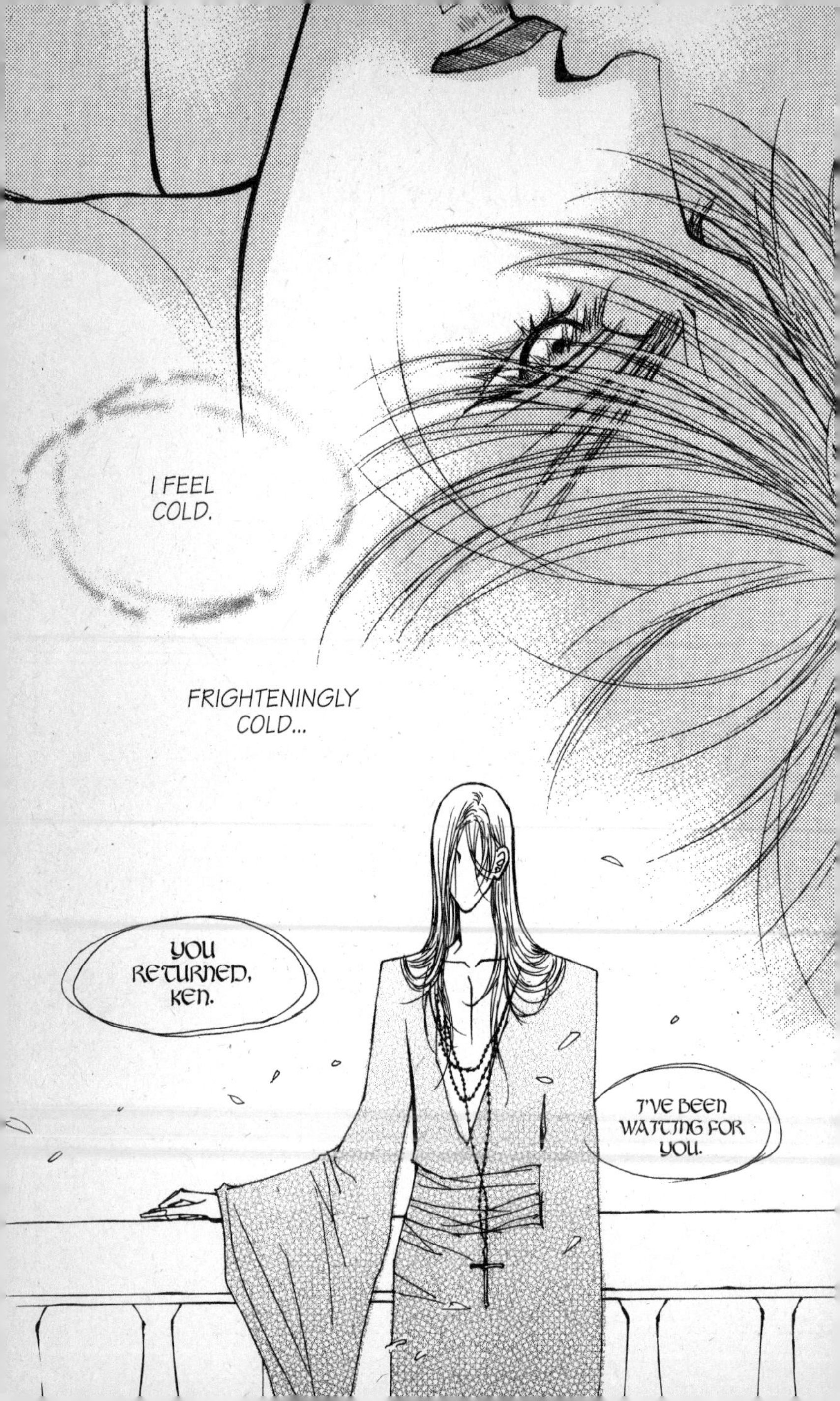
I FEEL COLD.
FRIGHTENINGLY COLD...
I'VE BEEN WAITING FOR YOU.
YOU RETURNED, KEN.

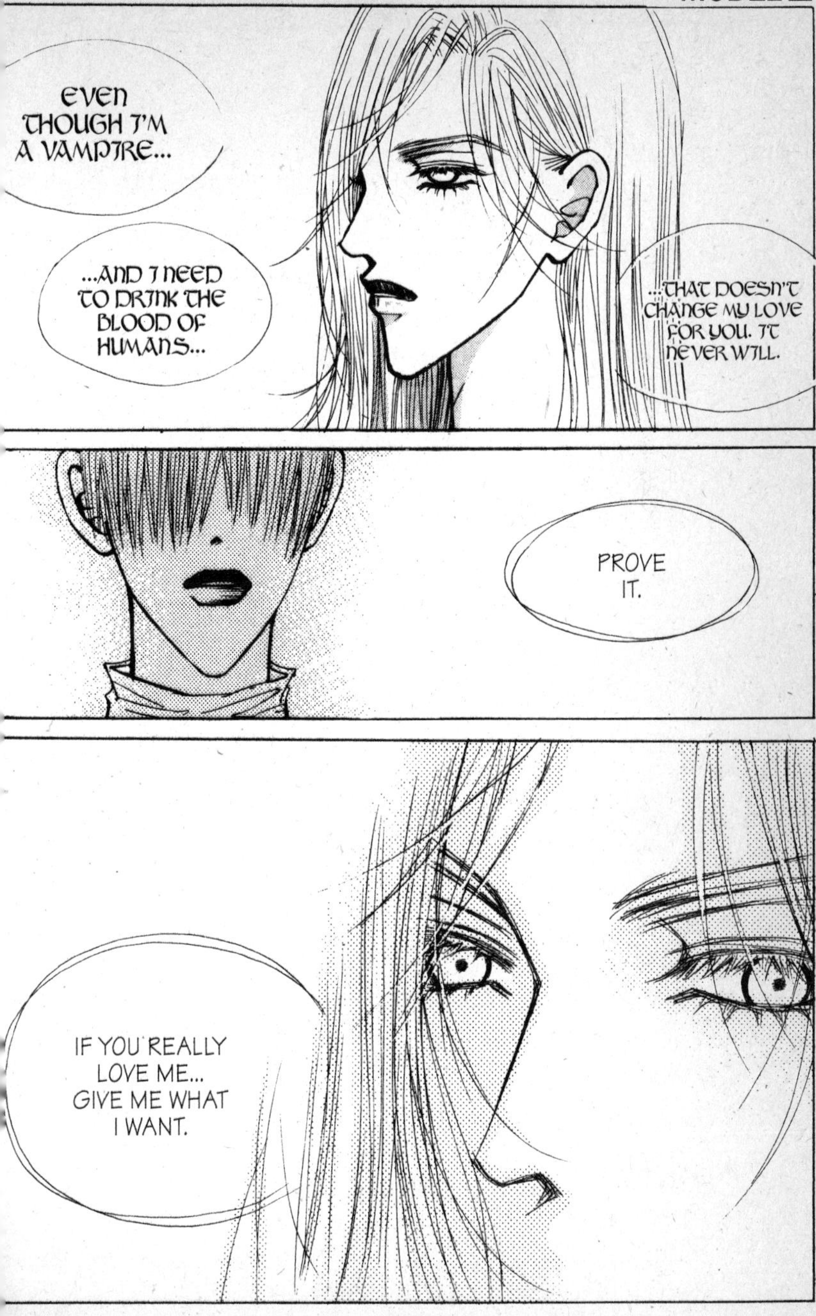
EVEN THOUGH I'M A VAMPIRE...
...AND I NEED TO DRINK THE BLOOD OF HUMANS...
...THAT DOESN'T CHANGE MY LOVE FOR YOU. IT NEVER WILL.
PROVE IT.
IF YOU REALLY LOVE ME... GIVE ME WHAT I WANT.

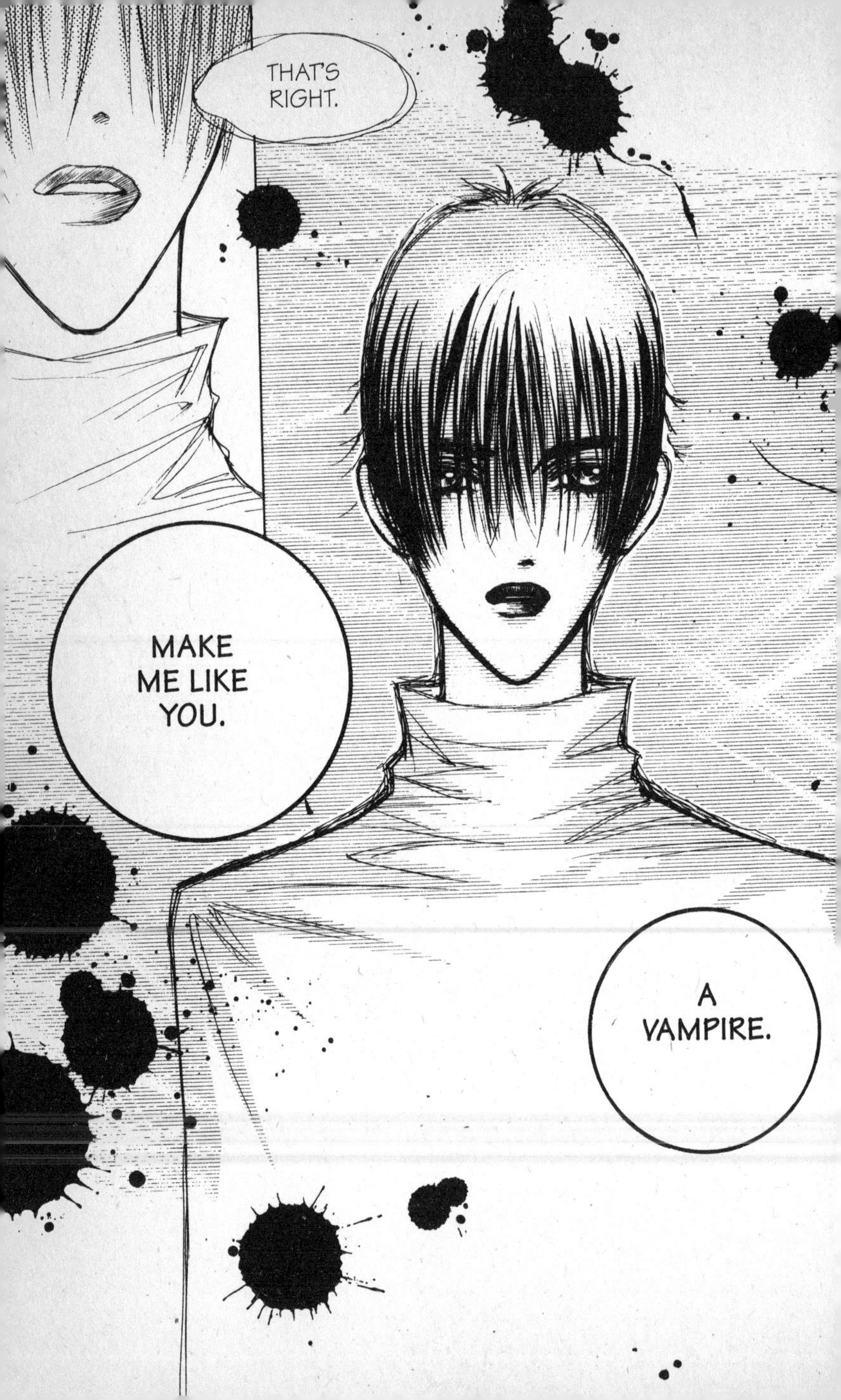
THAT'S RIGHT.
MAKE ME LIKE YOU.
A VAMPIRE.

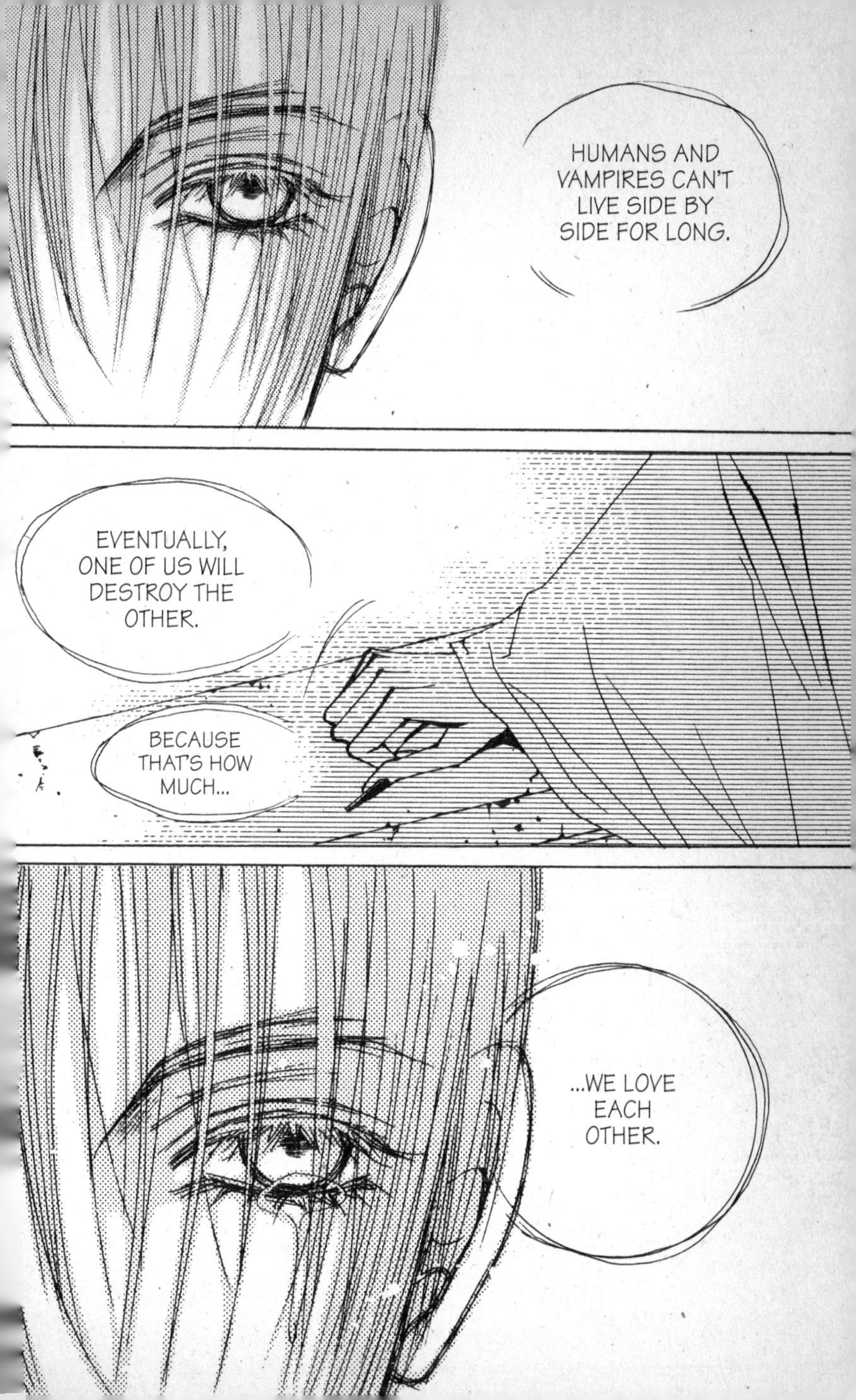
HUMANS AND VAMPIRES CAN'T LIVE SIDE BY SIDE FOR LONG.
EVENTUALLY, ONE OF US WILL DESTROY THE OTHER.
BECAUSE THAT'S HOW MUCH...
...WE LOVE EACH OTHER.

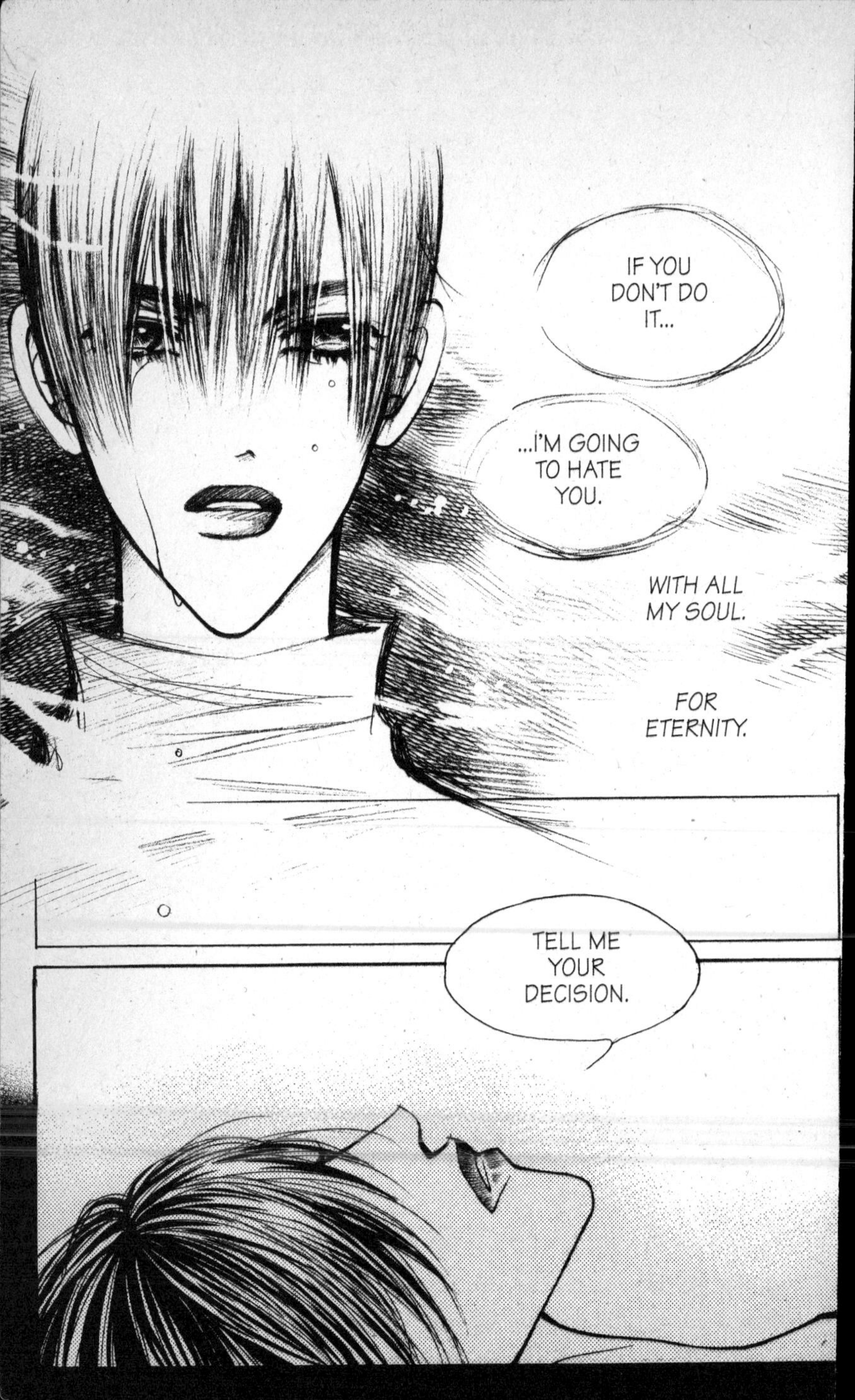
IF YOU DON'T DO IT...
...I'M GOING TO HATE YOU.
WITH ALL MY SOUL.
FOR ETERNITY.
TELL ME YOUR DECISION.

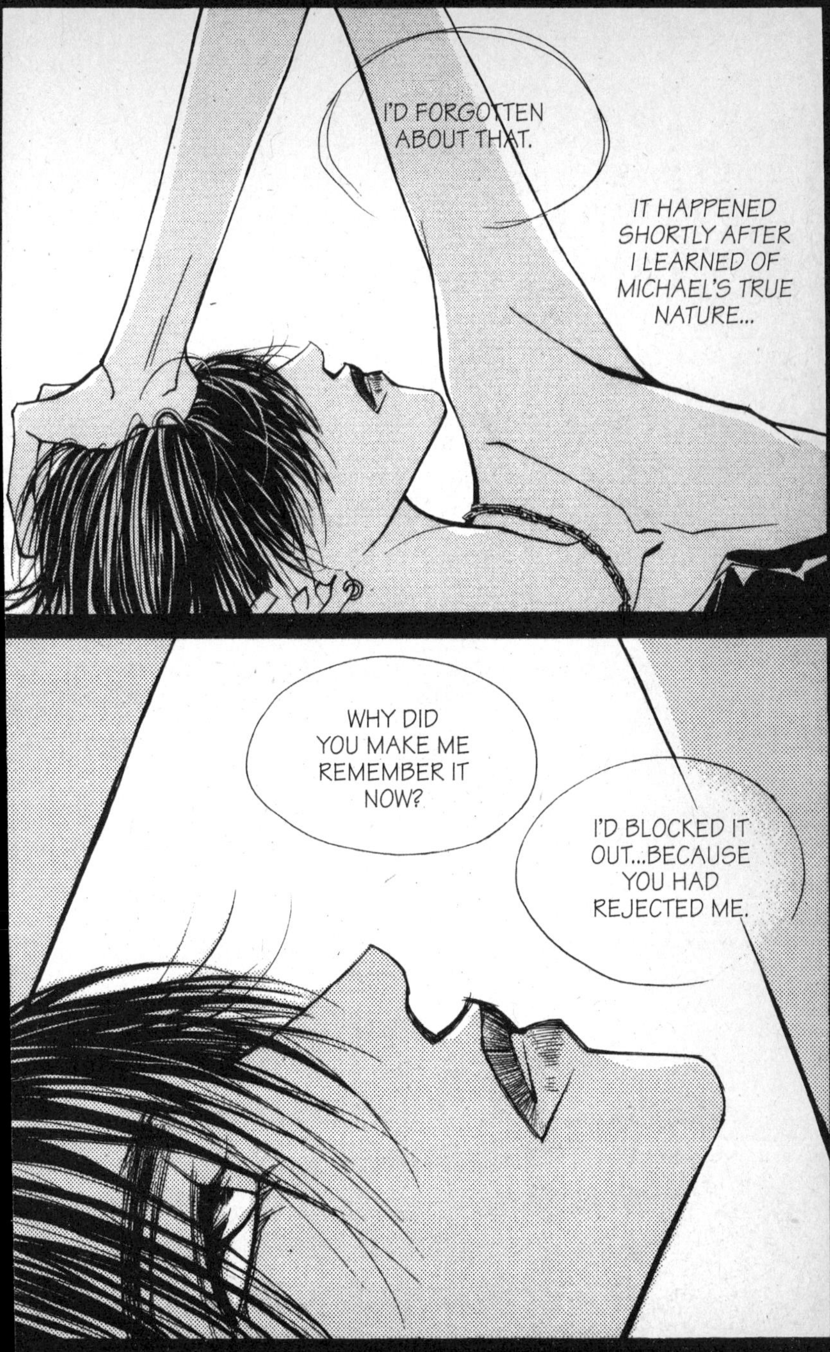
IT HAPPENED SHORTLY AFTER I LEARNED OF MICHAEL'S TRUE NATURE...
I'D FORGOTTEN ABOUT THAT.
I'D BLOCKED IT OUT...BECAUSE YOU HAD REJECTED ME.
WHY DID YOU MAKE ME REMEMBER IT NOW?

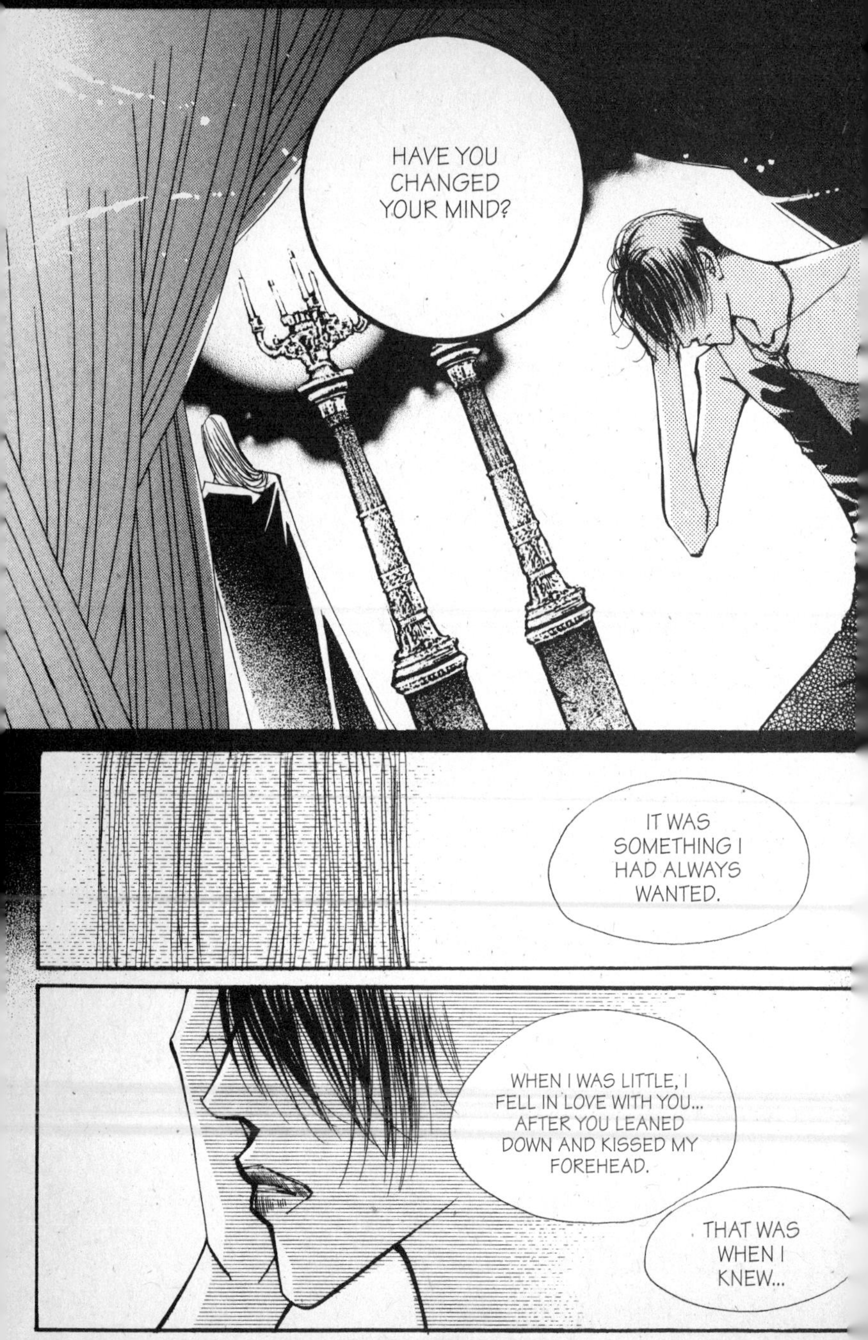
HAVE YOU CHANGED YOUR MIND?
IT WAS SOMETHING I HAD ALWAYS WANTED.
WHEN I WAS LITTLE, I FELL IN LOVE WITH YOU... AFTER YOU LEANED DOWN AND KISSED MY FOREHEAD.
THAT WAS WHEN I KNEW...

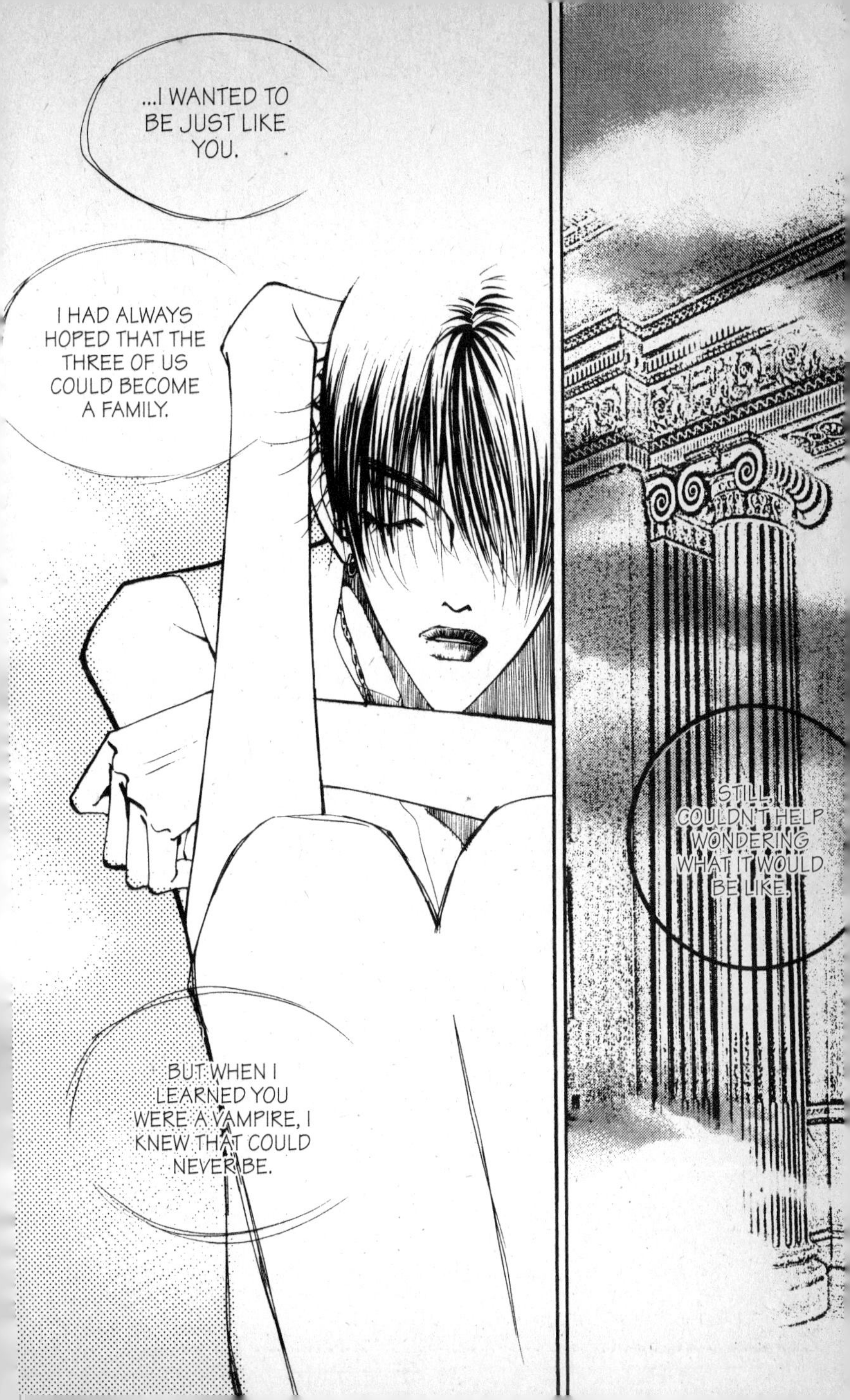
...I WANTED TO BE JUST LIKE YOU.
I HAD ALWAYS HOPED THAT THE THREE OF US COULD BECOME A FAMILY.
BUT WHEN I LEARNED YOU WERE A VAMPIRE, I KNEW THAT COULD NEVER BE.
STILL, I COULDN'T HELP WONDERING WHAT IT WOULD BE LIKE.

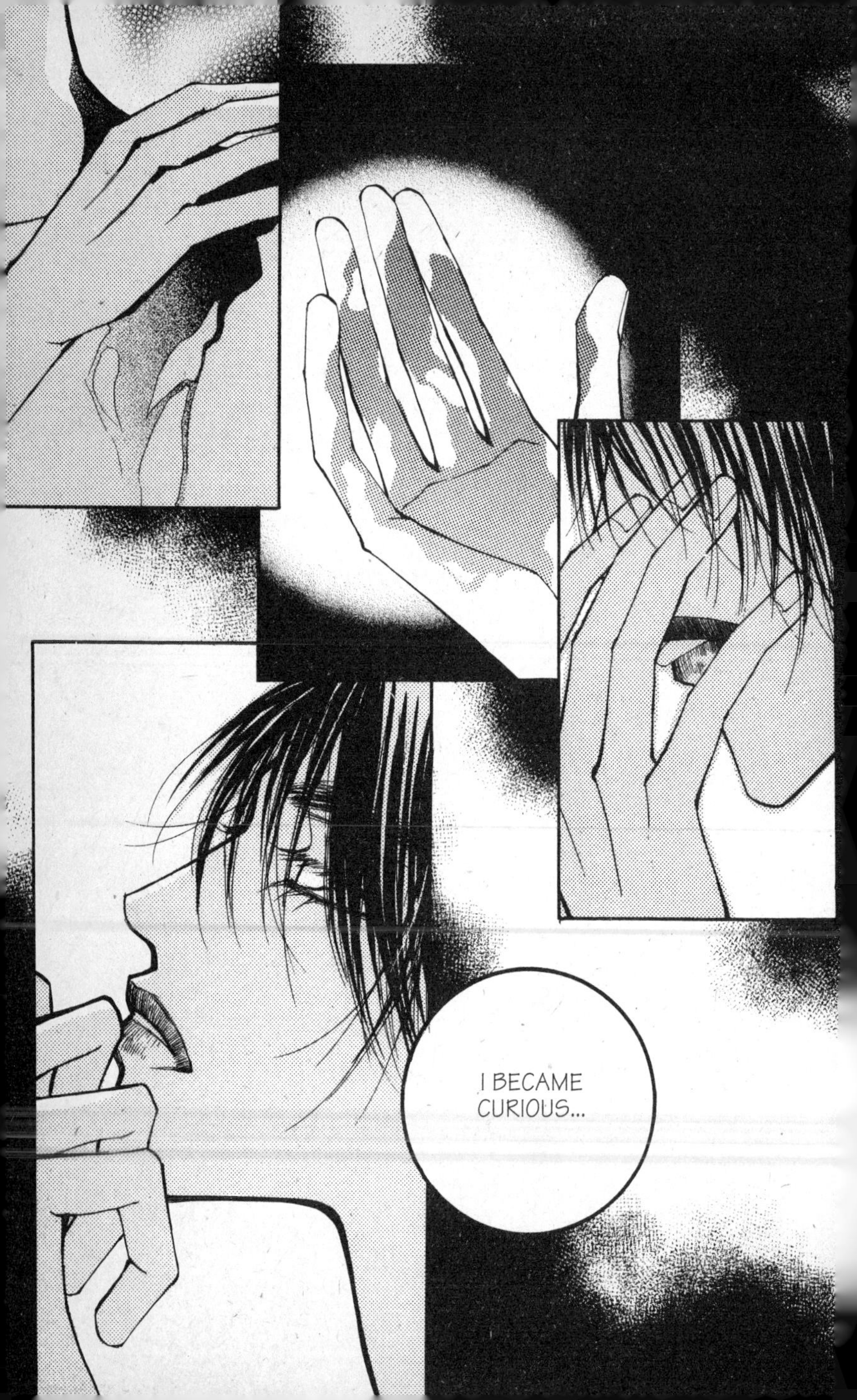
I BECAME CURIOUS...

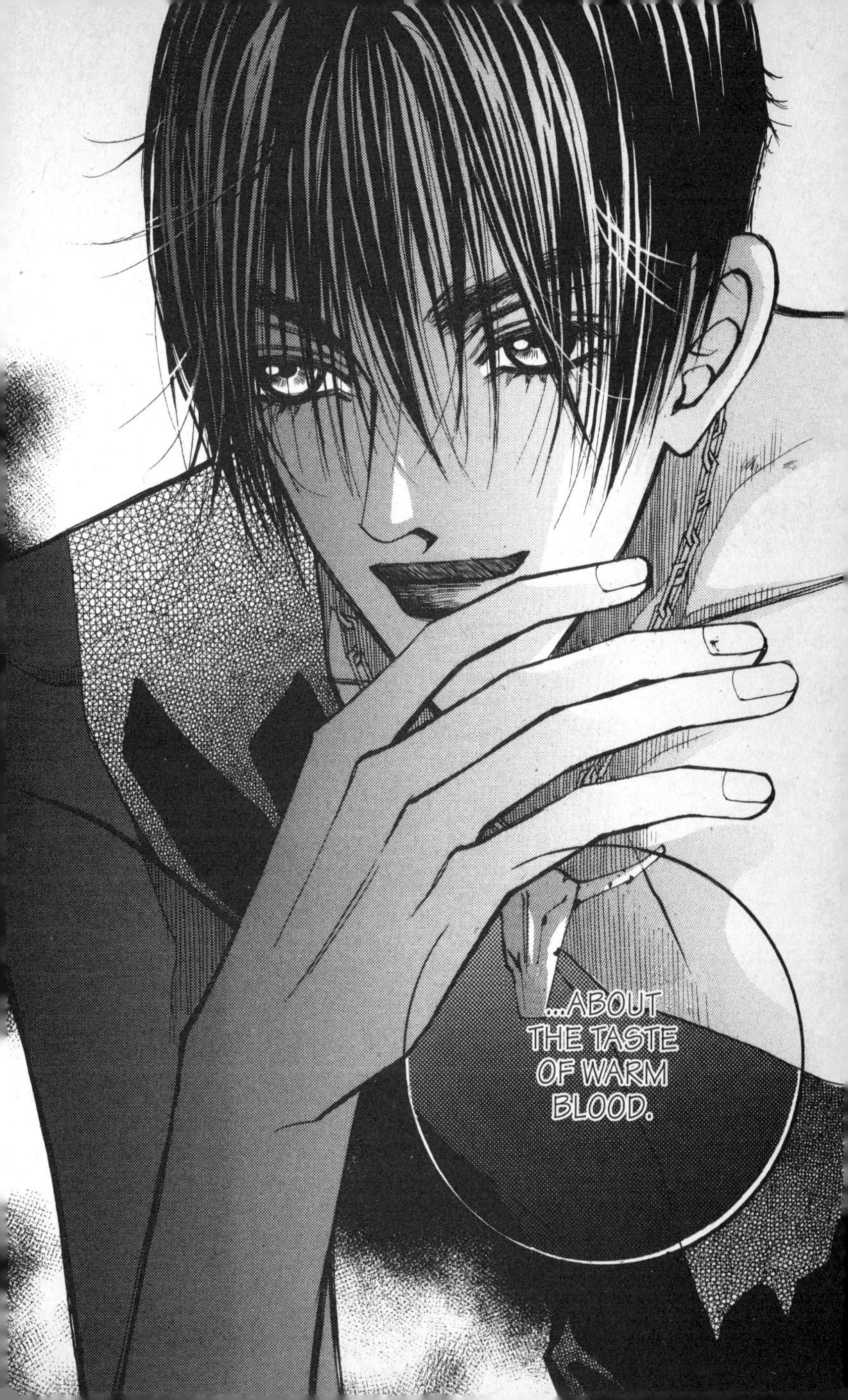
...ABOUT THE TASTE OF WARM BLOOD.

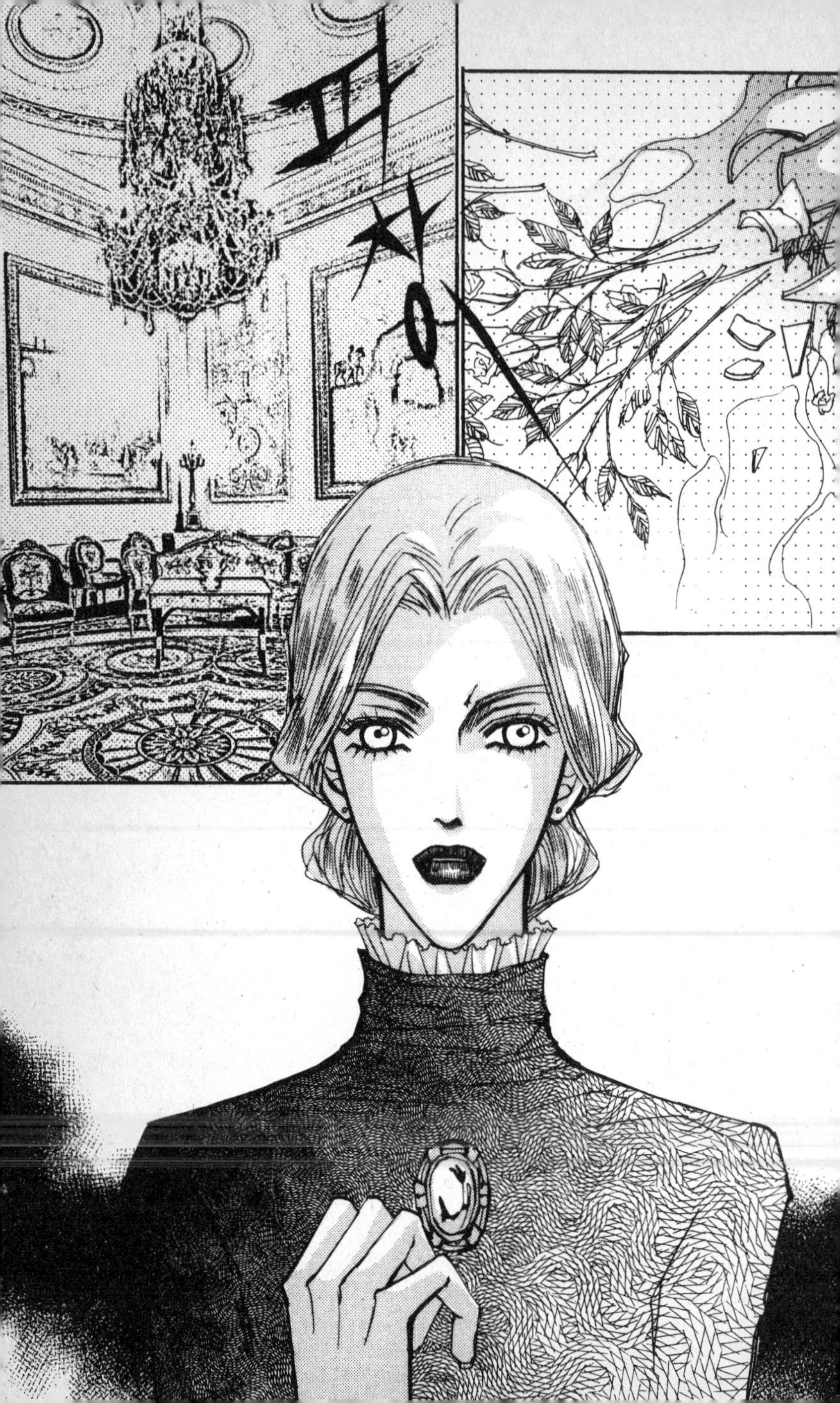
파창

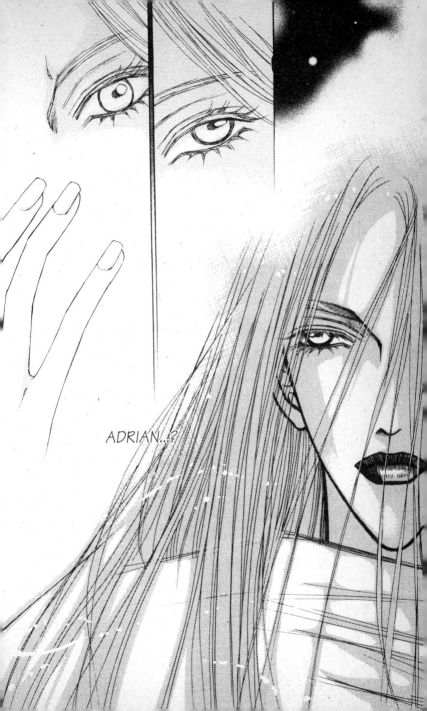

ADRIAN...!?

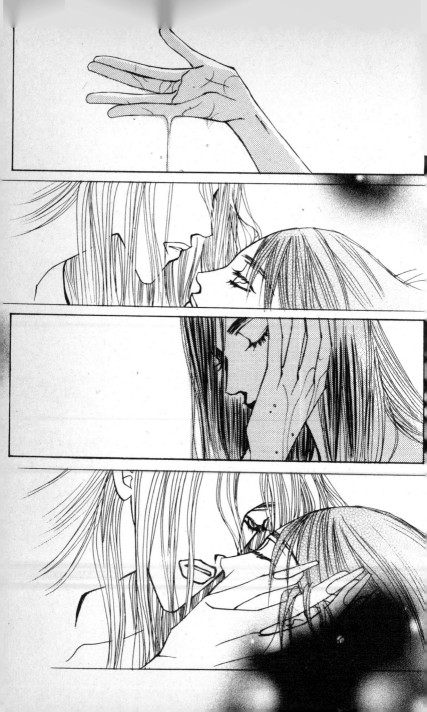

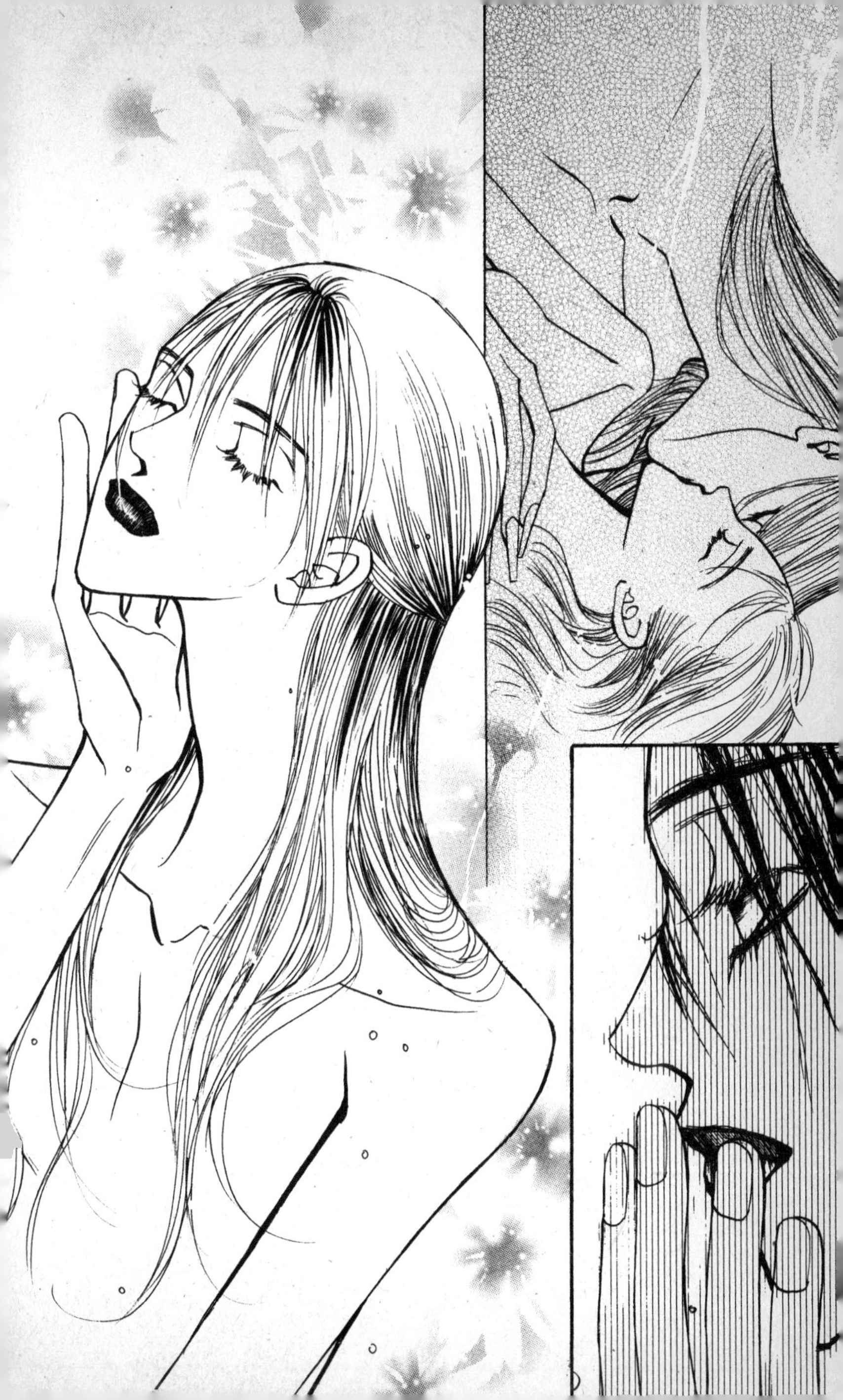

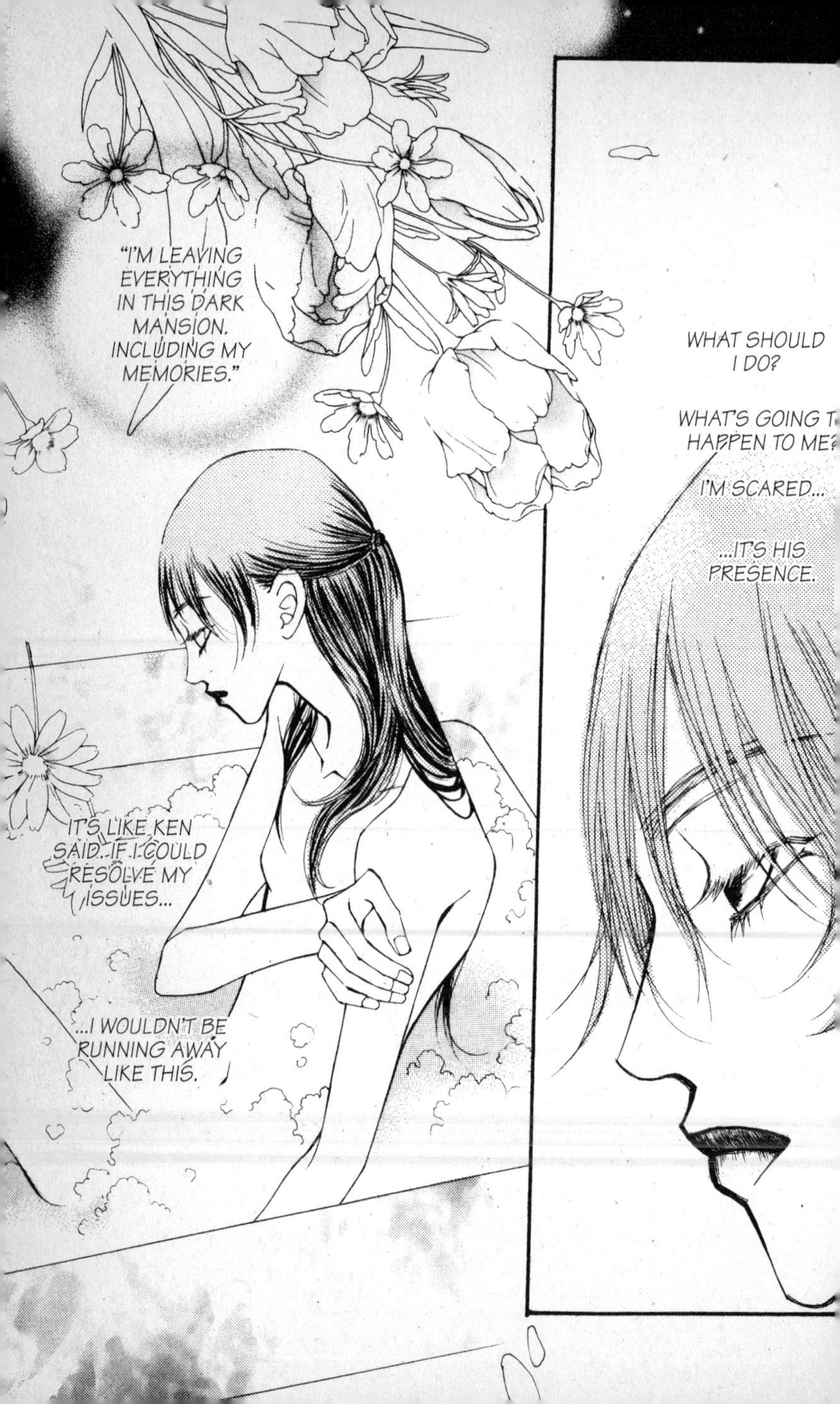
WHAT SHOULD I DO?
WHAT'S GOING T HAPPEN TO ME?
I'M SCARED...
...IT'S HIS PRESENCE.
"I'M LEAVING EVERYTHING IN THIS DARK MANSION. INCLUDING MY MEMORIES."
IT'S LIKE KEN SAID...IF I COULD RESOLVE MY ISSUES...
...I WOULDN'T BE RUNNING AWAY LIKE THIS.

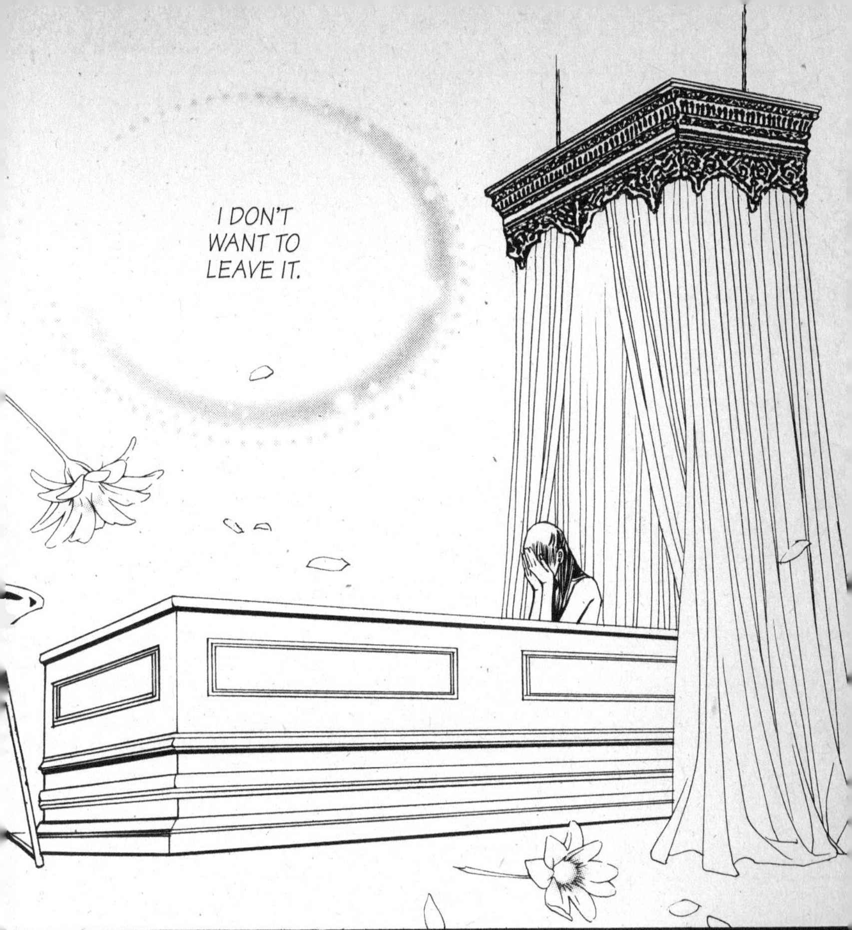
I DON'T
WANT TO
LEAVE IT.
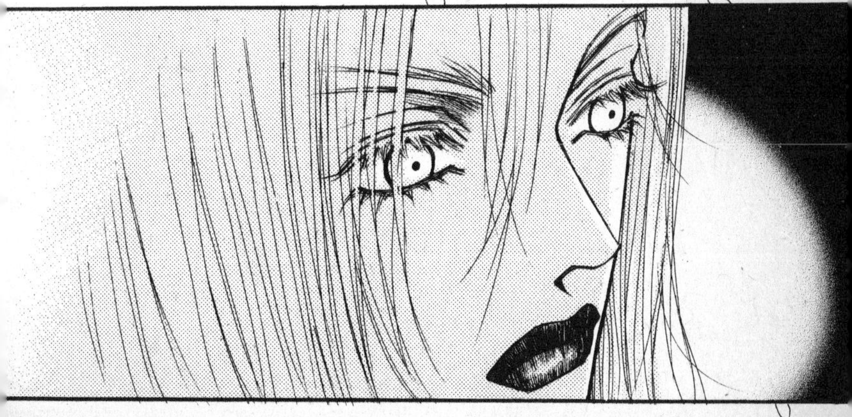

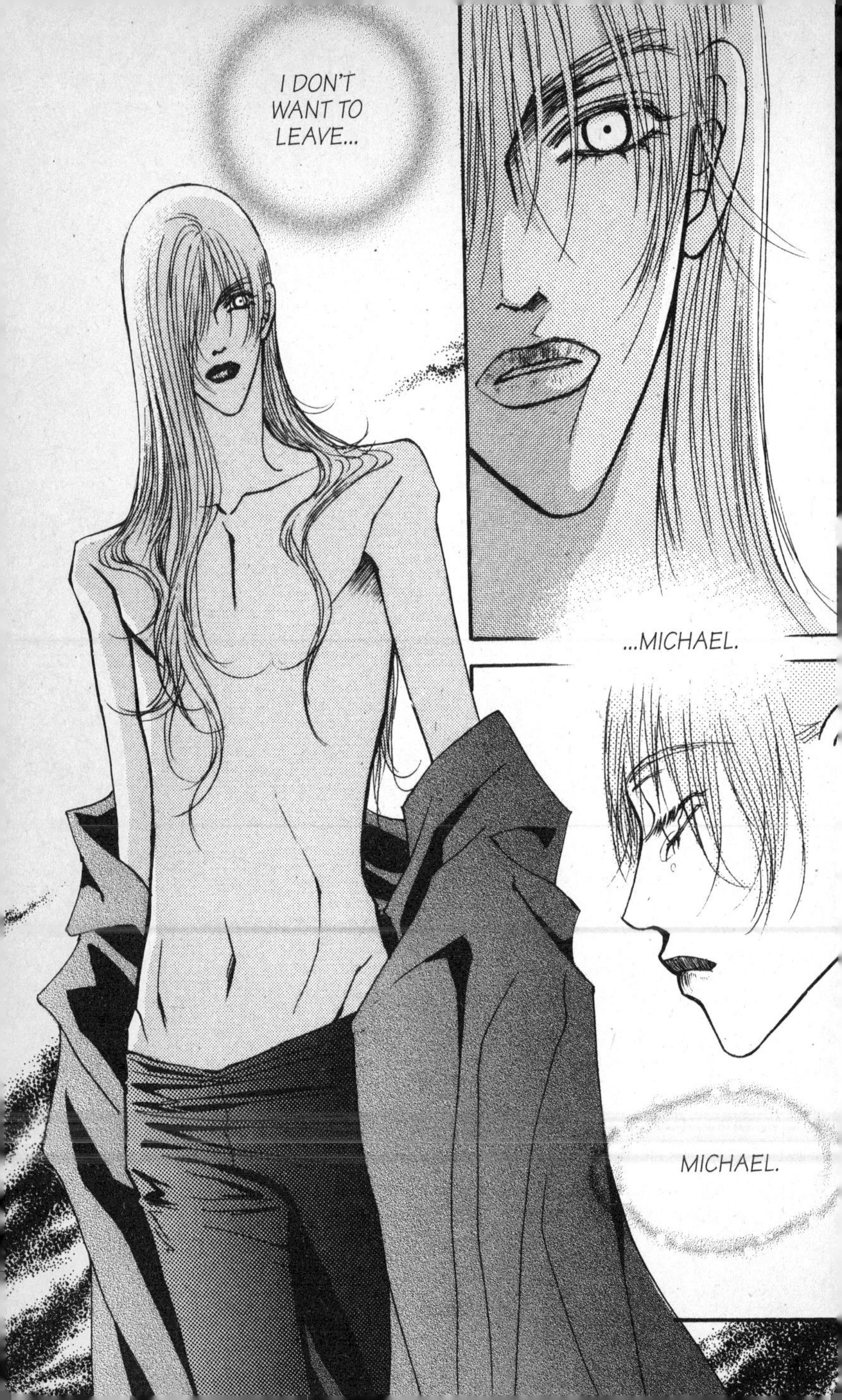
...MICHAEL.
MICHAEL.
I DON'T WANT TO LEAVE...

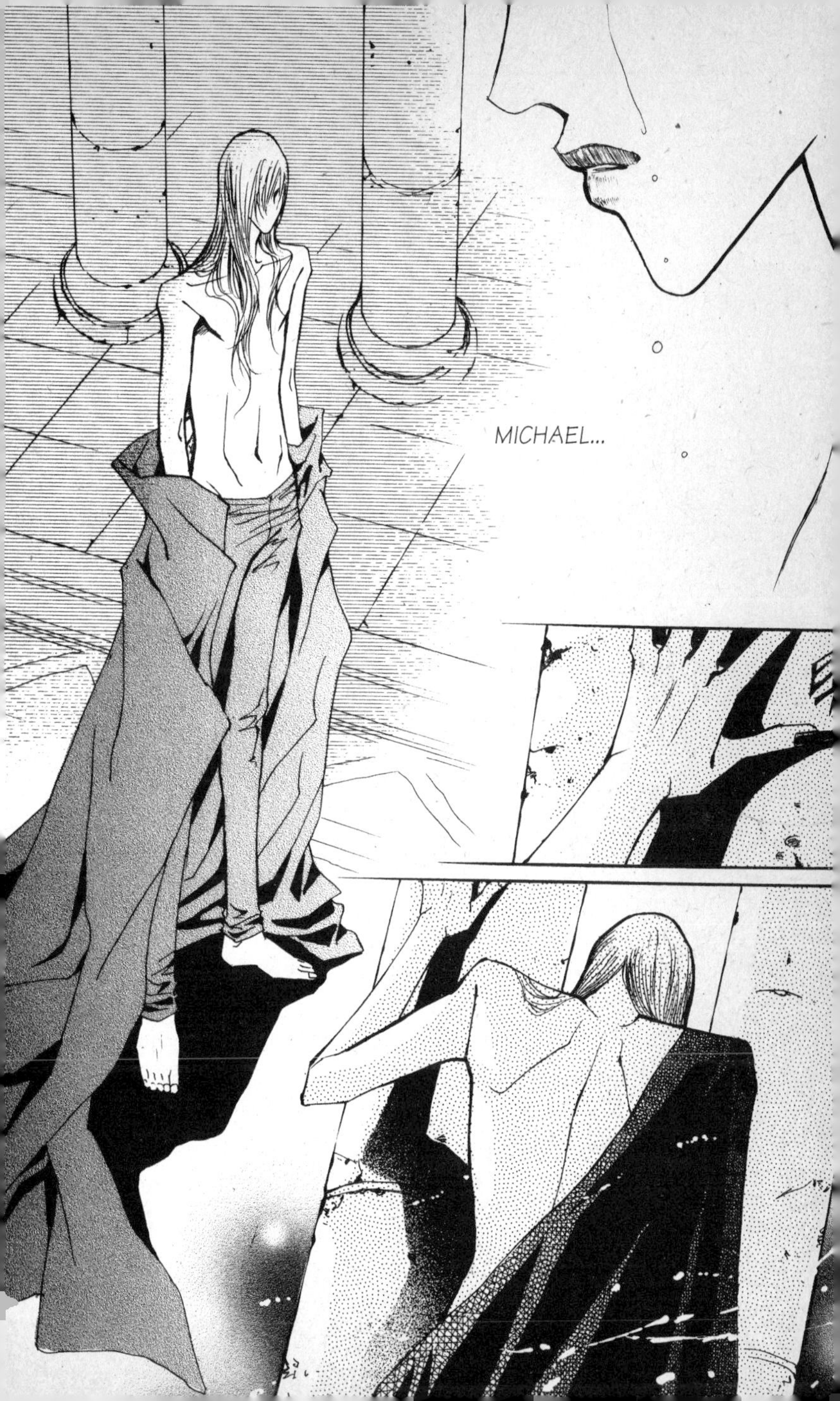
MICHAEL...

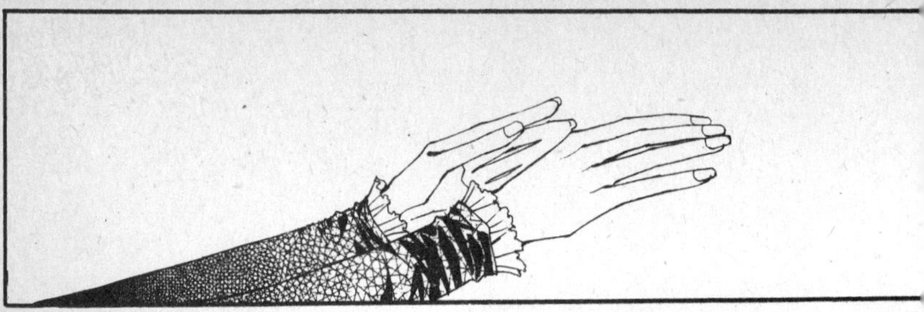
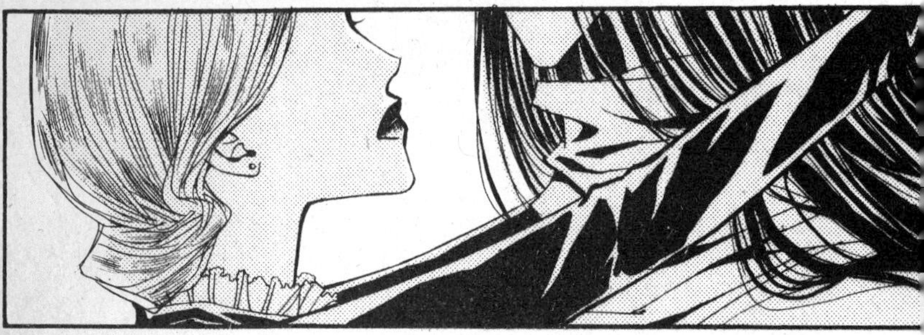
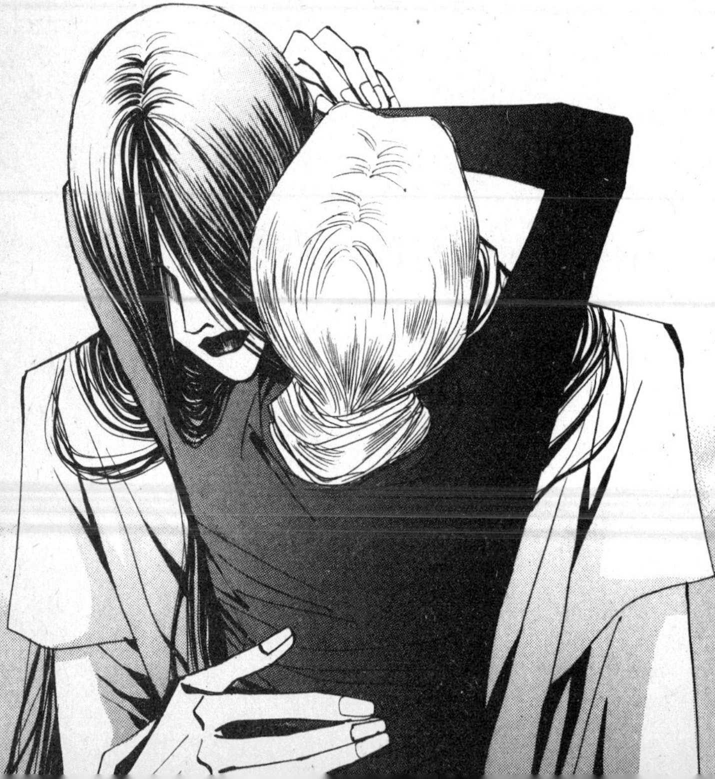

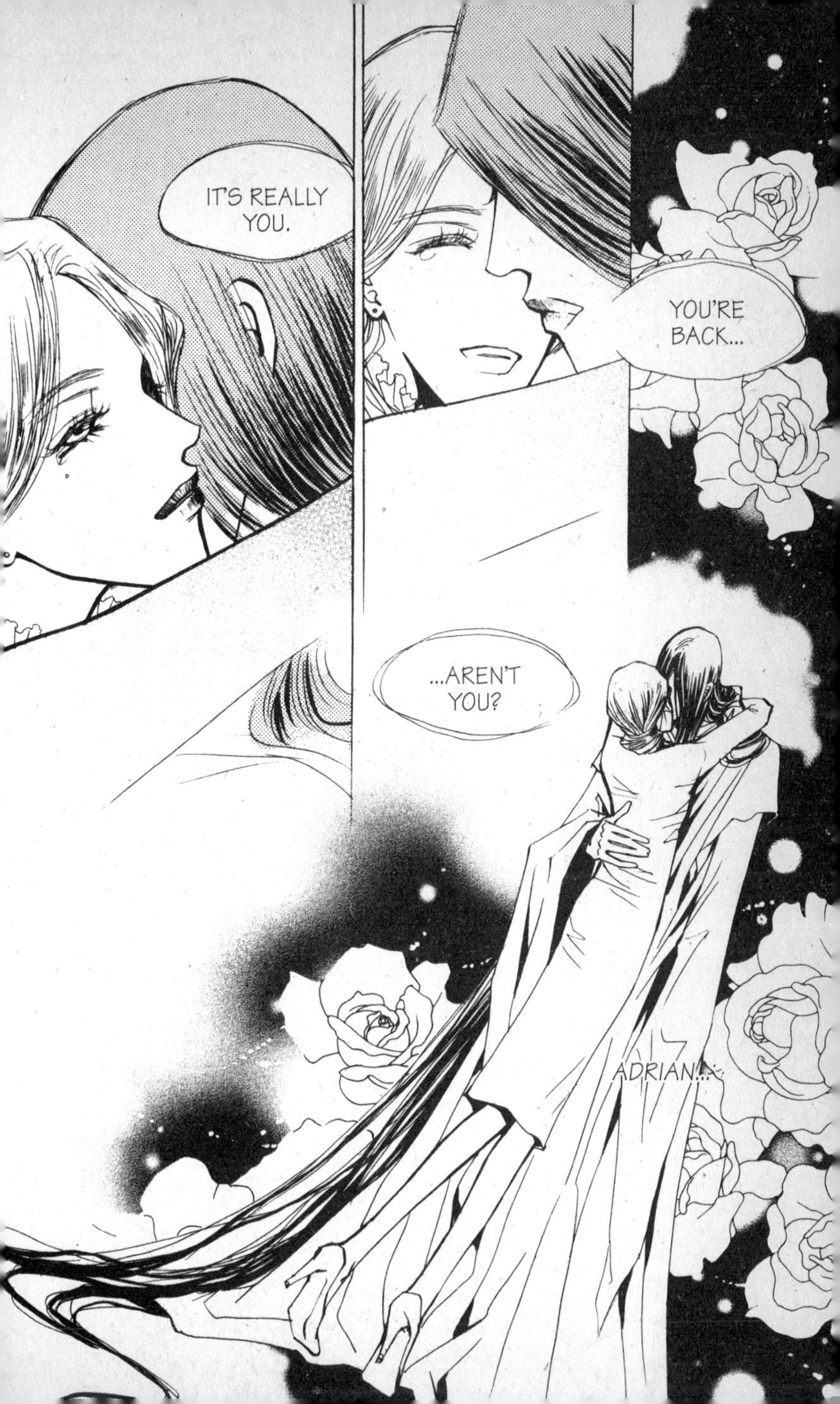
IT'S REALLY YOU.
YOU'RE BACK...
...AREN'T YOU?
ADRIAN!...

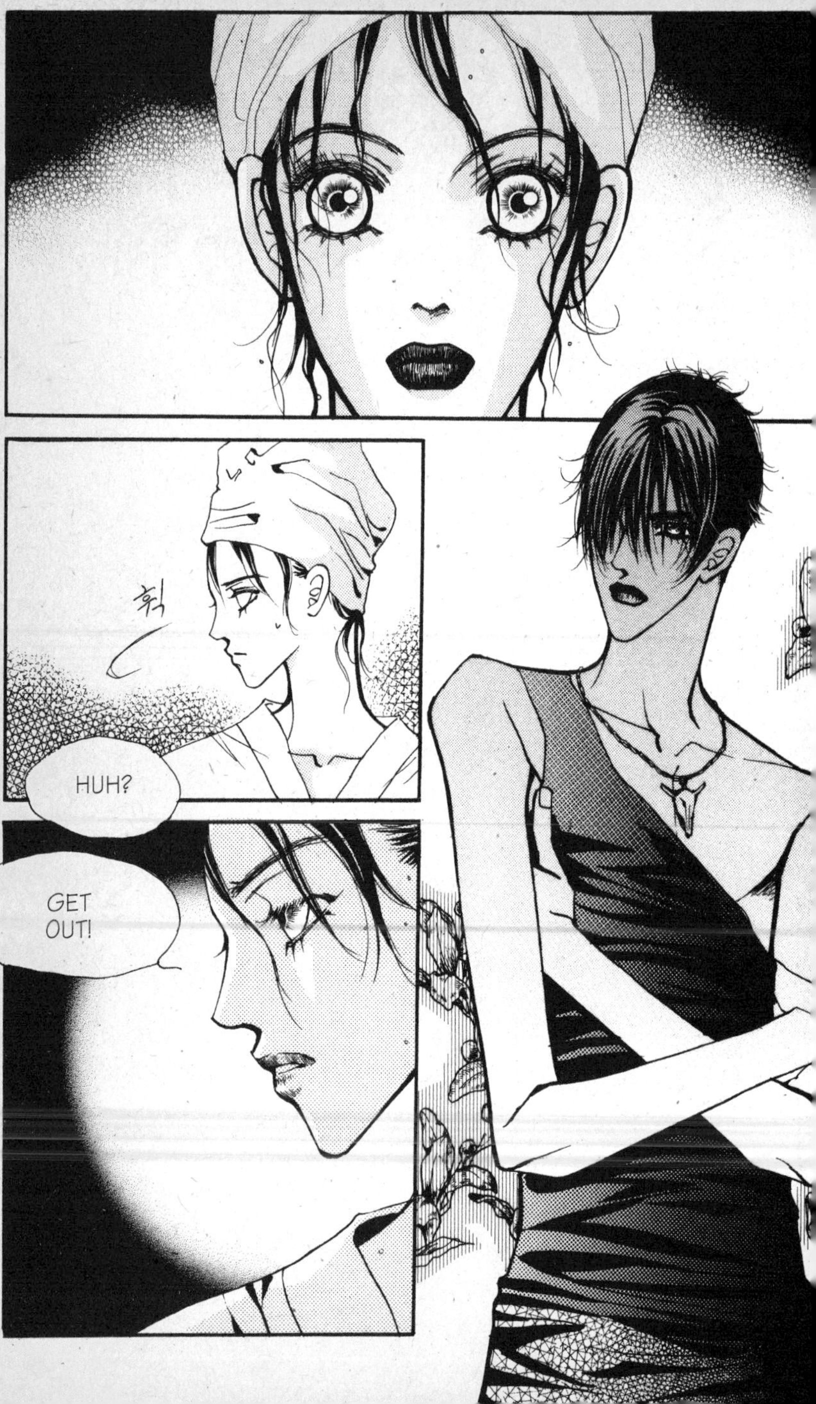
휙
HUH?
GET OUT!

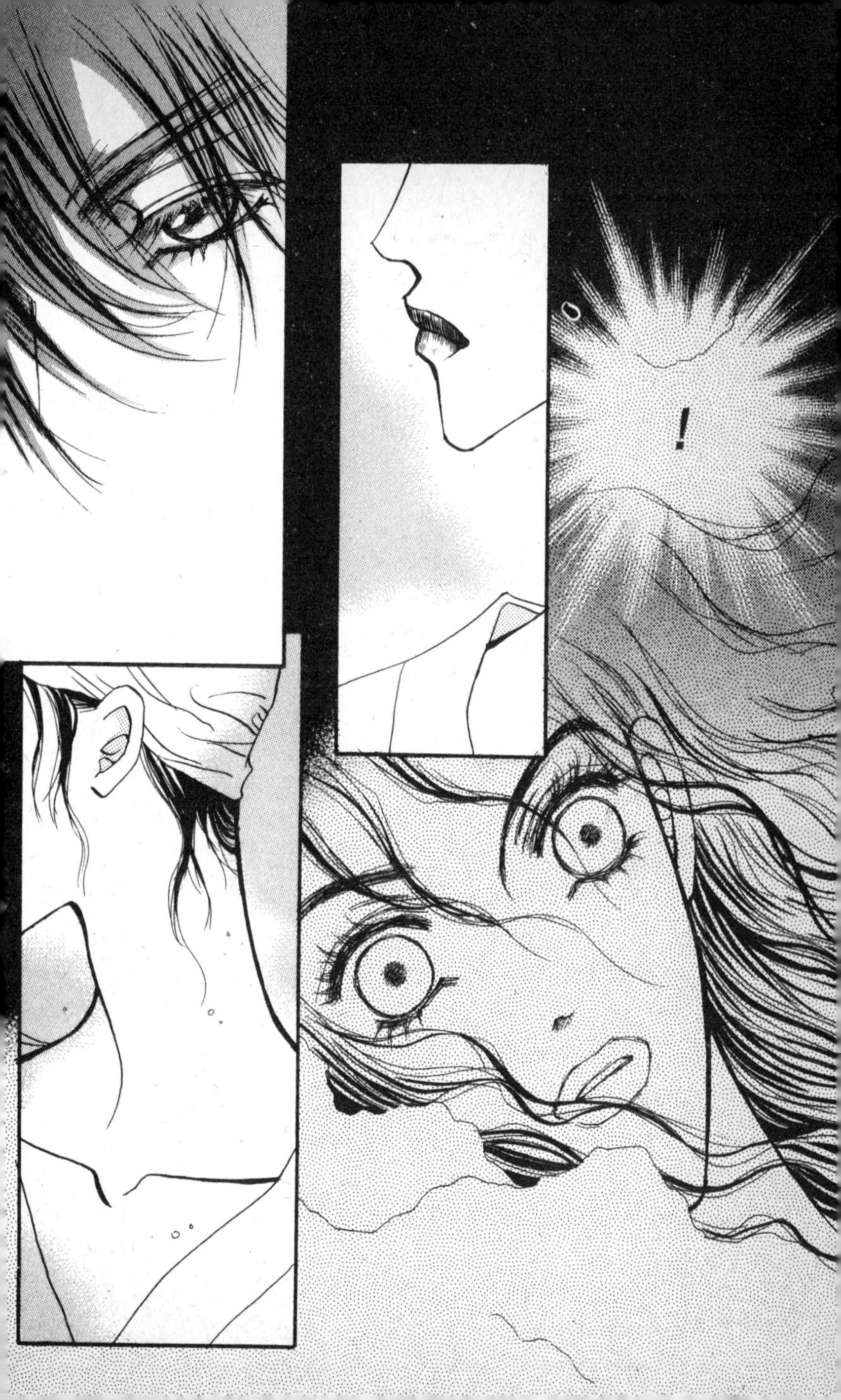
!

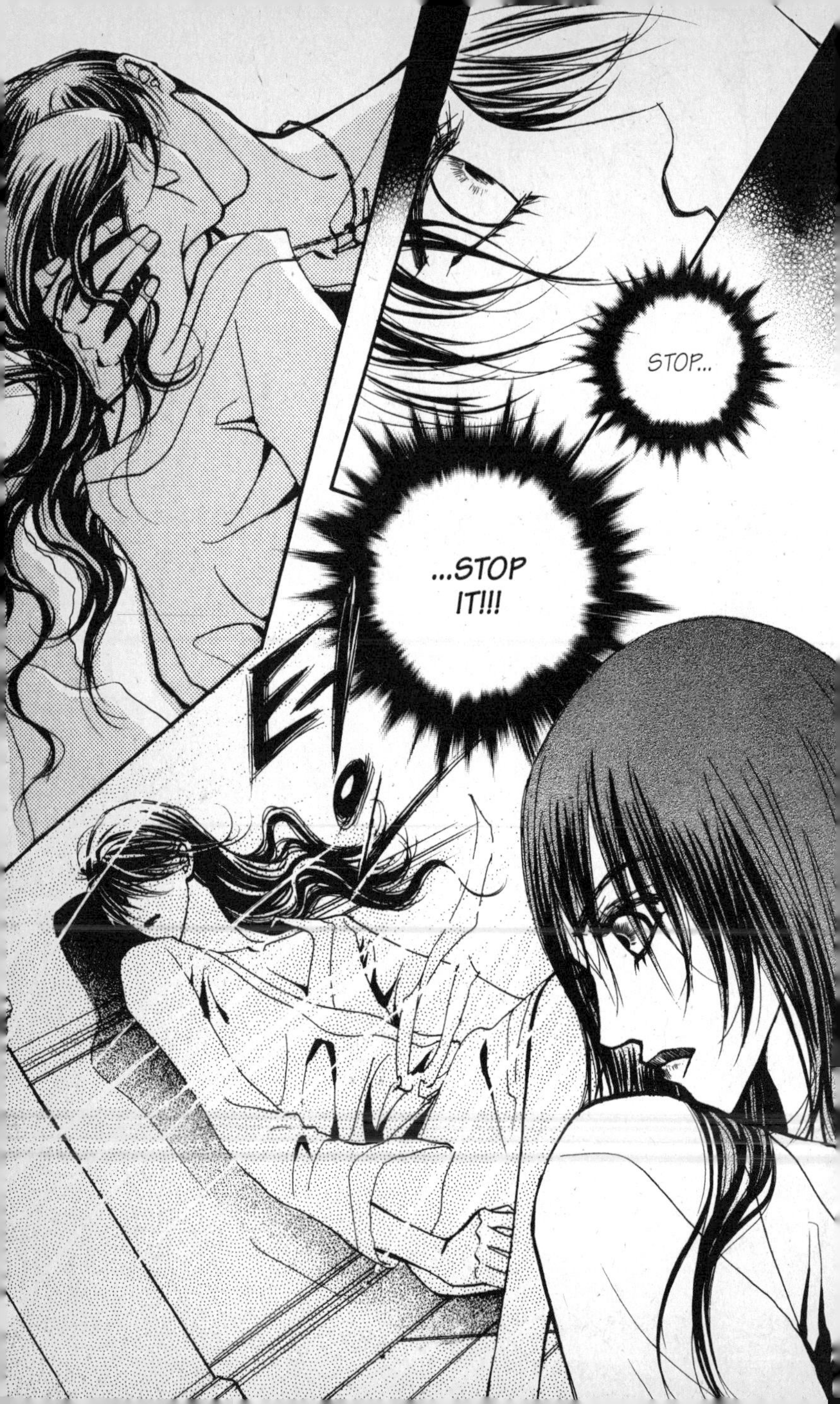
STOP...
...STOP IT!!!

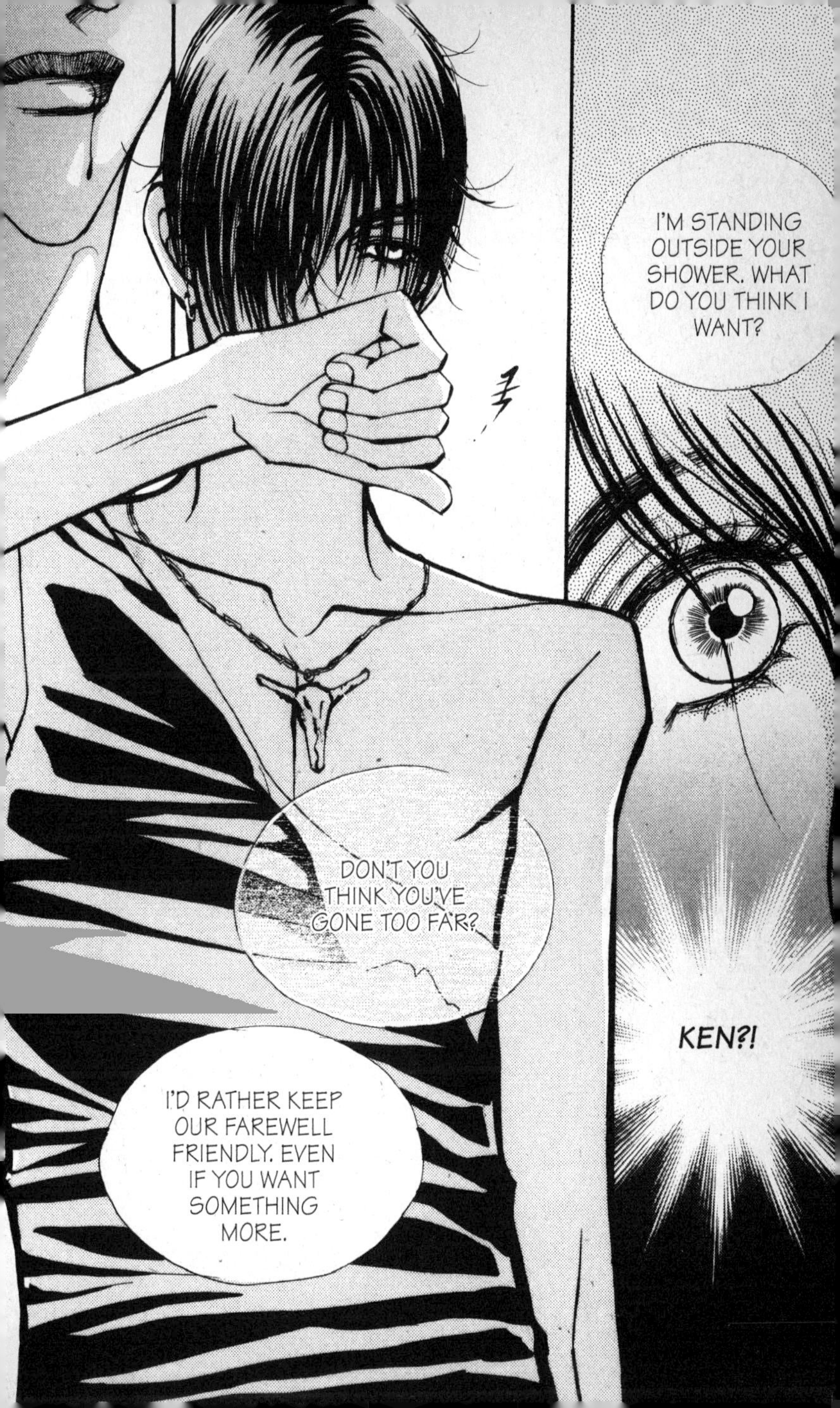
I'M STANDING OUTSIDE YOUR SHOWER. WHAT DO YOU THINK I WANT?
KEN?!
DON'T YOU THINK YOU'VE GONE TOO FAR?
I'D RATHER KEEP OUR FAREWELL FRIENDLY. EVEN IF YOU WANT SOMETHING MORE.

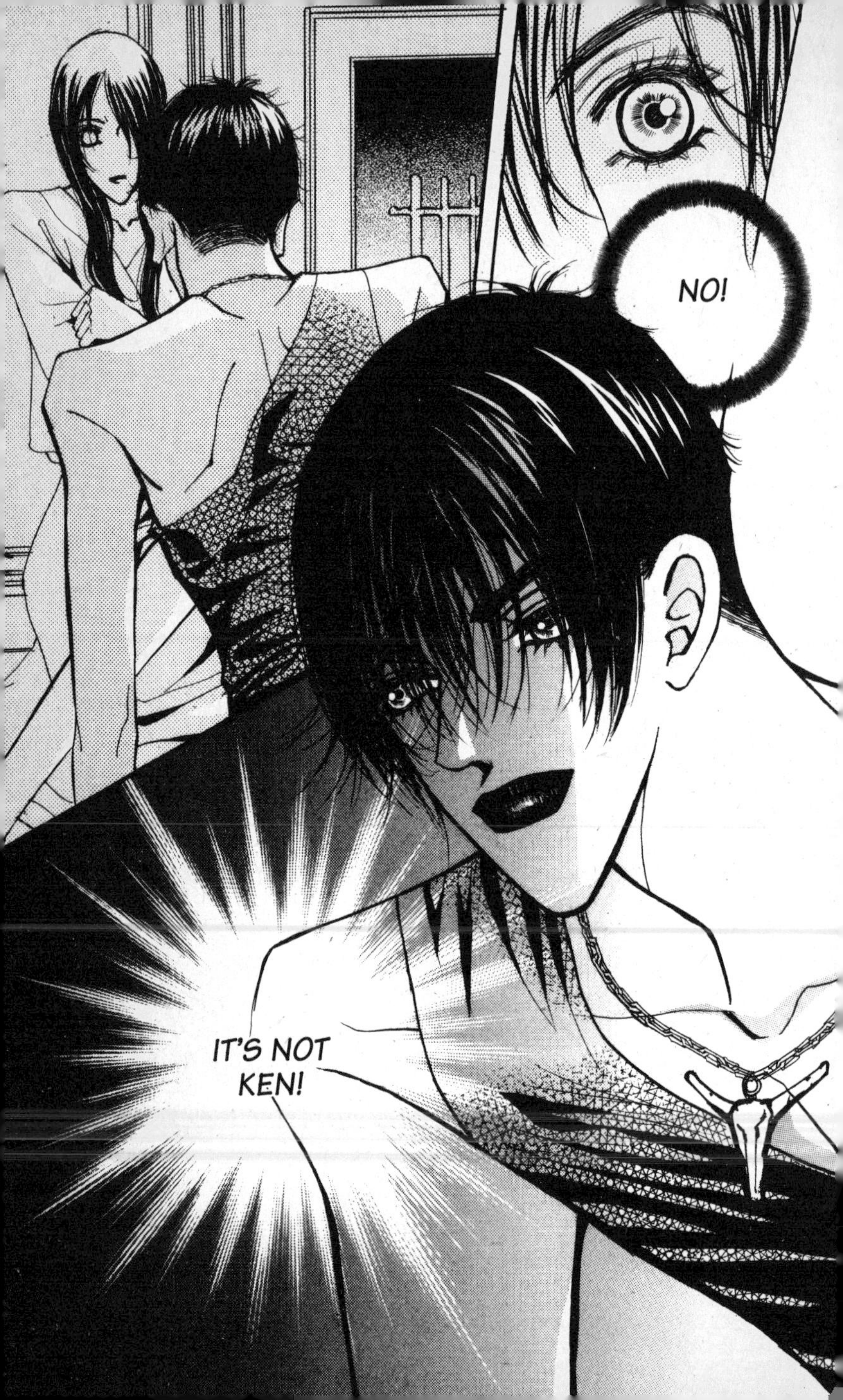
NO!
IT'S NOT KEN!

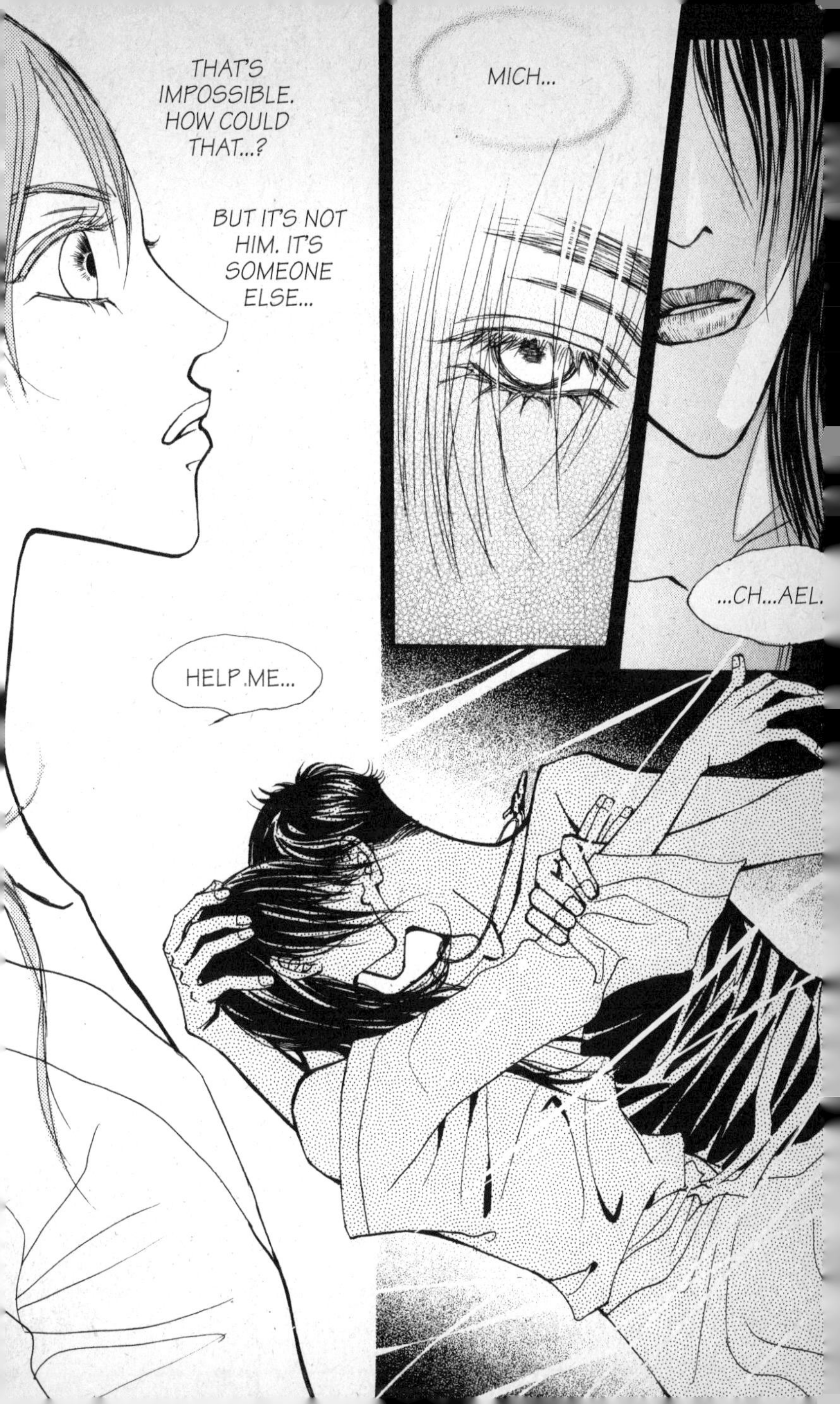
MICH...
...CH...AEL.
THAT'S IMPOSSIBLE. HOW COULD THAT...?
BUT IT'S NOT HIM. IT'S SOMEONE ELSE...
HELP.ME...

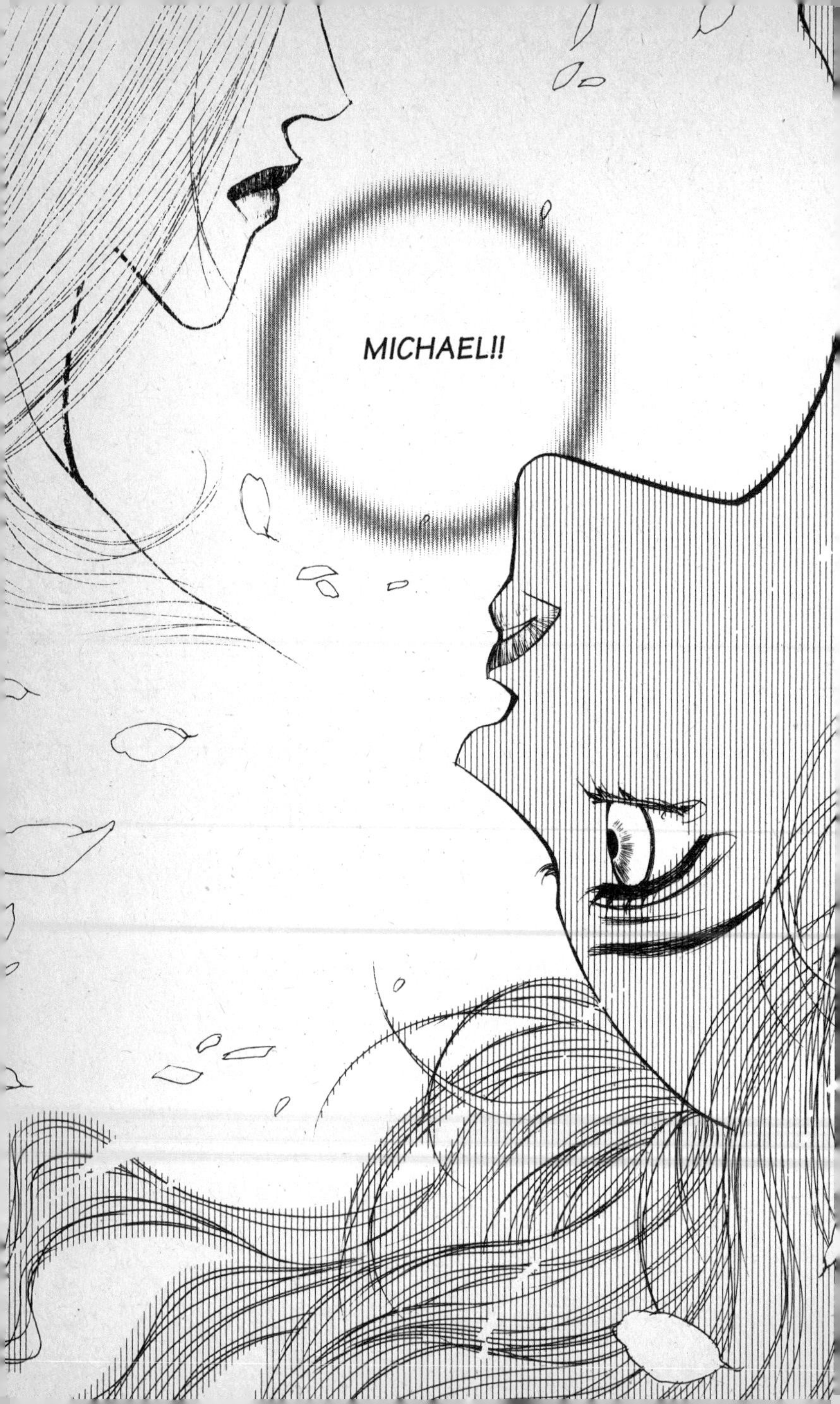
MICHAEL!!

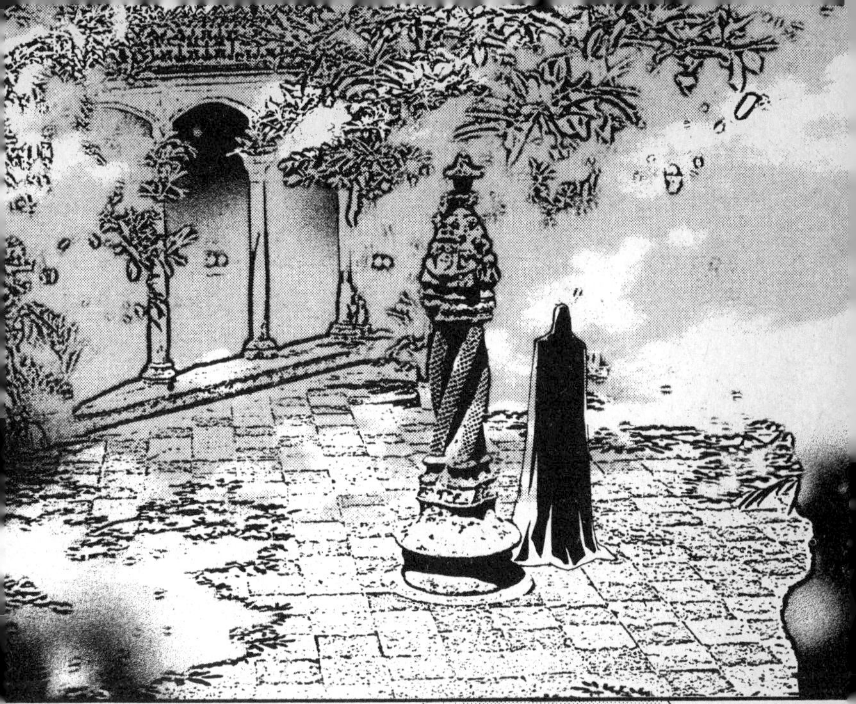

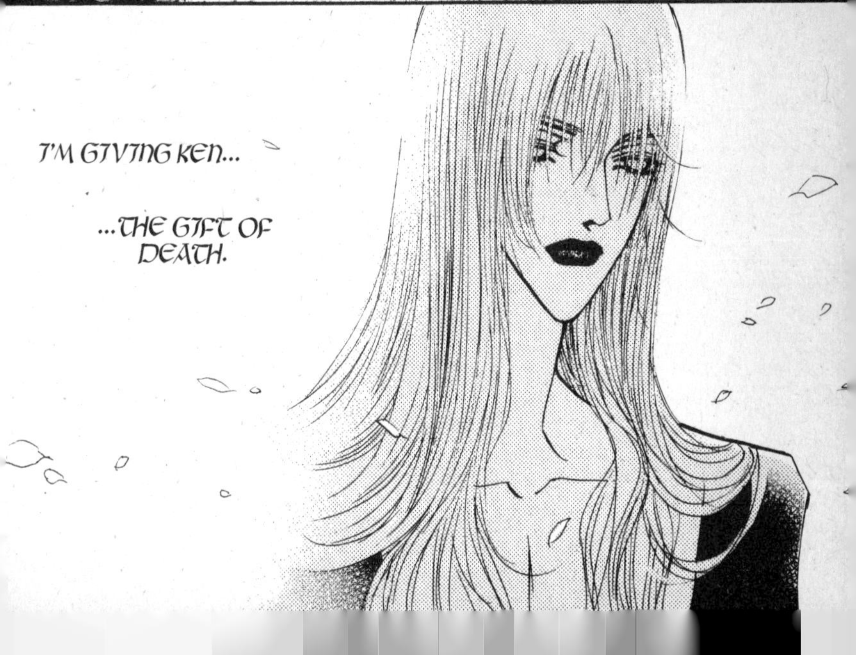
I'M GIVING KEN...
...THE GIFT OF DEATH.

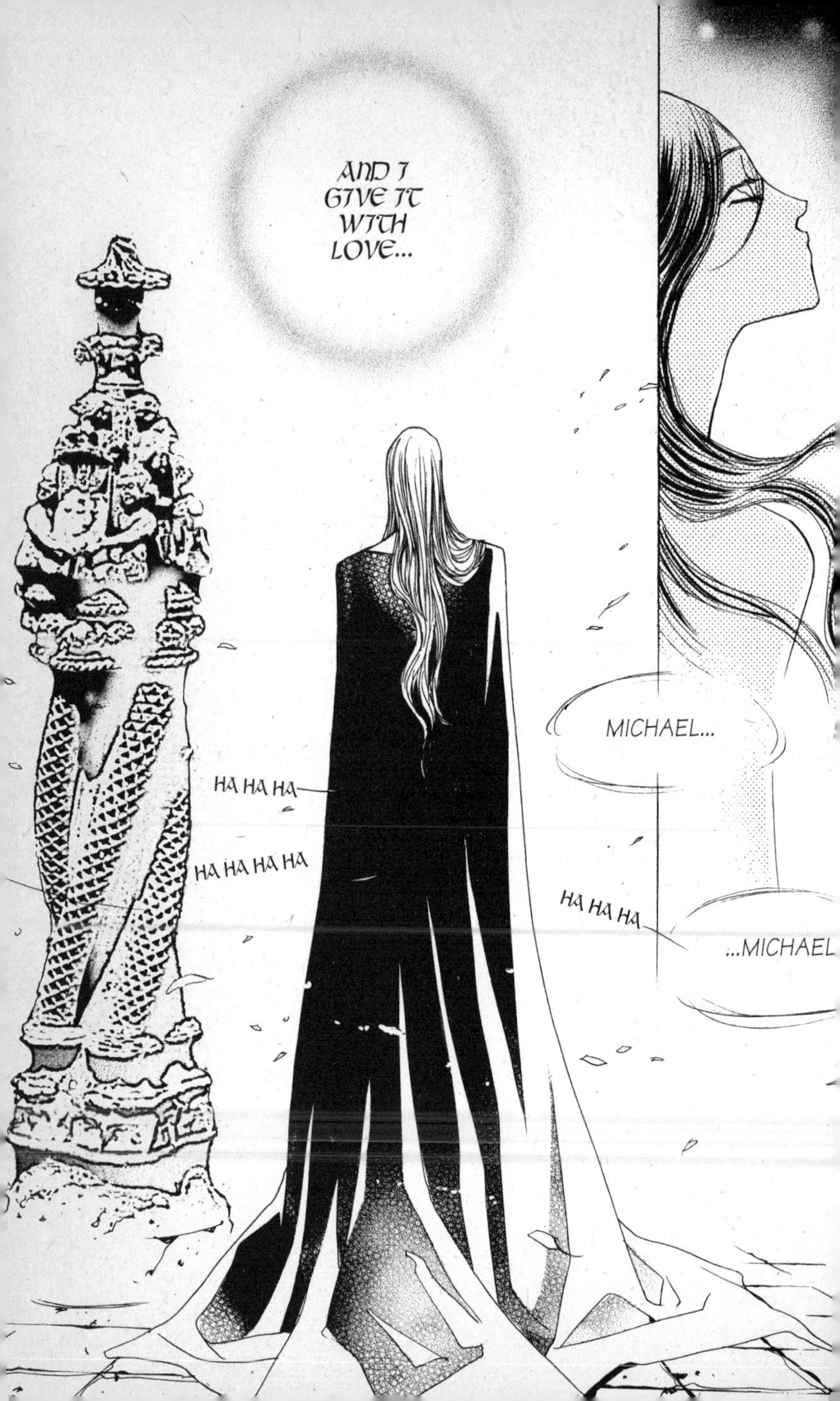
MICHAEL...
...MICHAEL
AND I GIVE IT WITH LOVE...
HA HA HA
HA HA HA—
HA HA HA HA

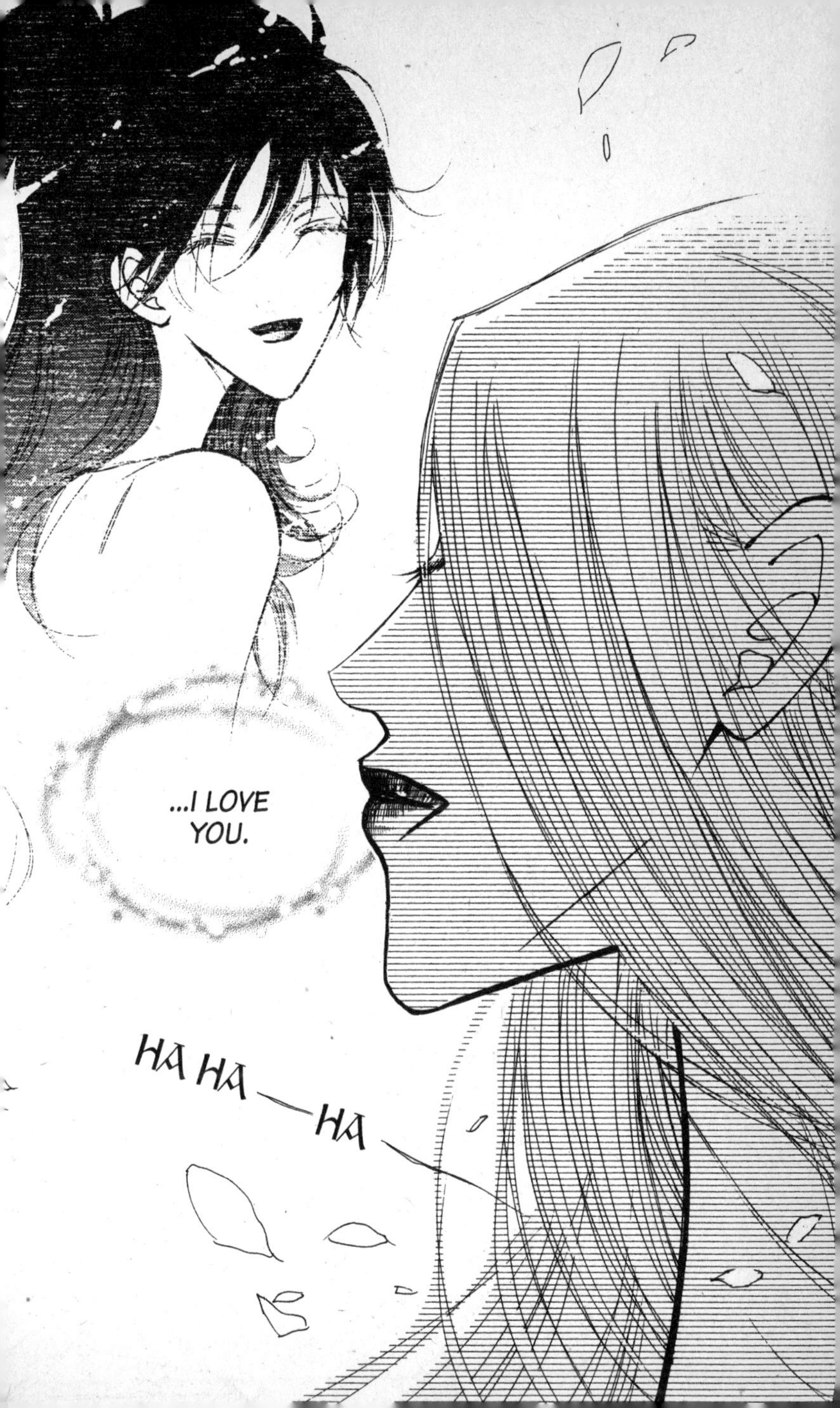
...I LOVE YOU.
HA HA—HA

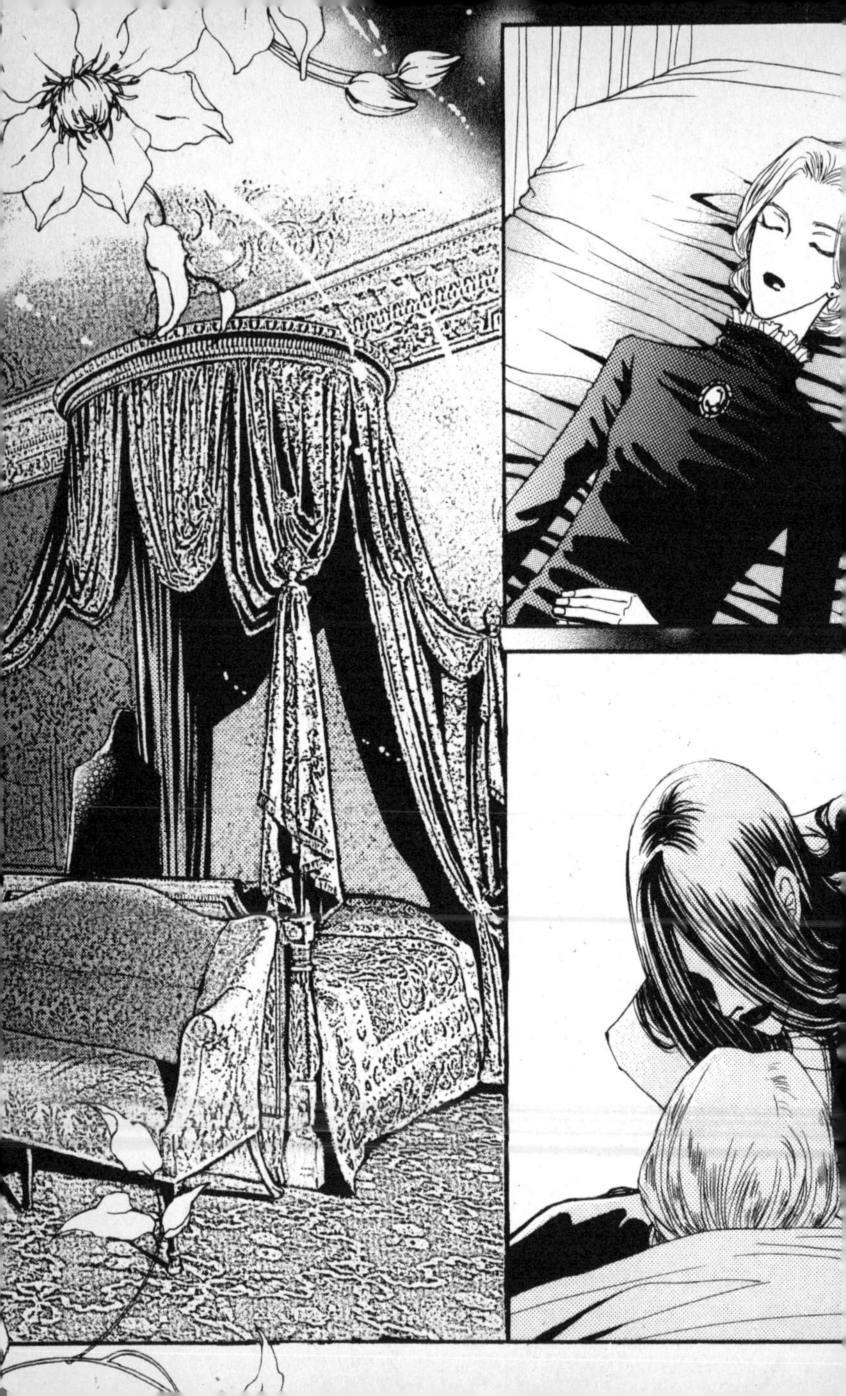

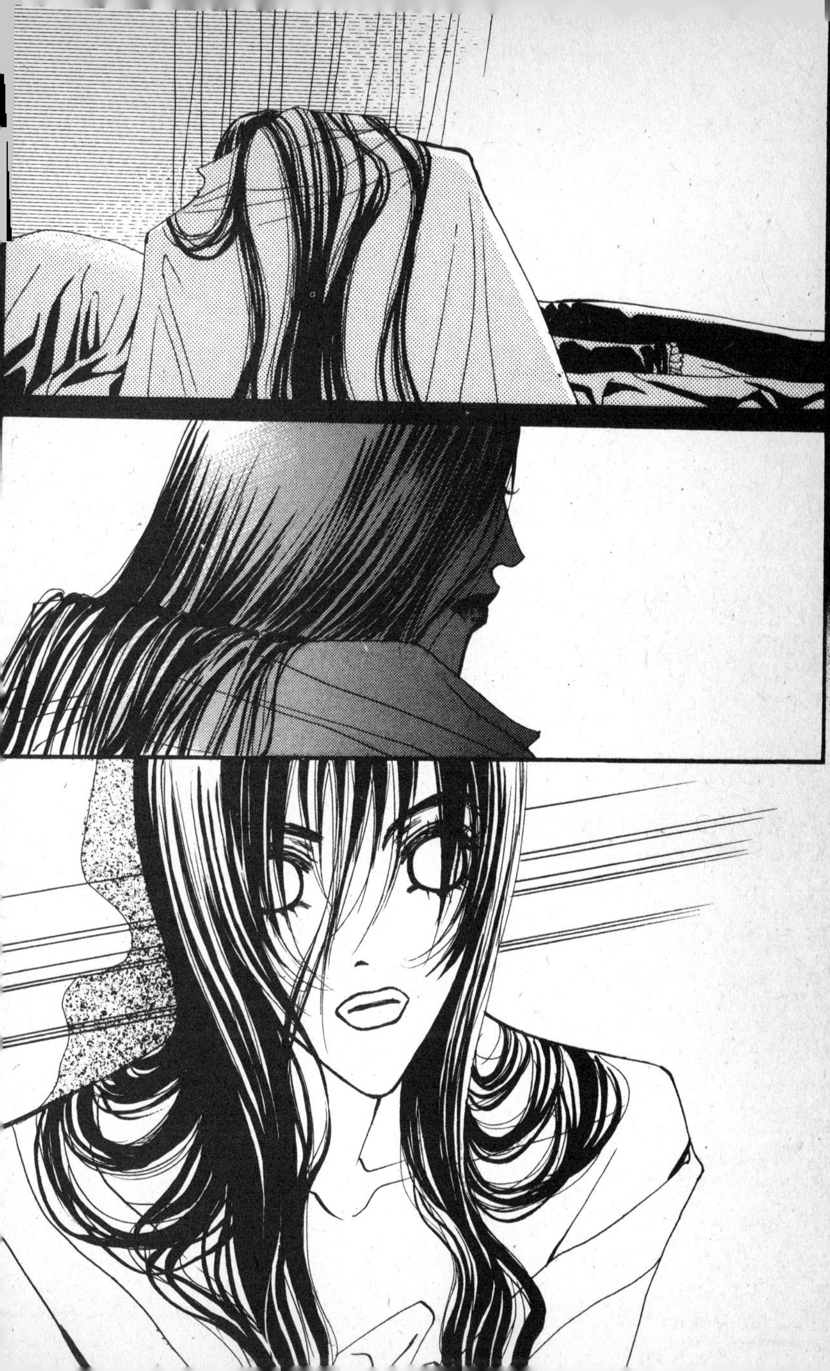

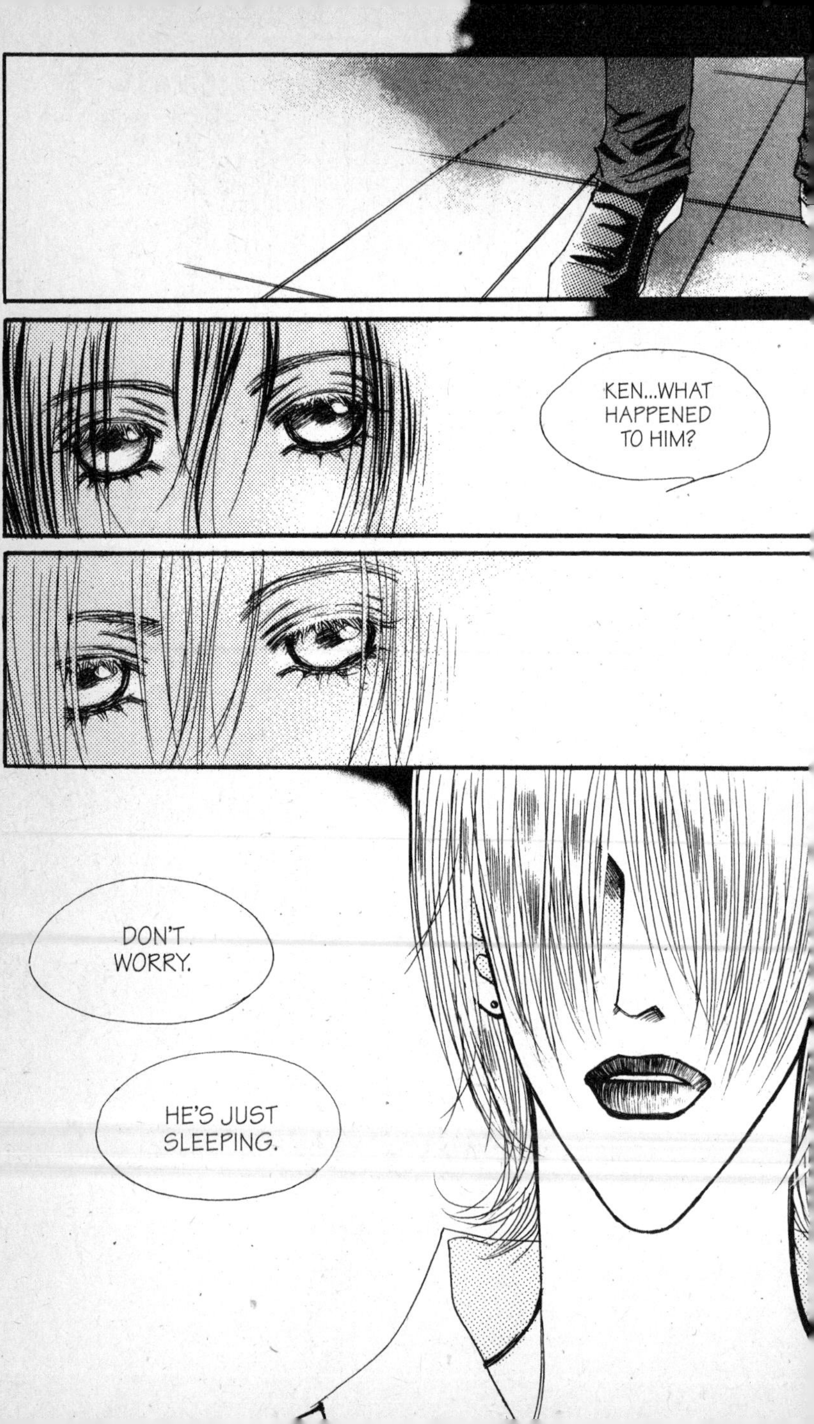
KEN...WHAT HAPPENED TO HIM?
DON'T WORRY.
HE'S JUST SLEEPING.

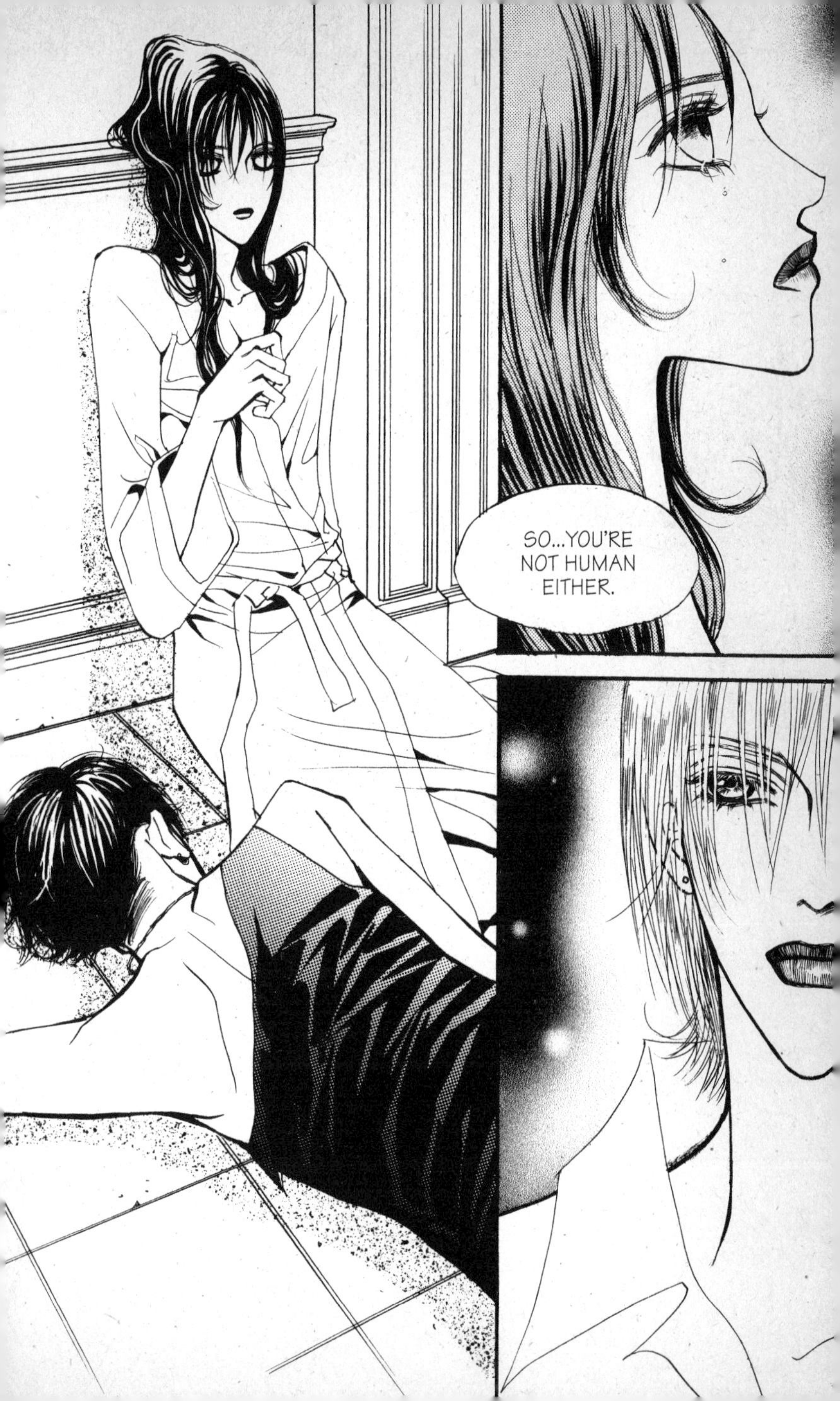
SO...YOU'RE NOT HUMAN EITHER.

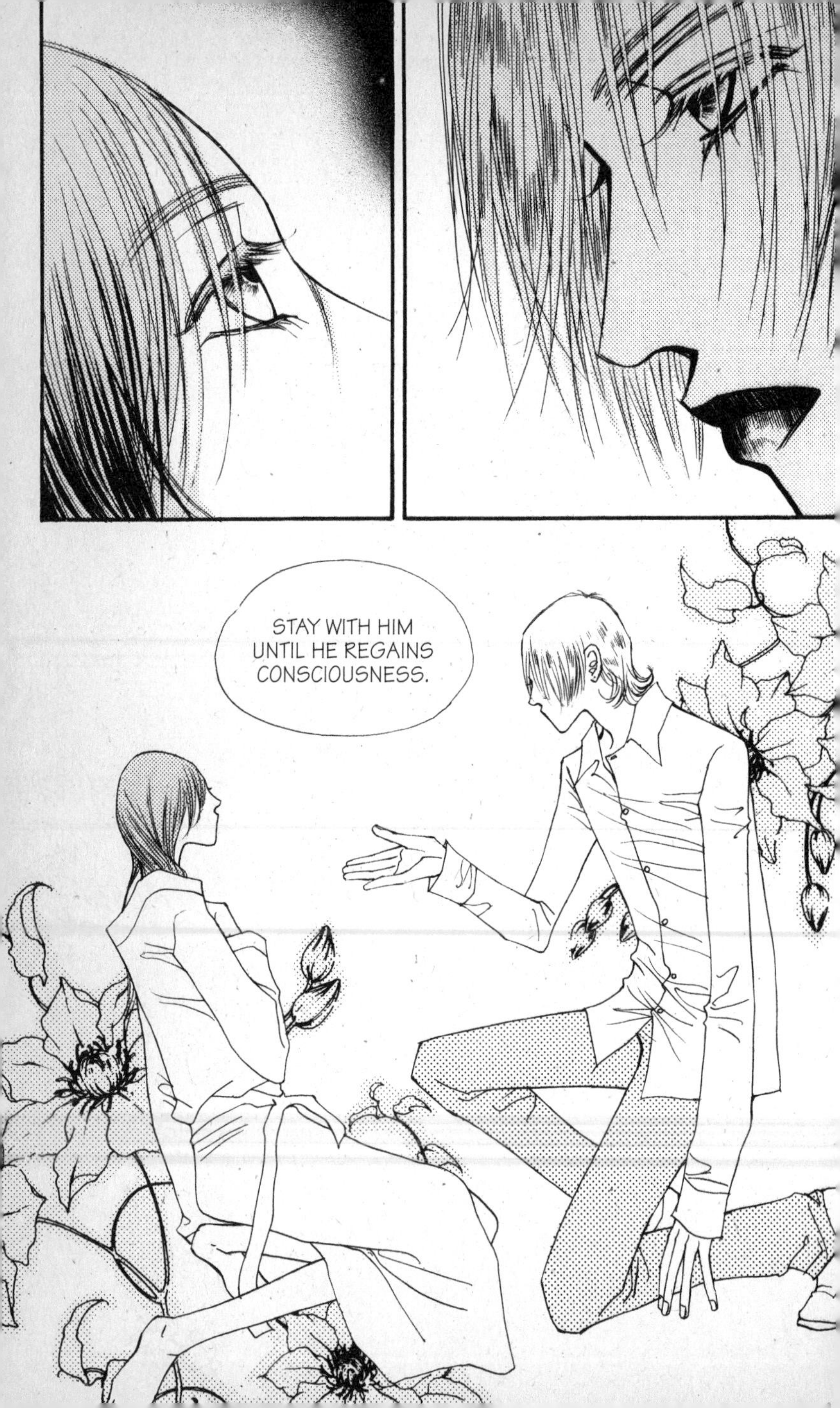
STAY WITH HIM UNTIL HE REGAINS CONSCIOUSNESS.

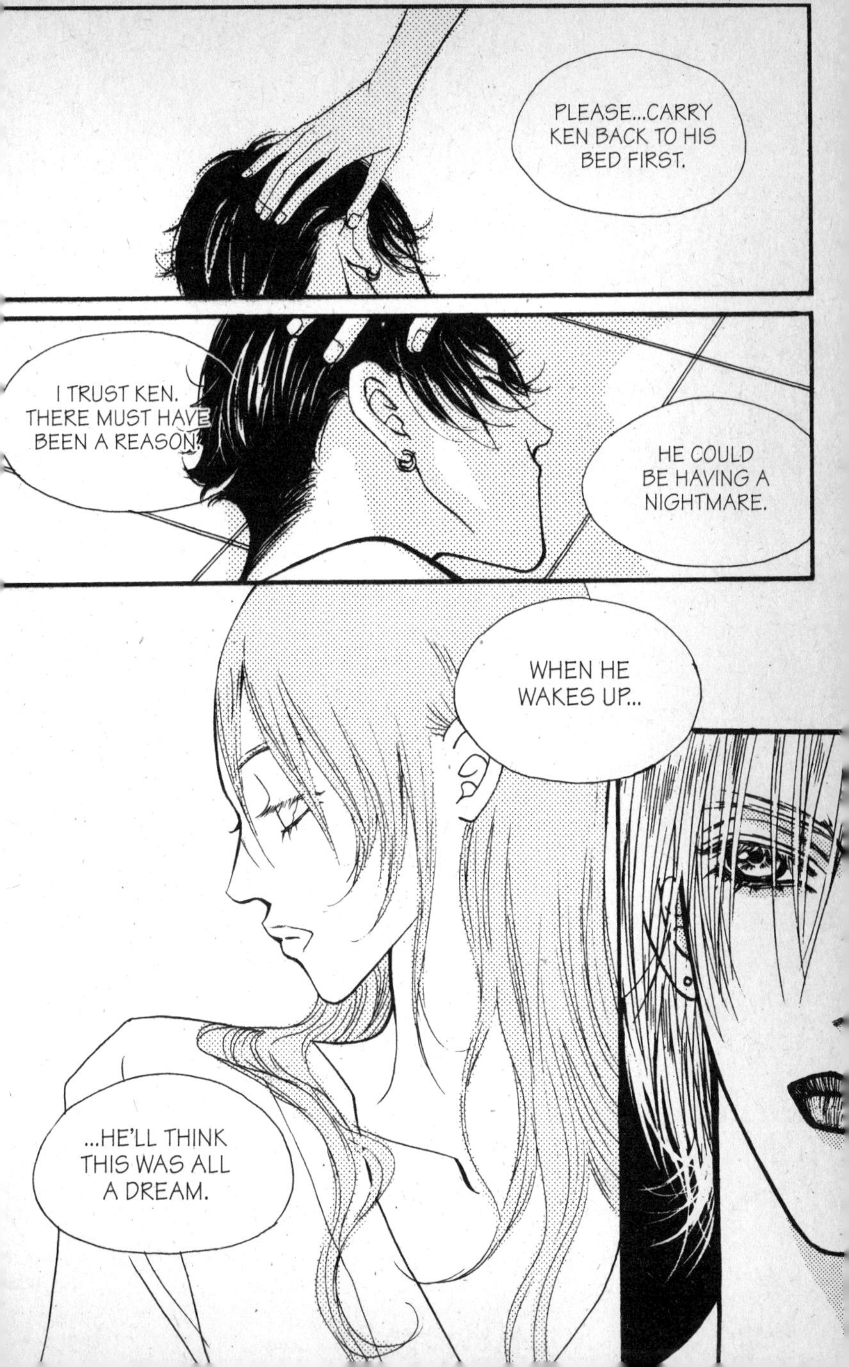
PLEASE...CARRY KEN BACK TO HIS BED FIRST.
HE COULD BE HAVING A NIGHTMARE.
I TRUST KEN. THERE MUST HAVE BEEN A REASON.
WHEN HE WAKES UP...
...HE'LL THINK THIS WAS ALL A DREAM.

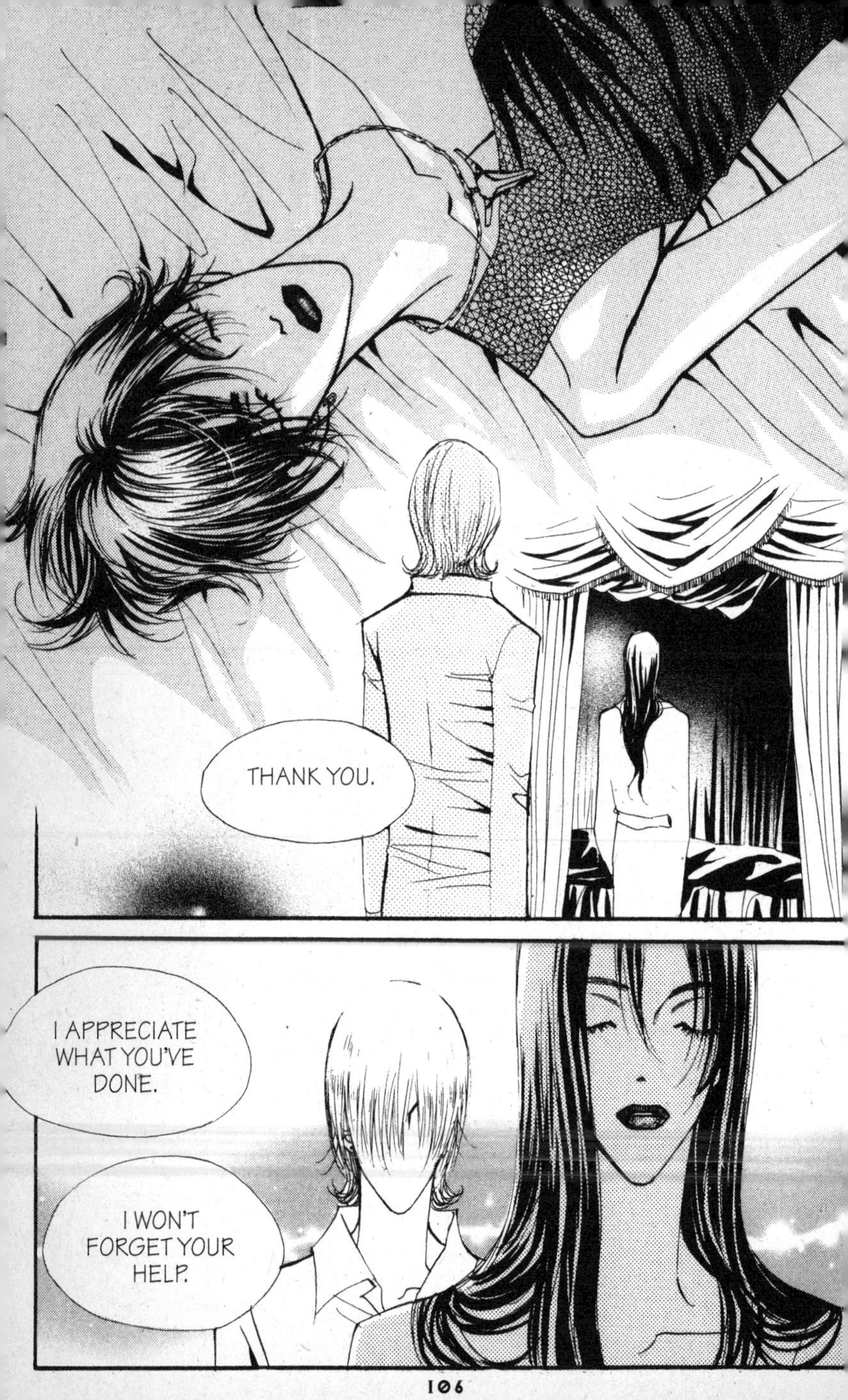
THANK YOU.
I APPRECIATE WHAT YOU'VE DONE.
I WON'T FORGET YOUR HELP.

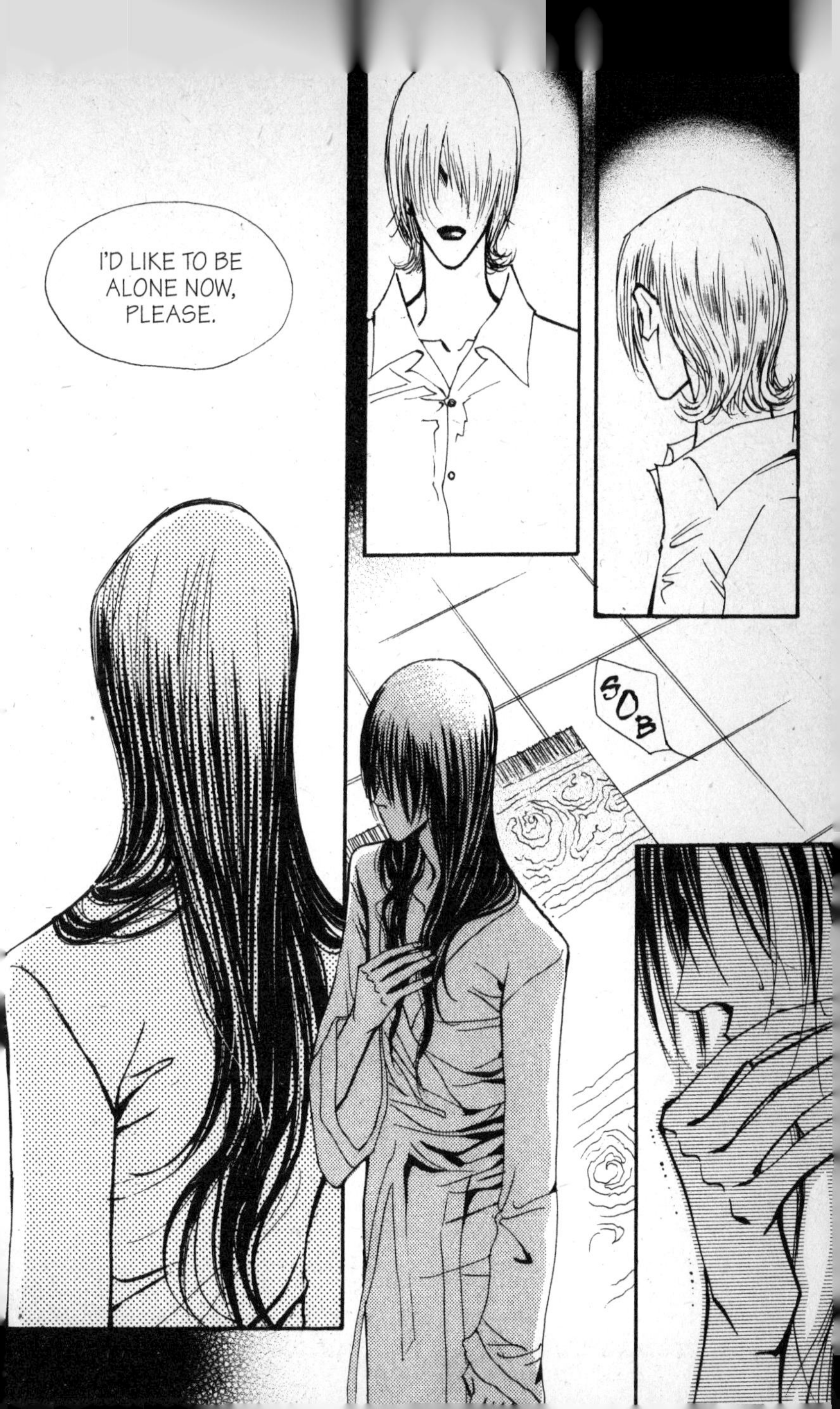
SOB
I'D LIKE TO BE ALONE NOW, PLEASE.

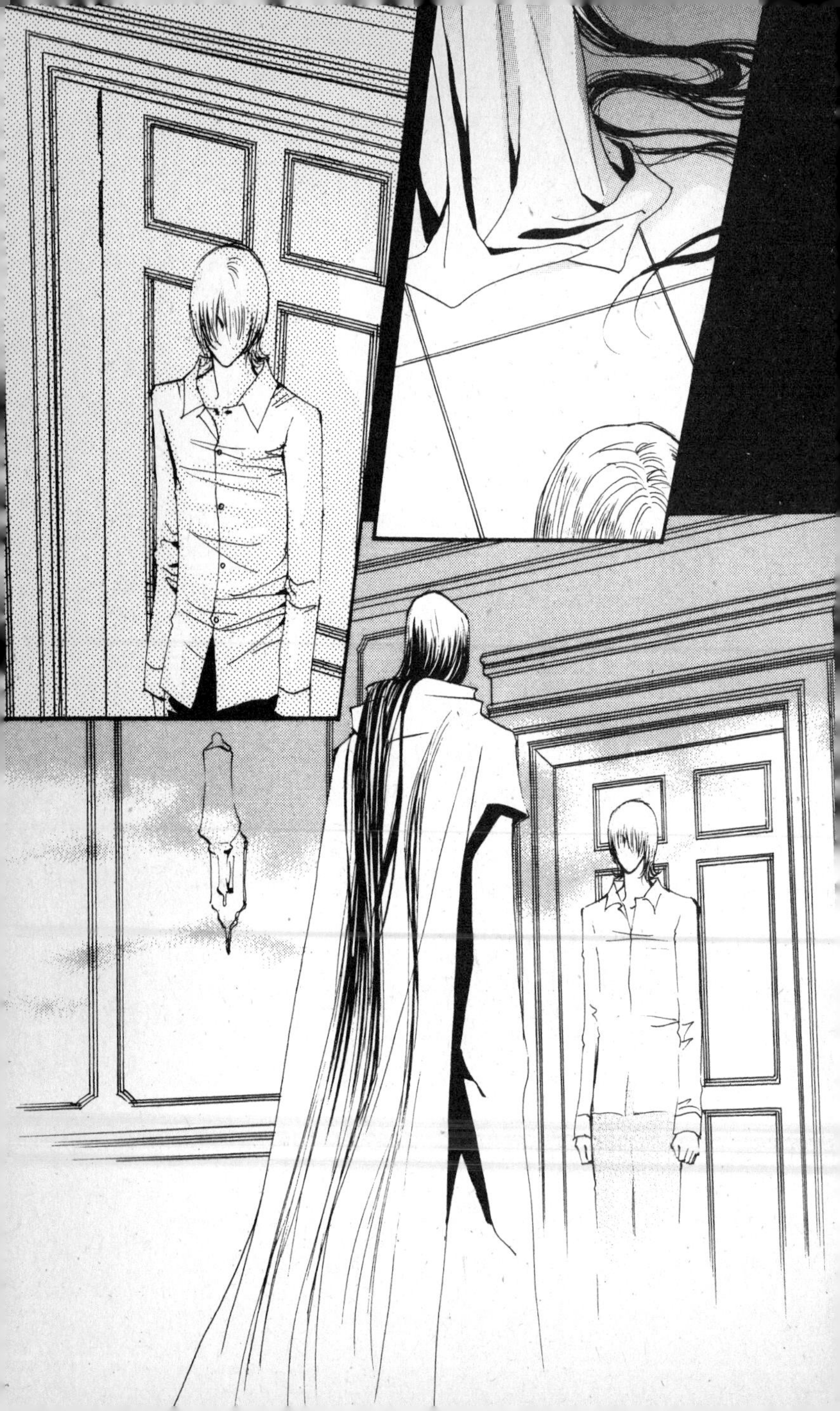

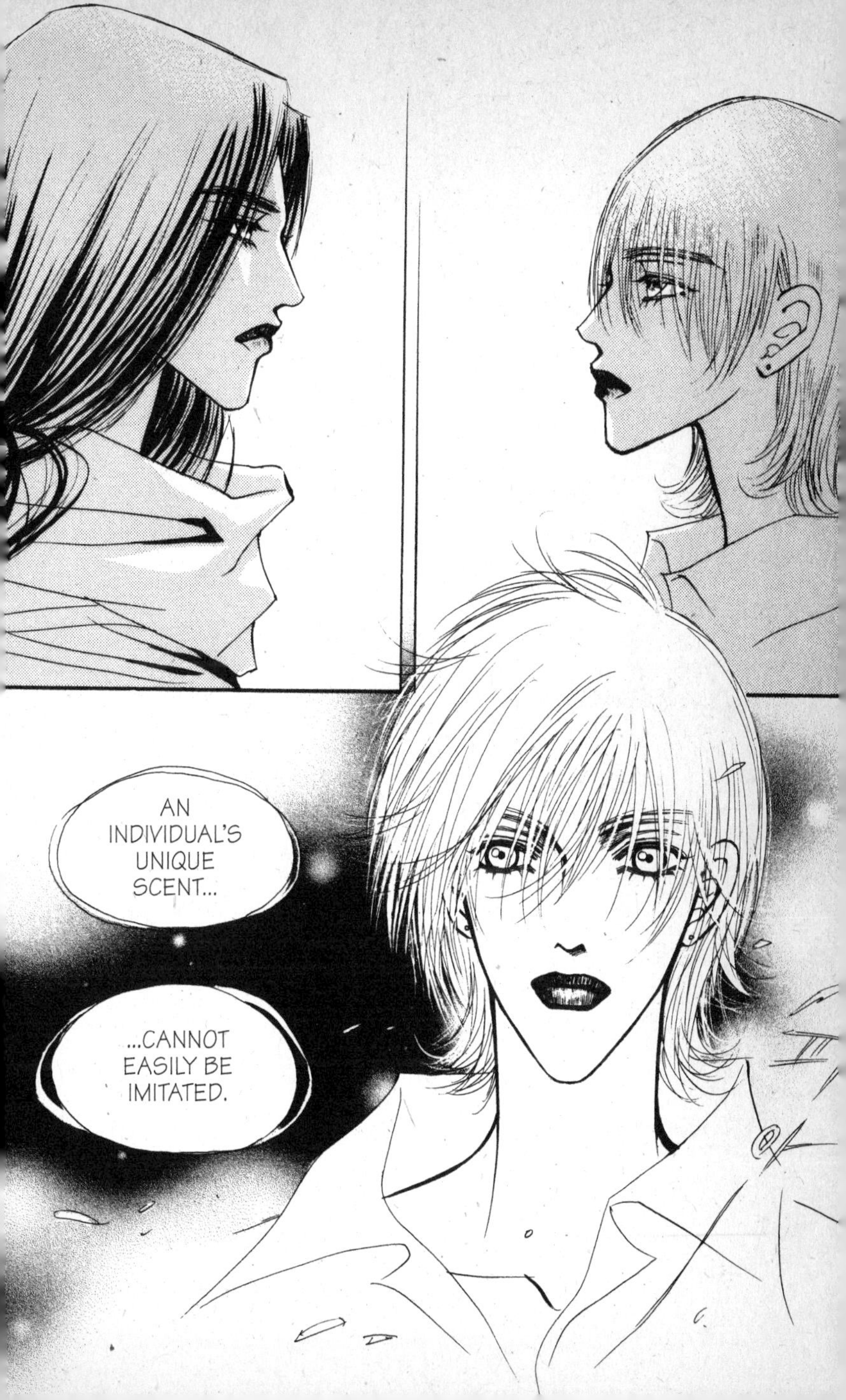
AN INDIVIDUAL'S UNIQUE SCENT...
...CANNOT EASILY BE IMITATED.

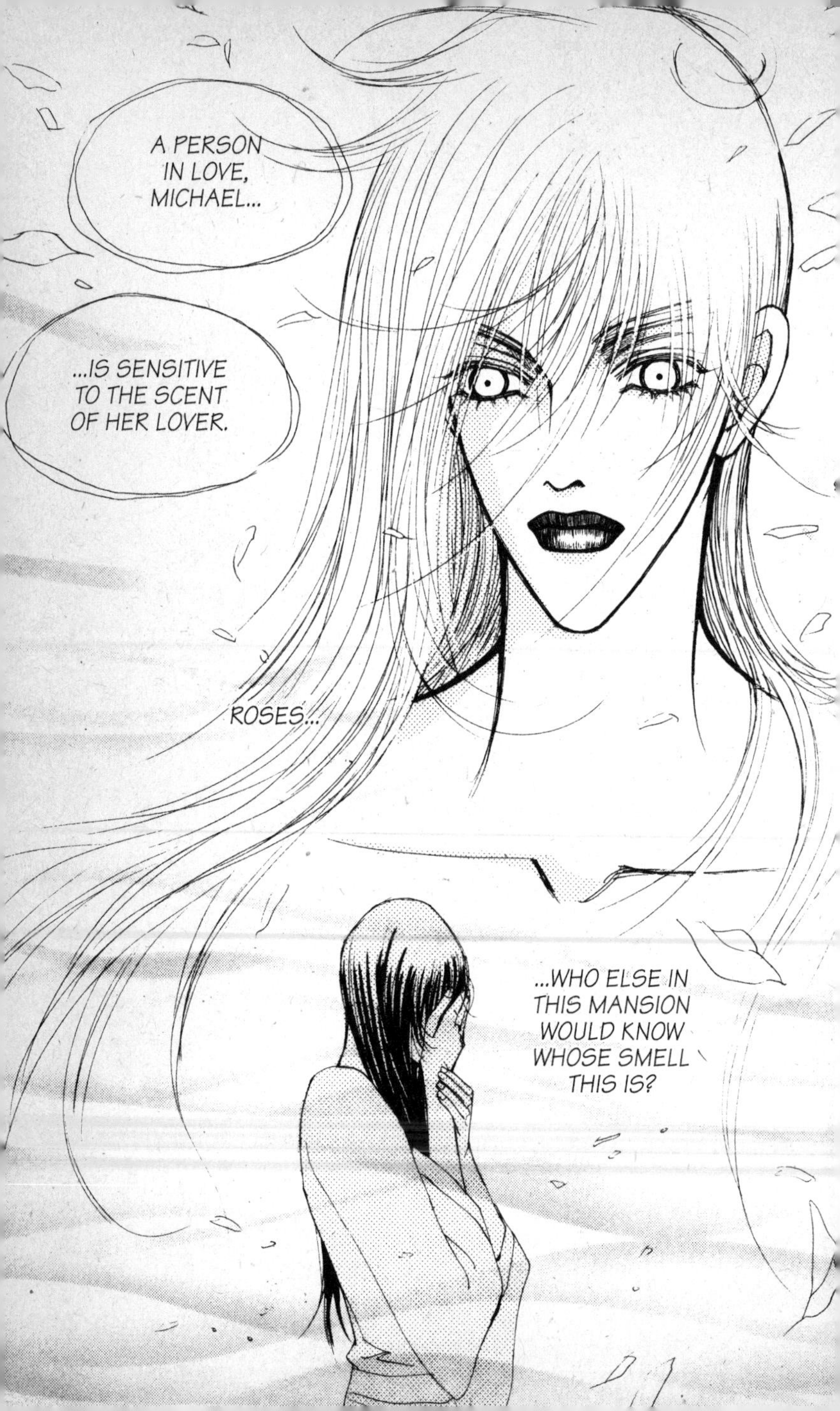
A PERSON IN LOVE, MICHAEL...
...IS SENSITIVE TO THE SCENT OF HER LOVER.
ROSES...
...WHO ELSE IN THIS MANSION WOULD KNOW WHOSE SMELL THIS IS?

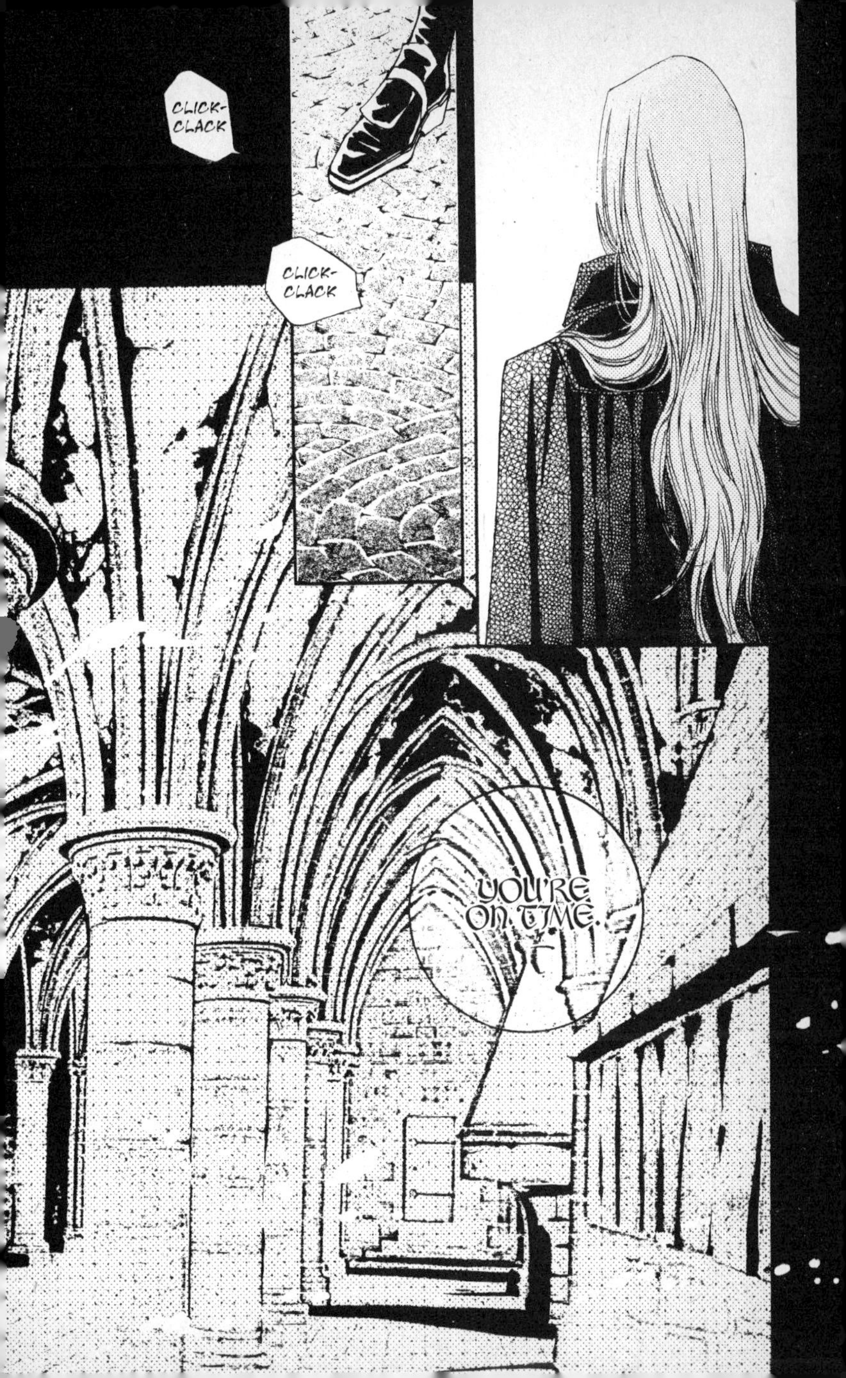
CLICK-CLACK
CLICK-CLACK
YOU'RE ON TIME.

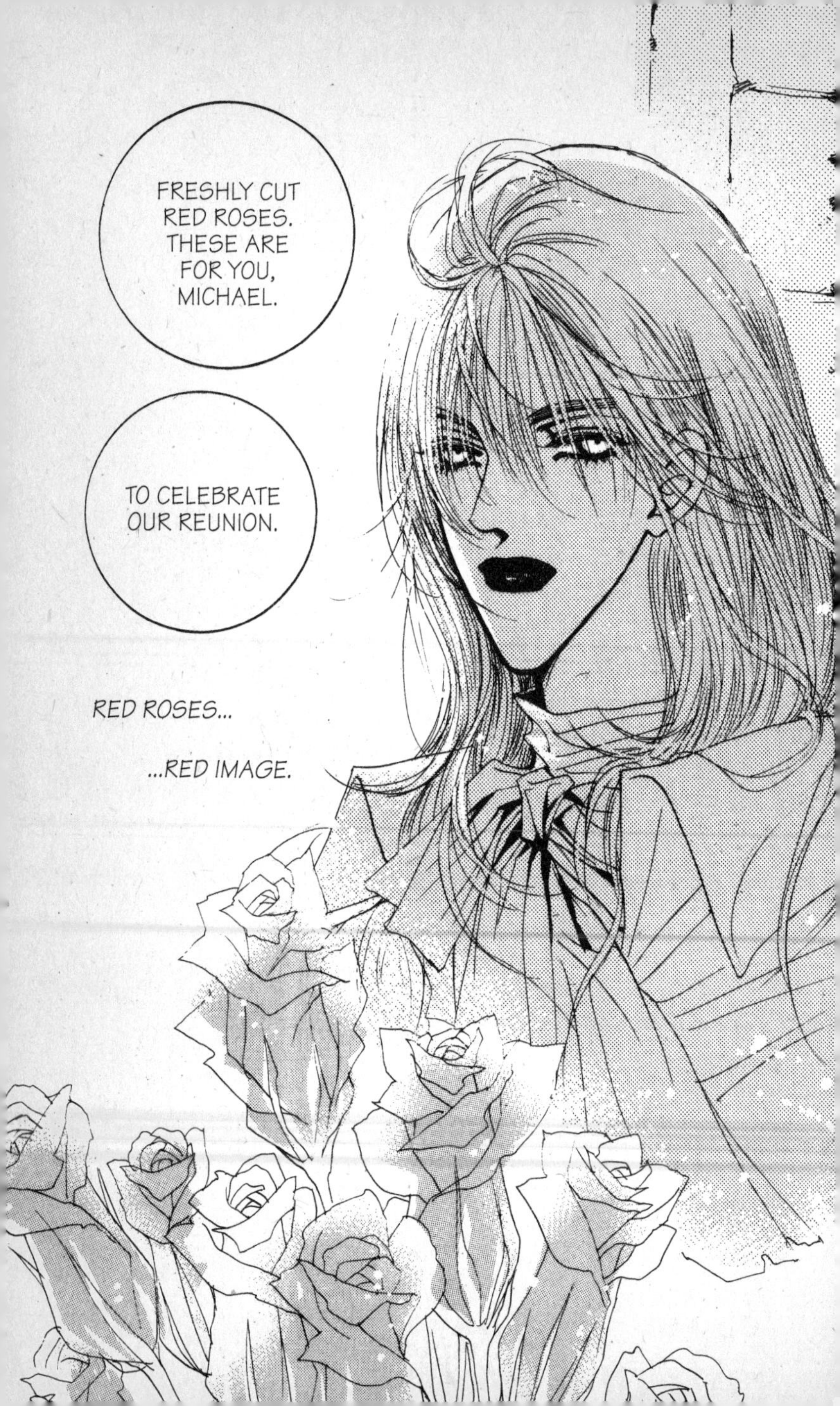
FRESHLY CUT RED ROSES. THESE ARE FOR YOU, MICHAEL.
TO CELEBRATE OUR REUNION.
RED ROSES...
...RED IMAGE.

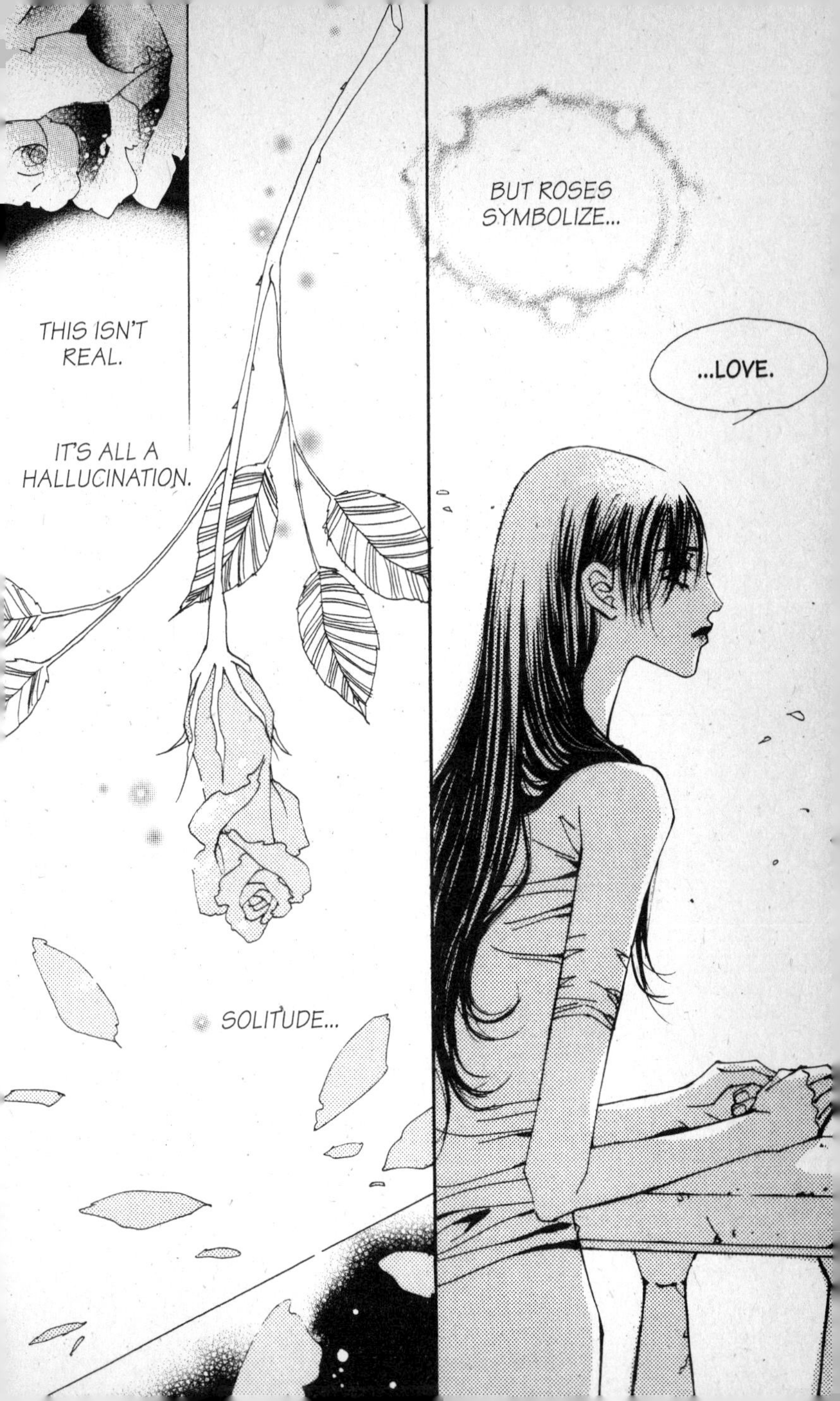
THIS ISN'T REAL.
IT'S ALL A HALLUCINATION.
SOLITUDE...
BUT ROSES SYMBOLIZE...
...LOVE.

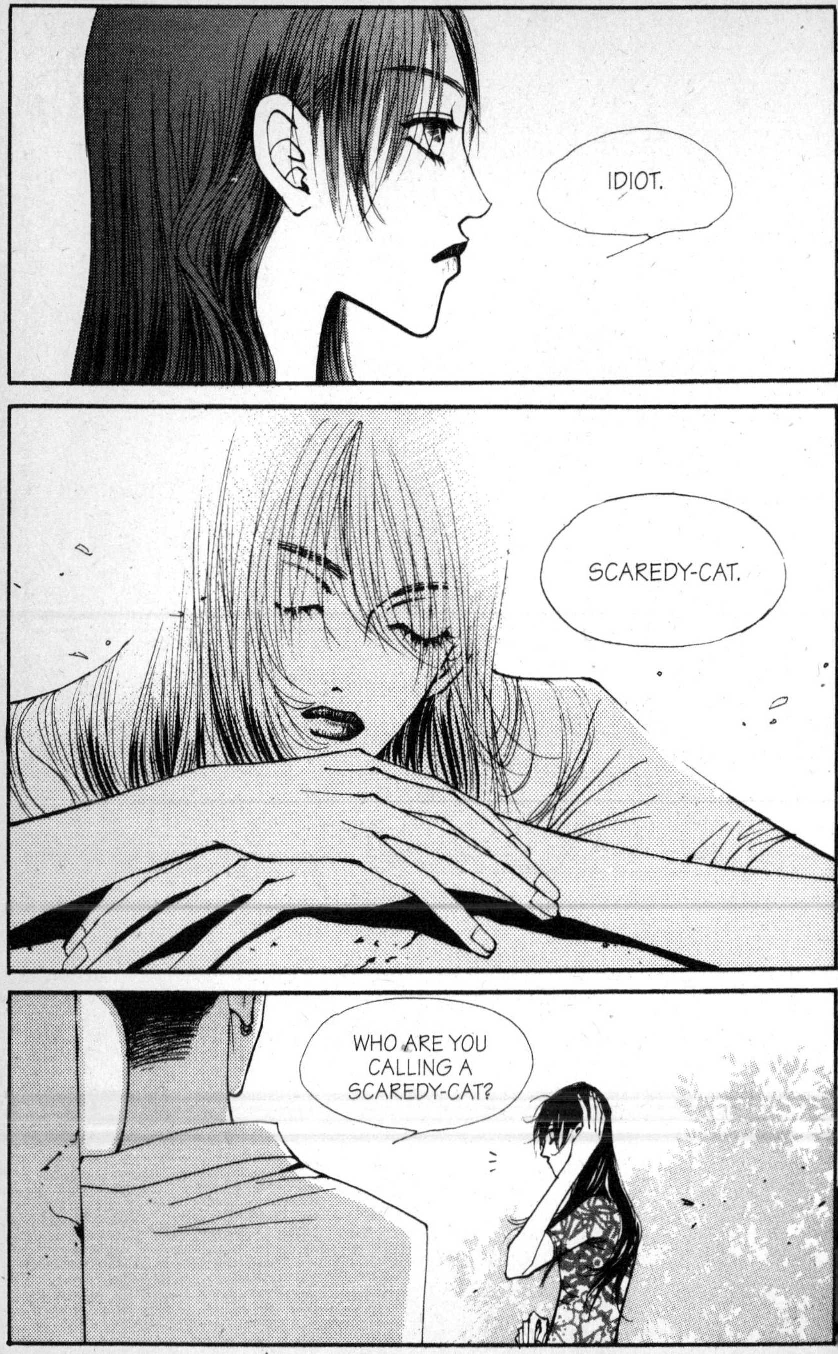
IDIOT.
SCAREDY-CAT.
WHO ARE YOU CALLING A SCAREDY-CAT?

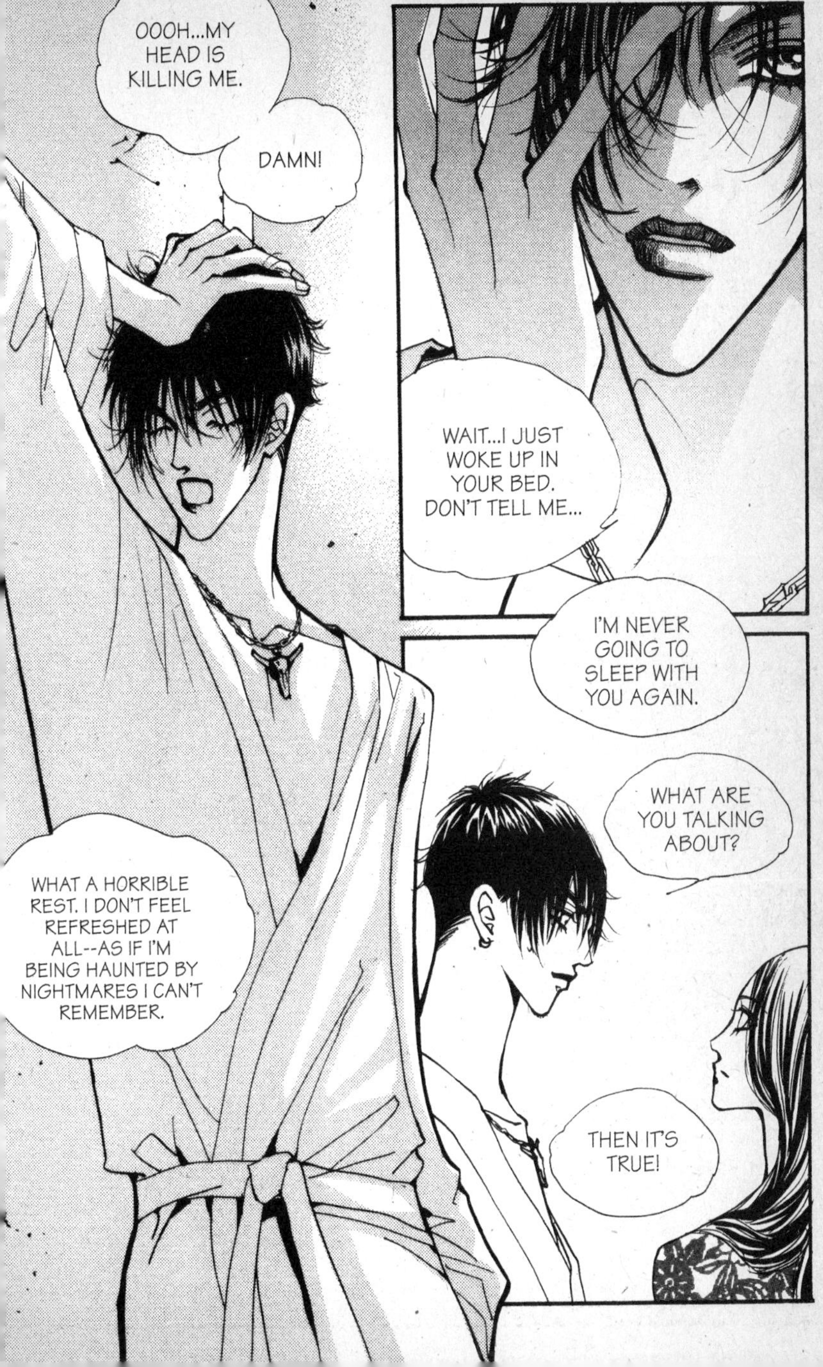
OOOH...MY HEAD IS KILLING ME.
DAMN!
WHAT A HORRIBLE REST. I DON'T FEEL REFRESHED AT ALL--AS IF I'M BEING HAUNTED BY NIGHTMARES I CAN'T REMEMBER.
WAIT...I JUST WOKE UP IN YOUR BED. DON'T TELL ME...
I'M NEVER GOING TO SLEEP WITH YOU AGAIN.
WHAT ARE YOU TALKING ABOUT?
THEN IT'S TRUE!

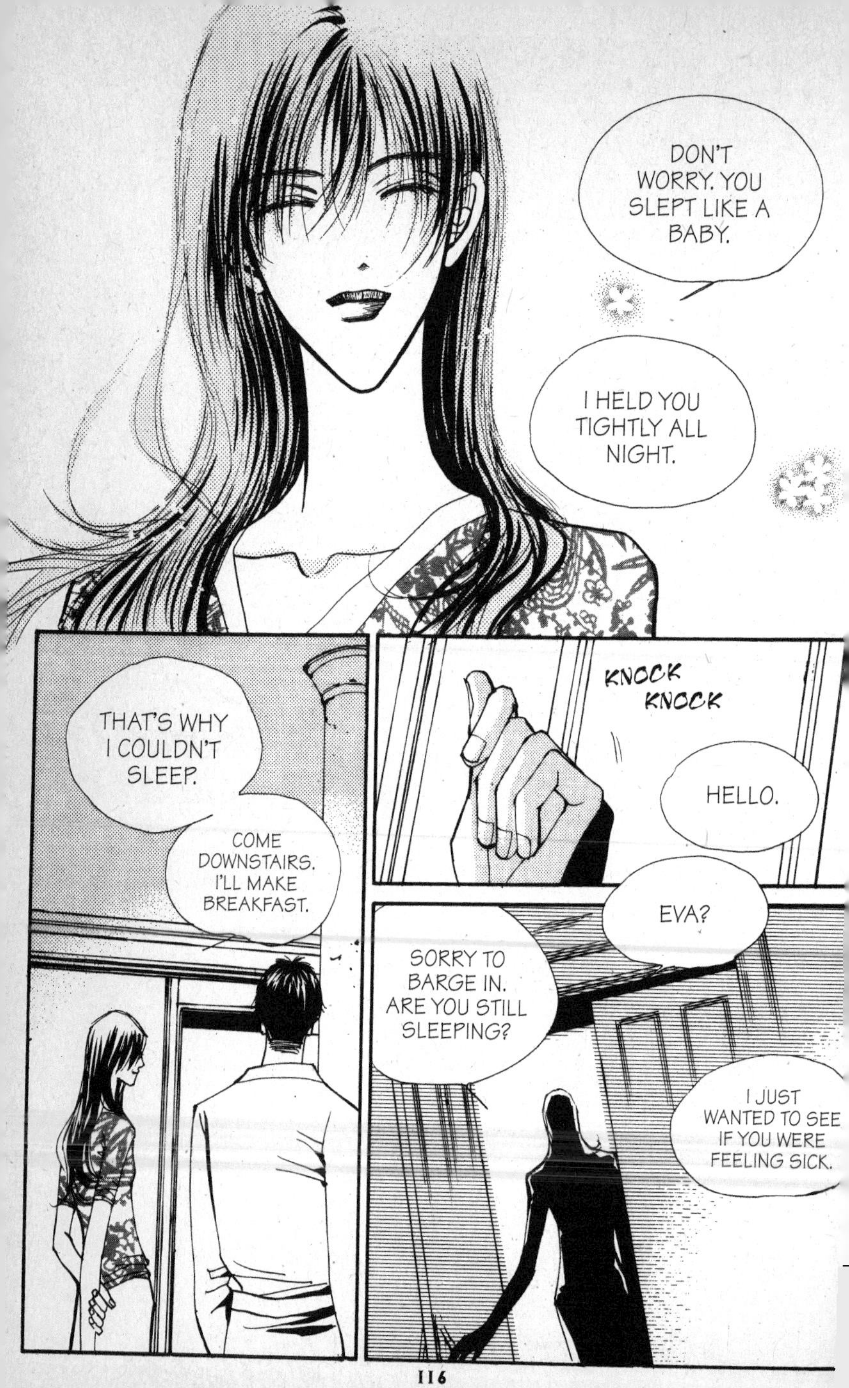
DON'T WORRY. YOU SLEPT LIKE A BABY.
I HELD YOU TIGHTLY ALL NIGHT.
THAT'S WHY I COULDN'T SLEEP.
COME DOWNSTAIRS. I'LL MAKE BREAKFAST.
KNOCK KNOCK
HELLO.
EVA?
SORRY TO BARGE IN. ARE YOU STILL SLEEPING?
I JUST WANTED TO SEE IF YOU WERE FEELING SICK.

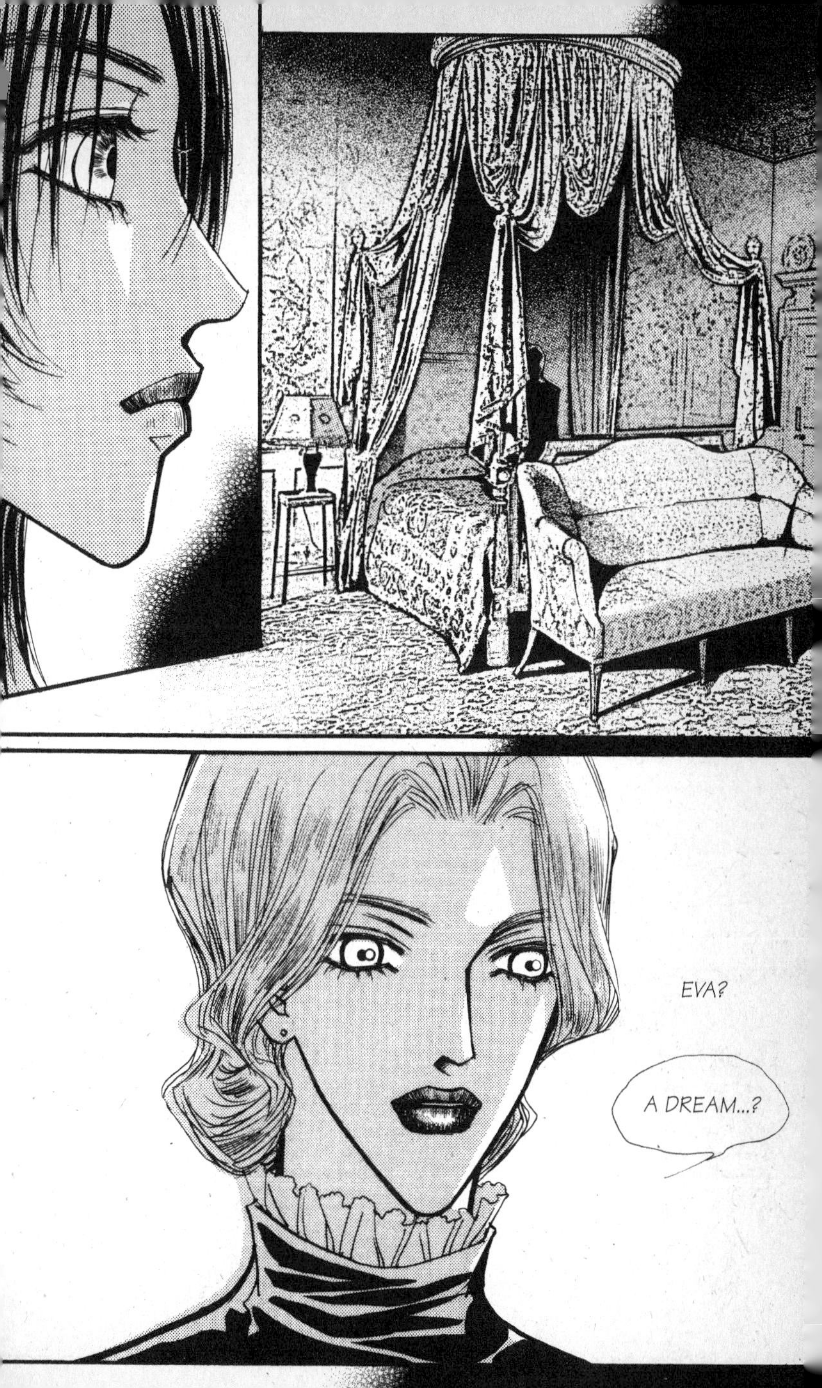
EVA?
A DREAM...?

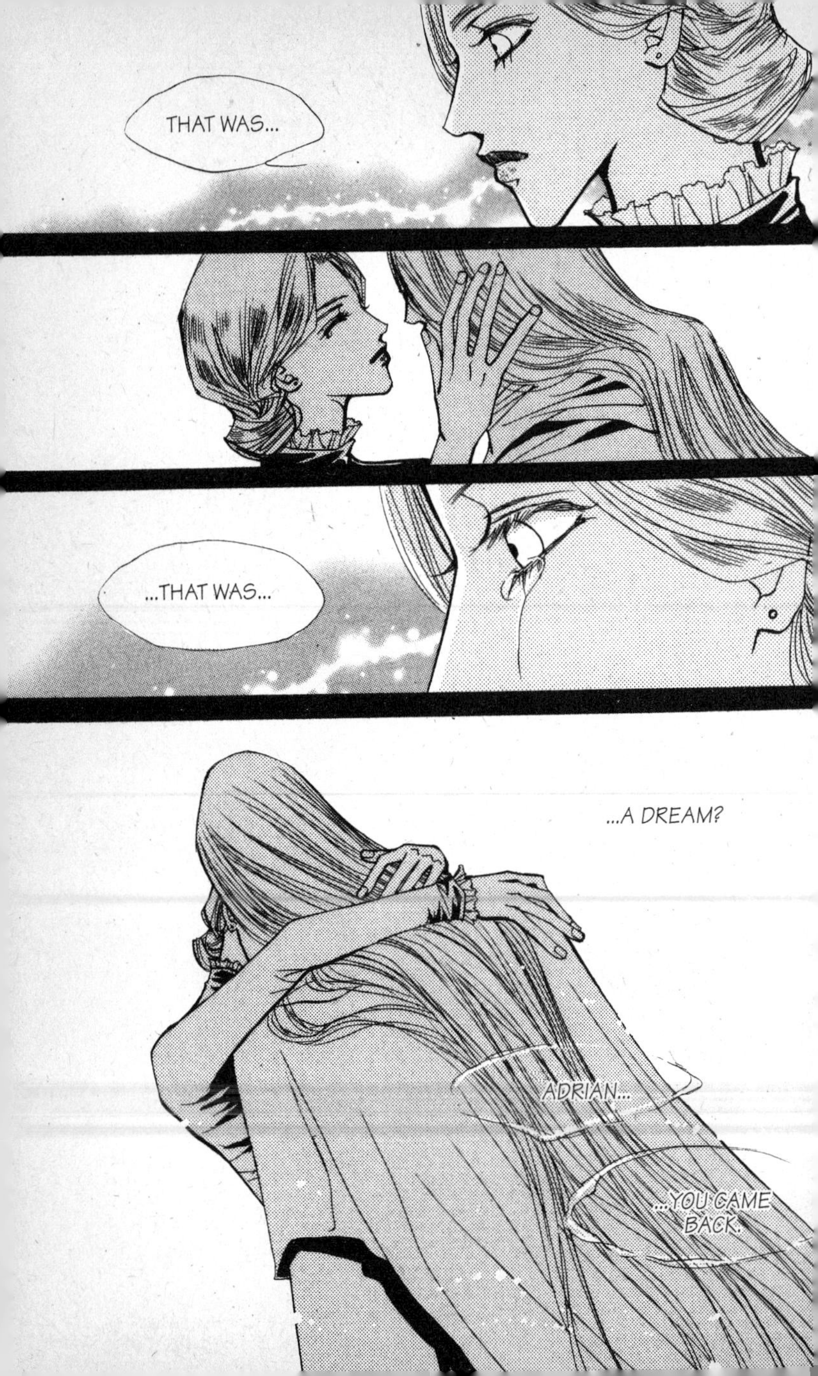
THAT WAS...
...THAT WAS...
...A DREAM?
ADRIAN...
...YOU CAME BACK.

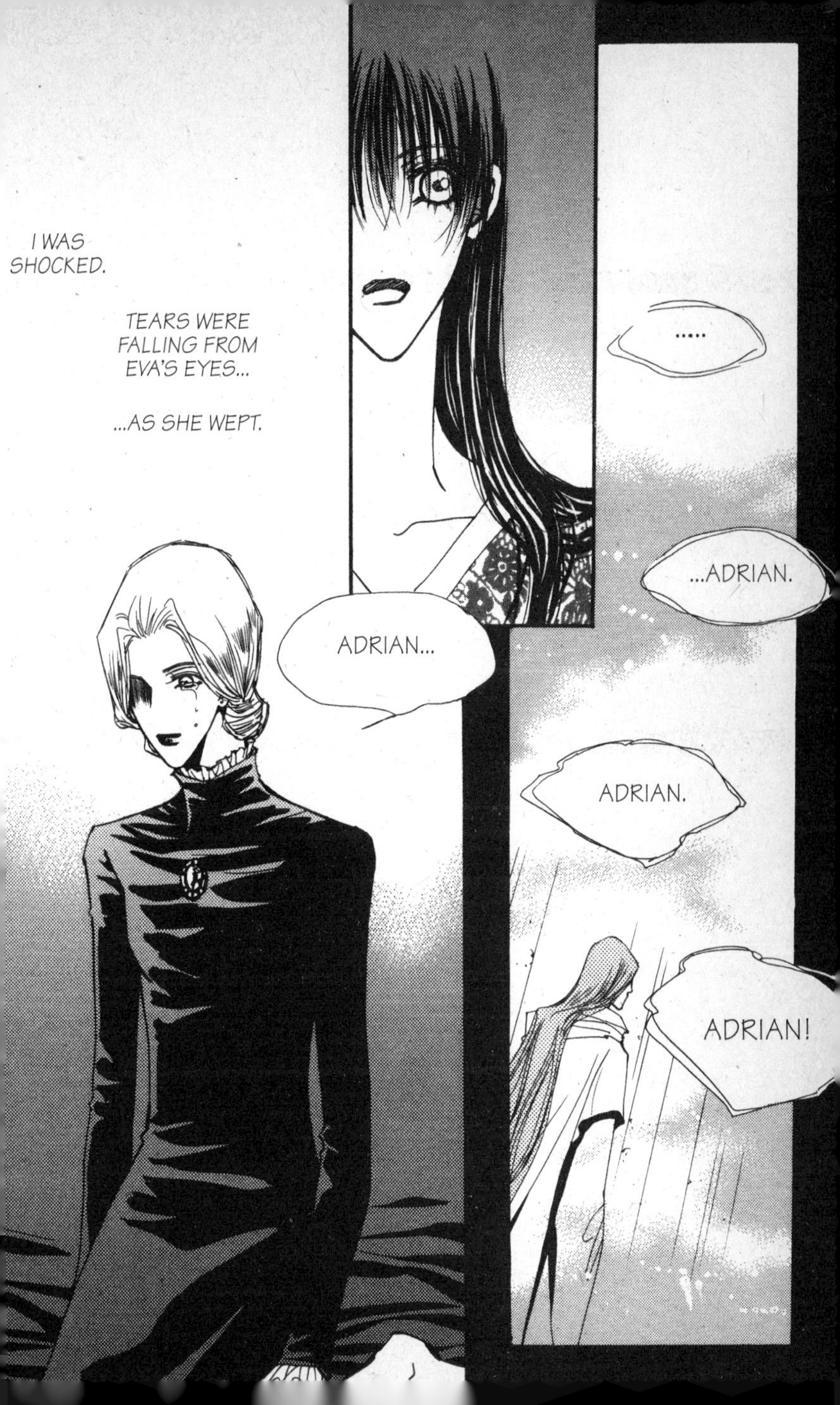
I WAS SHOCKED.
TEARS WERE FALLING FROM EVA'S EYES...
...AS SHE WEPT.
.....
ADRIAN...
...ADRIAN.
ADRIAN.
ADRIAN!

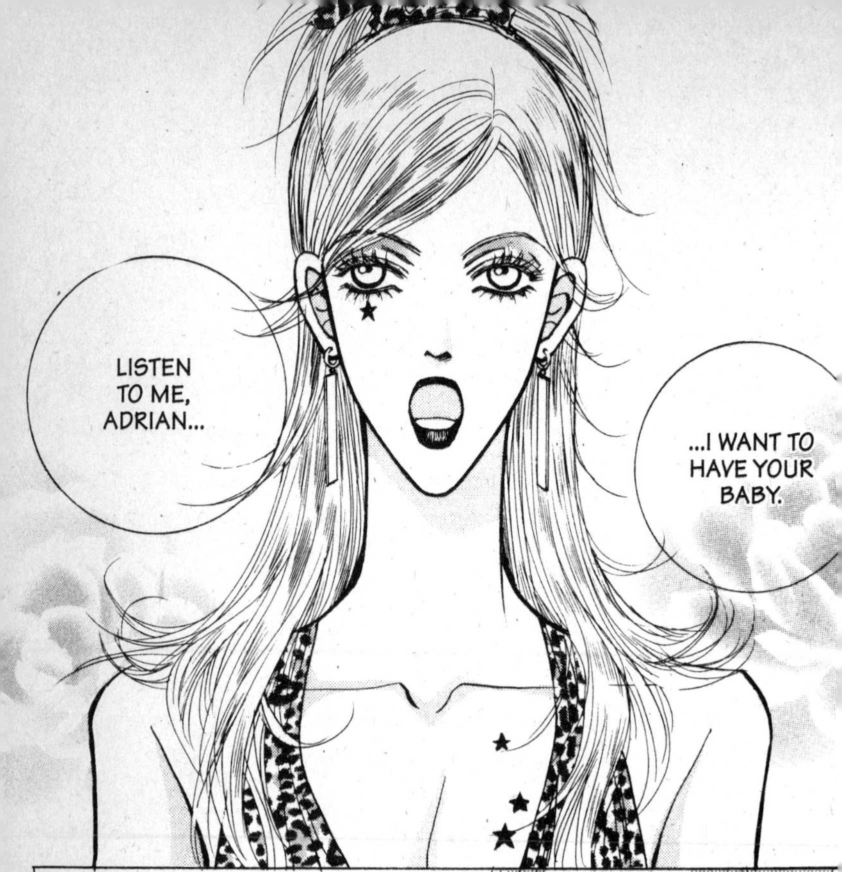
LISTEN TO ME, ADRIAN...
...I WANT TO HAVE YOUR BABY.

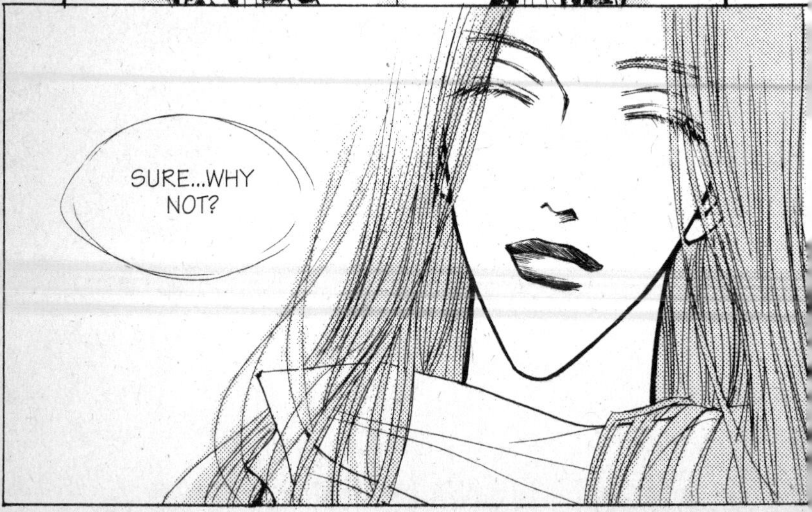
SURE...WHY NOT?

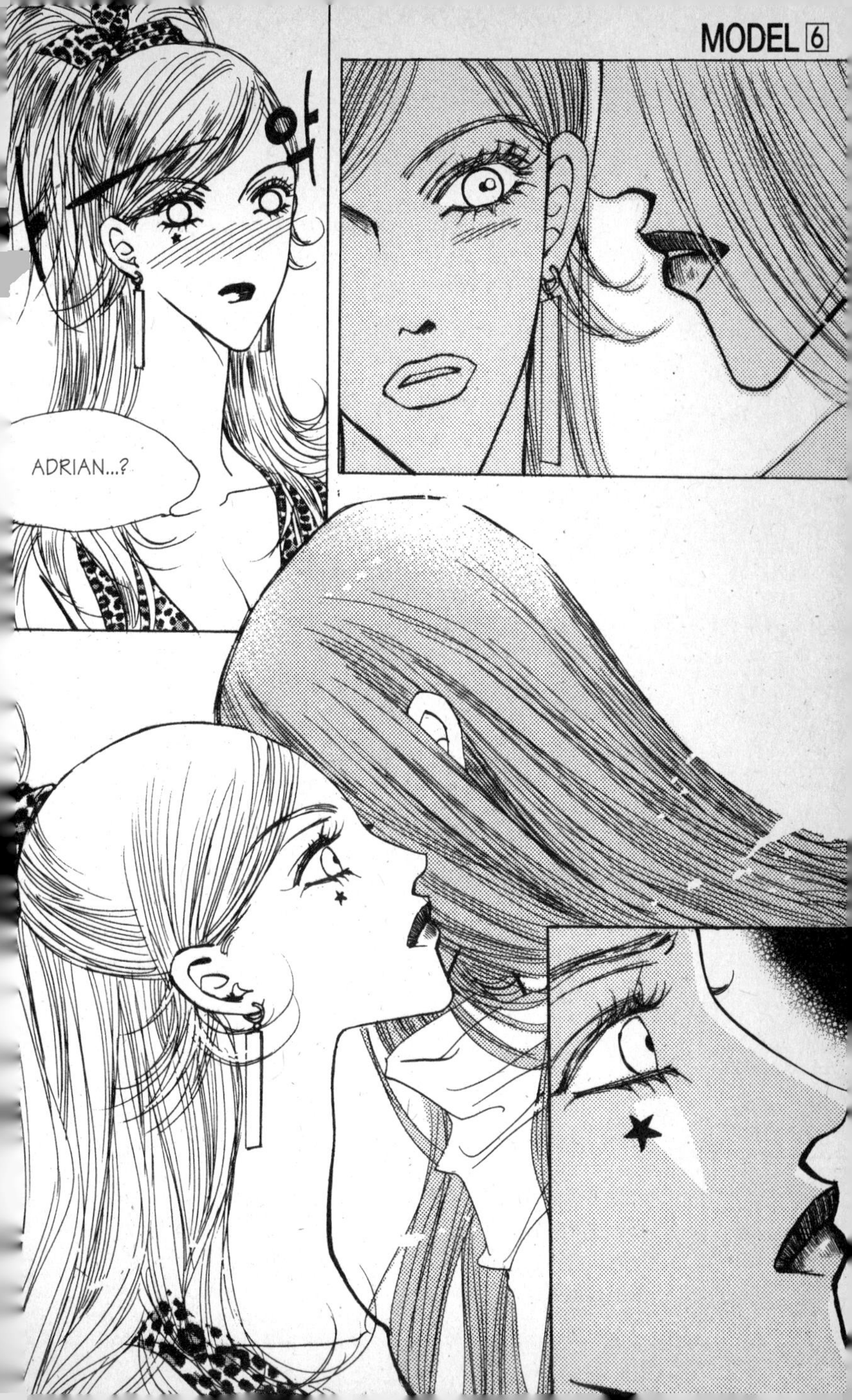
ADRIAN...?

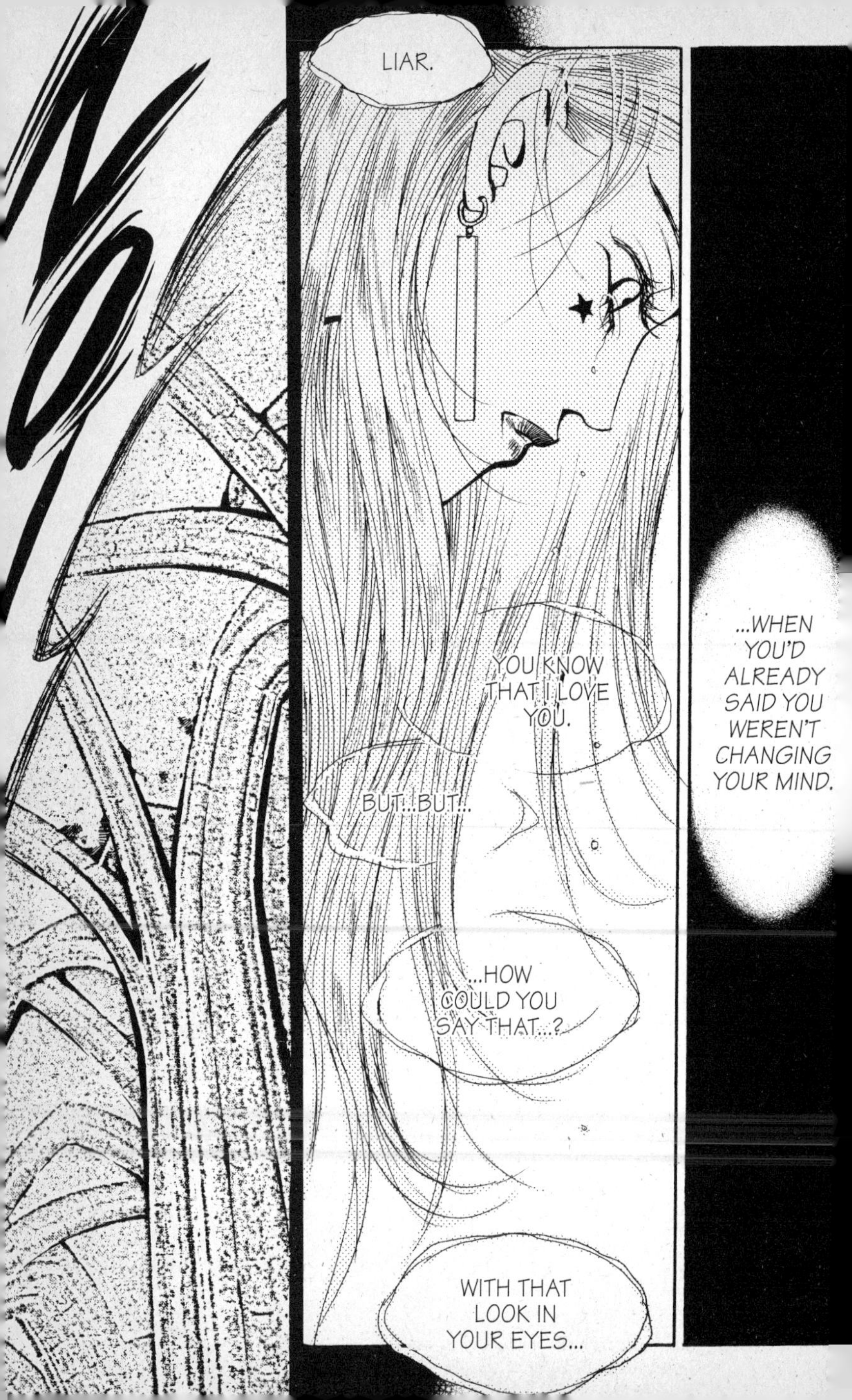
LIAR.
YOU KNOW THAT I LOVE YOU.
BUT...BUT...
...HOW COULD YOU SAY THAT...?
WITH THAT LOOK IN YOUR EYES...
...WHEN YOU'D ALREADY SAID YOU WEREN'T CHANGING YOUR MIND.

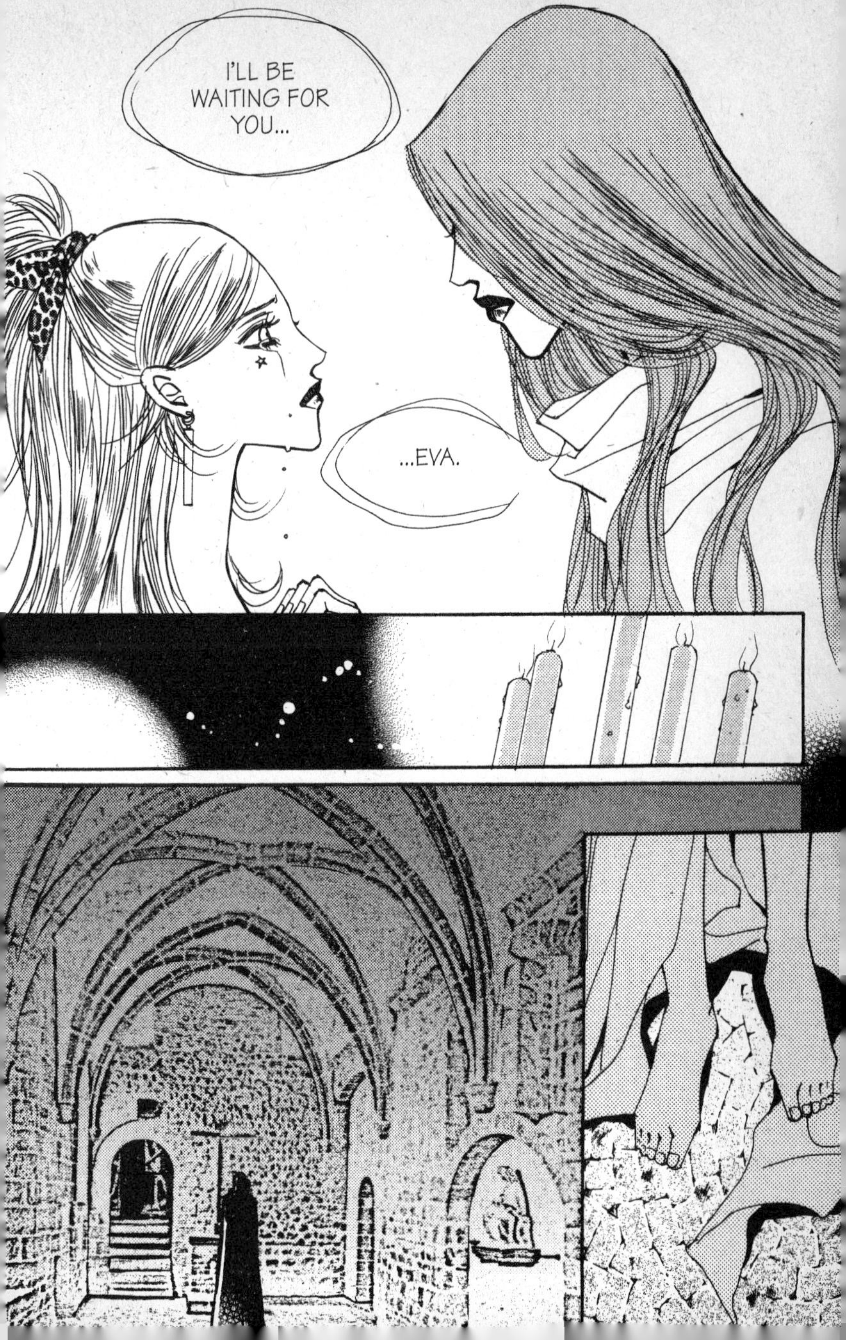
I'LL BE WAITING FOR YOU...
...EVA.

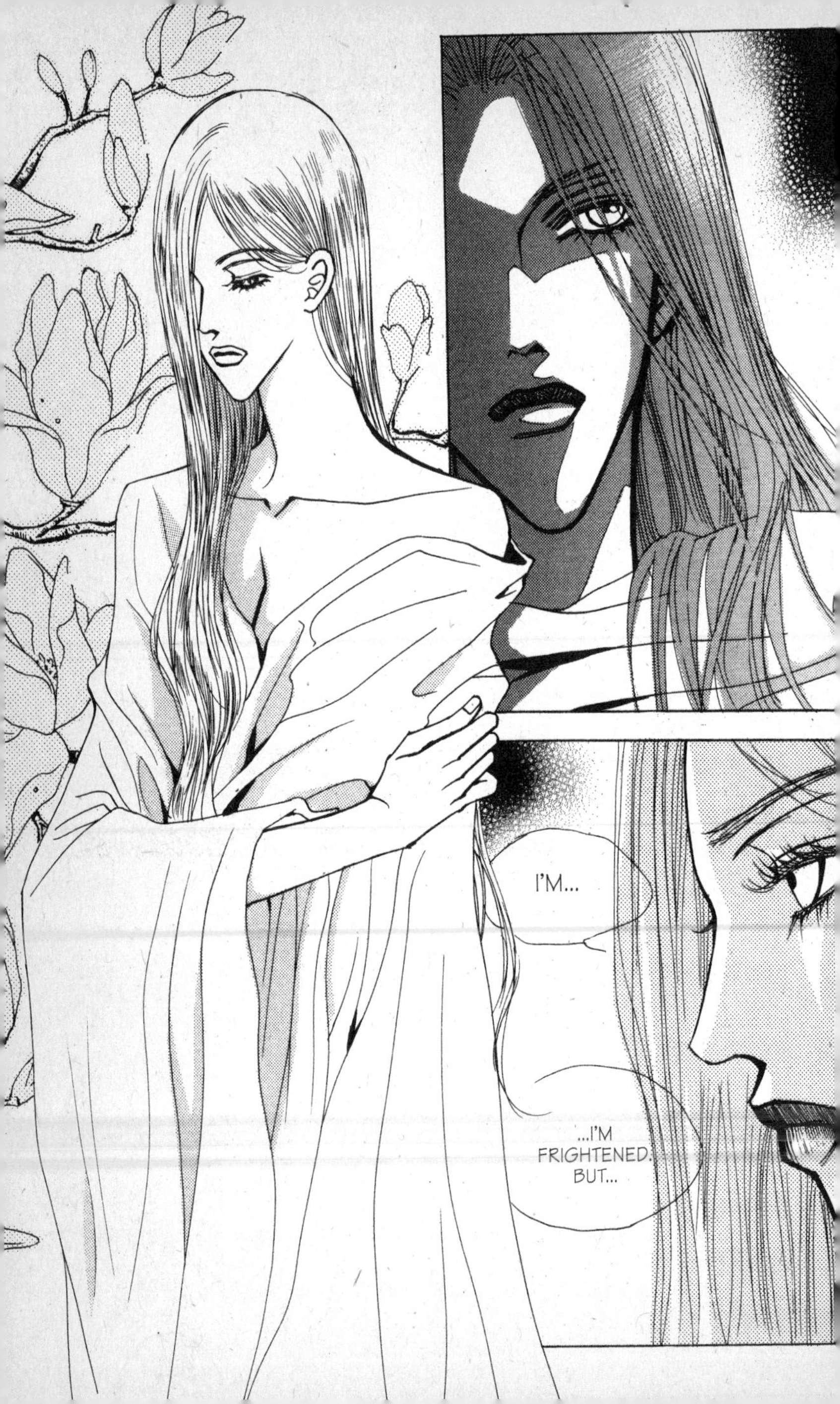
I'M...
...I'M FRIGHTENED. BUT...

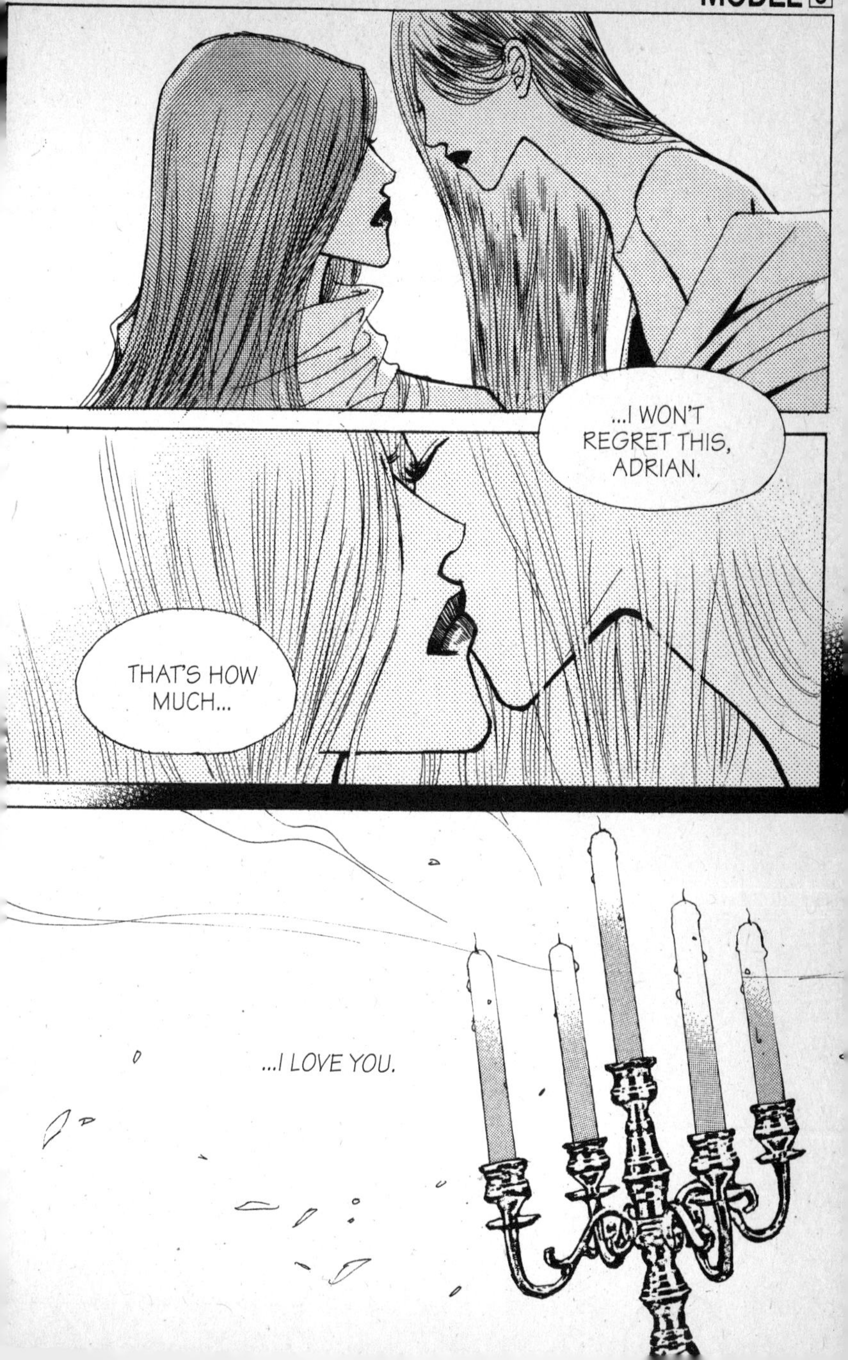
...I WON'T REGRET THIS, ADRIAN.
THAT'S HOW MUCH...
...I LOVE YOU.

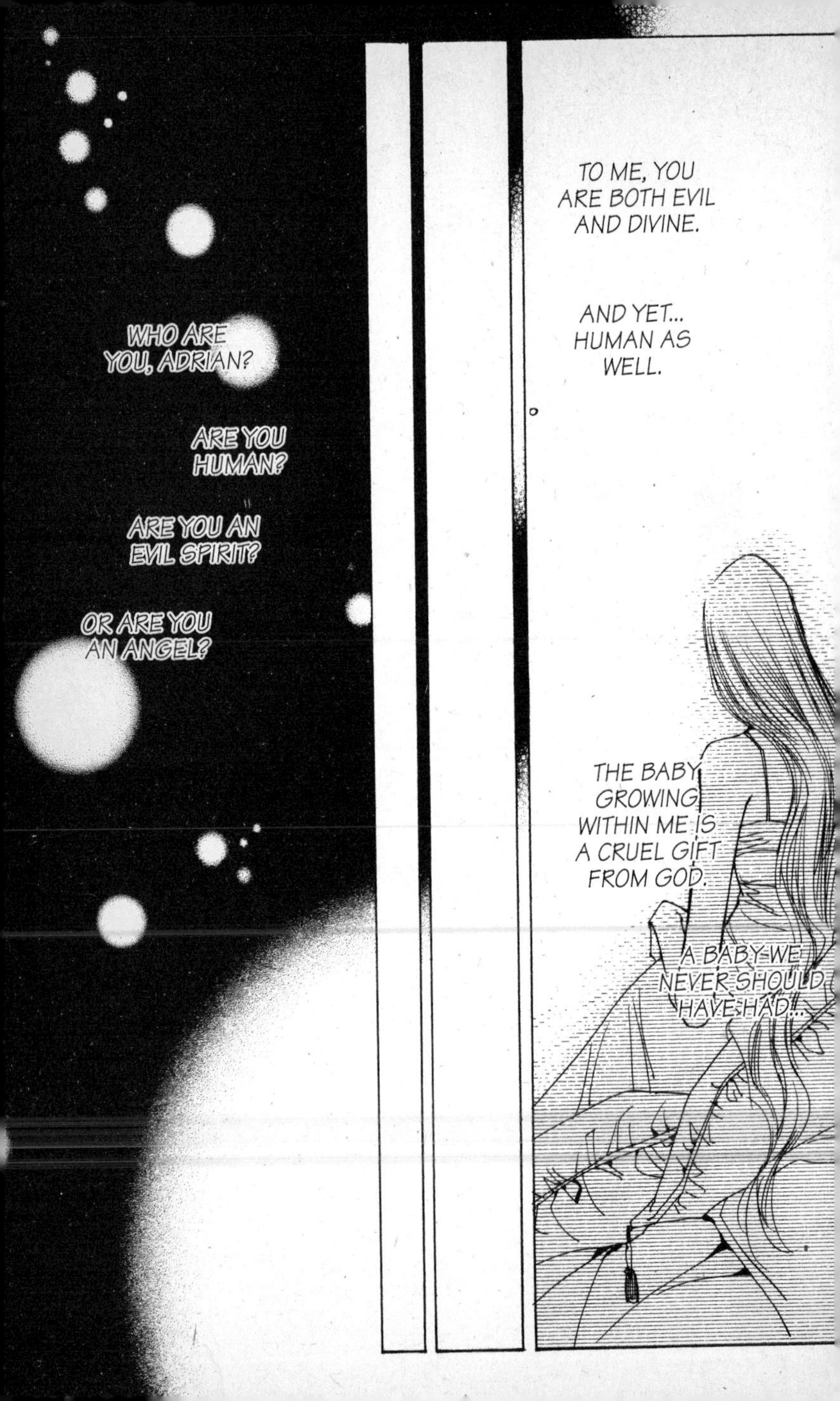
TO ME, YOU ARE BOTH EVIL AND DIVINE.
AND YET... HUMAN AS WELL.
THE BABY GROWING WITHIN ME IS A CRUEL GIFT FROM GOD.
A BABY WE NEVER SHOULD HAVE HAD!...
WHO ARE YOU, ADRIAN?
ARE YOU HUMAN?
ARE YOU AN EVIL SPIRIT?
OR ARE YOU AN ANGEL?

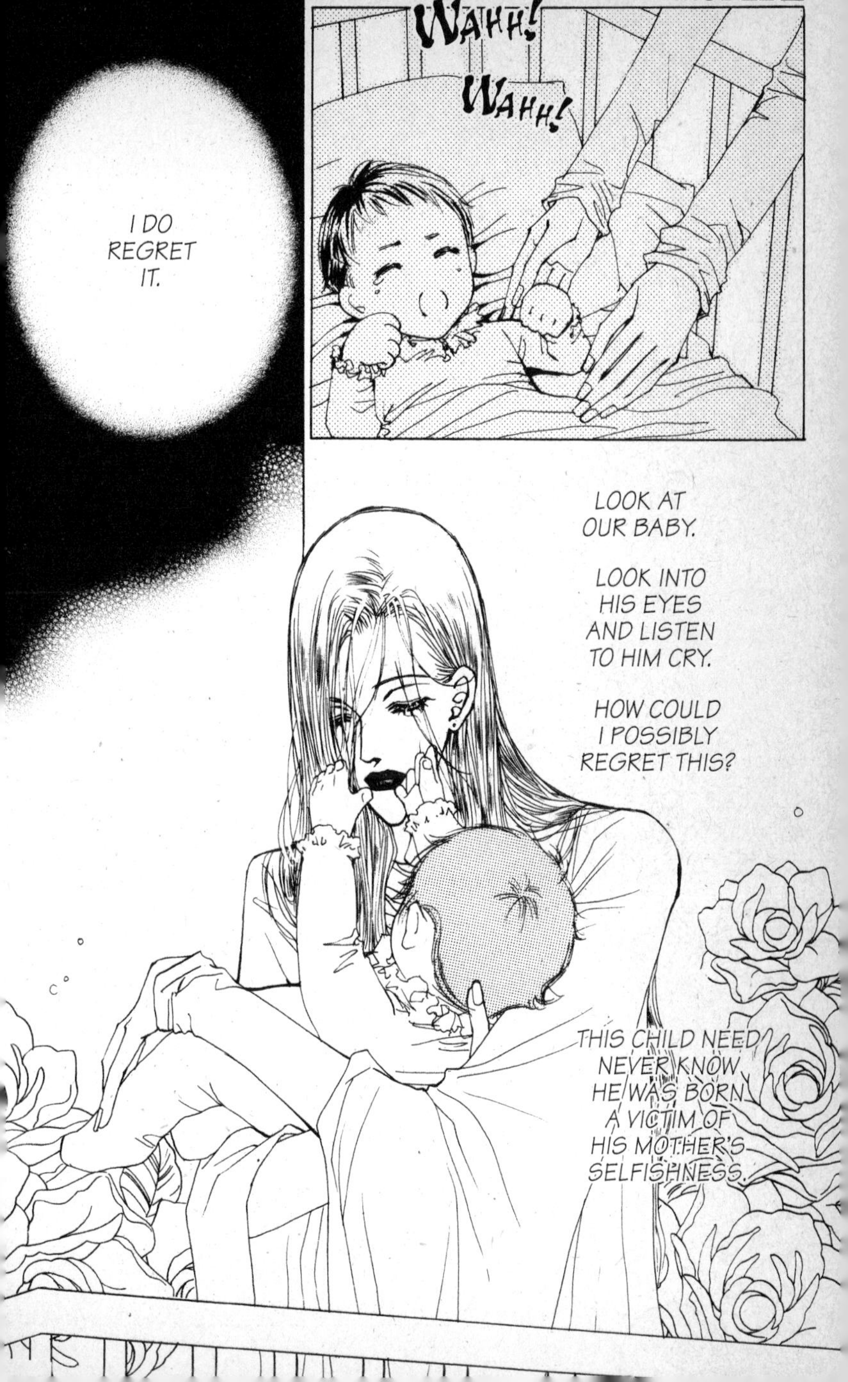
WAHH!
WAHH!
I DO REGRET IT.
LOOK AT OUR BABY.
LOOK INTO HIS EYES AND LISTEN TO HIM CRY.
HOW COULD I POSSIBLY REGRET THIS?
THIS CHILD NEED NEVER KNOW HE WAS BORN A VICTIM OF HIS MOTHER'S SELFISHNESS.

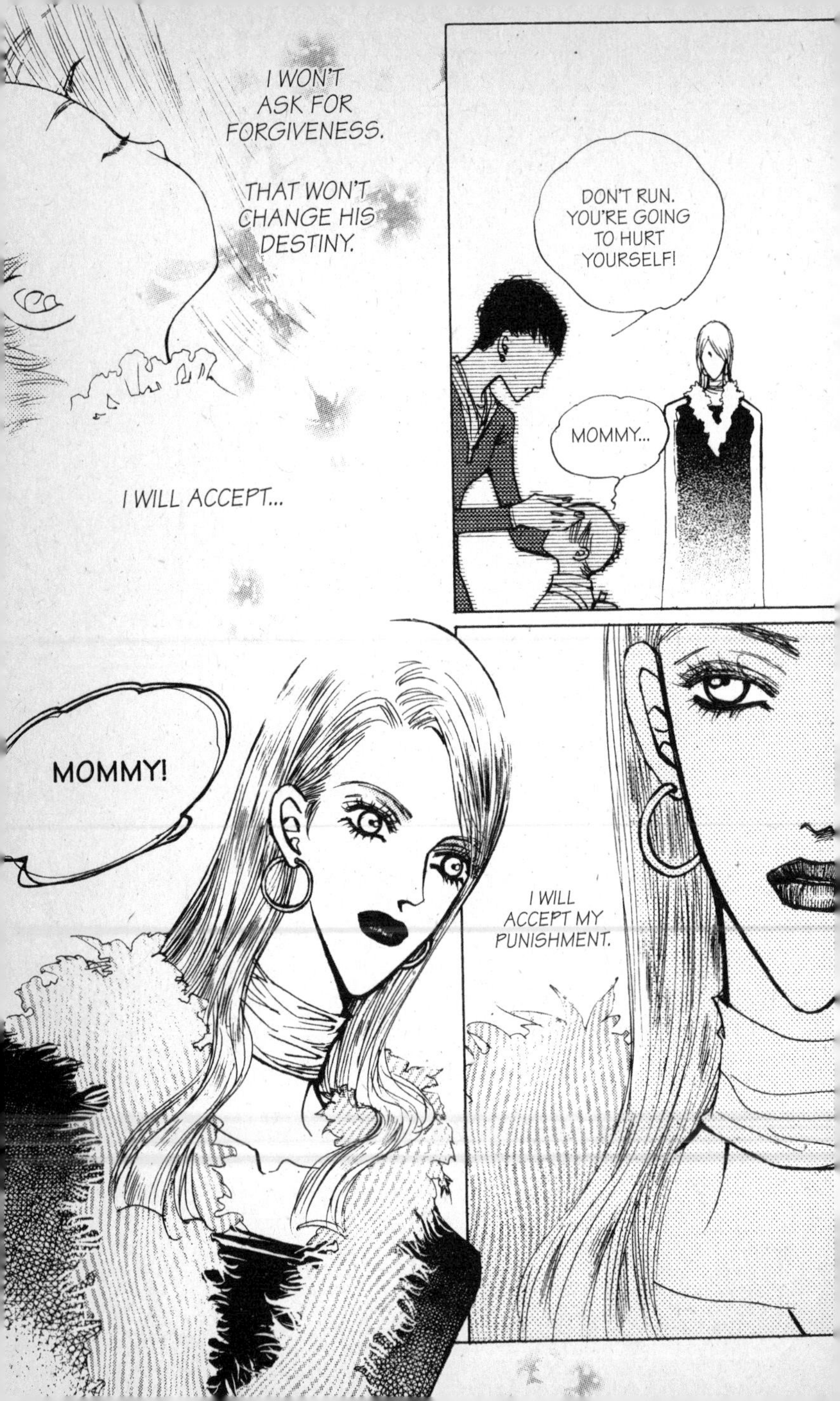
DON'T RUN. YOU'RE GOING TO HURT YOURSELF!
MOMMY...
I WON'T ASK FOR FORGIVENESS.
THAT WON'T CHANGE HIS DESTINY.
I WILL ACCEPT...
I WILL ACCEPT MY PUNISHMENT.
MOMMY!

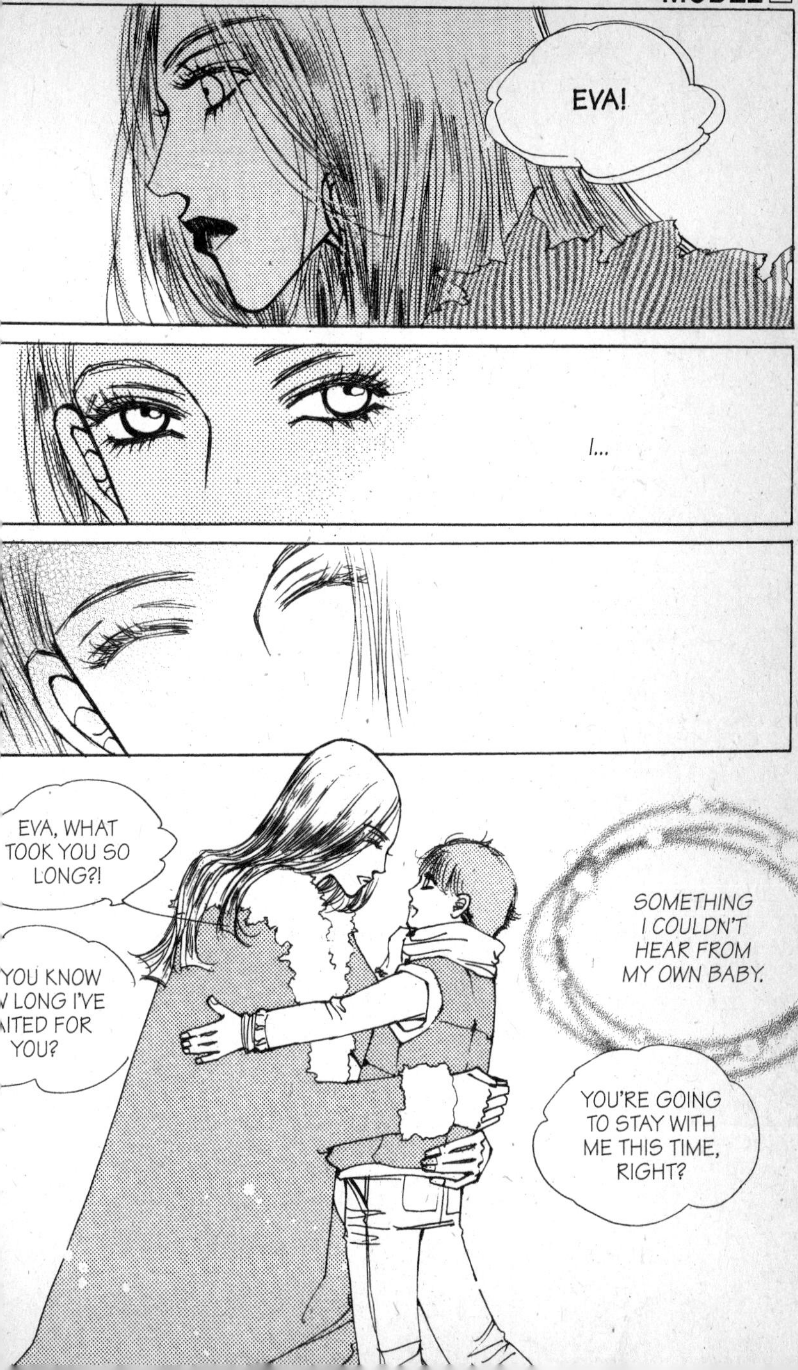
EVA!
I...
SOMETHING I COULDN'T HEAR FROM MY OWN BABY.
EVA, WHAT TOOK YOU SO LONG?!
YOU KNOW LONG I'VE ITED FOR YOU?
YOU'RE GOING TO STAY WITH ME THIS TIME, RIGHT?

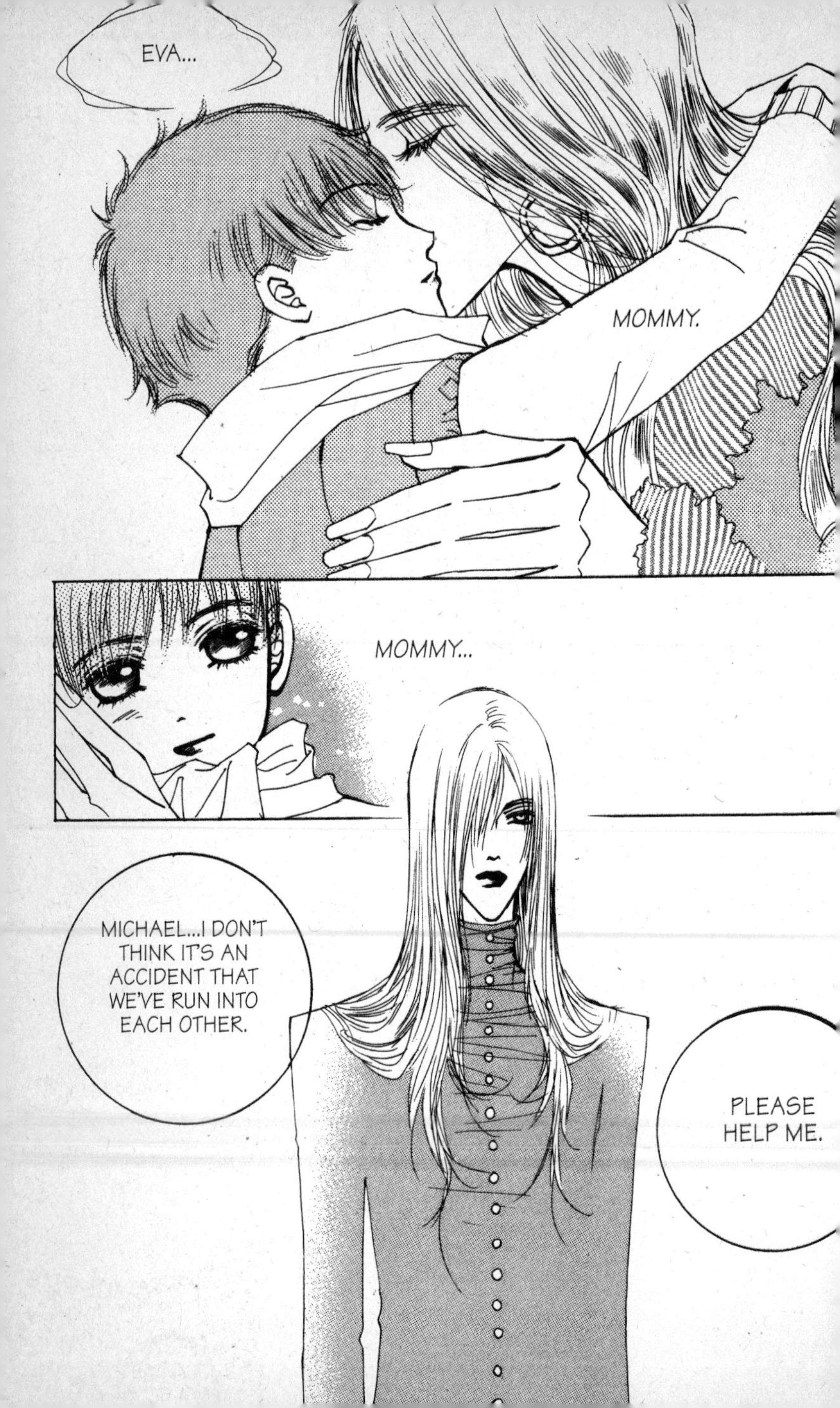
EVA...
MOMMY.
MOMMY...
PLEASE HELP ME.
MICHAEL...I DON'T THINK IT'S AN ACCIDENT THAT WE'VE RUN INTO EACH OTHER.

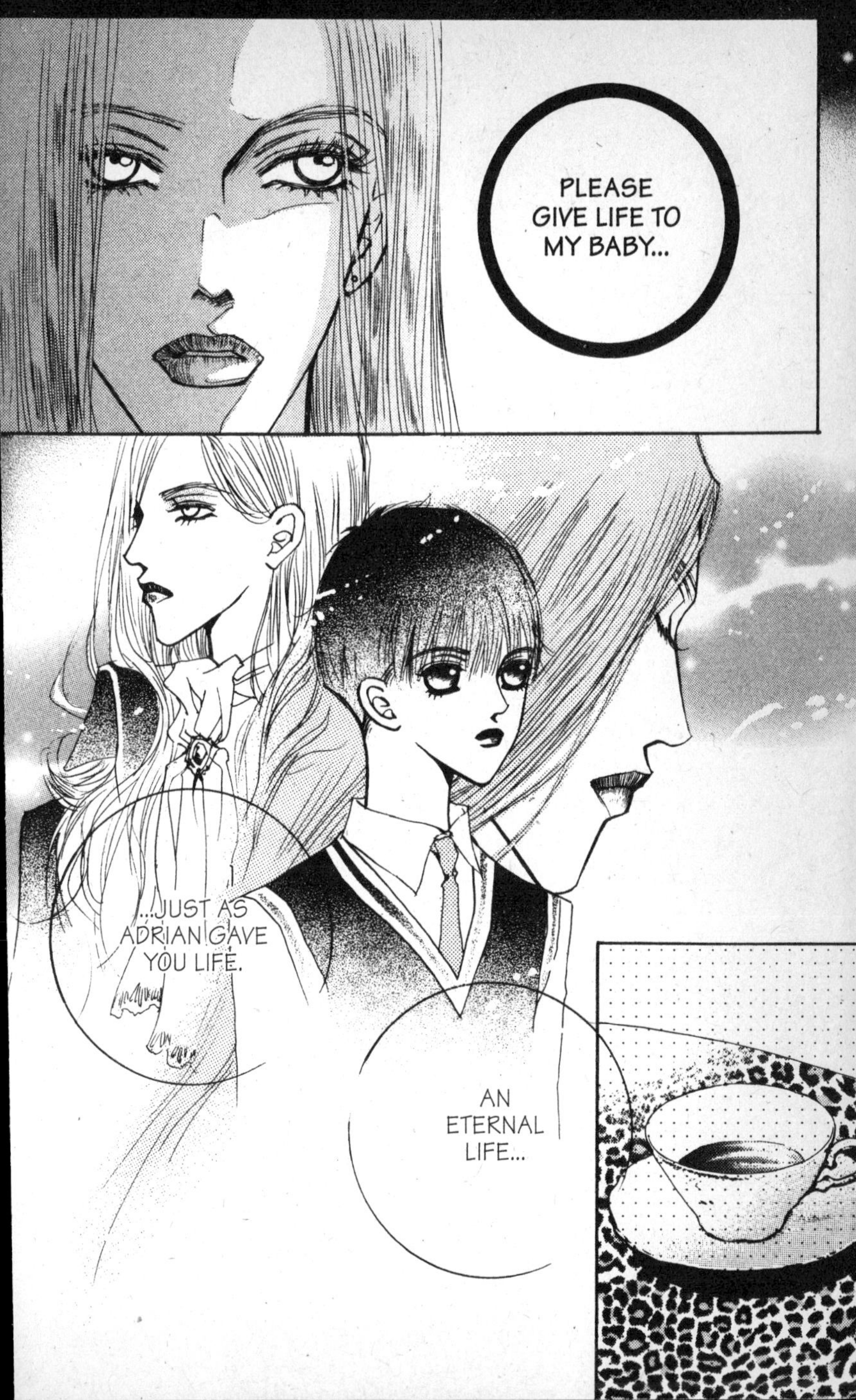
PLEASE GIVE LIFE TO MY BABY...
...JUST AS ADRIAN GAVE YOU LIFE.
AN ETERNAL LIFE...

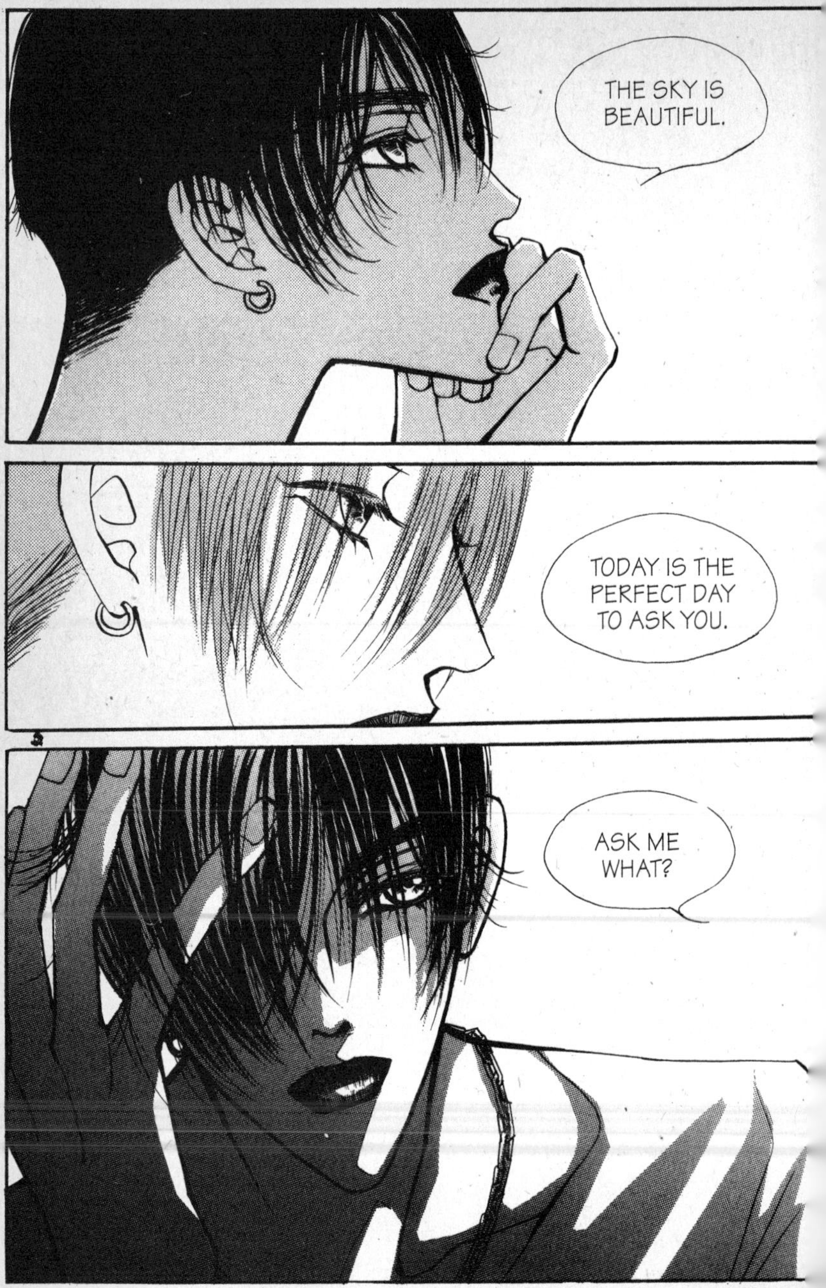
THE SKY IS BEAUTIFUL.
TODAY IS THE PERFECT DAY TO ASK YOU.
ASK ME WHAT?

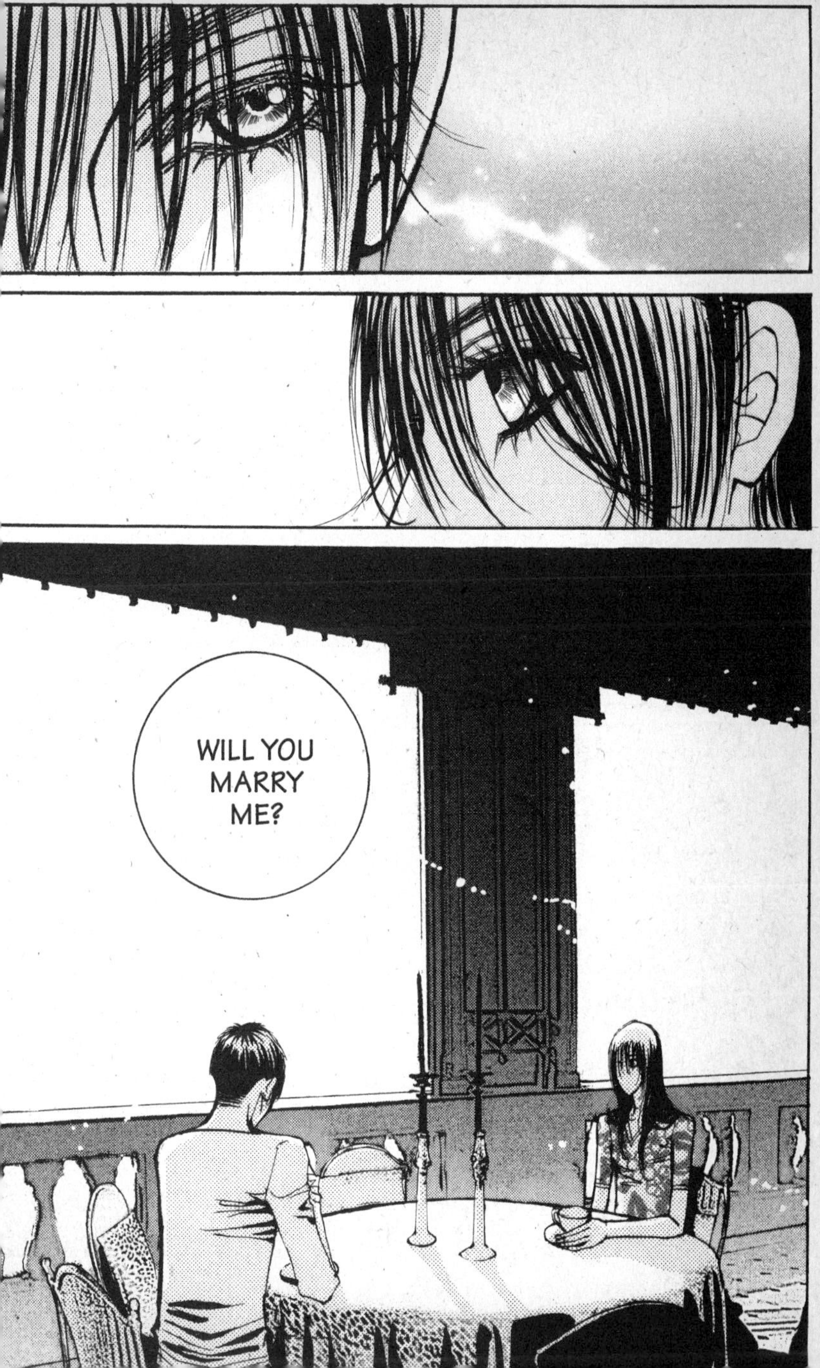
WILL YOU MARRY ME?

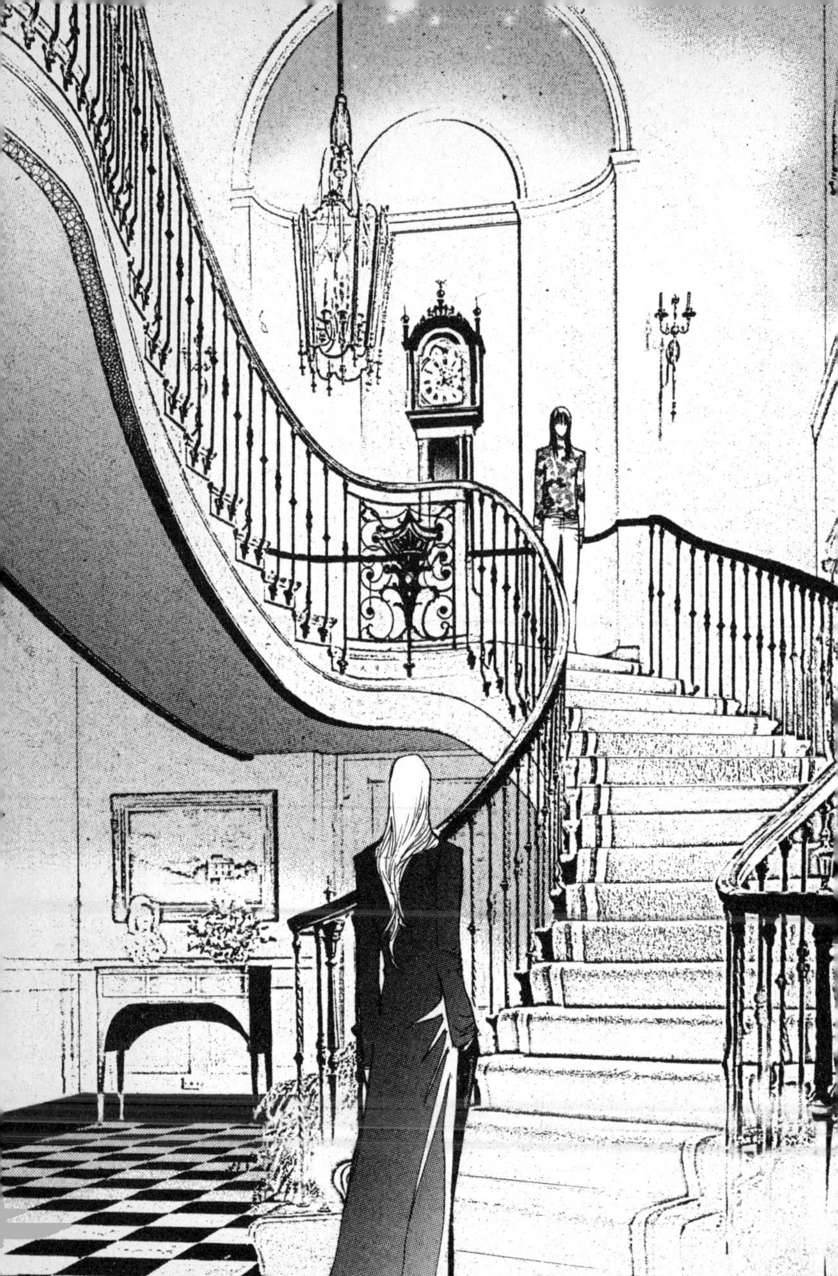

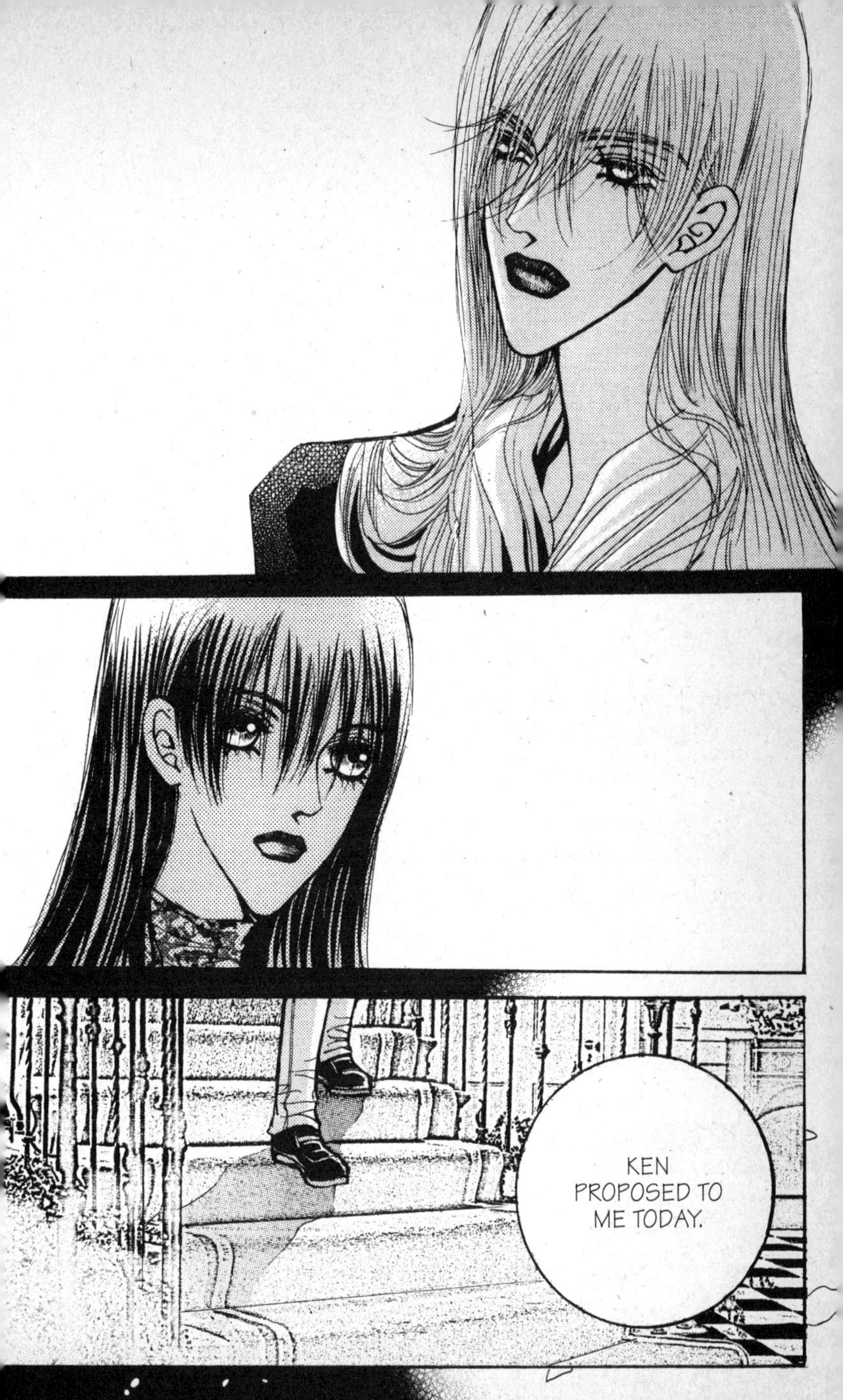
KEN PROPOSED TO ME TODAY.

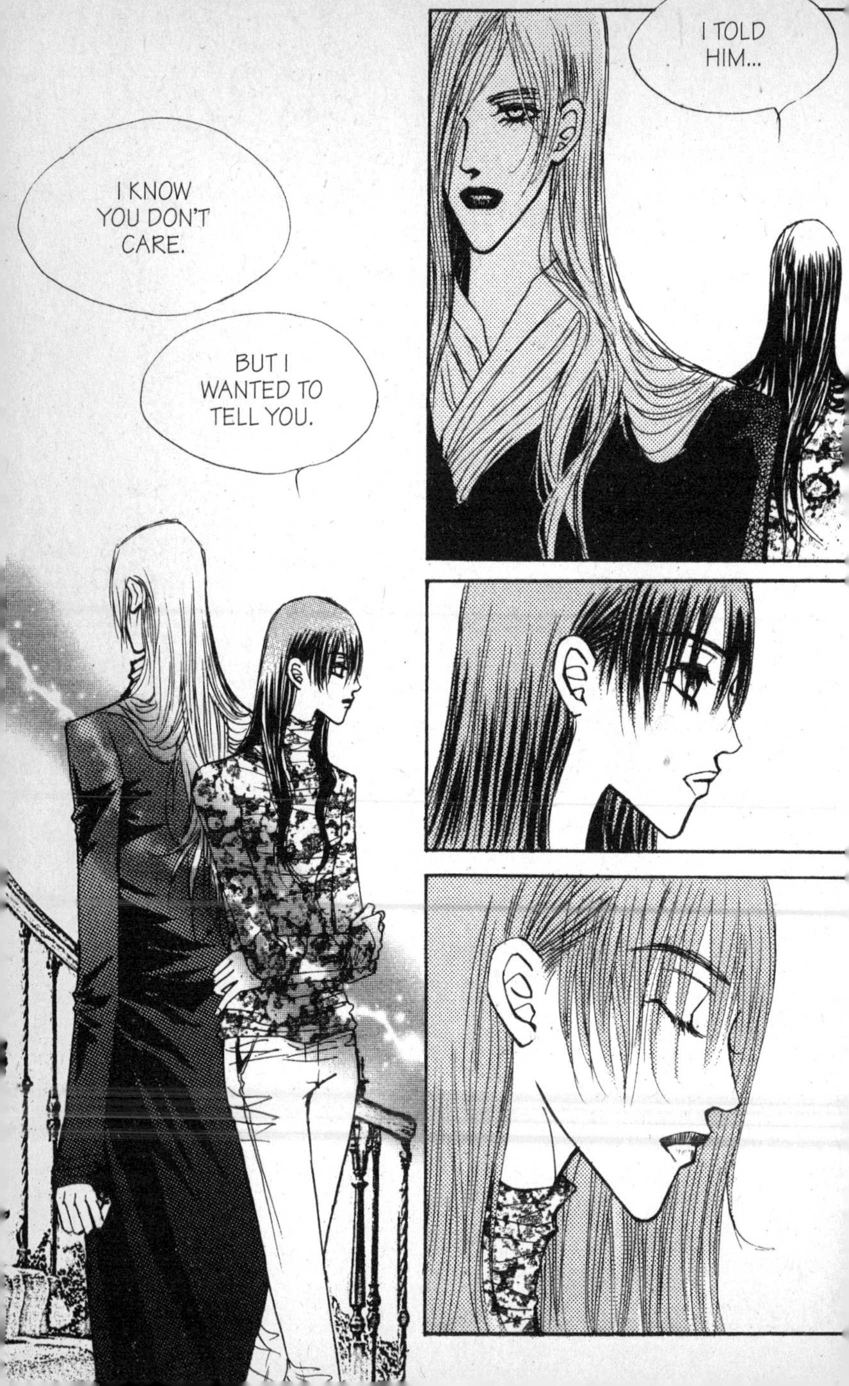
I TOLD HIM...
I KNOW YOU DON'T CARE.
BUT I WANTED TO TELL YOU.

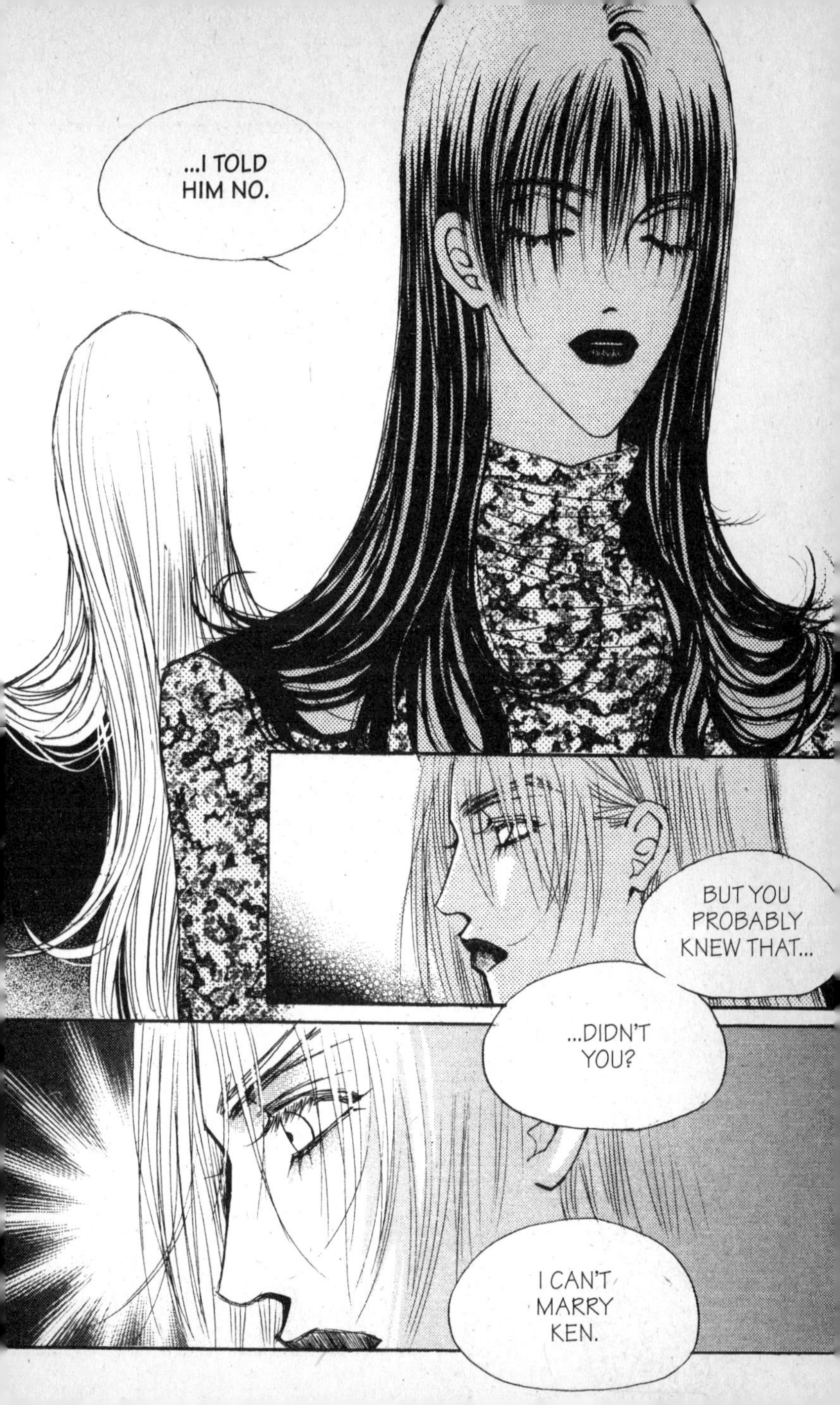
...I TOLD HIM NO.
BUT YOU PROBABLY KNEW THAT...
...DIDN'T YOU?
I CAN'T MARRY KEN.

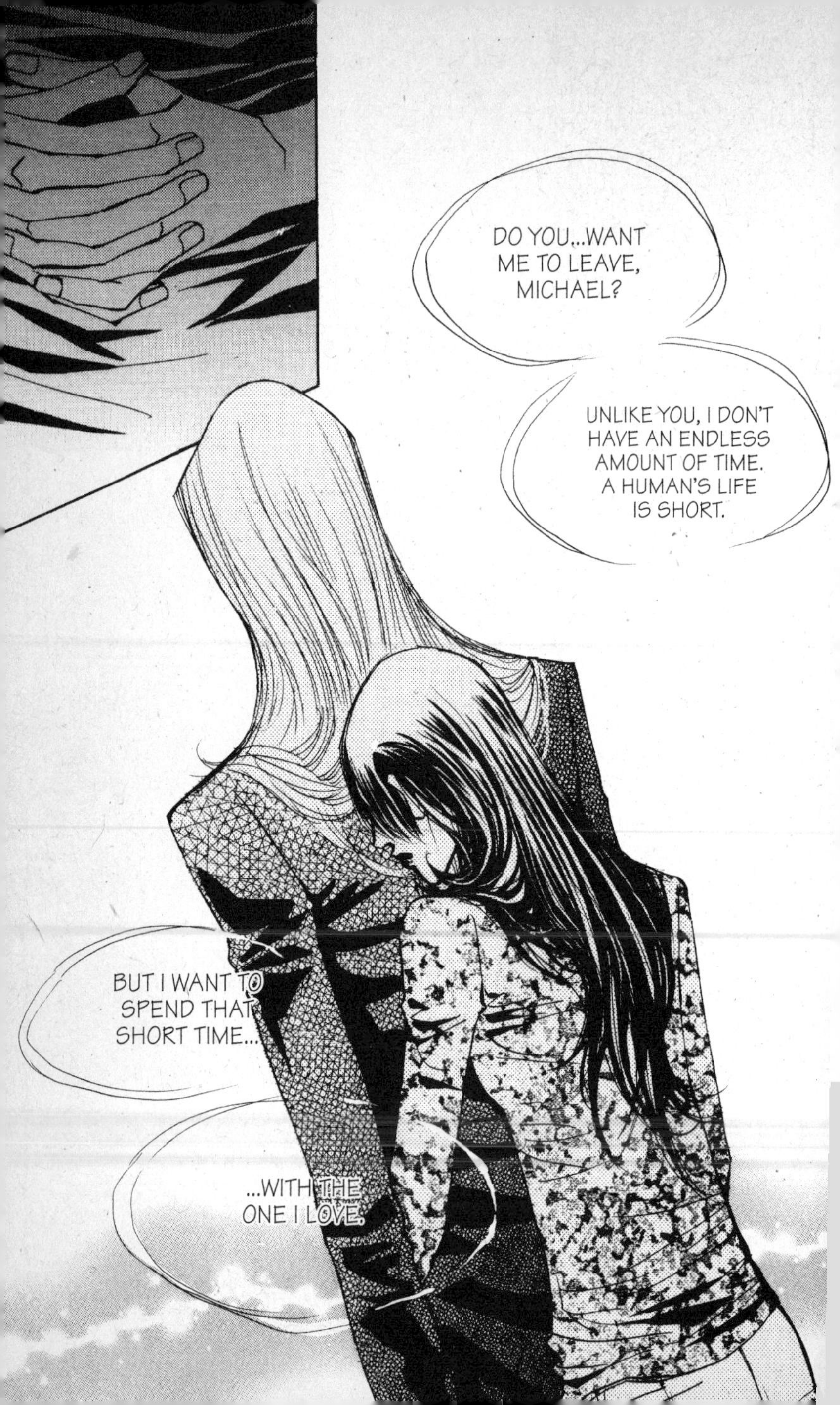
DO YOU...WANT ME TO LEAVE, MICHAEL?
UNLIKE YOU, I DON'T HAVE AN ENDLESS AMOUNT OF TIME. A HUMAN'S LIFE IS SHORT.
BUT I WANT TO SPEND THAT SHORT TIME...
...WITH THE ONE I LOVE.

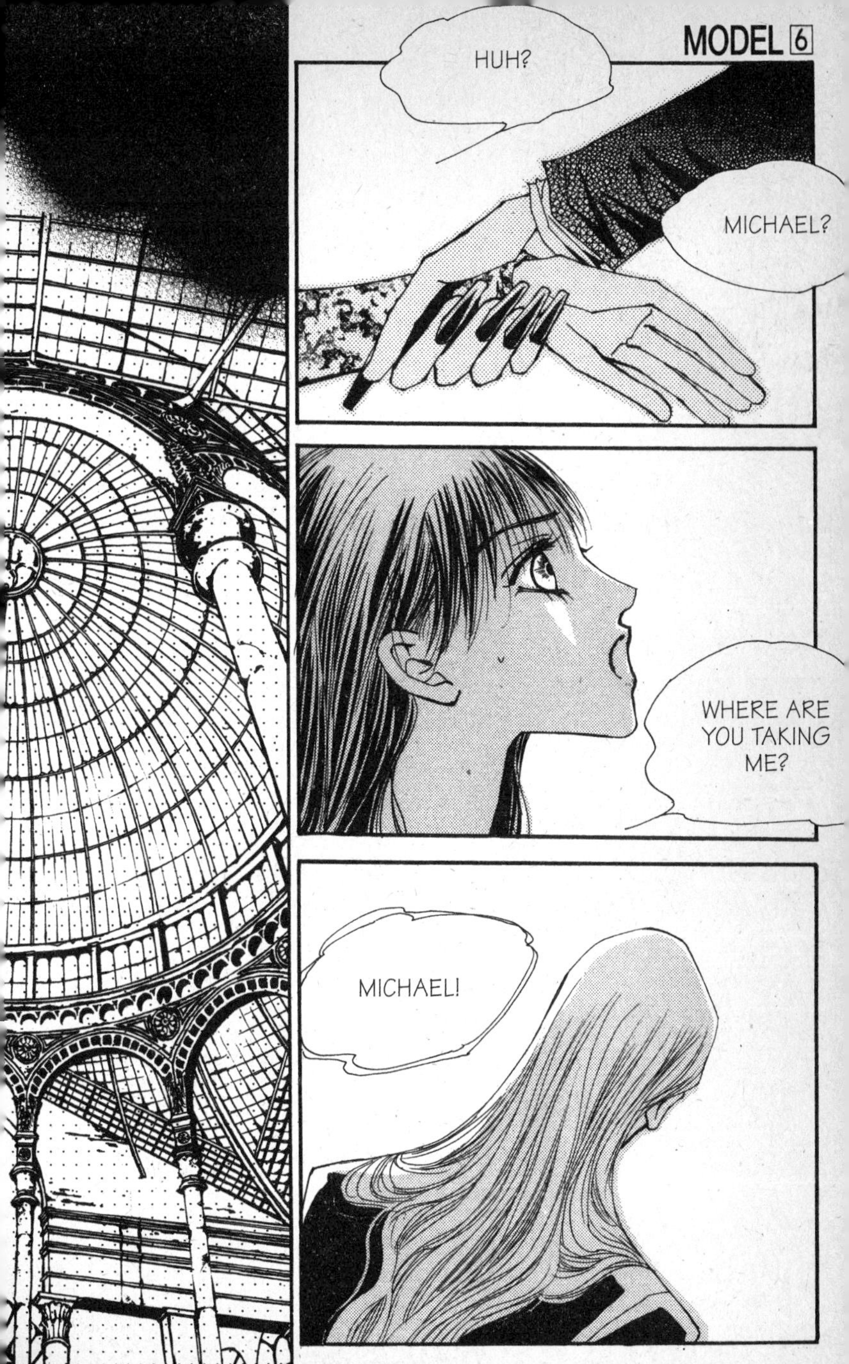
HUH?
MICHAEL?
WHERE ARE YOU TAKING ME?
MICHAEL!

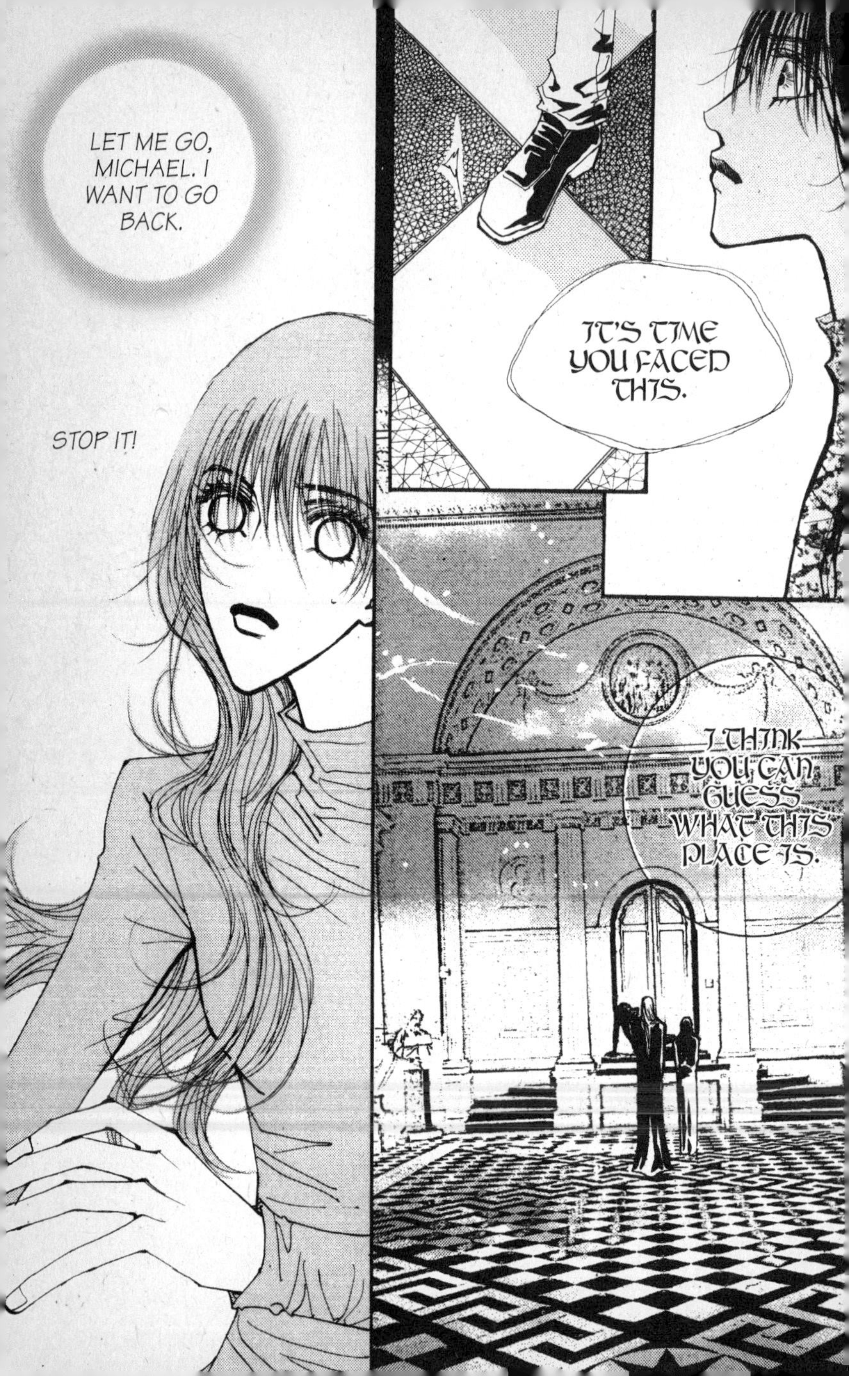
IT'S TIME YOU FACED THIS.
I THINK YOU CAN GUESS WHAT THIS PLACE IS.
LET ME GO, MICHAEL. I WANT TO GO BACK.
STOP IT!

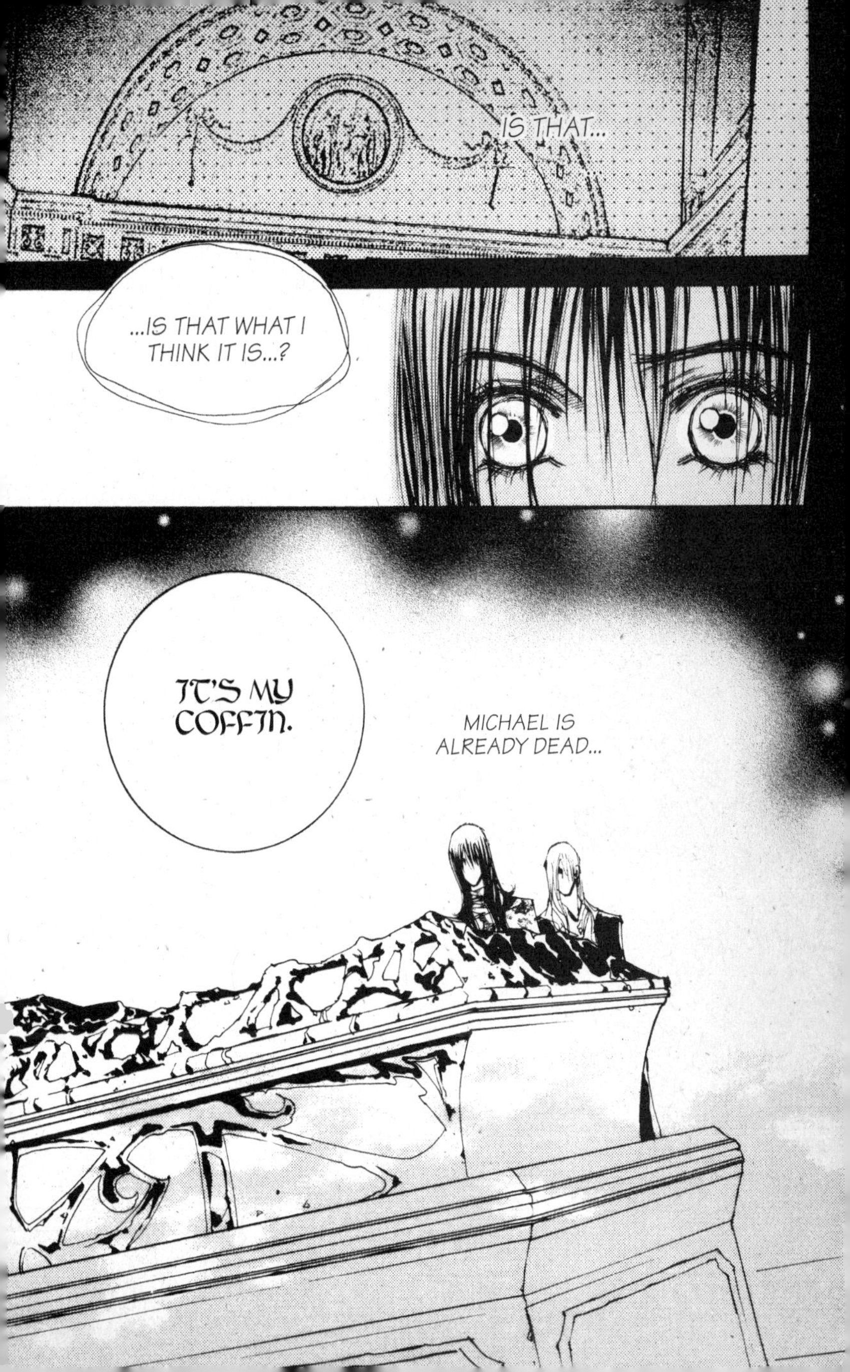
IS THAT...
...IS THAT WHAT I THINK IT IS...?
IT'S MY COFFIN.
MICHAEL IS ALREADY DEAD...

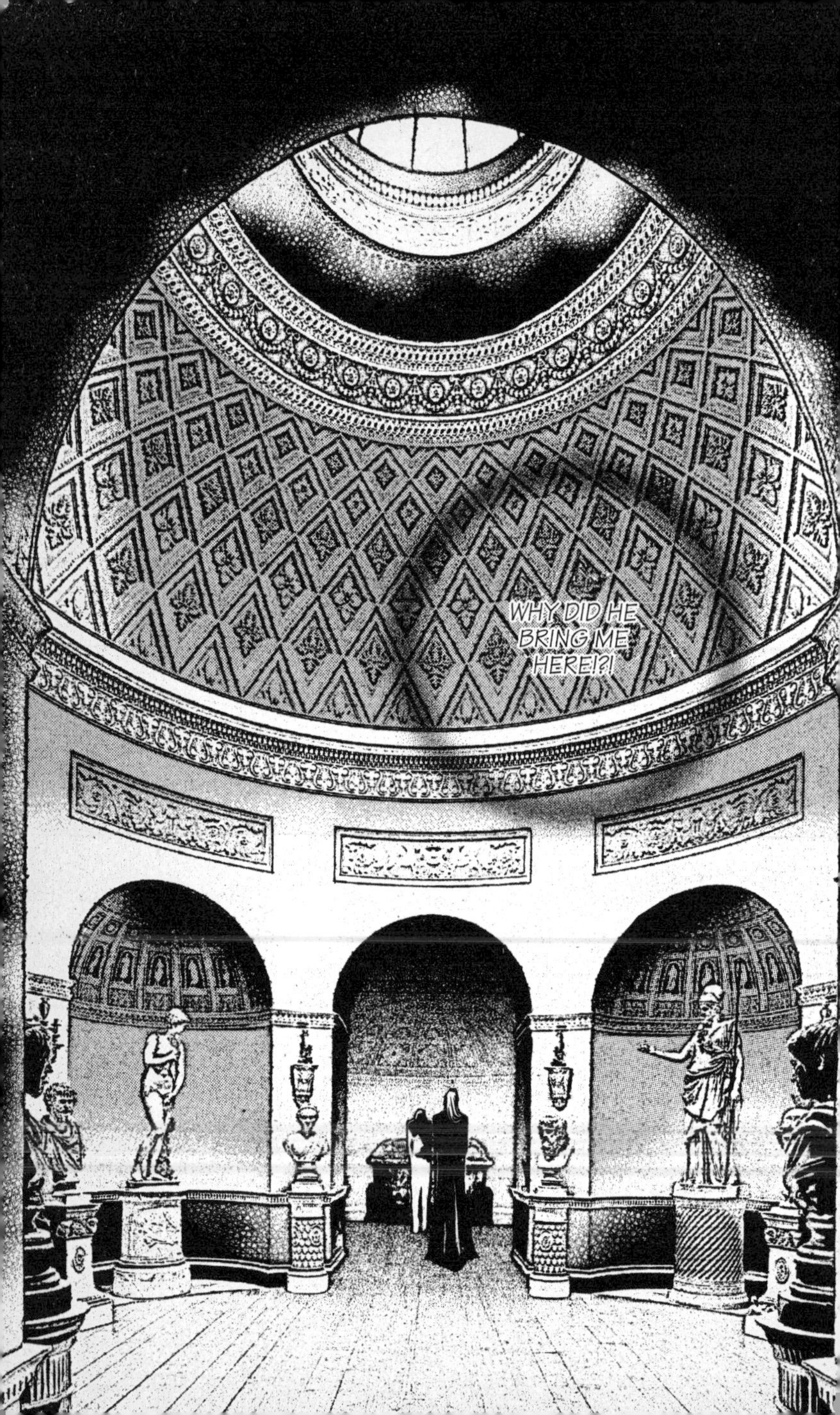
WHY DID HE BRING ME HERE!?!

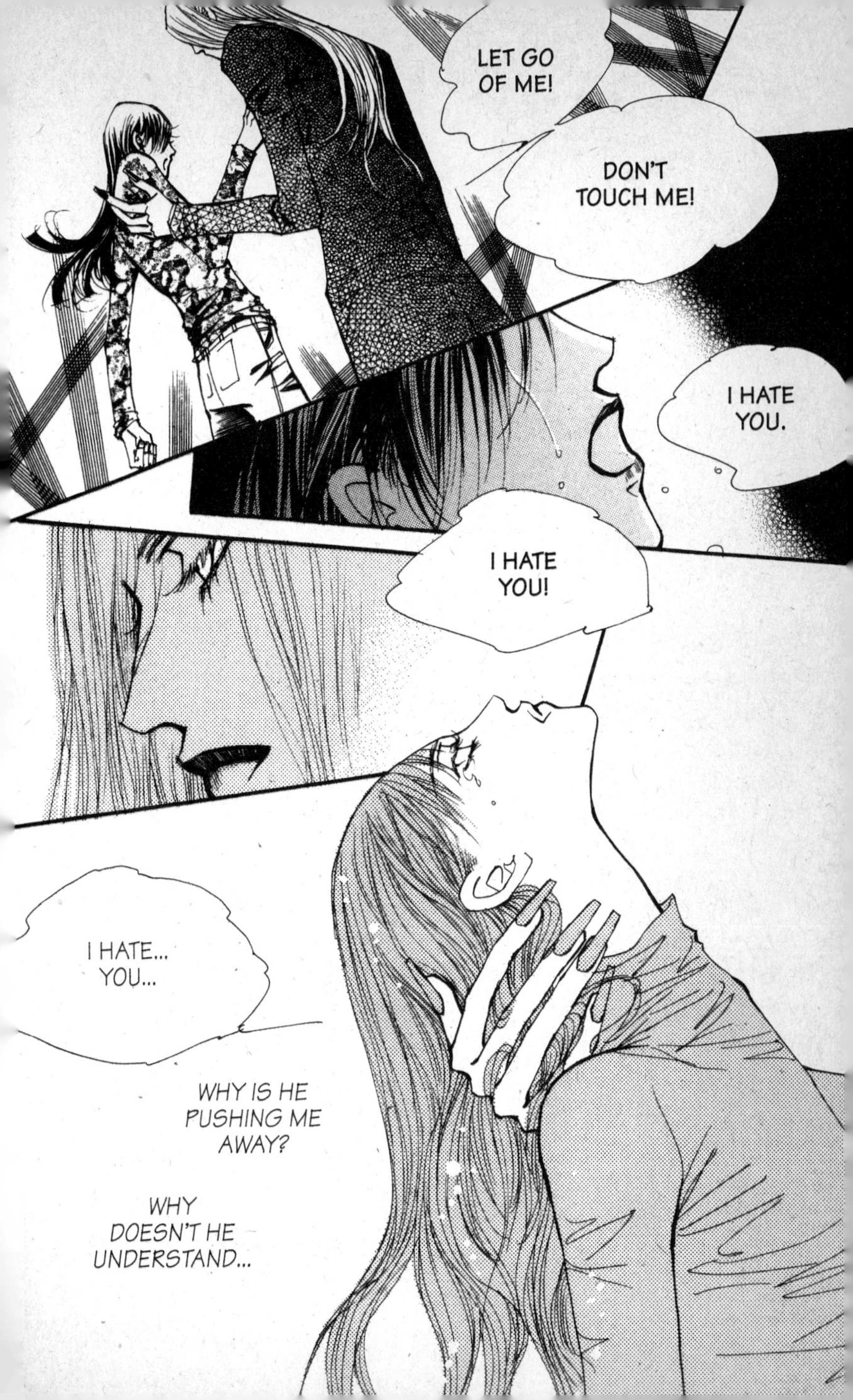
LET GO OF ME!
DON'T TOUCH ME!
I HATE YOU.
I HATE YOU!
I HATE... YOU...
WHY IS HE PUSHING ME AWAY?
WHY DOESN'T HE UNDERSTAND...

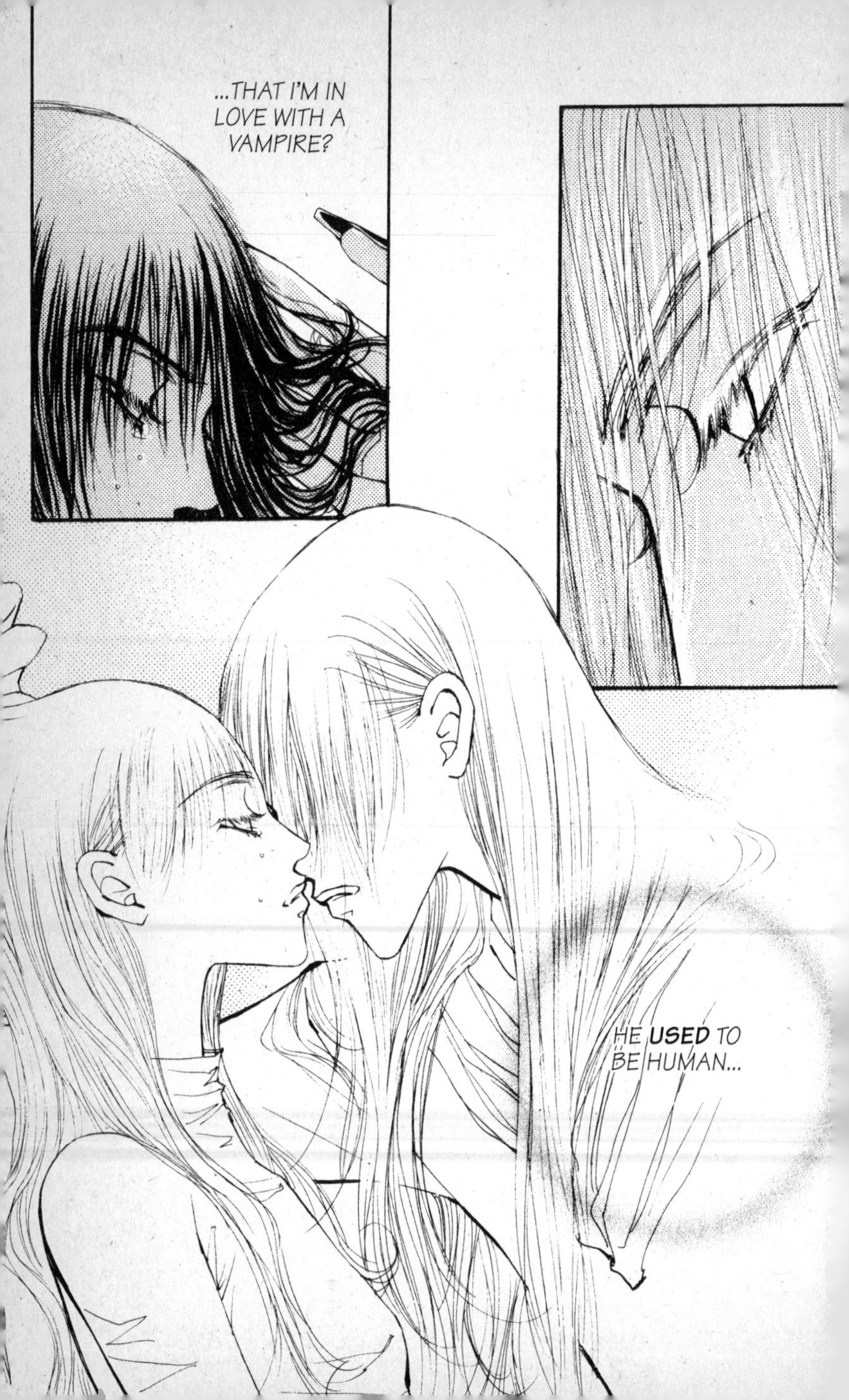
...THAT I'M IN LOVE WITH A VAMPIRE?
HE **USED** TO BE HUMAN...

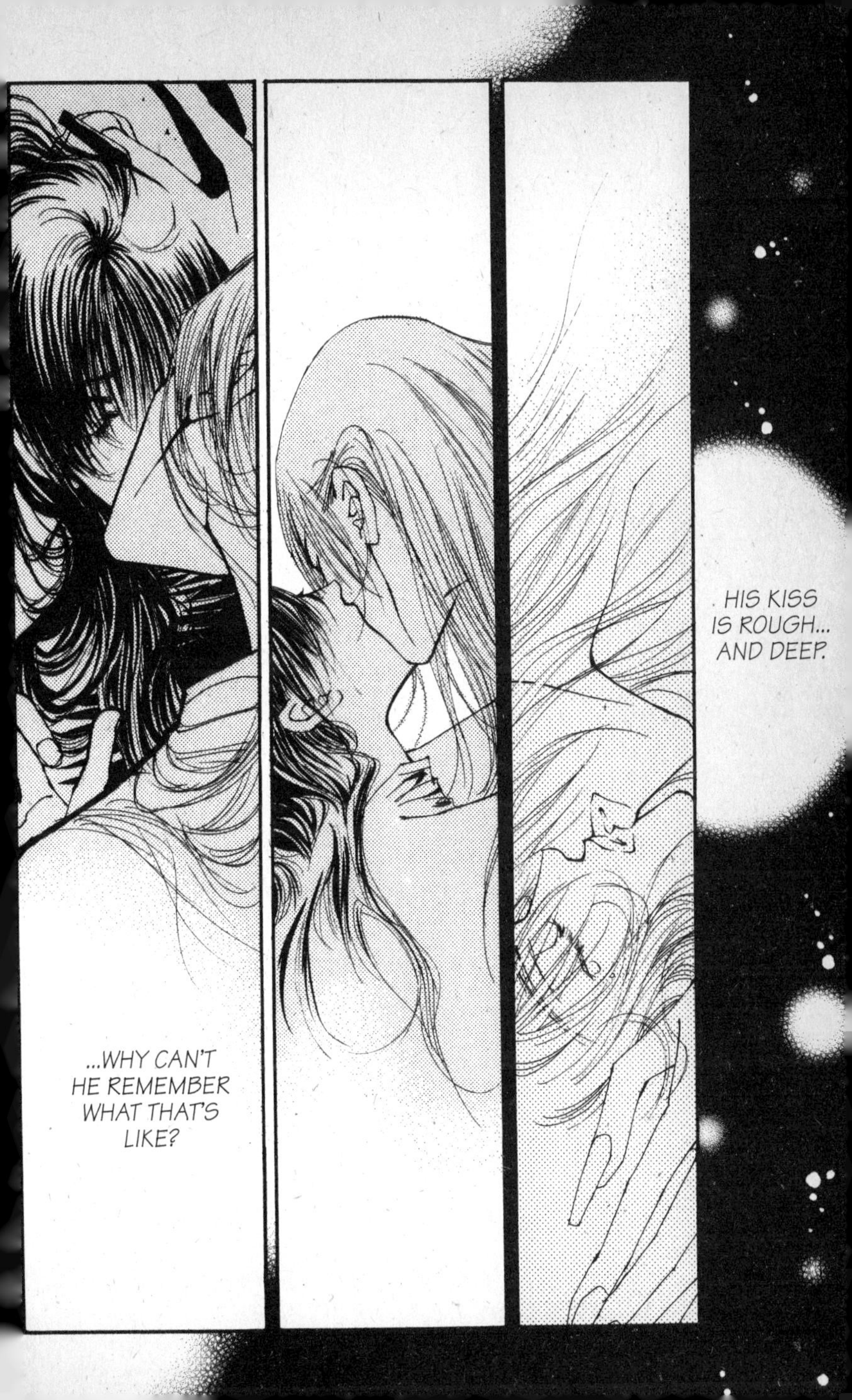
HIS KISS IS ROUGH... AND DEEP.
...WHY CAN'T HE REMEMBER WHAT THAT'S LIKE?

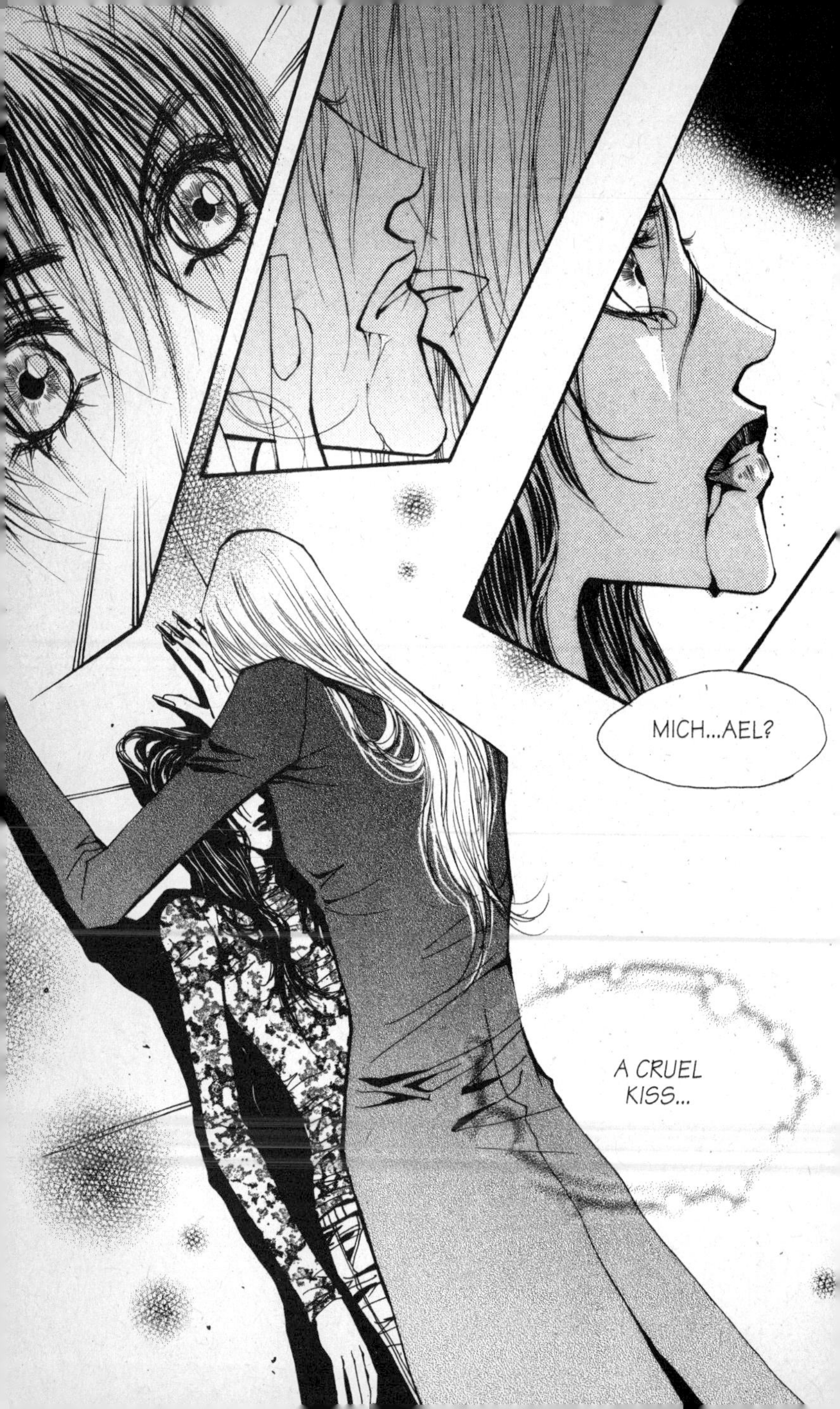
MICH...AEL?
A CRUEL KISS...

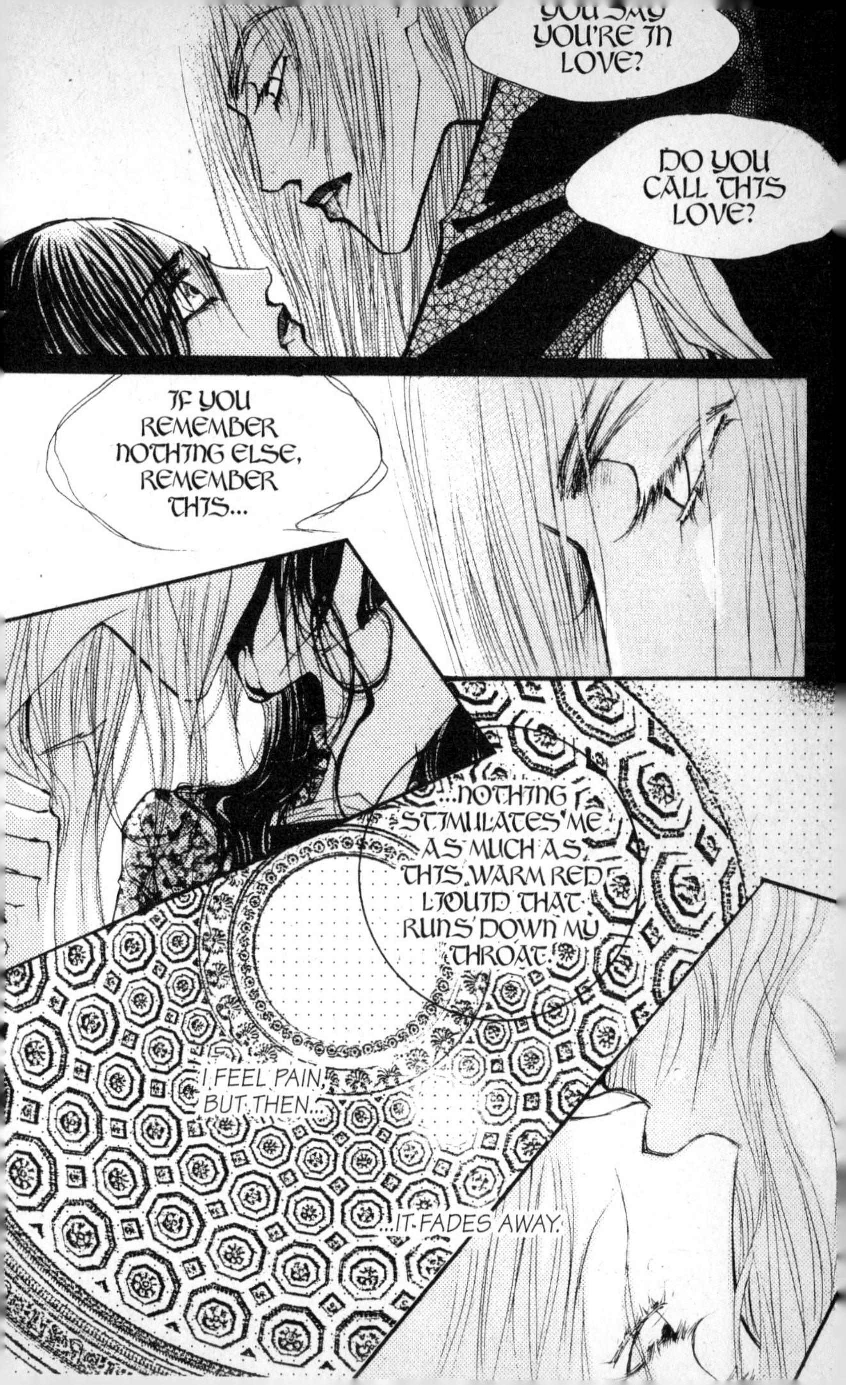
YOU SAY YOU'RE IN LOVE?
DO YOU CALL THIS LOVE?
IF YOU REMEMBER NOTHING ELSE, REMEMBER THIS...
...NOTHING STIMULATES ME AS MUCH AS THIS WARM RED LIQUID THAT RUNS DOWN MY THROAT.
I FEEL PAIN, BUT THEN...
...IT FADES AWAY.

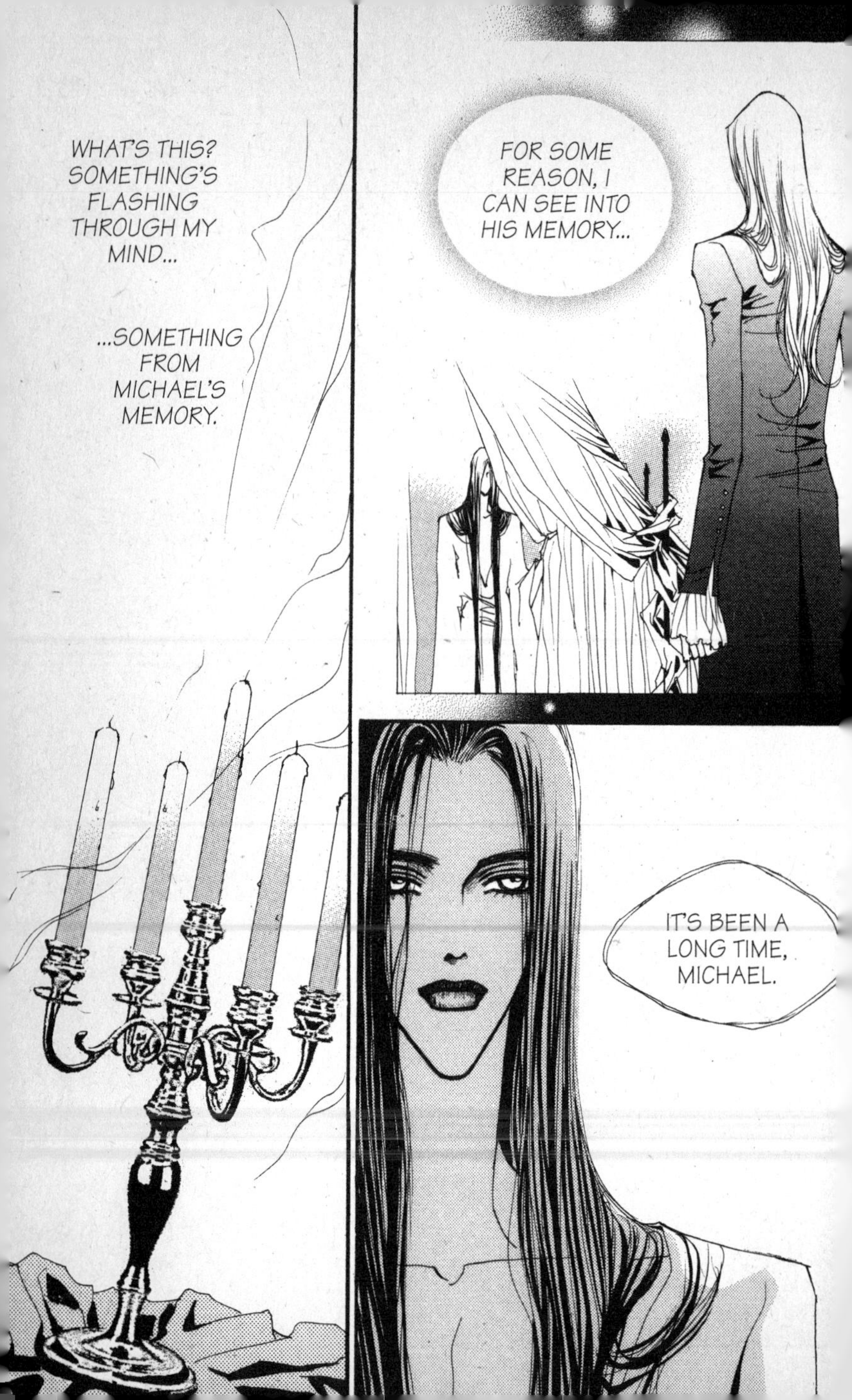
WHAT'S THIS? SOMETHING'S FLASHING THROUGH MY MIND...
...SOMETHING FROM MICHAEL'S MEMORY.
FOR SOME REASON, I CAN SEE INTO HIS MEMORY...
IT'S BEEN A LONG TIME, MICHAEL.

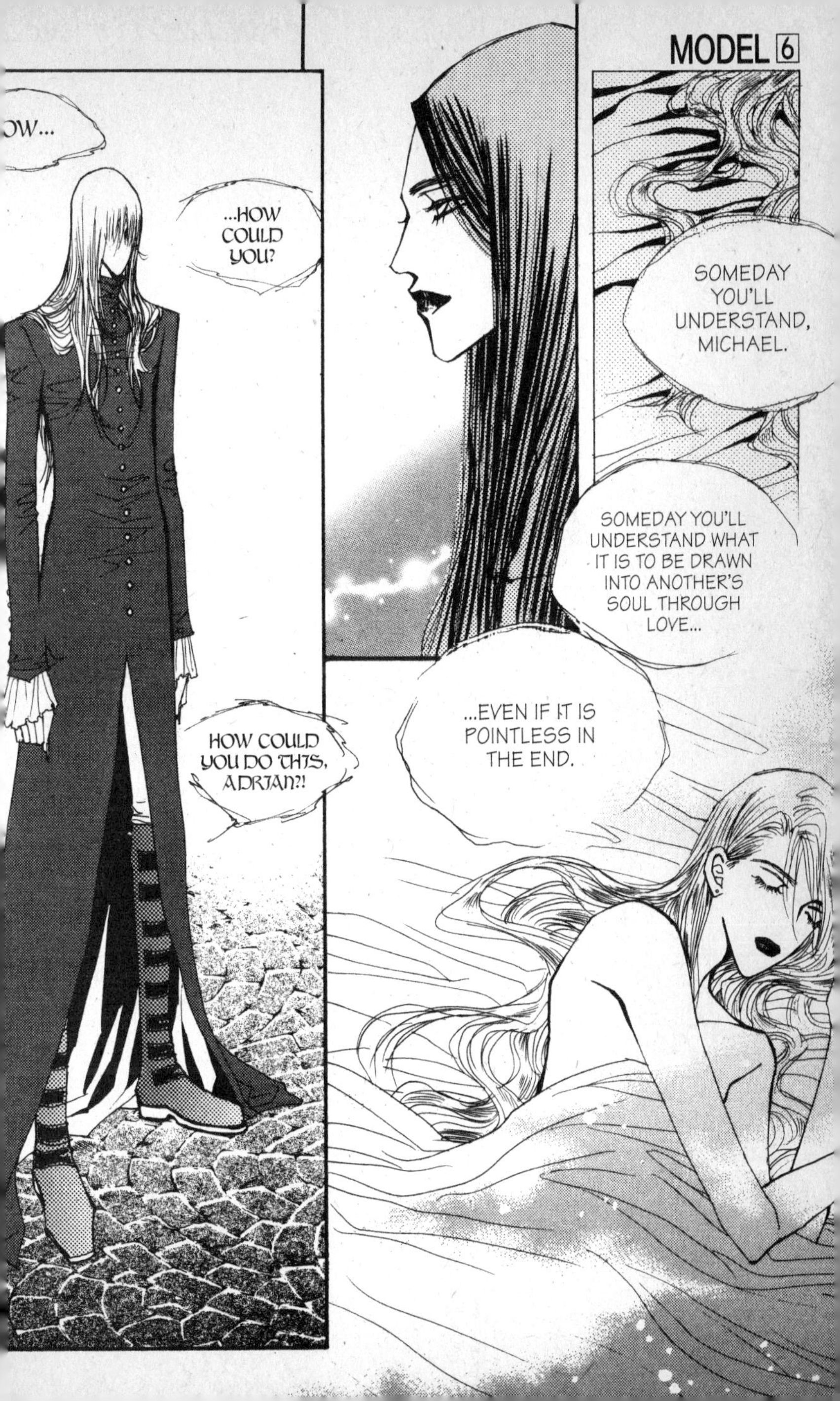
SOMEDAY YOU'LL UNDERSTAND, MICHAEL.
SOMEDAY YOU'LL UNDERSTAND WHAT IT IS TO BE DRAWN INTO ANOTHER'S SOUL THROUGH LOVE...
...EVEN IF IT IS POINTLESS IN THE END.
OW...
...HOW COULD YOU?
HOW COULD YOU DO THIS, ADRIAN?!

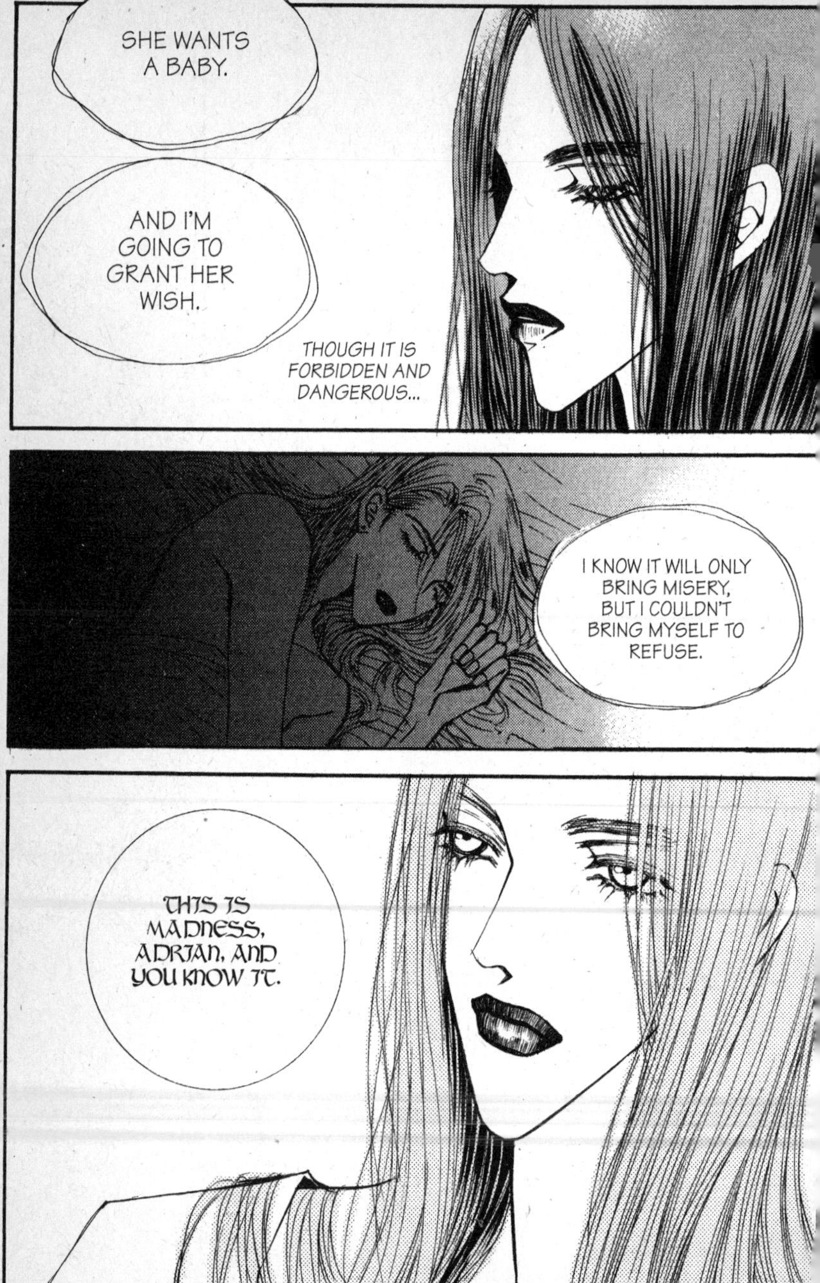
SHE WANTS A BABY.
AND I'M GOING TO GRANT HER WISH.
THOUGH IT IS FORBIDDEN AND DANGEROUS...
I KNOW IT WILL ONLY BRING MISERY, BUT I COULDN'T BRING MYSELF TO REFUSE.
THIS IS MADNESS, ADRIAN, AND YOU KNOW IT.

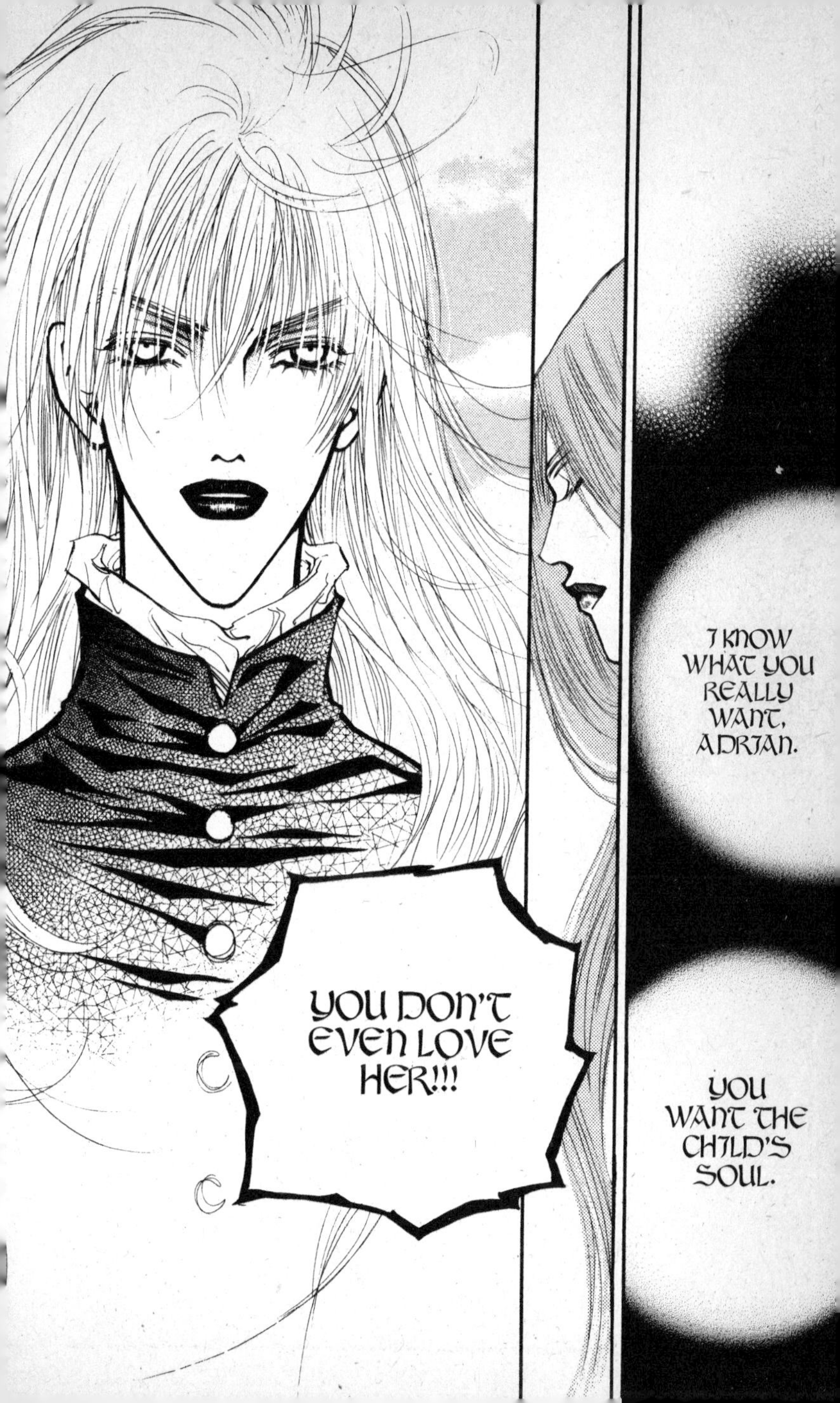
I KNOW WHAT YOU REALLY WANT, ADRIAN.
YOU WANT THE CHILD'S SOUL.
YOU DON'T EVEN LOVE HER!!!

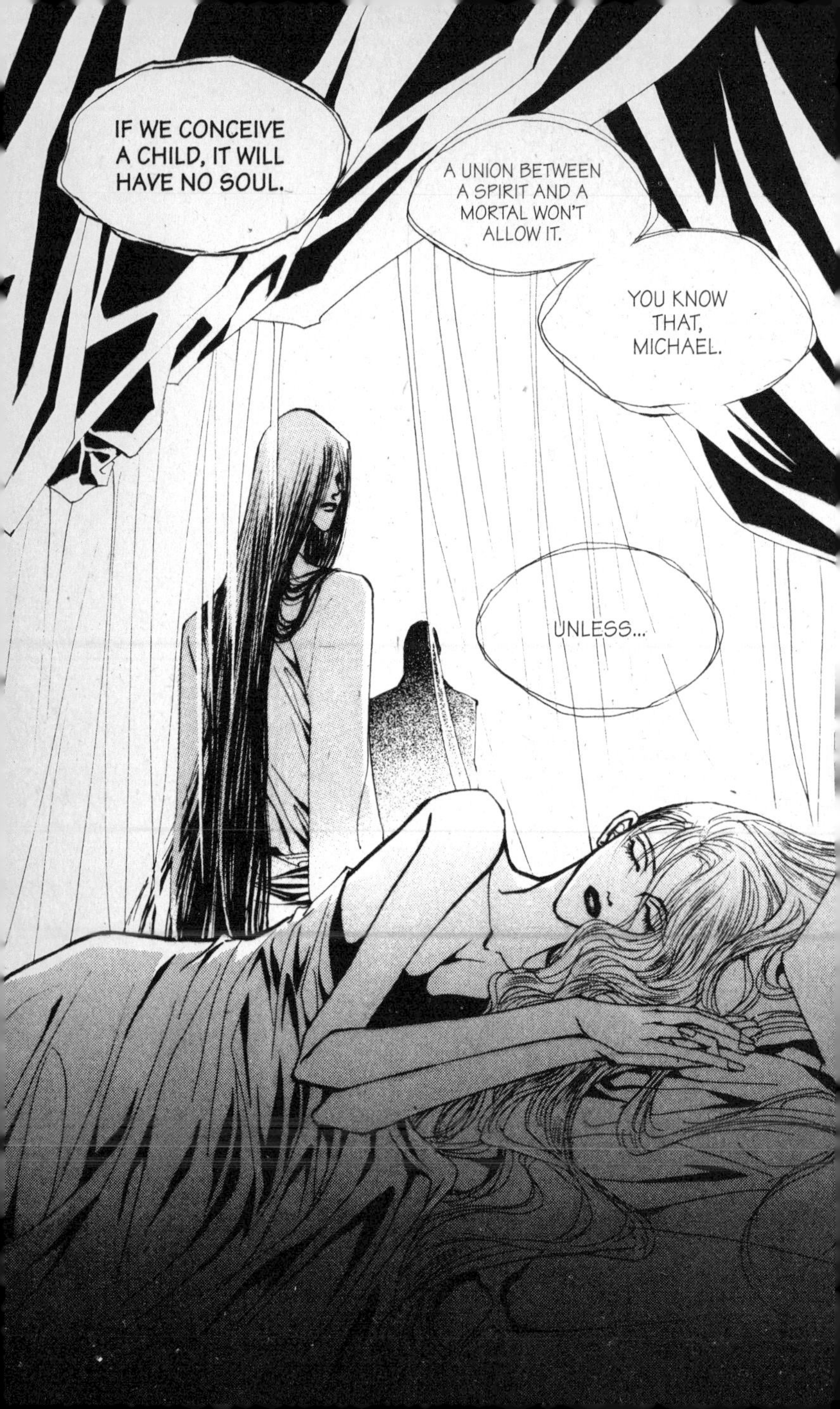
IF WE CONCEIVE A CHILD, IT WILL HAVE NO SOUL.
A UNION BETWEEN A SPIRIT AND A MORTAL WON'T ALLOW IT.
YOU KNOW THAT, MICHAEL.
UNLESS...

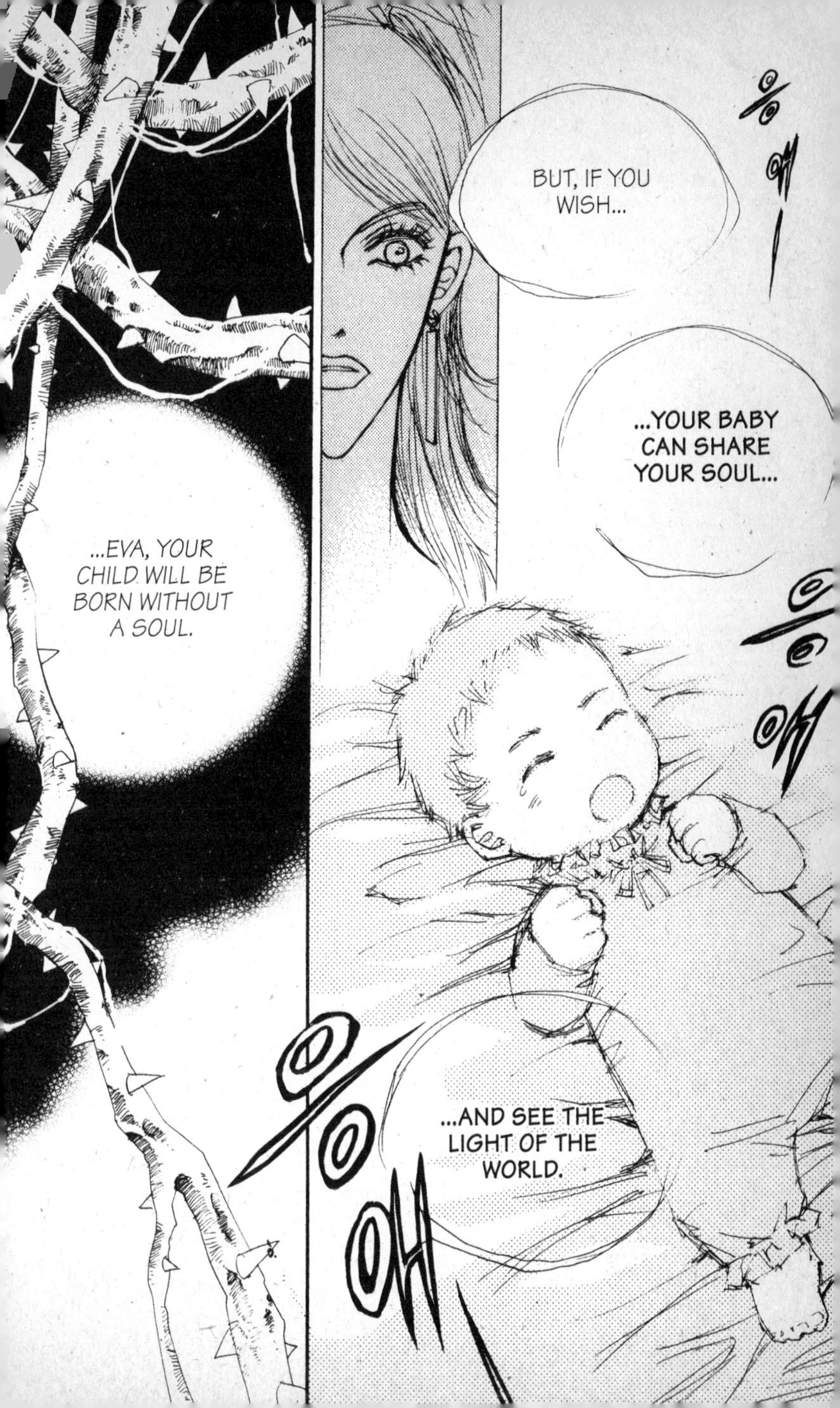
...EVA, YOUR CHILD WILL BE BORN WITHOUT A SOUL.
BUT, IF YOU WISH...
...YOUR BABY CAN SHARE YOUR SOUL...
...AND SEE THE LIGHT OF THE WORLD.

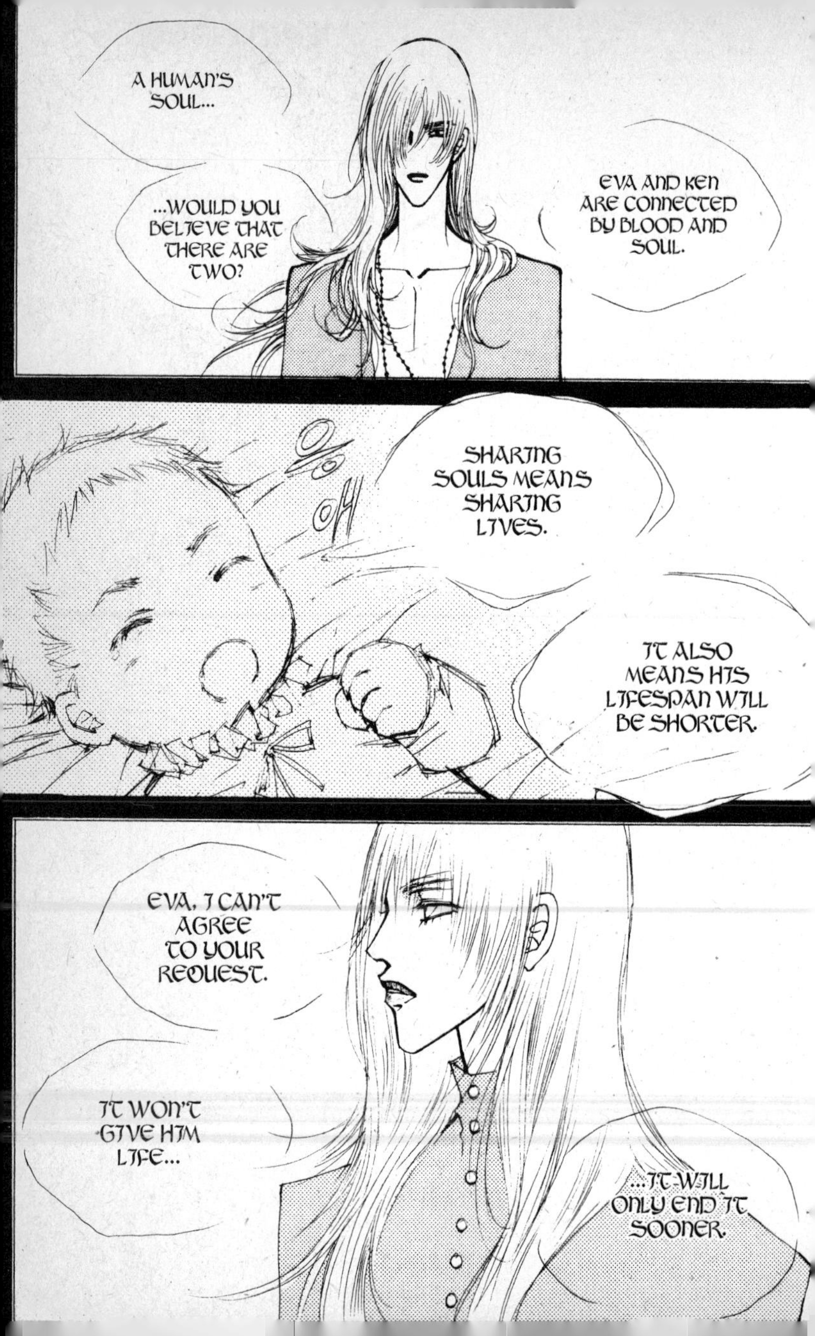
A HUMAN'S SOUL...
...WOULD YOU BELIEVE THAT THERE ARE TWO?
EVA AND KEN ARE CONNECTED BY BLOOD AND SOUL.
SHARING SOULS MEANS SHARING LIVES.
IT ALSO MEANS HIS LIFESPAN WILL BE SHORTER.
EVA, I CAN'T AGREE TO YOUR REQUEST.
IT WON'T GIVE HIM LIFE...
...IT WILL ONLY END IT SOONER.

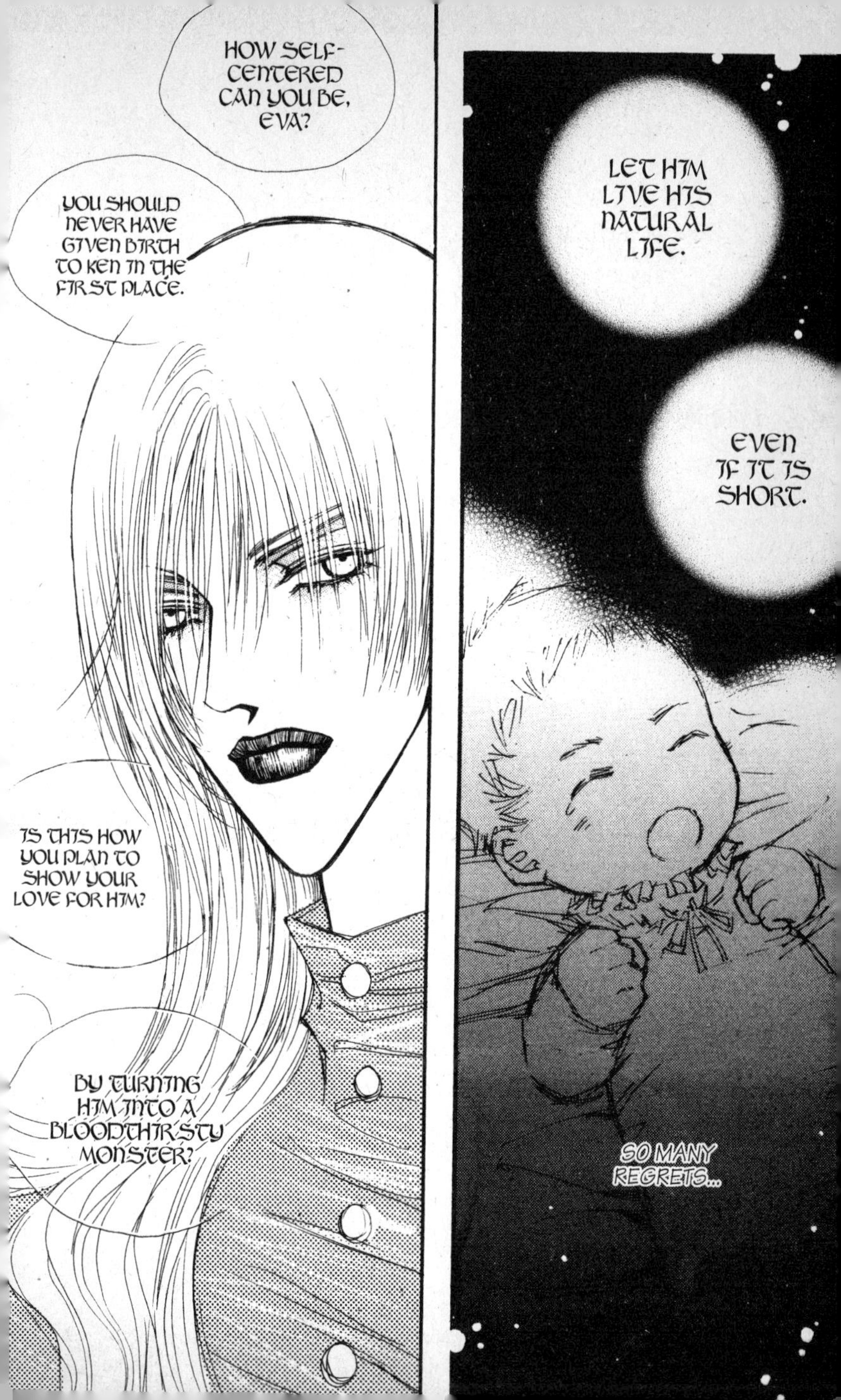
HOW SELF-CENTERED CAN YOU BE, EVA?
YOU SHOULD NEVER HAVE GIVEN BIRTH TO KEN IN THE FIRST PLACE.
IS THIS HOW YOU PLAN TO SHOW YOUR LOVE FOR HIM?
BY TURNING HIM INTO A BLOODTHIRSTY MONSTER?
LET HIM LIVE HIS NATURAL LIFE.
EVEN IF IT IS SHORT.
SO MANY REGRETS...

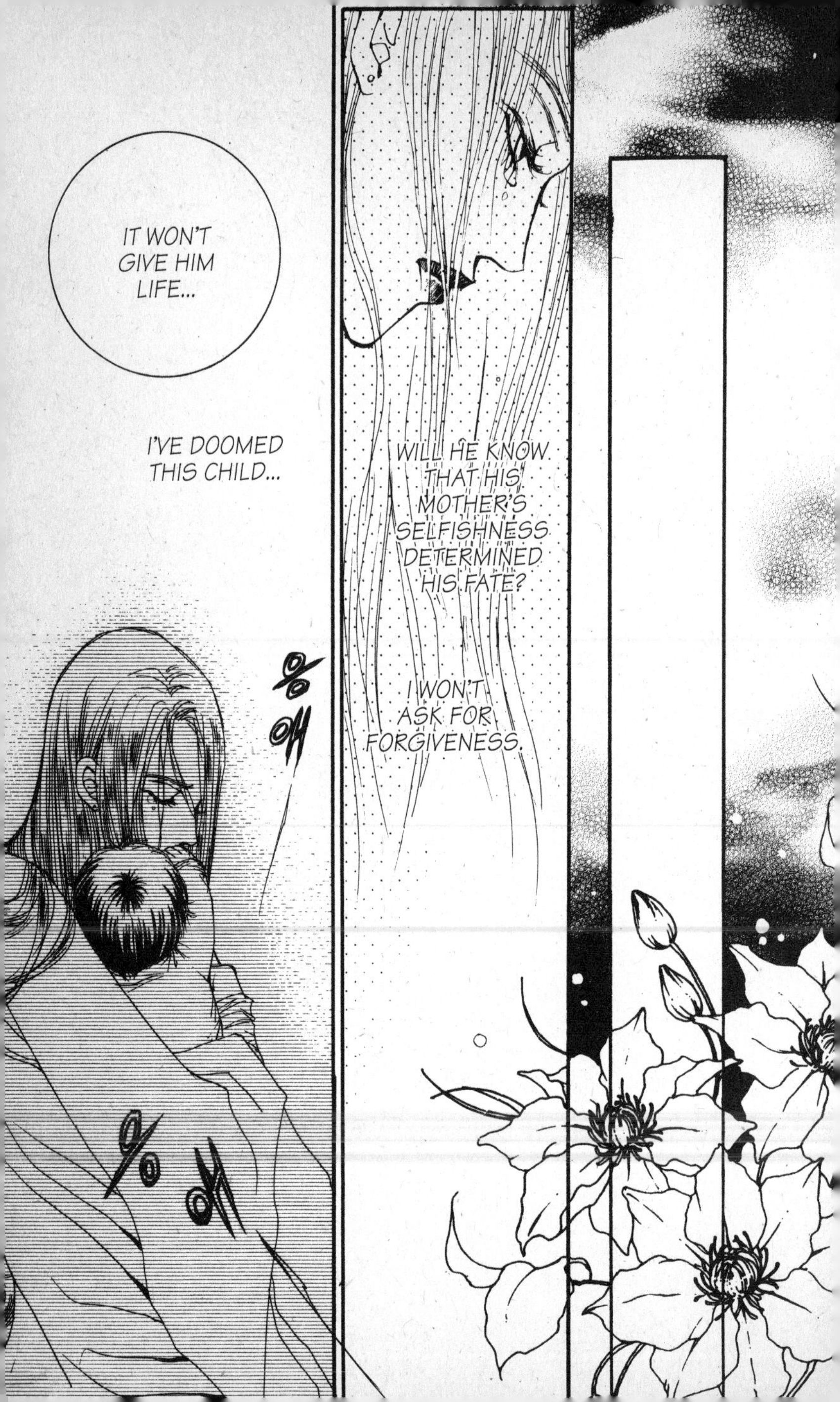
IT WON'T GIVE HIM LIFE...
I'VE DOOMED THIS CHILD...
응애
응애
WILL HE KNOW THAT HIS MOTHER'S SELFISHNESS DETERMINED HIS FATE?
I WON'T ASK FOR FORGIVENESS.

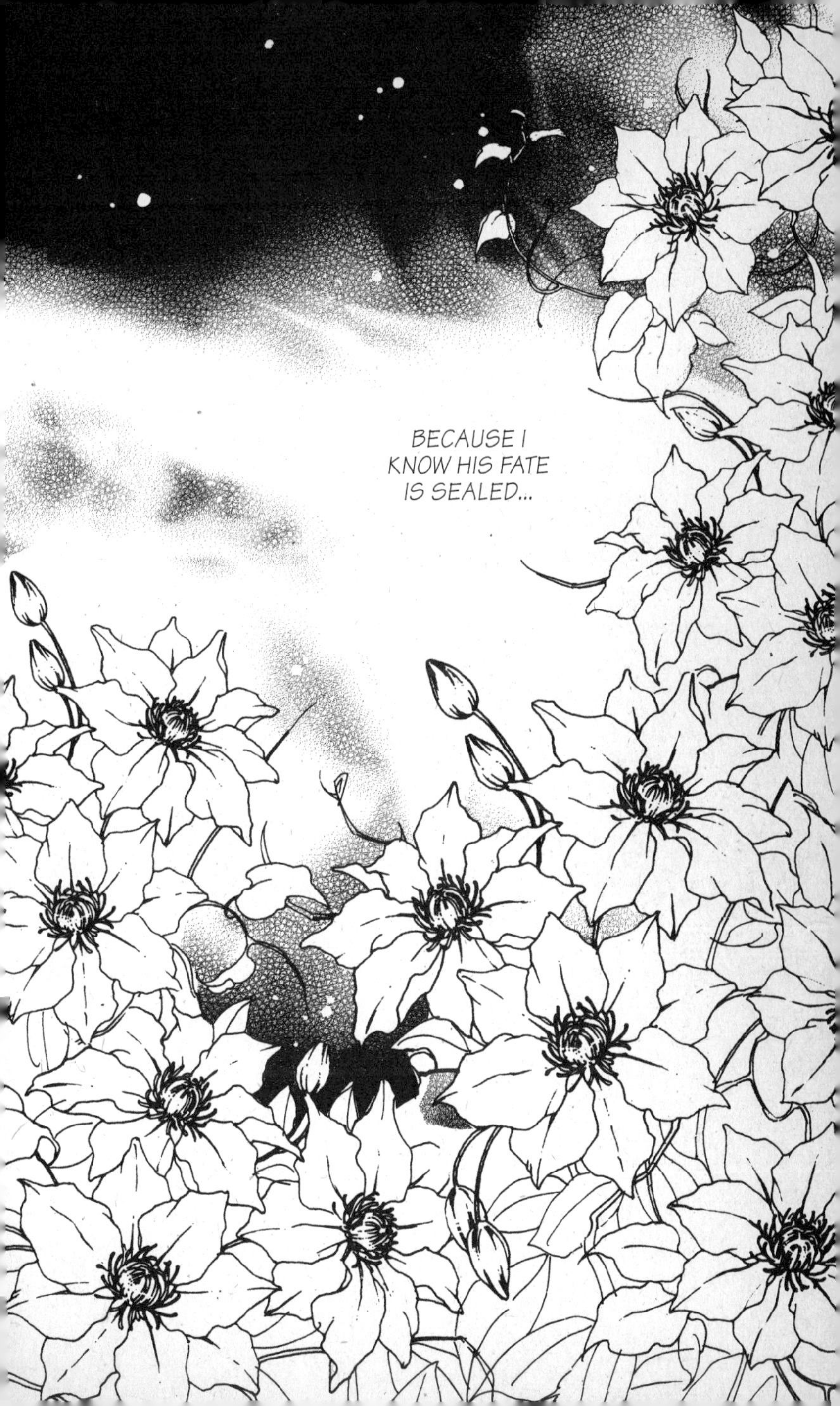
BECAUSE I KNOW HIS FATE IS SEALED...

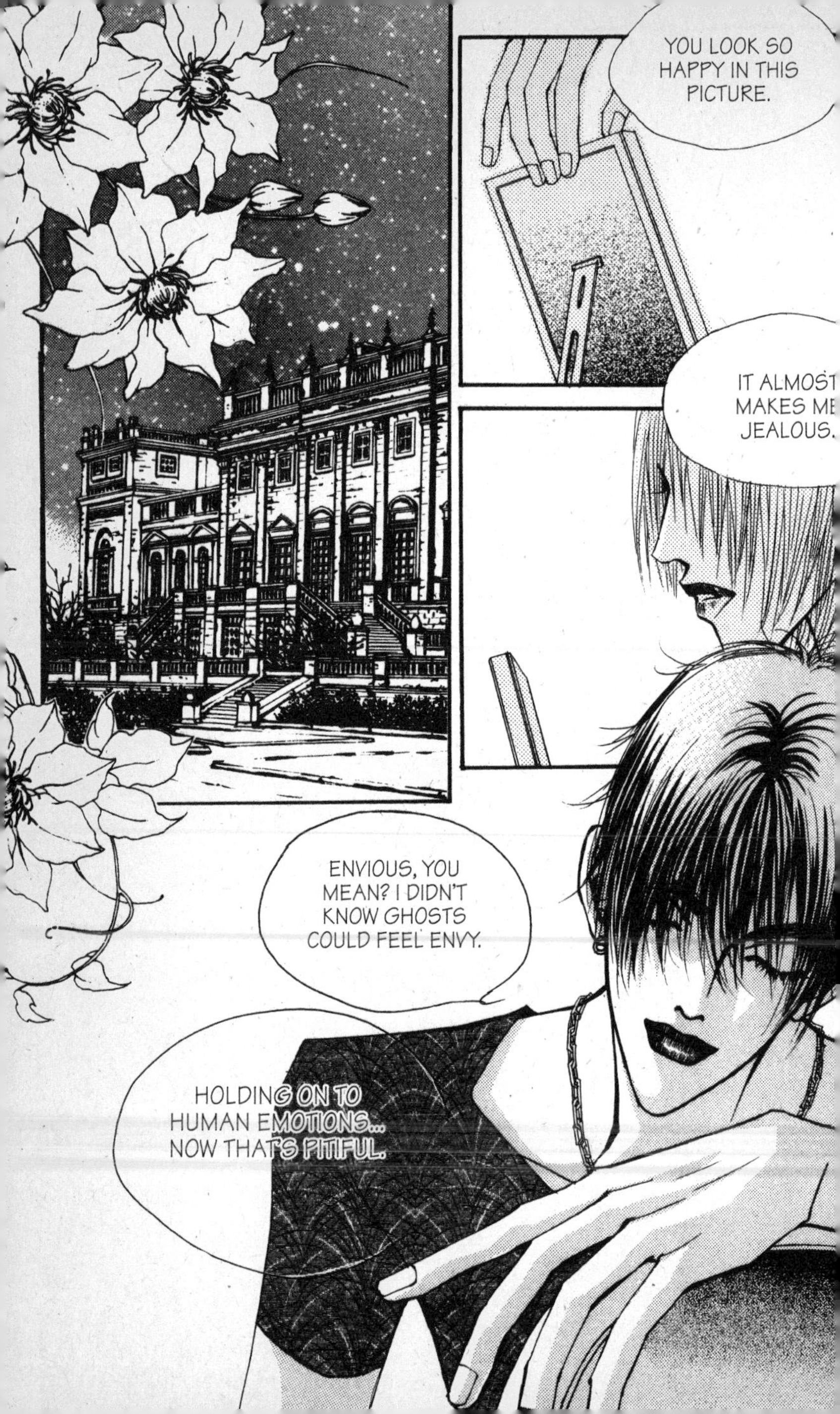
YOU LOOK SO HAPPY IN THIS PICTURE.
IT ALMOST MAKES ME JEALOUS.
ENVIOUS, YOU MEAN? I DIDN'T KNOW GHOSTS COULD FEEL ENVY.
HOLDING ON TO HUMAN EMOTIONS... NOW THAT'S PITIFUL.

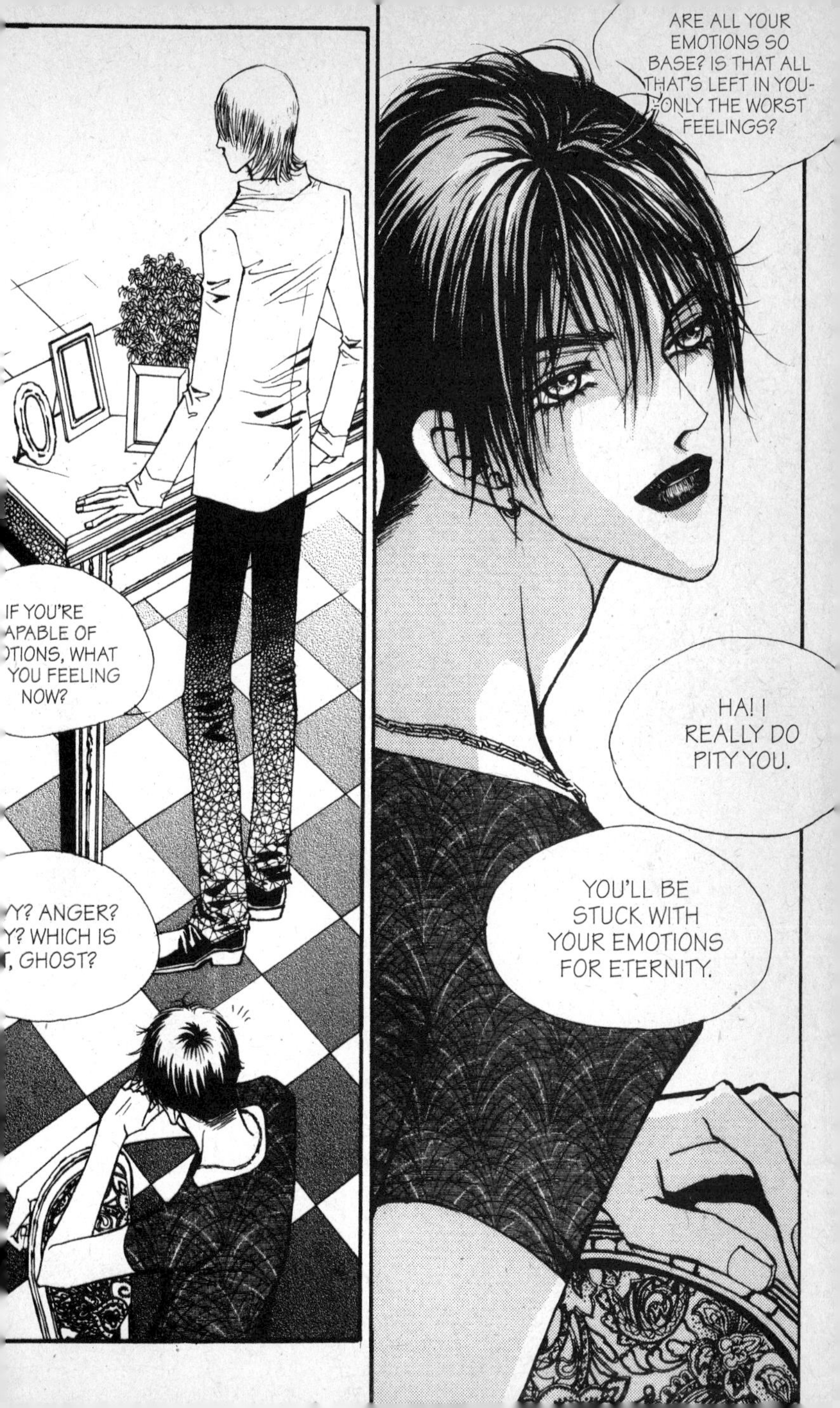
ARE ALL YOUR EMOTIONS SO BASE? IS THAT ALL THAT'S LEFT IN YOU--ONLY THE WORST FEELINGS?
HA! I REALLY DO PITY YOU.
YOU'LL BE STUCK WITH YOUR EMOTIONS FOR ETERNITY.
IF YOU'RE APABLE OF TIONS, WHAT YOU FEELING NOW?
Y? ANGER? Y? WHICH IS , GHOST?

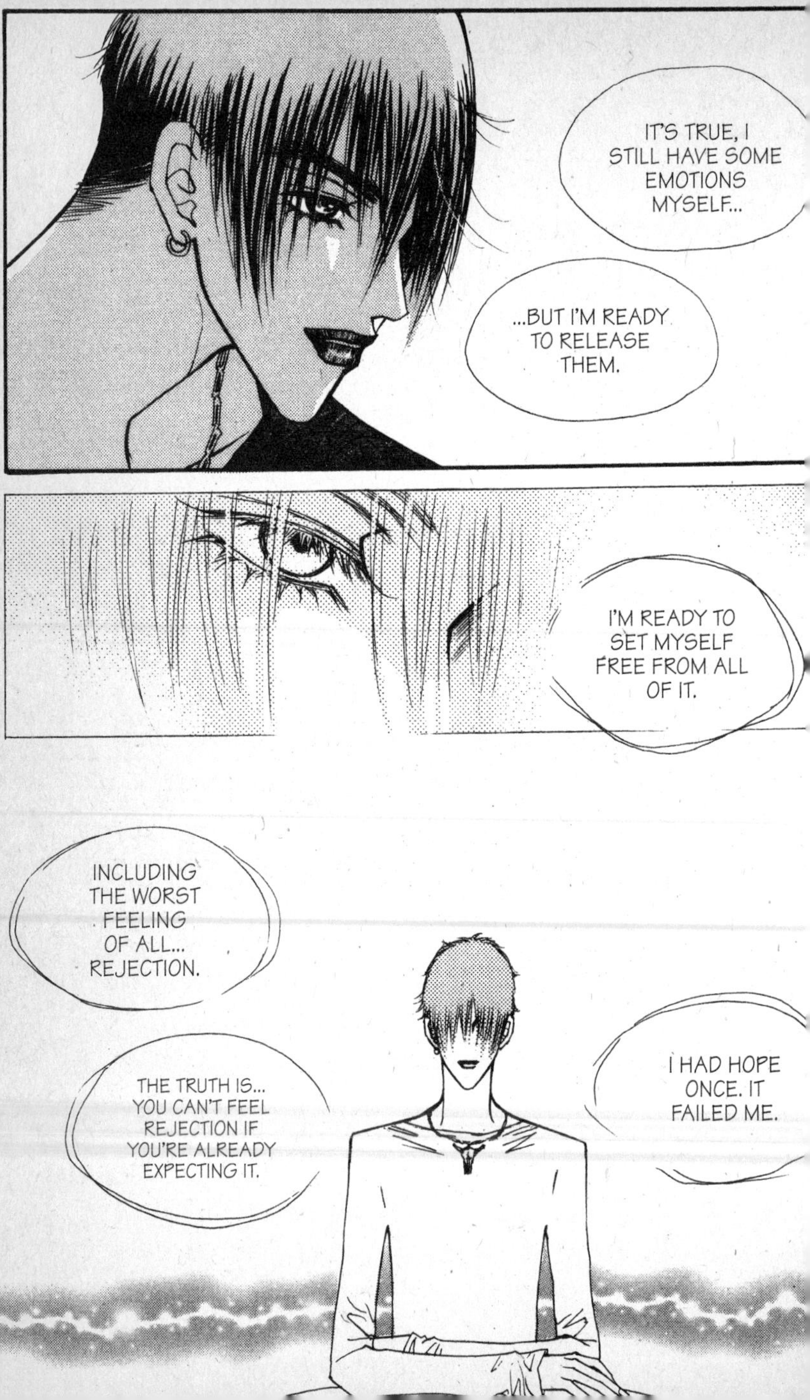
IT'S TRUE, I STILL HAVE SOME EMOTIONS MYSELF...
...BUT I'M READY TO RELEASE THEM.
I'M READY TO SET MYSELF FREE FROM ALL OF IT.
INCLUDING THE WORST FEELING OF ALL... REJECTION.
I HAD HOPE ONCE. IT FAILED ME.
THE TRUTH IS... YOU CAN'T FEEL REJECTION IF YOU'RE ALREADY EXPECTING IT.

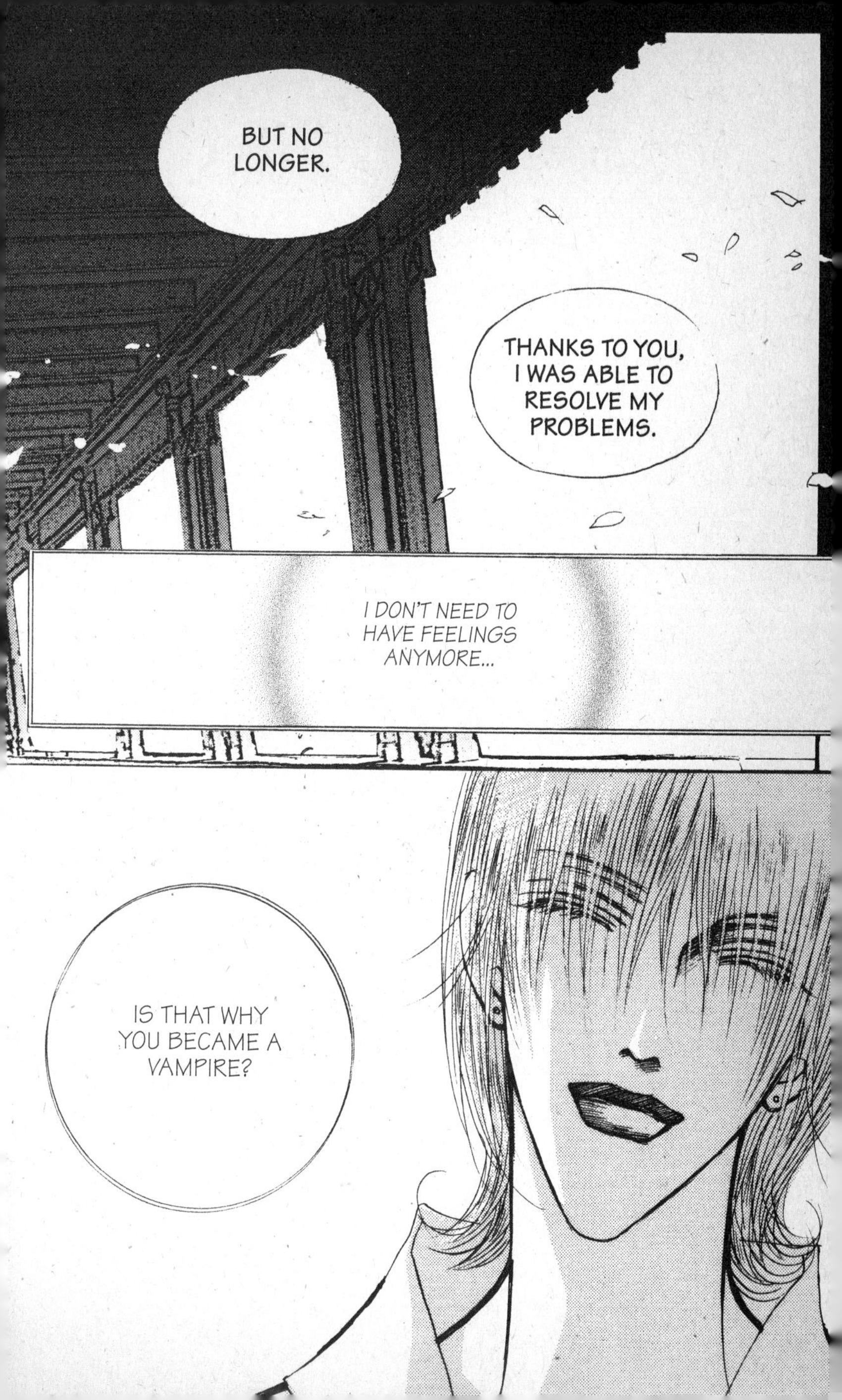
BUT NO LONGER.
THANKS TO YOU, I WAS ABLE TO RESOLVE MY PROBLEMS.
I DON'T NEED TO HAVE FEELINGS ANYMORE...
IS THAT WHY YOU BECAME A VAMPIRE?

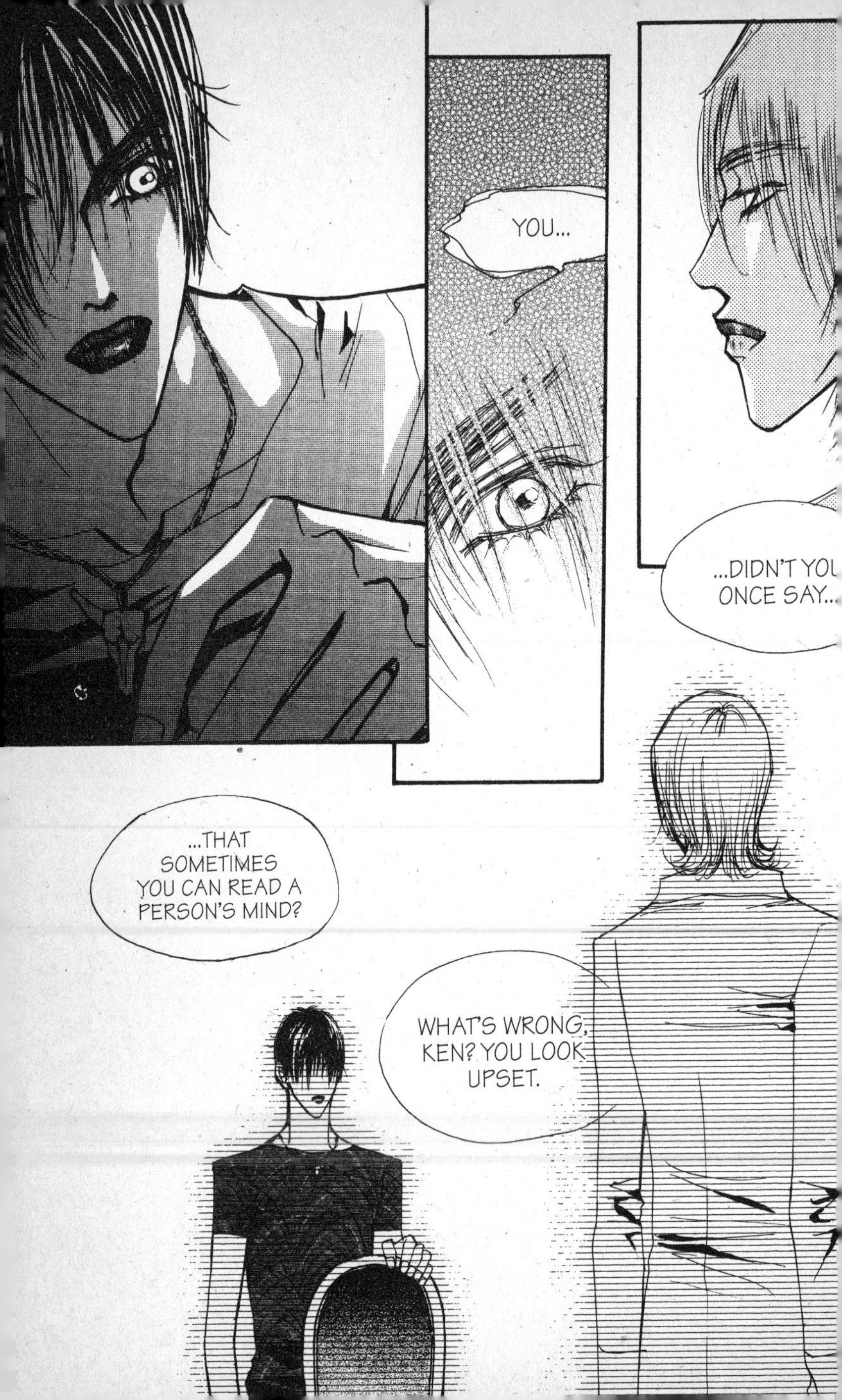
...DIDN'T YOU ONCE SAY...
YOU...
...THAT SOMETIMES YOU CAN READ A PERSON'S MIND?
WHAT'S WRONG, KEN? YOU LOOK UPSET.

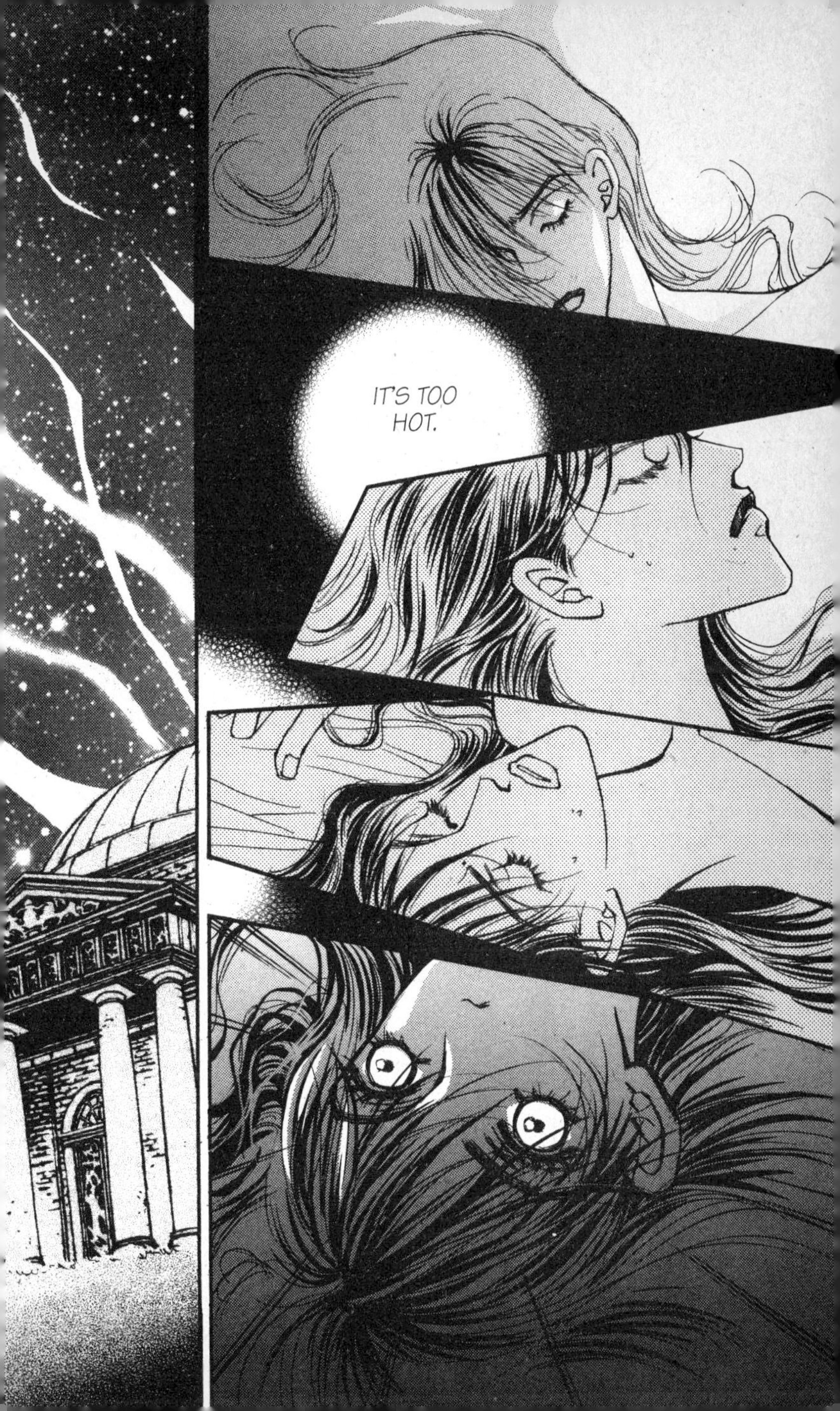
IT'S TOO HOT.

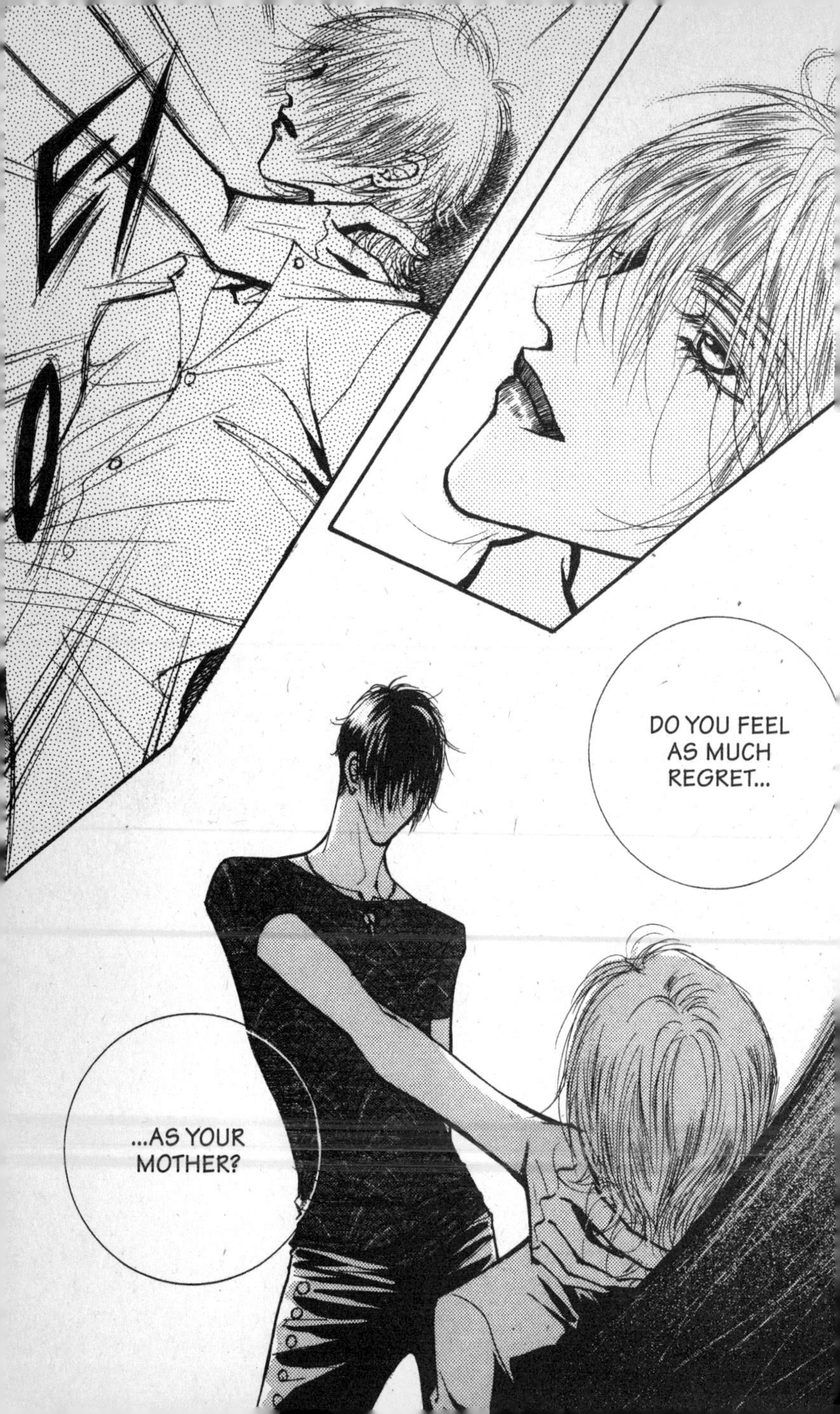
DO YOU FEEL AS MUCH REGRET...
...AS YOUR MOTHER?

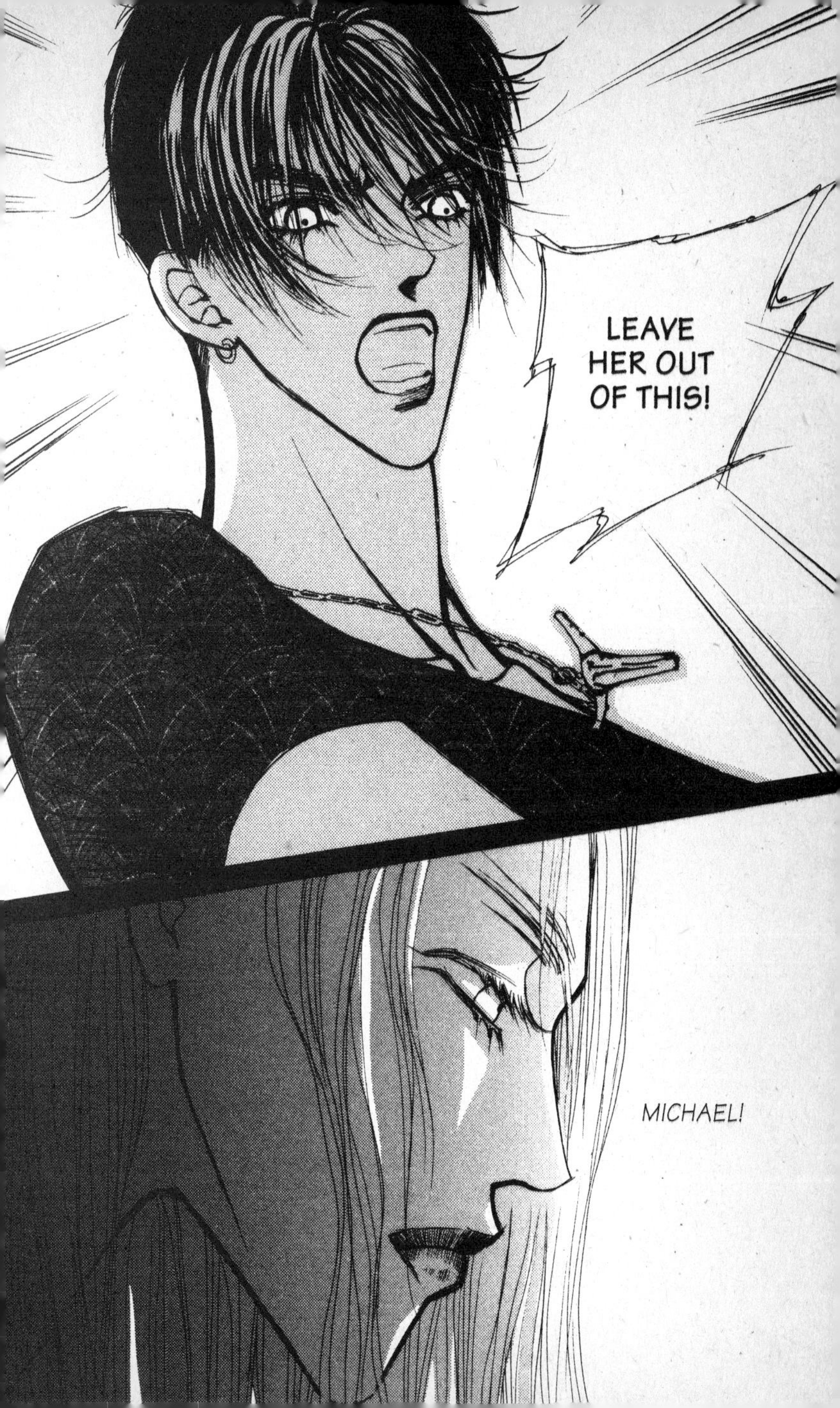
LEAVE HER OUT OF THIS!
MICHAEL!

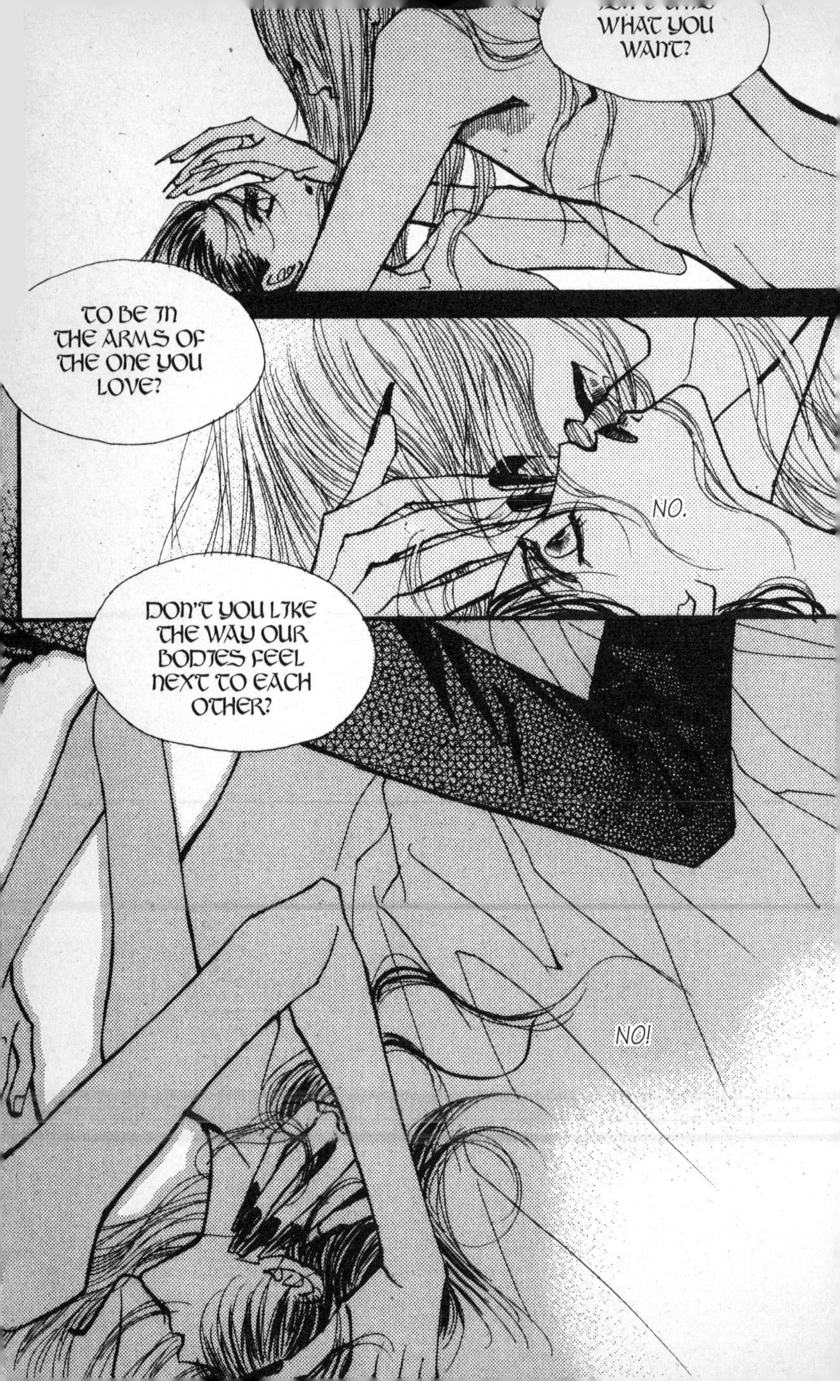
WHAT YOU WANT?
TO BE IN THE ARMS OF THE ONE YOU LOVE?
NO.
DON'T YOU LIKE THE WAY OUR BODIES FEEL NEXT TO EACH OTHER?
NO!

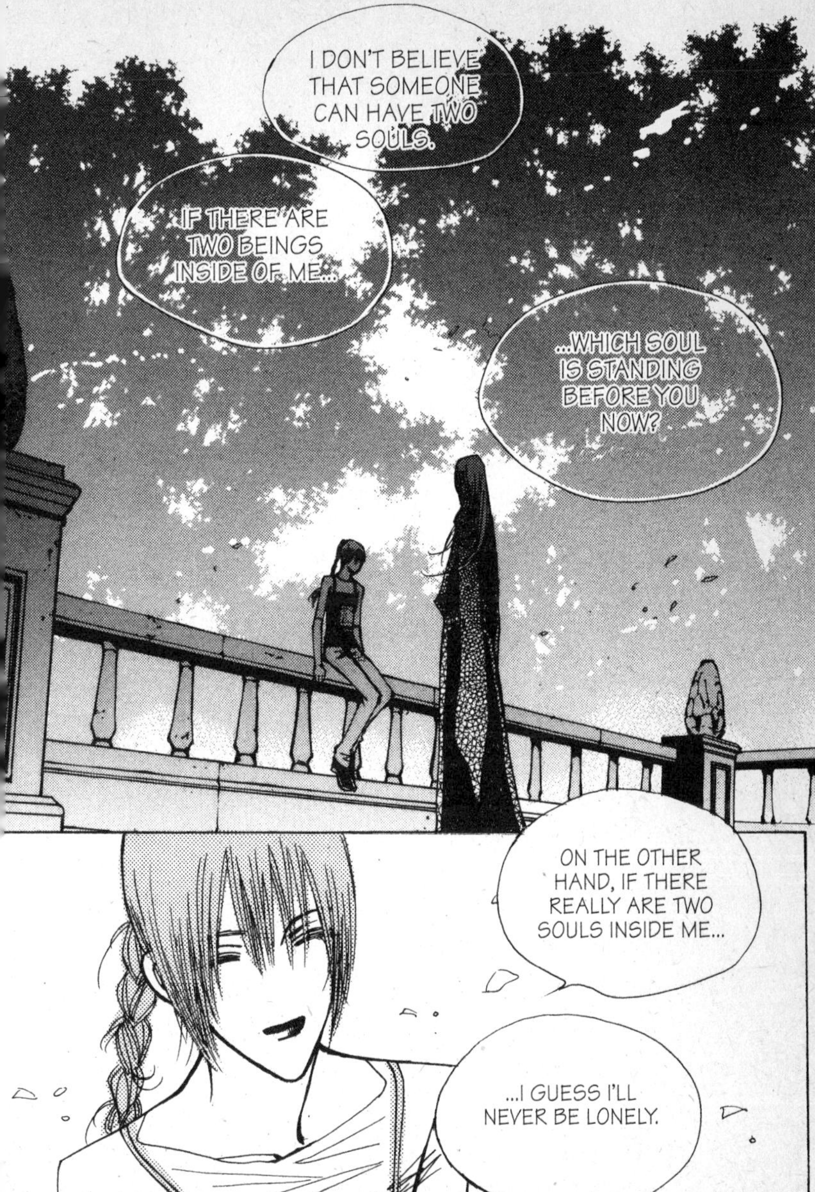
I DON'T BELIEVE THAT SOMEONE CAN HAVE TWO SOULS.
IF THERE ARE TWO BEINGS INSIDE OF ME...
...WHICH SOUL IS STANDING BEFORE YOU NOW?
ON THE OTHER HAND, IF THERE REALLY ARE TWO SOULS INSIDE ME...
...I GUESS I'LL NEVER BE LONELY.

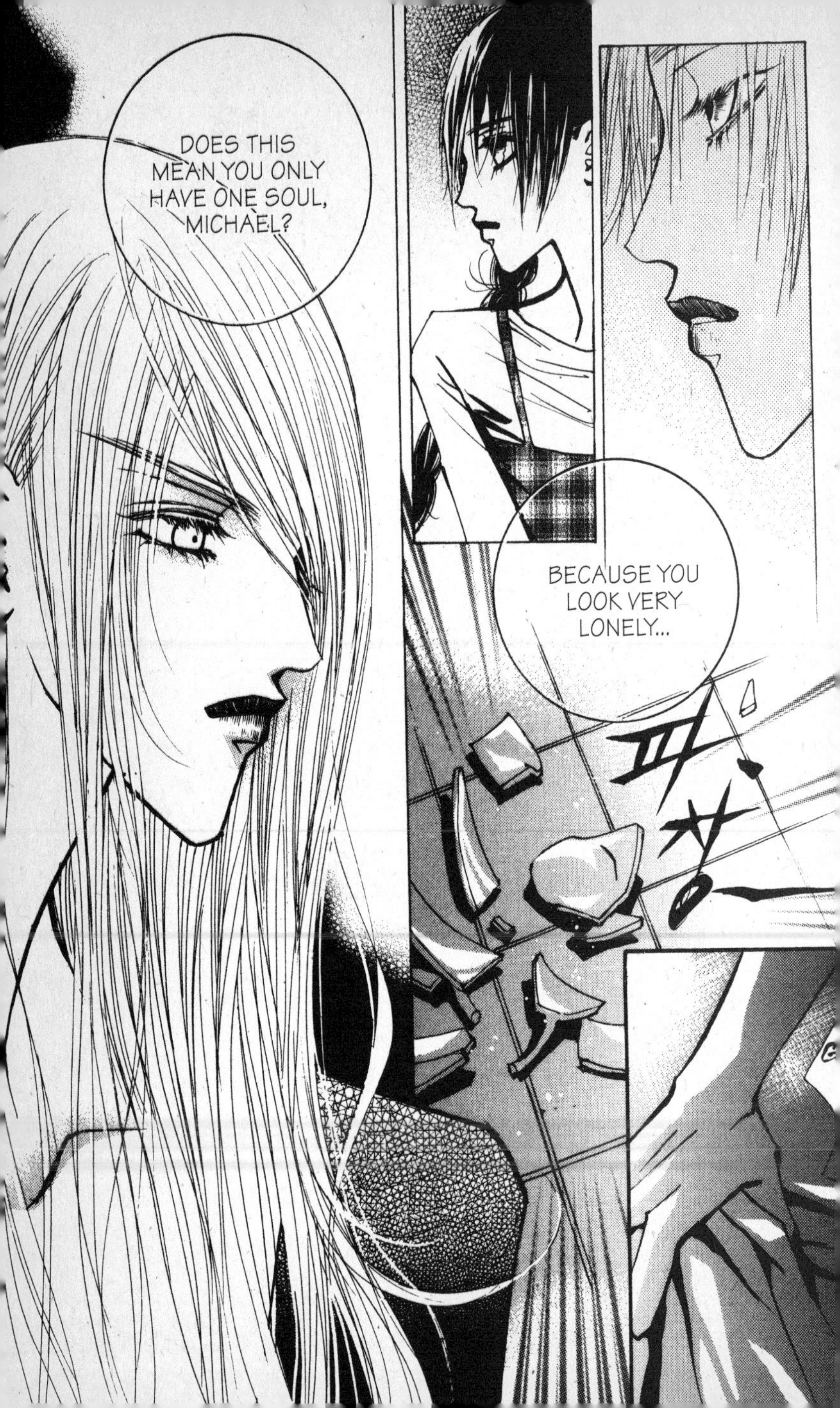
DOES THIS MEAN YOU ONLY HAVE ONE SOUL, MICHAEL?
BECAUSE YOU LOOK VERY LONELY...

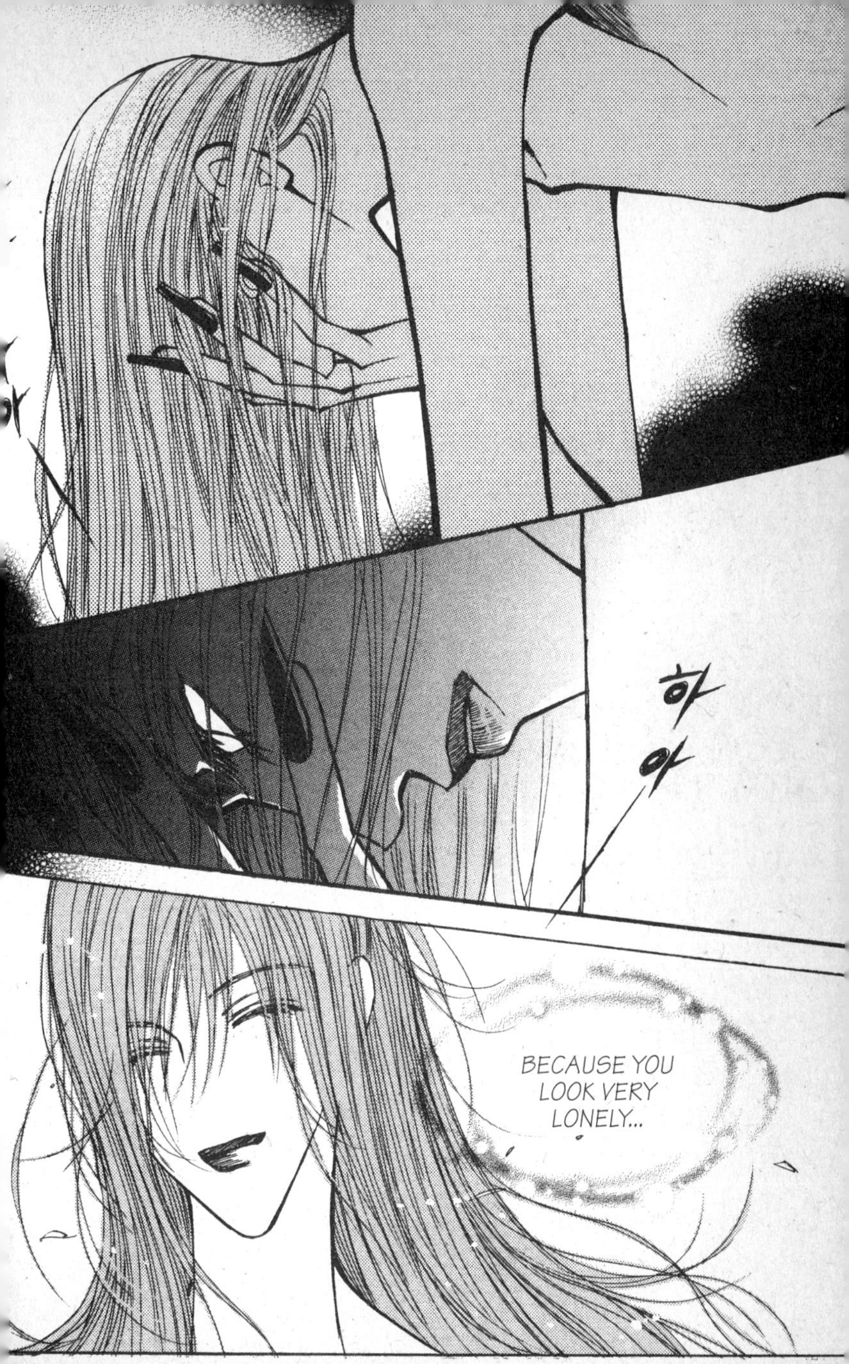
하아
BECAUSE YOU LOOK VERY LONELY...

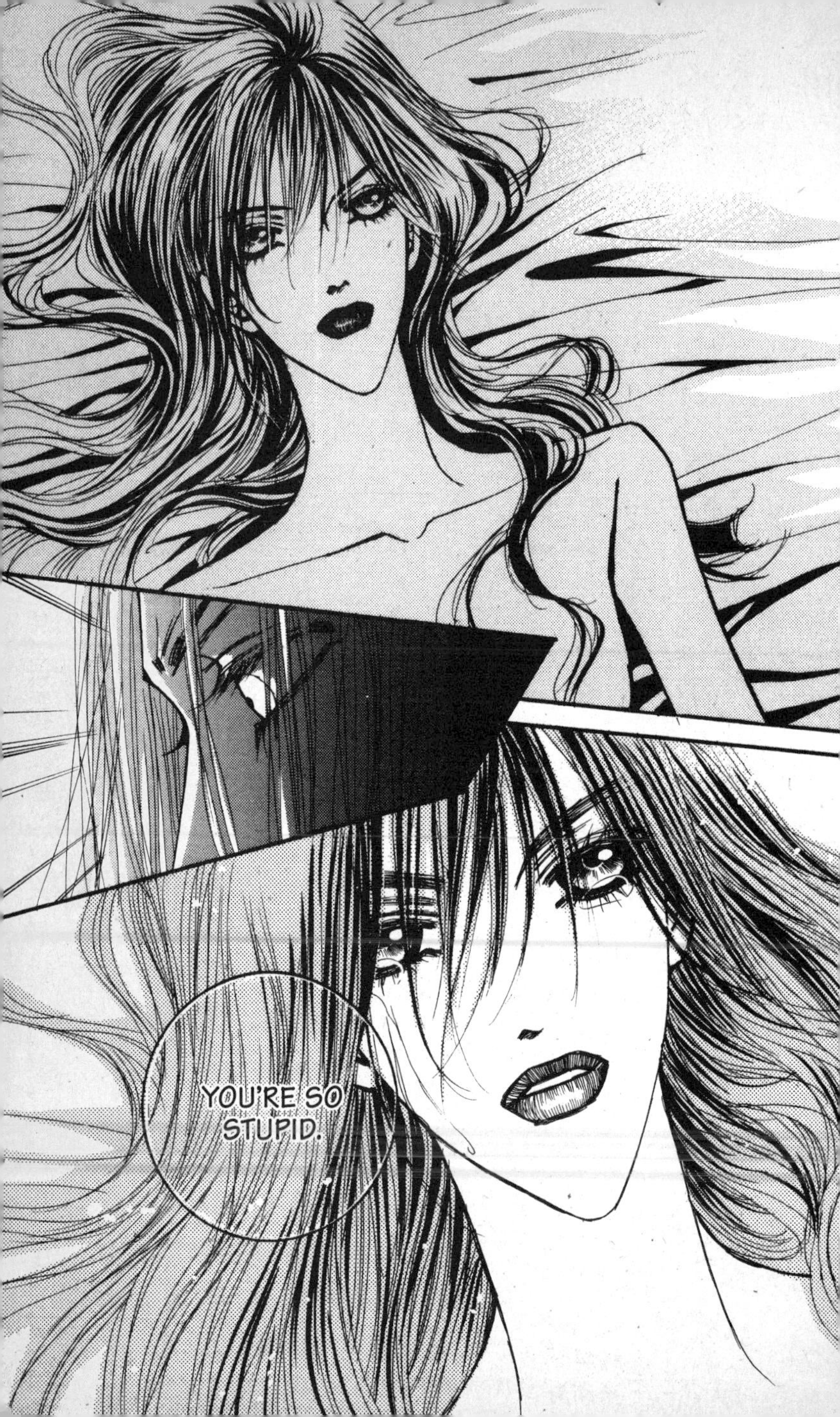
YOU'RE SO STUPID.

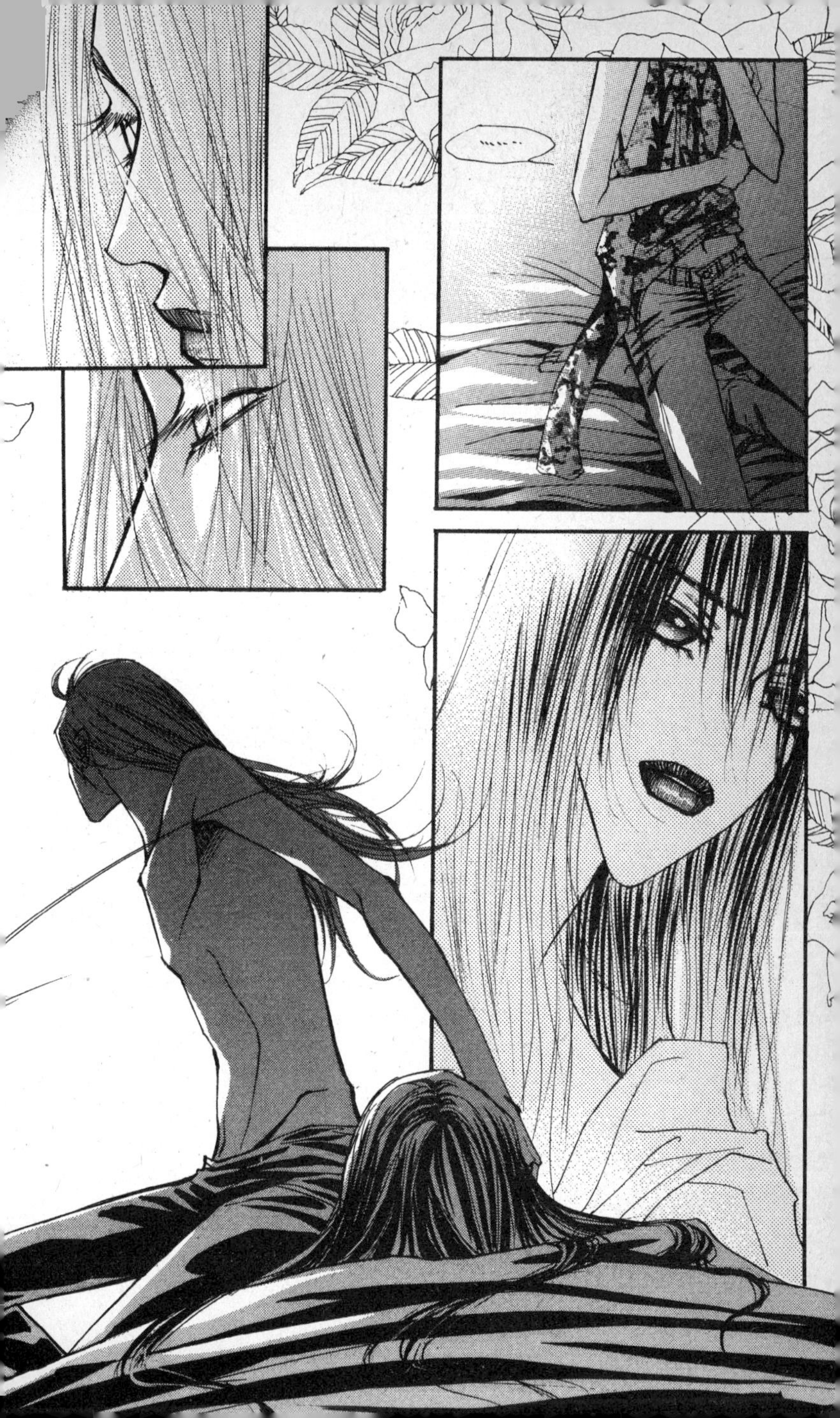
......

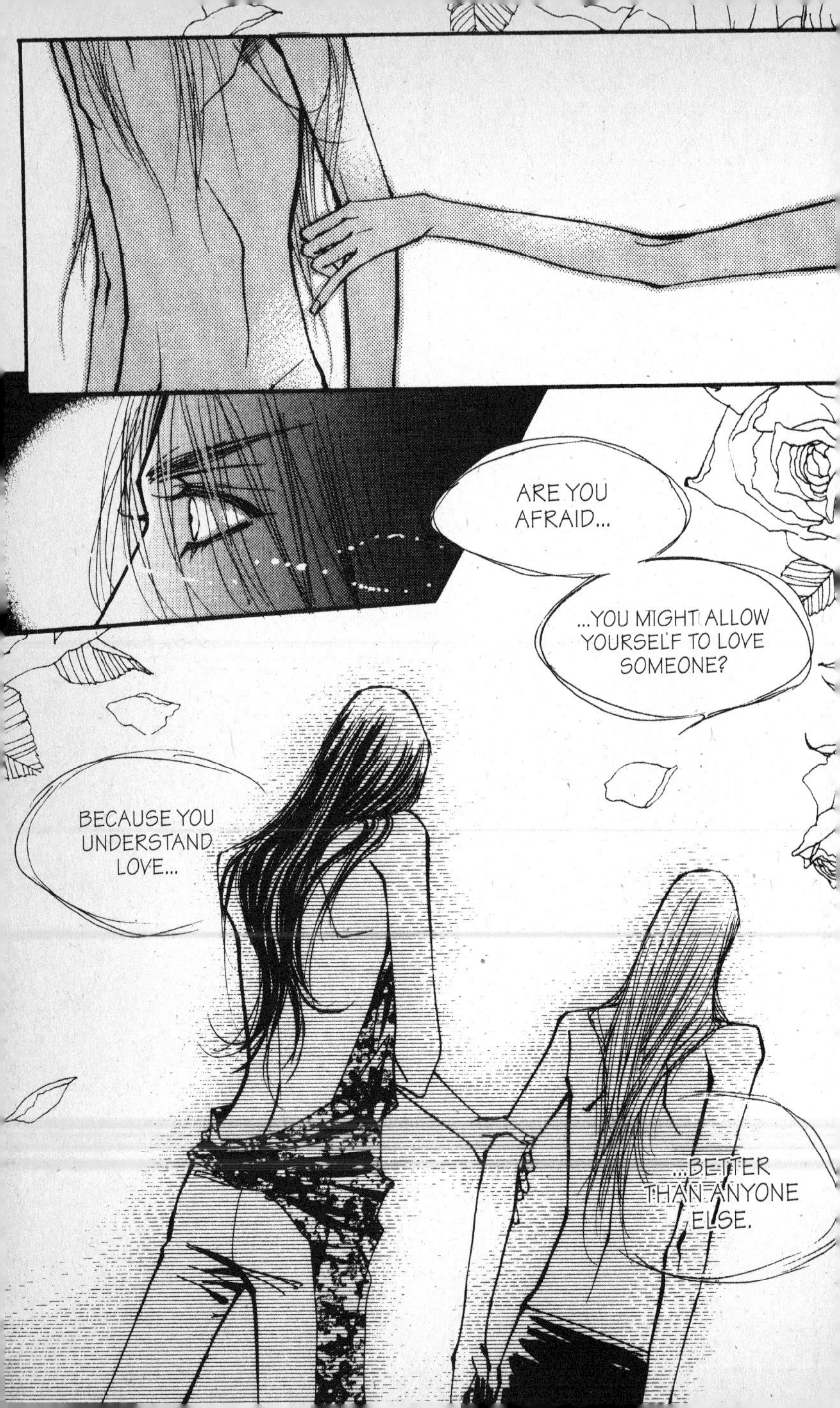
ARE YOU AFRAID...
...YOU MIGHT ALLOW YOURSELF TO LOVE SOMEONE?
BECAUSE YOU UNDERSTAND LOVE...
...BETTER THAN ANYONE ELSE.

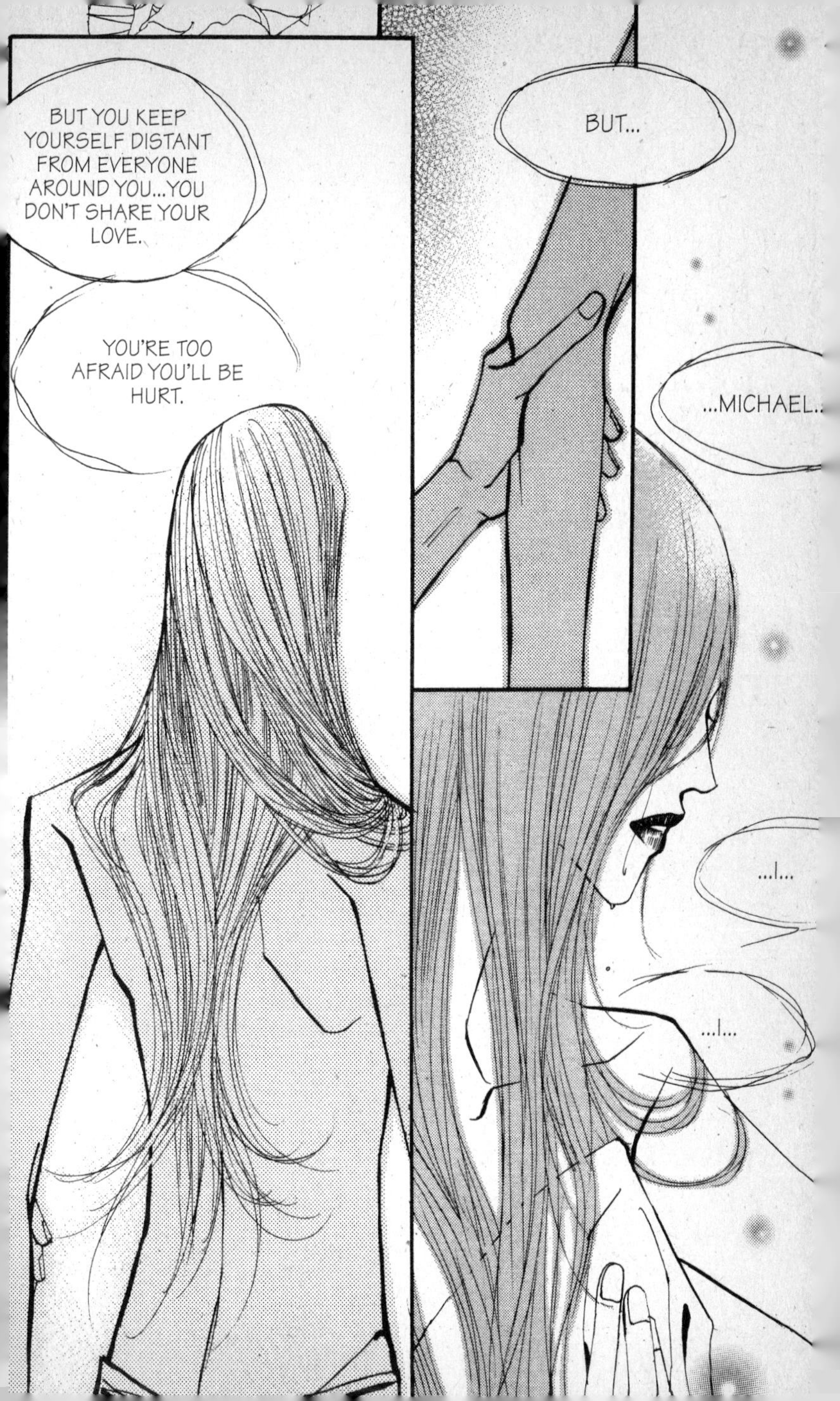
BUT YOU KEEP YOURSELF DISTANT FROM EVERYONE AROUND YOU...YOU DON'T SHARE YOUR LOVE.
YOU'RE TOO AFRAID YOU'LL BE HURT.
BUT...
...MICHAEL...
...I...
...I...

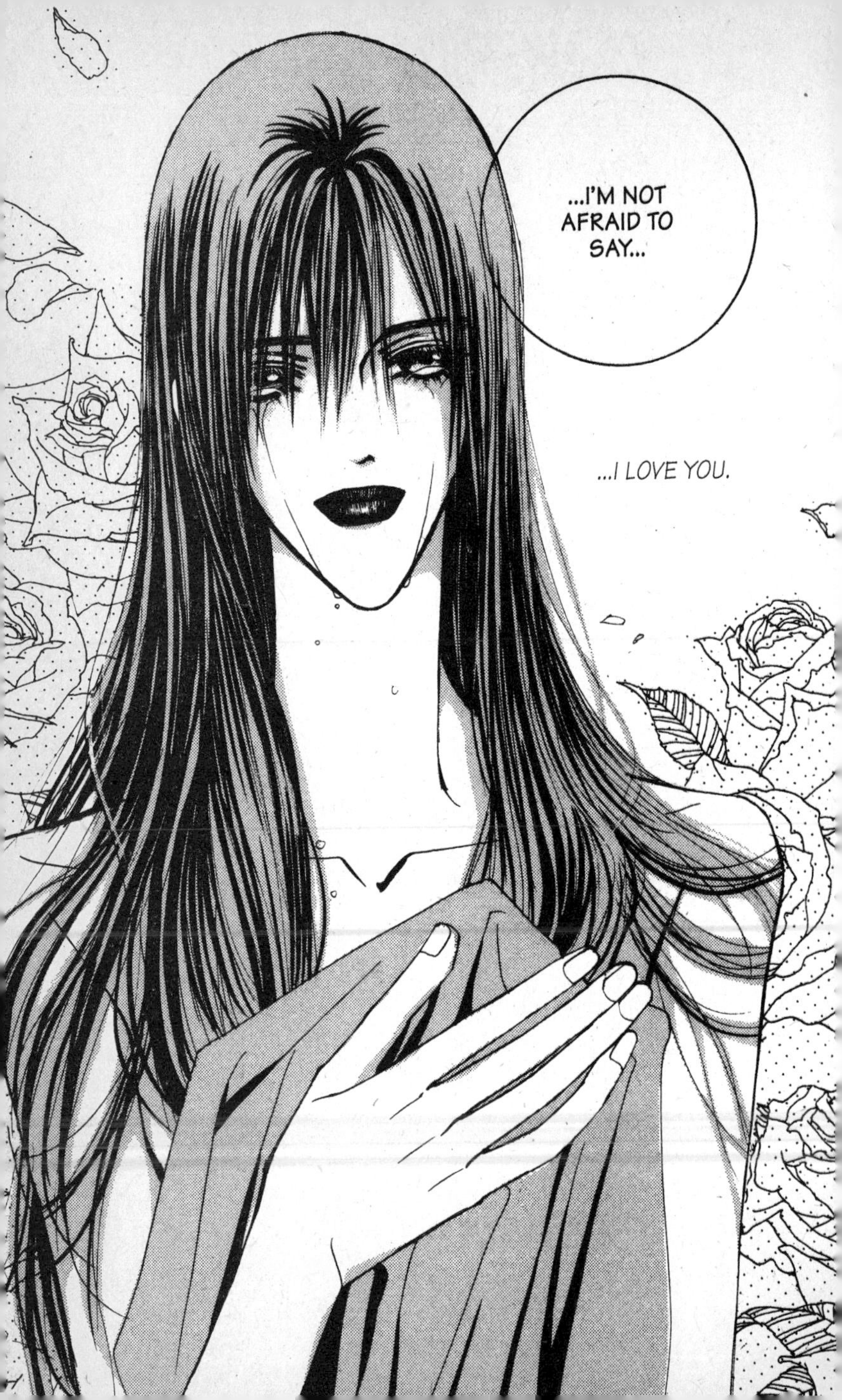
...I'M NOT AFRAID TO SAY...
...I LOVE YOU.

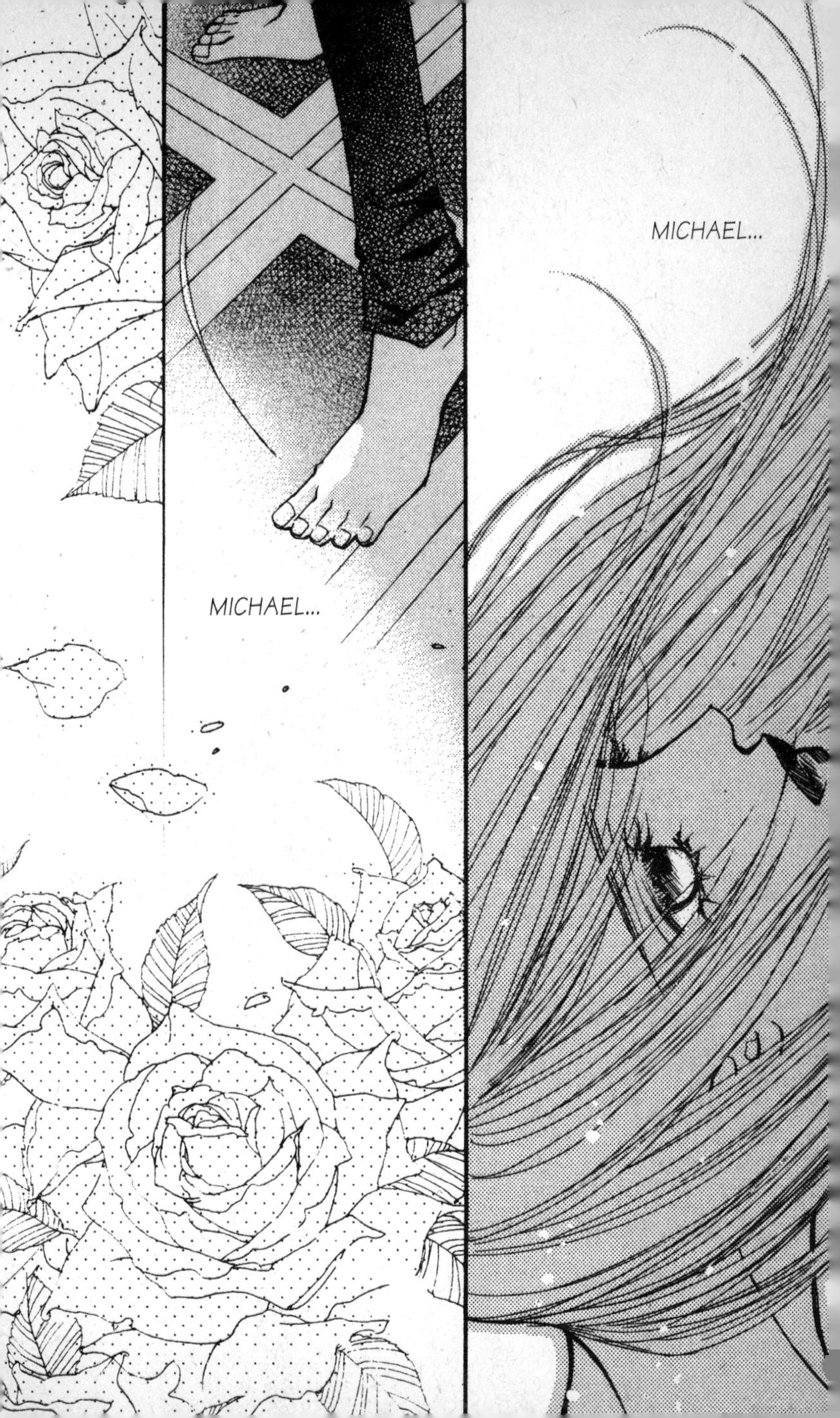
MICHAEL...
MICHAEL...

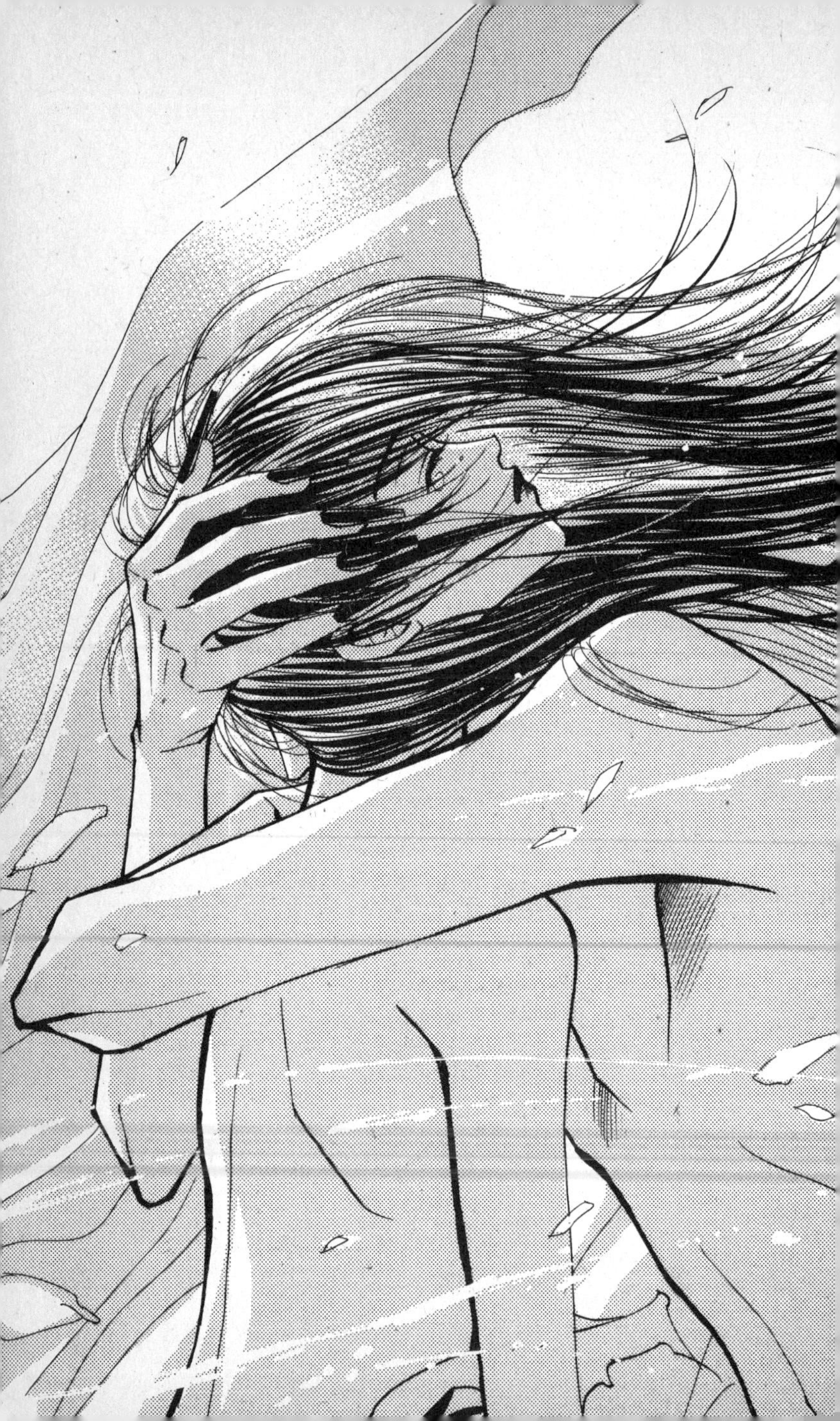

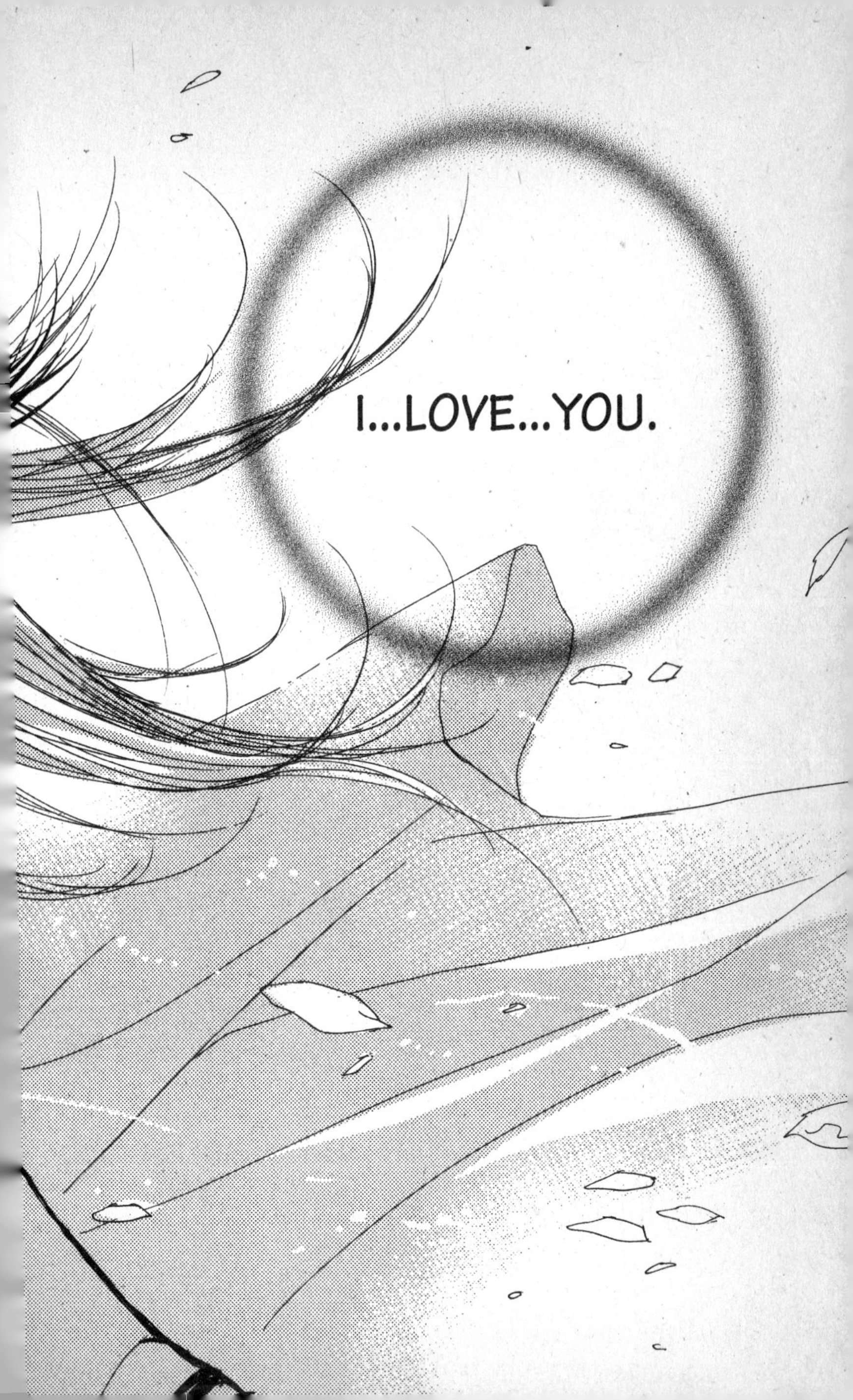
I...LOVE...YOU.

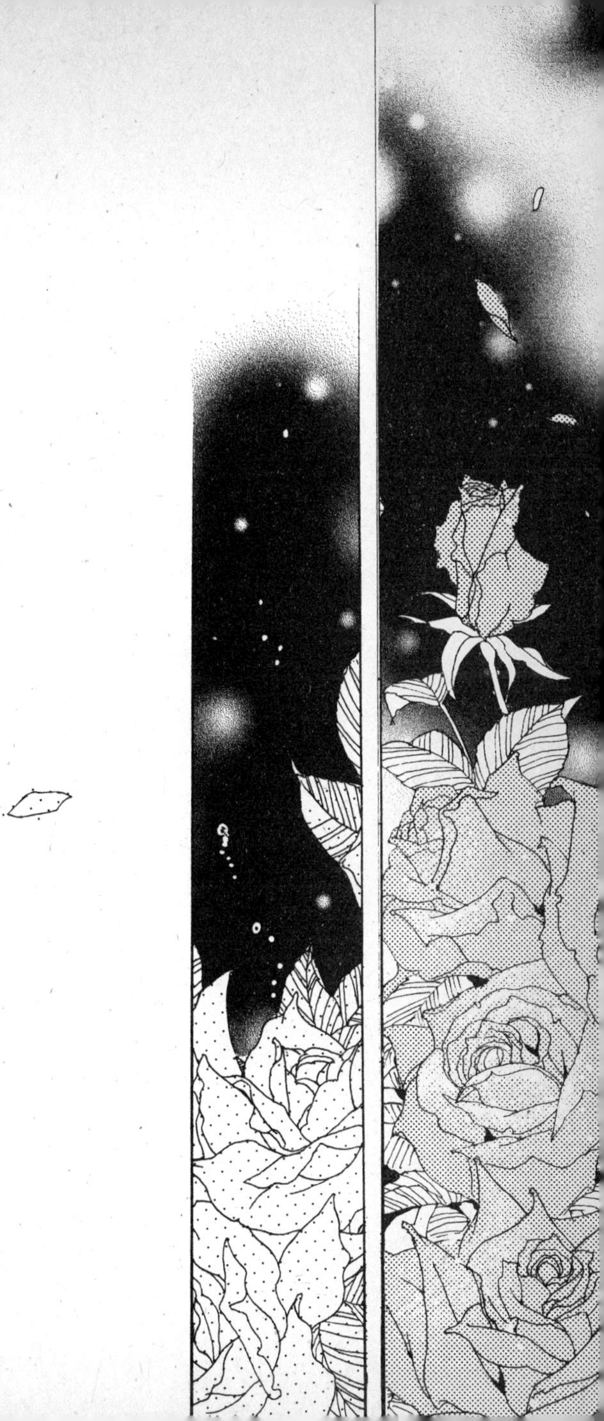

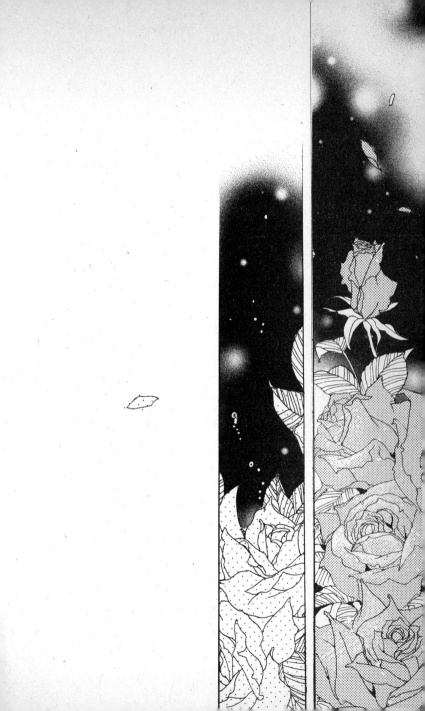

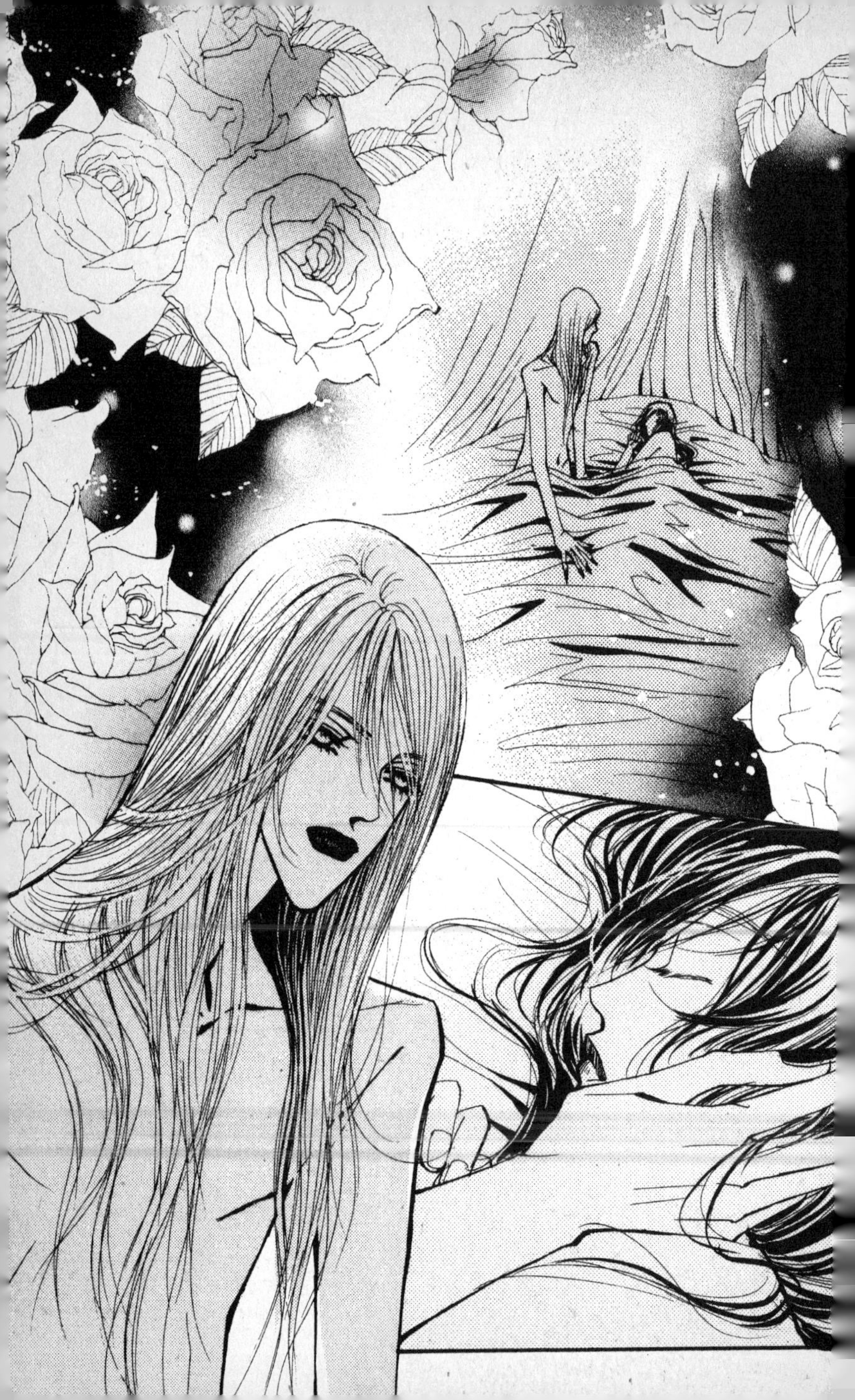

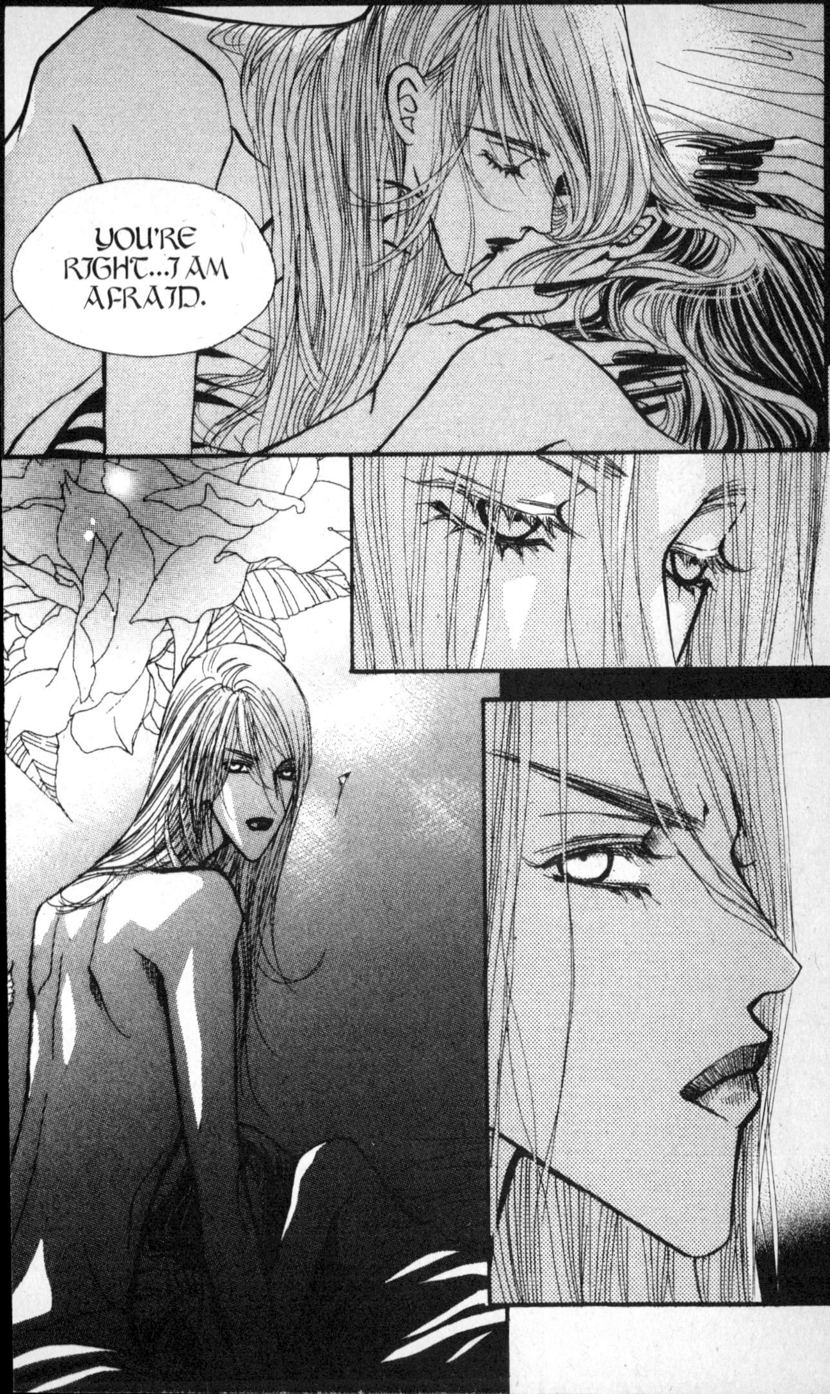
YOU'RE RIGHT...I AM AFRAID.

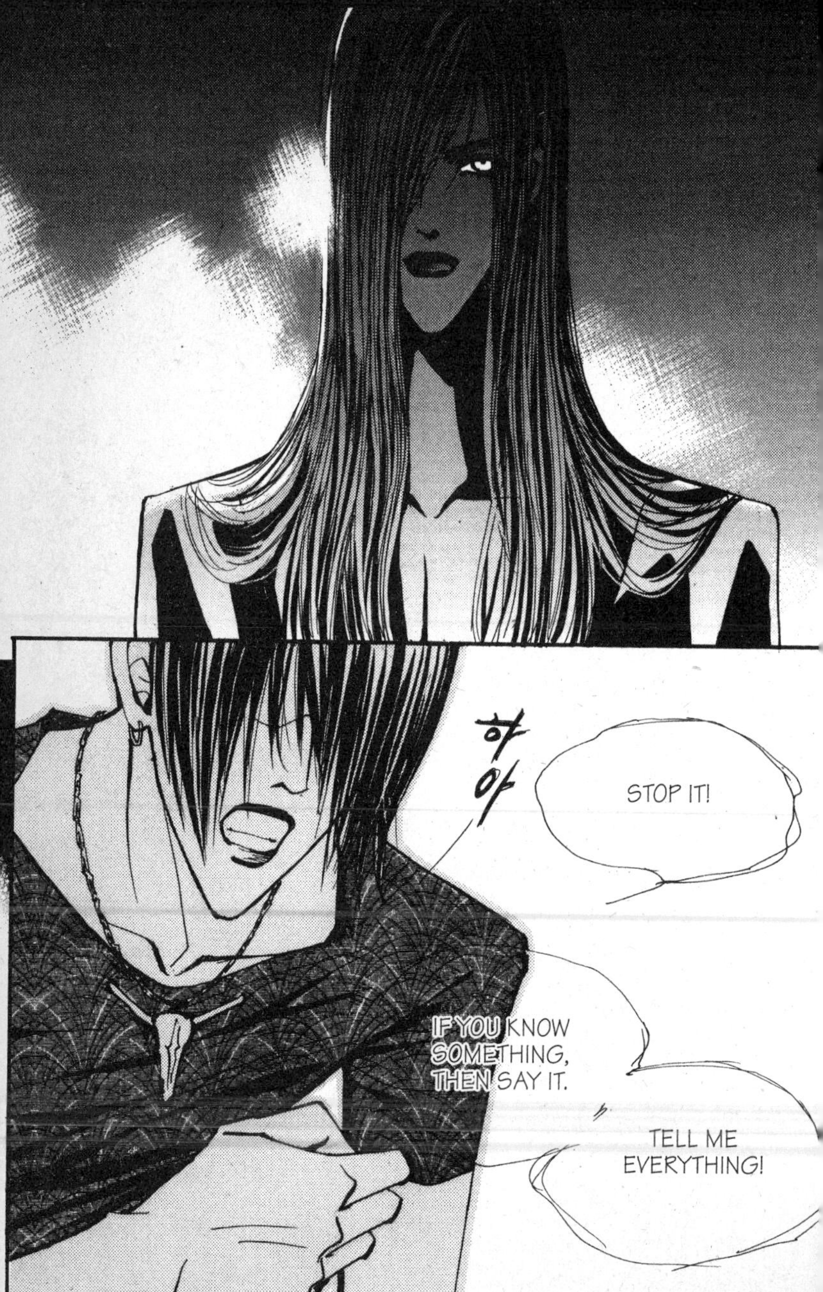
하아
STOP IT!
IF YOU KNOW SOMETHING, THEN SAY IT.
TELL ME EVERYTHING!

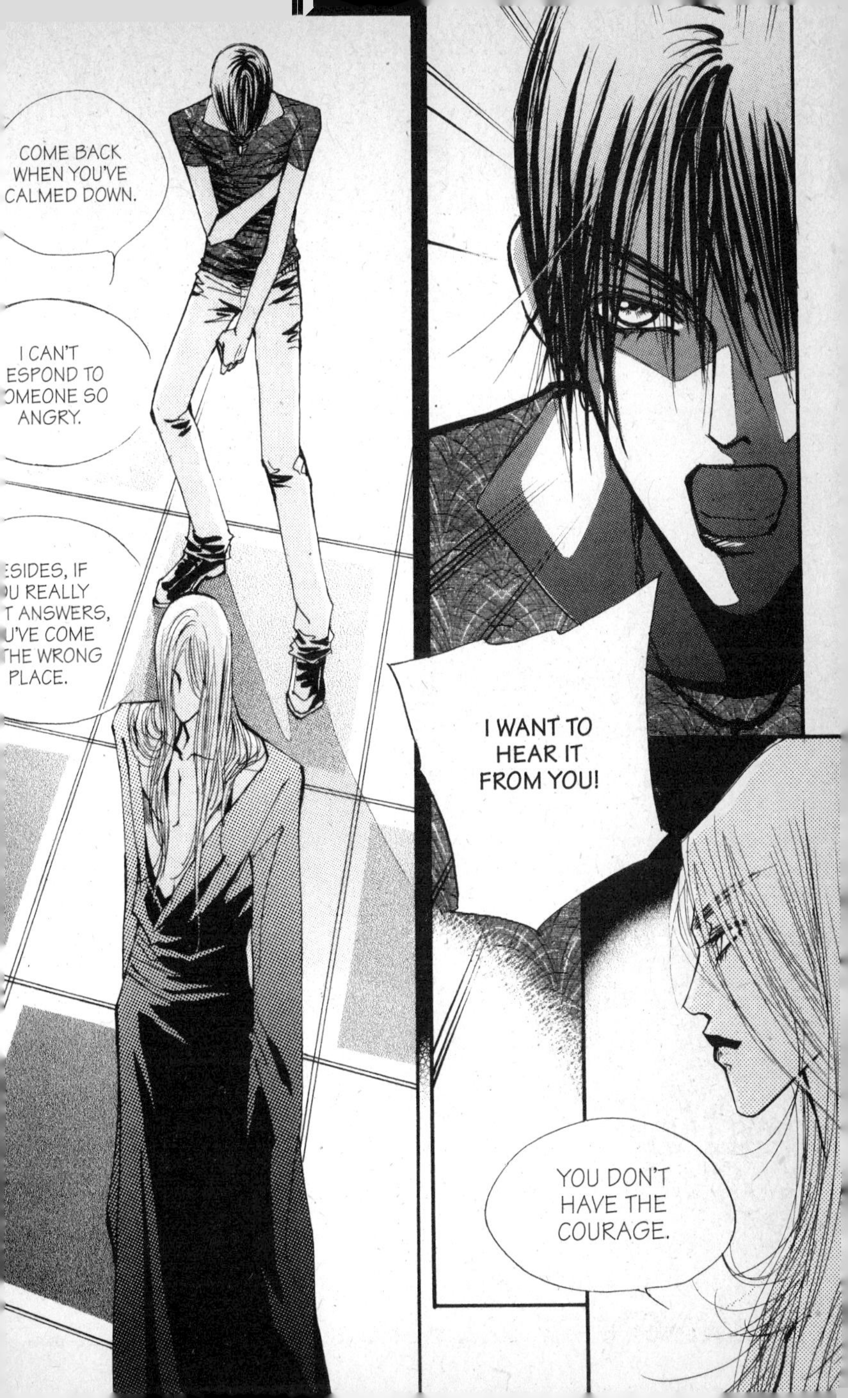
I WANT TO HEAR IT FROM YOU!
YOU DON'T HAVE THE COURAGE.
COME BACK WHEN YOU'VE CALMED DOWN.
I CAN'T ESPOND TO OMEONE SO ANGRY.
ESIDES, IF U REALLY T ANSWERS, U'VE COME THE WRONG PLACE.

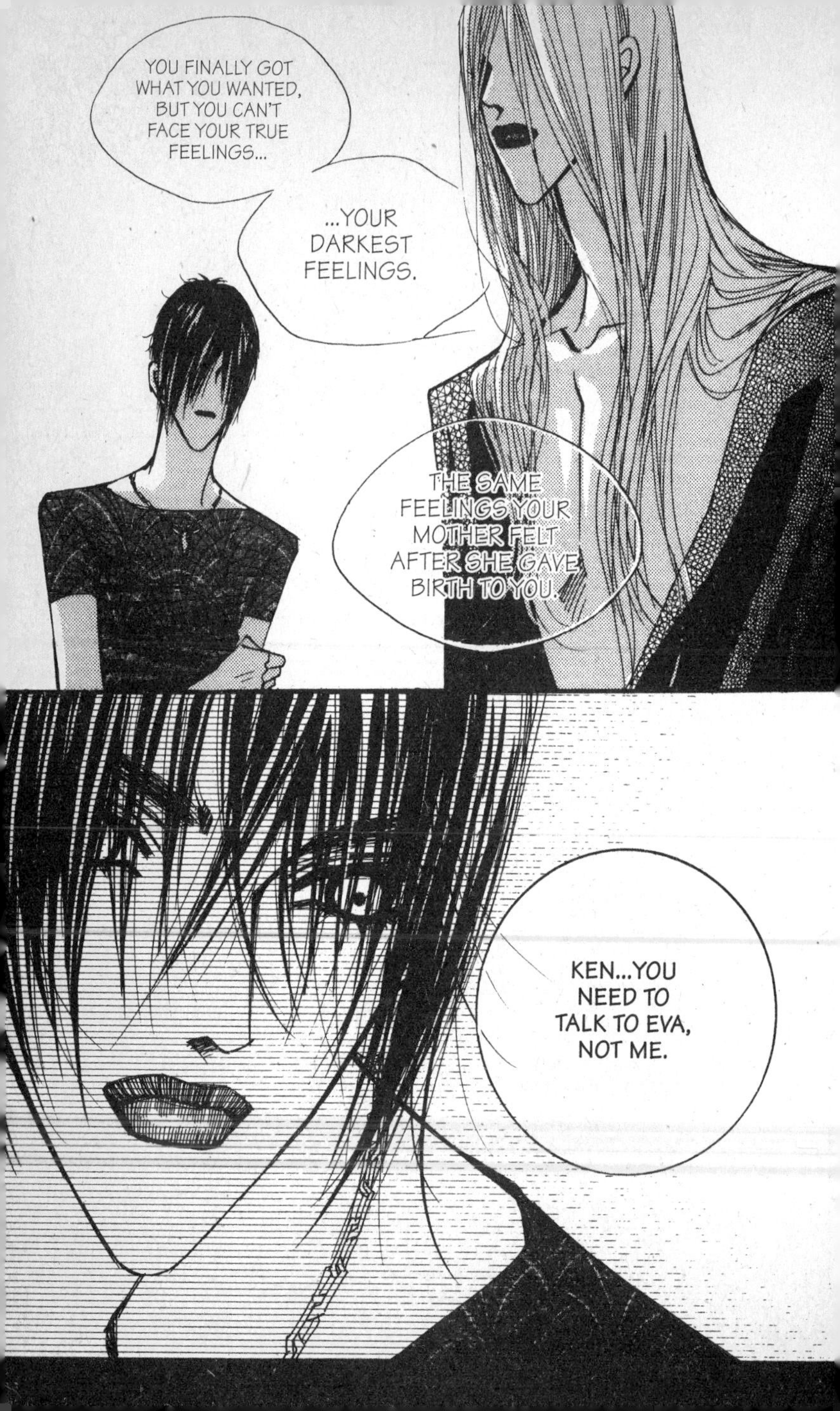
YOU FINALLY GOT WHAT YOU WANTED, BUT YOU CAN'T FACE YOUR TRUE FEELINGS...
...YOUR DARKEST FEELINGS.
THE SAME FEELINGS YOUR MOTHER FELT AFTER SHE GAVE BIRTH TO YOU.
KEN...YOU NEED TO TALK TO EVA, NOT ME.

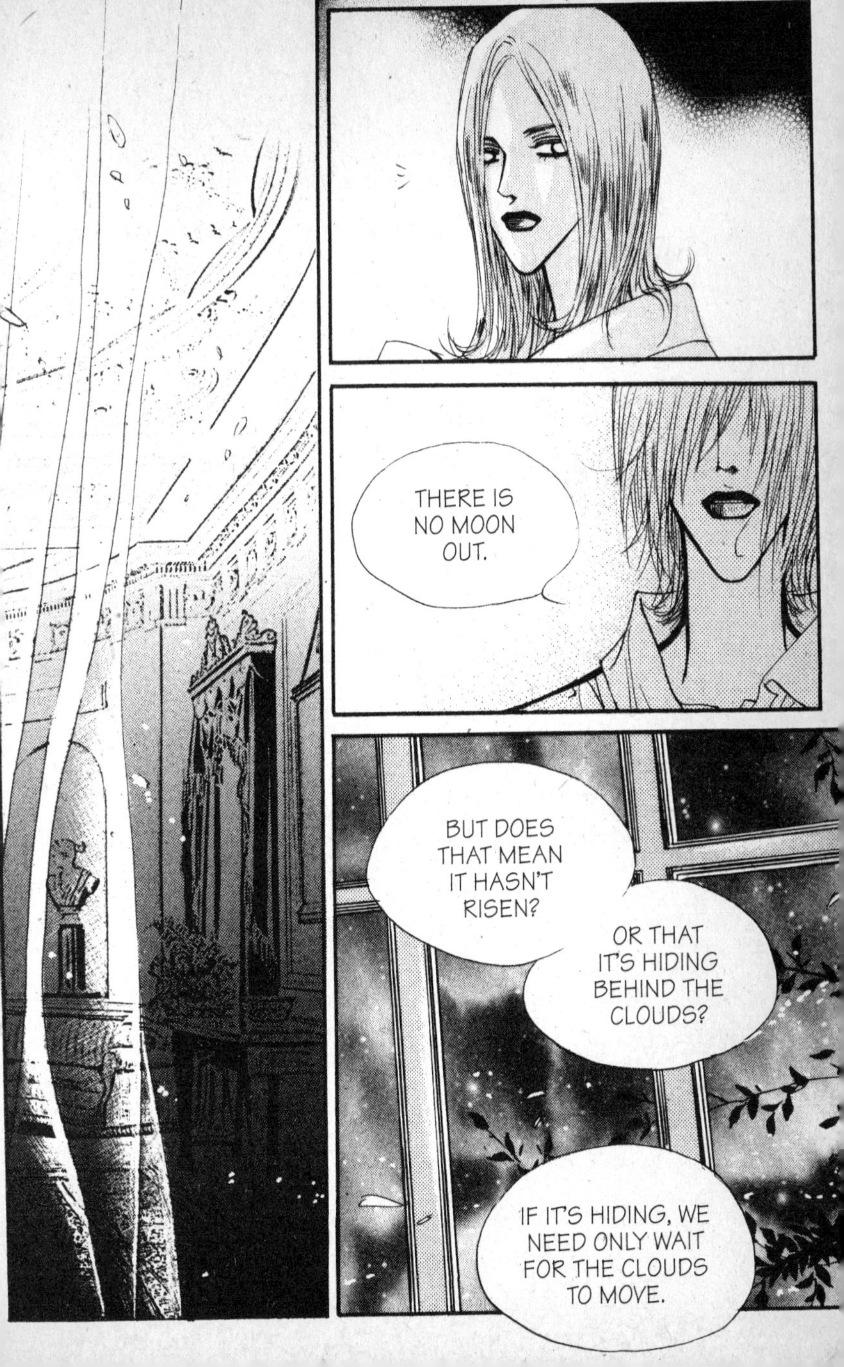
THERE IS NO MOON OUT.
BUT DOES THAT MEAN IT HASN'T RISEN?
OR THAT IT'S HIDING BEHIND THE CLOUDS?
IF IT'S HIDING, WE NEED ONLY WAIT FOR THE CLOUDS TO MOVE.

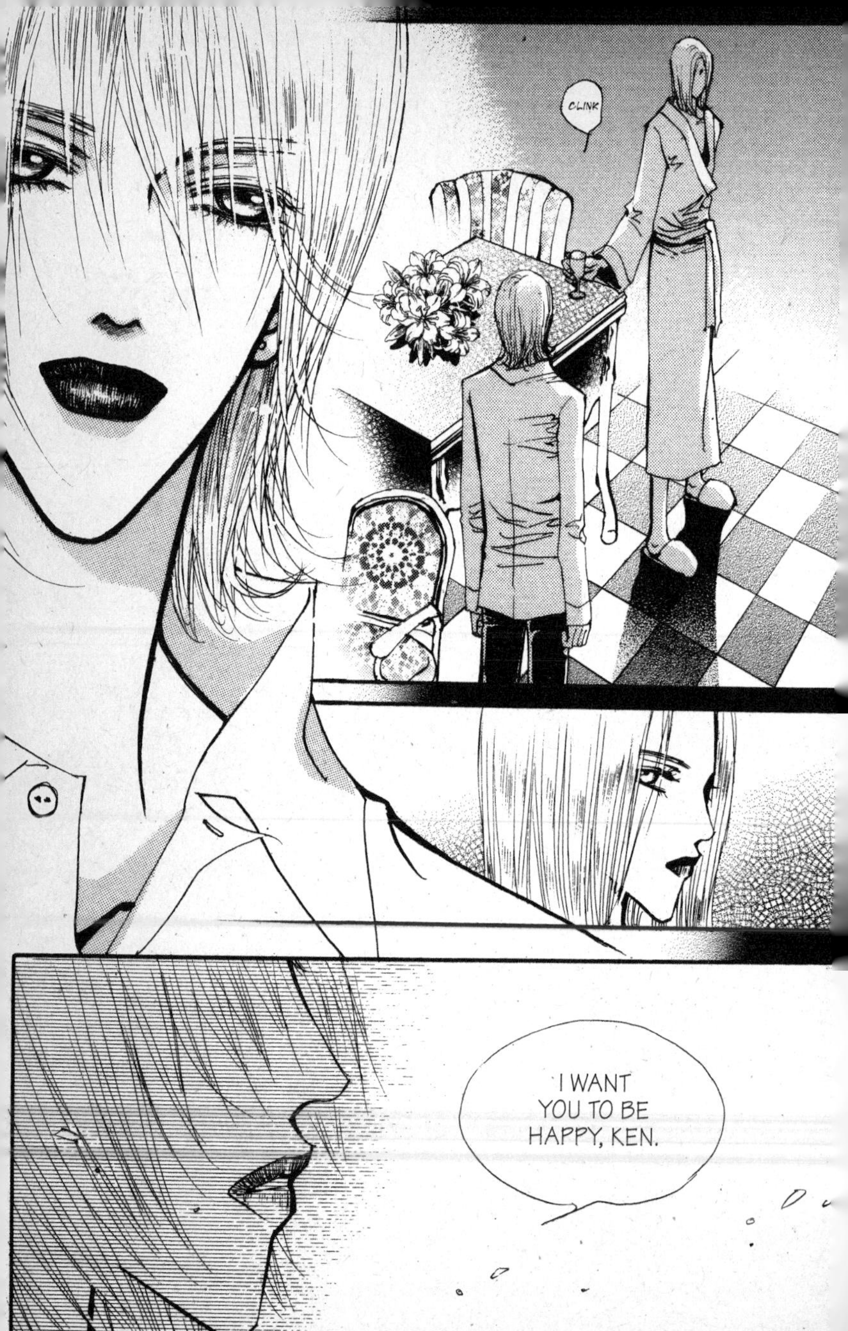
CLINK
I WANT YOU TO BE HAPPY, KEN.

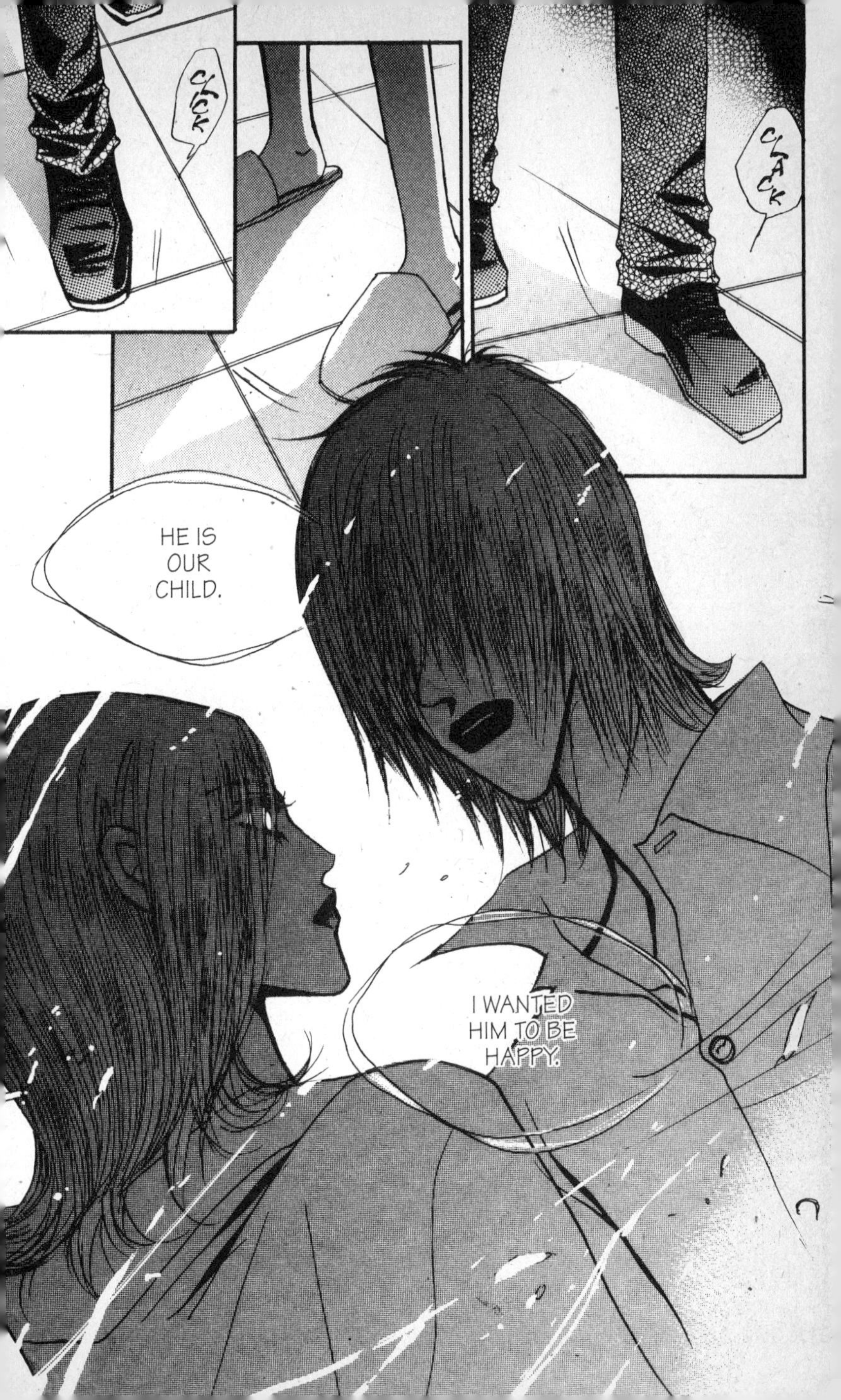
CLACK
CLACK
HE IS OUR CHILD.
I WANTED HIM TO BE HAPPY.

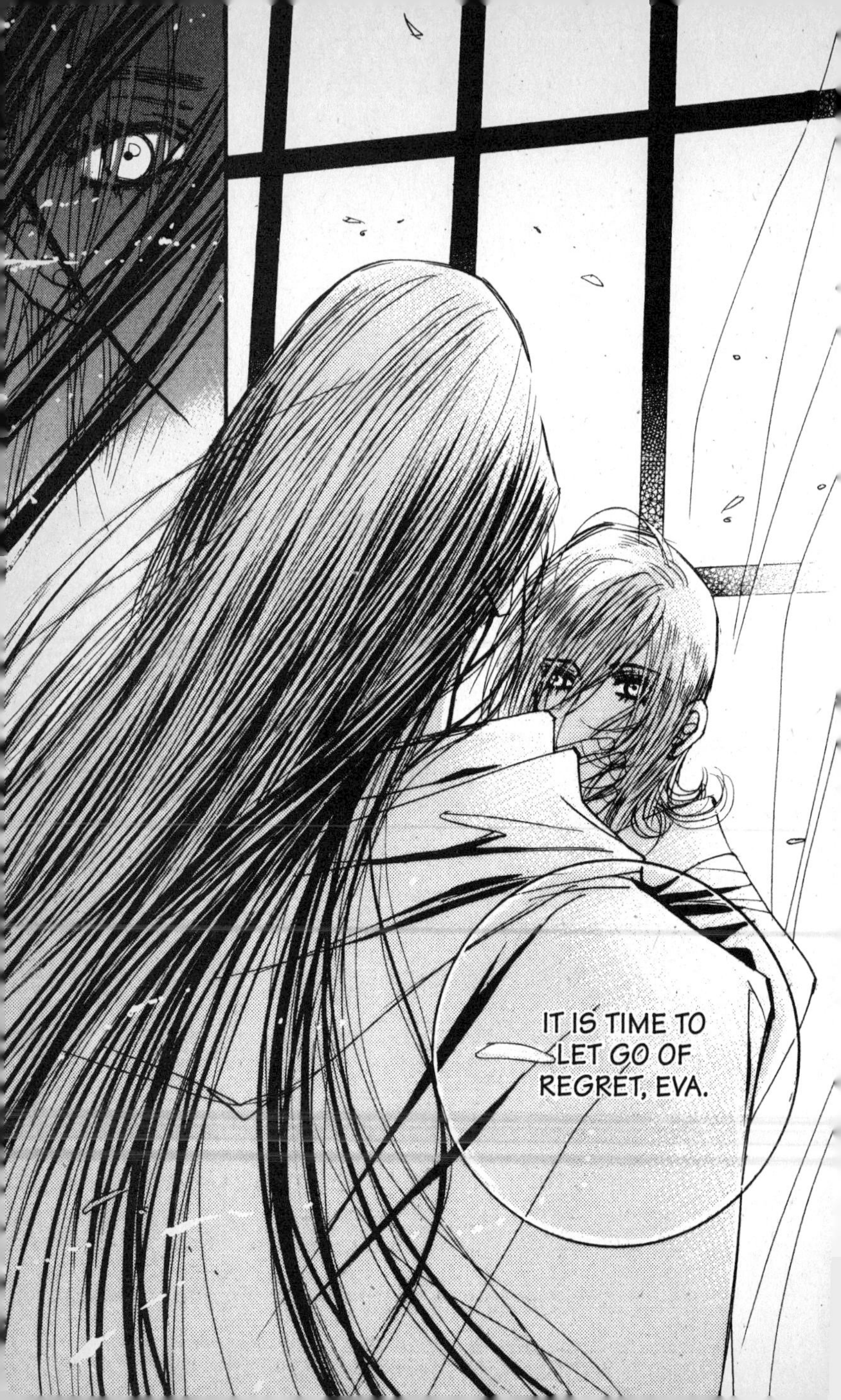
IT IS TIME TO LET GO OF REGRET, EVA.

'MODEL CHAPTER 6' THE END.

# MESSAGES FROM THE MAUSOLEUM

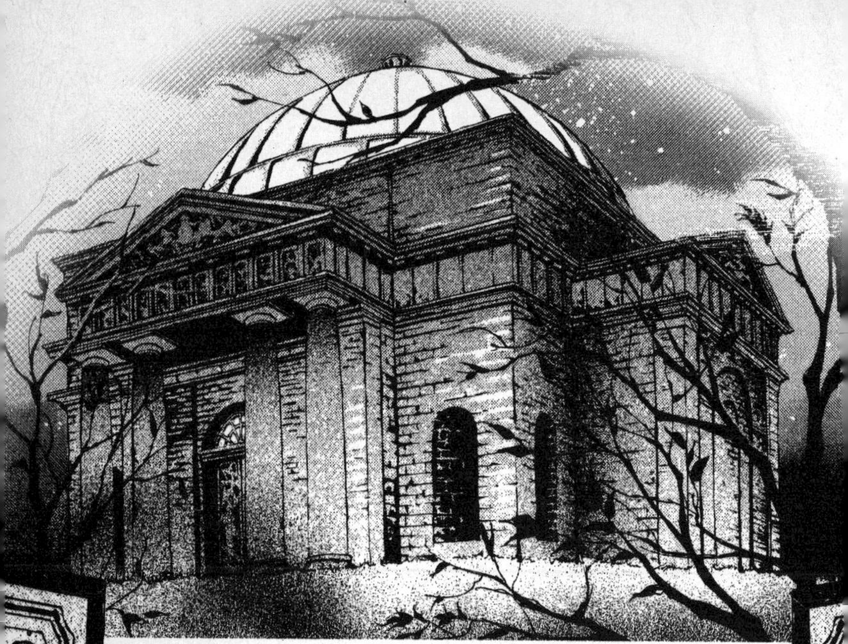

IT IS TIME FOR AN INEVITABLE PARTING OF COMPANY. JAE MUST RESOLVE HER FEELINGS FOR MICHAEL. KEN MUST DECIDE WHETHER TO RELEASE THE POWERS HIS FATHER PASSED ON TO HIM. EVA MUST DECIDE WHETHER TO JOIN HER LOST LOVE. AND KEN AND JAE KNOW THEY MUST LEAVE MICHAEL'S ESTATE. BUT MICHAEL HAS ONE MORE SURPRISE FOR JAE BEFORE SHE GOES... IN THE FINAL VOLUME OF MODEL.

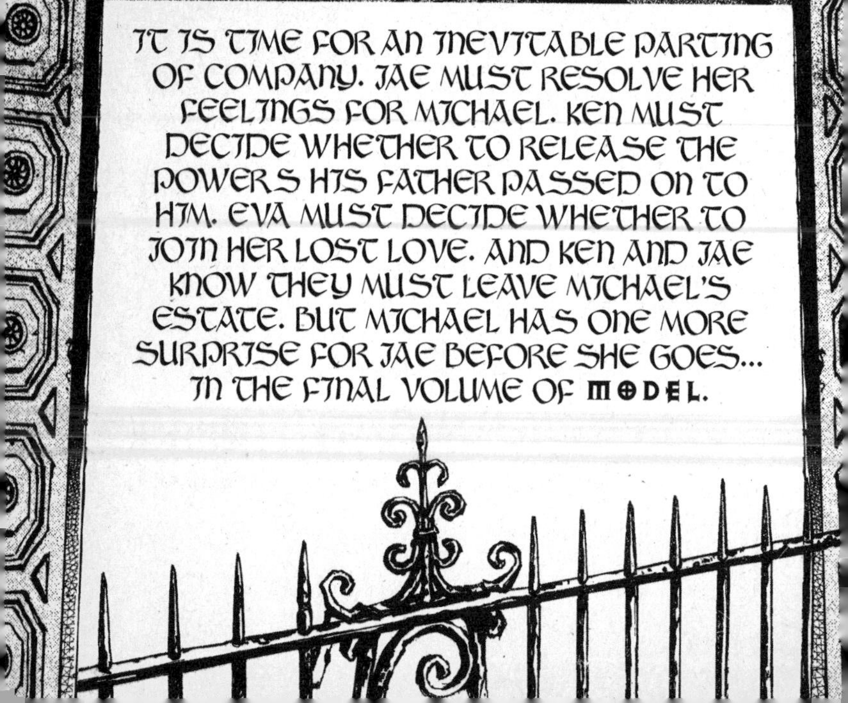

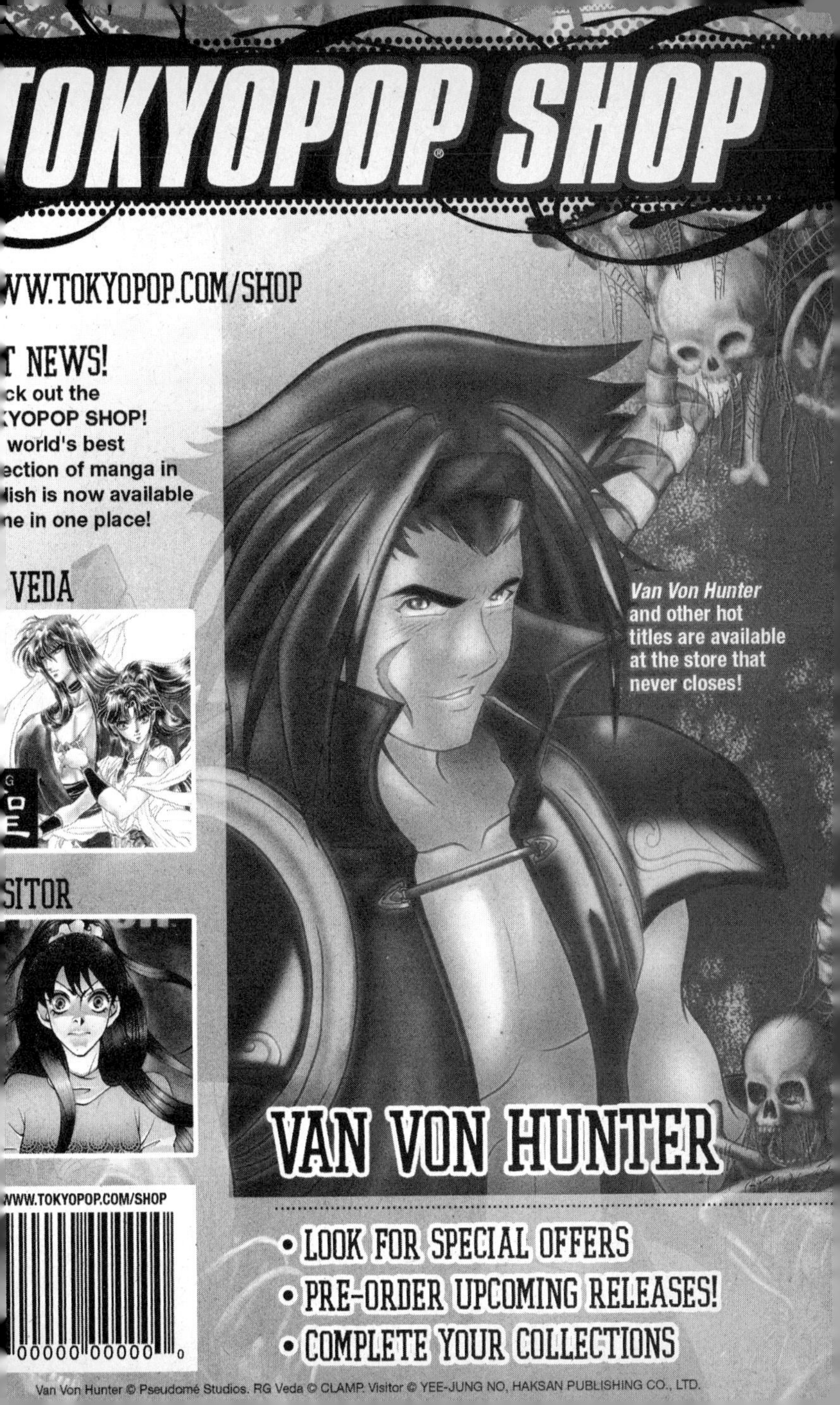

TOKYOPOP® SHOP
WWW.TOKYOPOP.COM/SHOP
T NEWS!
ck out the
YOPOP SHOP!
world's best
ection of manga in
lish is now available
ne in one place!
VEDA
SITOR
Van Von Hunter and other hot titles are available at the store that never closes!
VAN VON HUNTER
WWW.TOKYOPOP.COM/SHOP
00000 00000 0
• LOOK FOR SPECIAL OFFERS
• PRE-ORDER UPCOMING RELEASES!
• COMPLETE YOUR COLLECTIONS
Van Von Hunter © Pseudomé Studios. RG Veda © CLAMP. Visitor © YEE-JUNG NO, HAKSAN PUBLISHING CO., LTD.

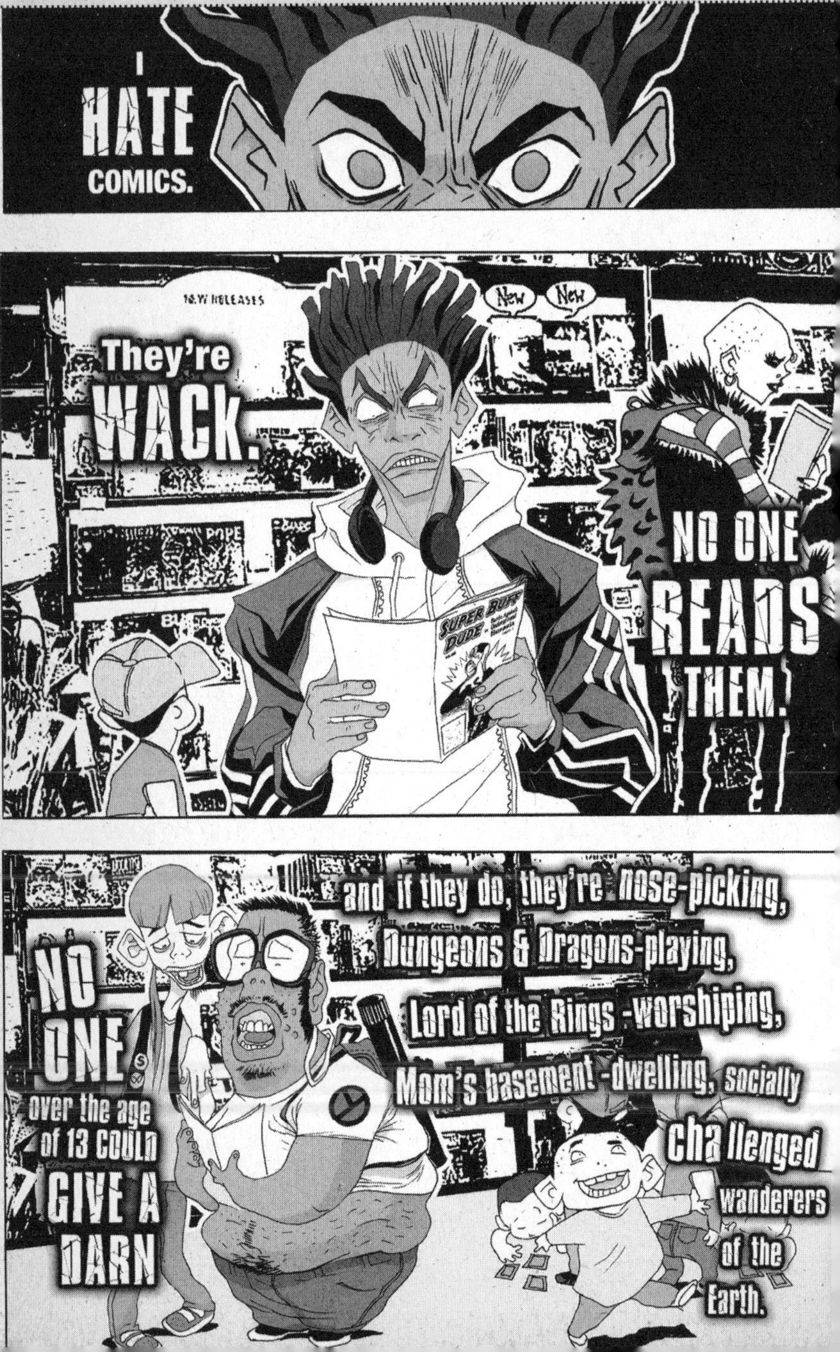
I HATE COMICS.
They're WACK.
New
New
SUPER BUFF DUDE
NO ONE READS THEM.
NO ONE over the age of 13 COULD GIVE A DARN
and if they do, they're nose-picking, Dungeons & Dragons-playing, Lord of the Rings-worshiping, Mom's basement-dwelling, socially challenged wanderers of the Earth.

## BLAZIN' BARRELS

Sting may look harmless and naïve, but he's really an excellent fighter and a wannab
bounty hunter in the futuristic Wild West. When he comes across a notice that advertise
a reward for the criminal outfit named Gold Romany, he decides that capturing th
all-girl gang of bad guys is his ticket to fame and fortune!

## MIN-SEO PARK HAS CREATED ONE WILD TUMBLEWEED TALE FILLED WITH ADVENTURE GALORE AND PLENTY OF SHOTGUN ACTION!

© MIN-SEO PARK, DAIWON C.I. Inc.

# EDITORS' PICKS

BY LEE VIN

BY MI-YOUNG NOH

## ONE

Like American Idol? Then you'll love *One*, an energetic manga that gives you a sneak peek into the pop music industry. Lee Vin, who also created *Crazy Love Story*, is an amazingly accomplished artist! The story centers on the boy band One, a powerhouse of good looks, hot moves, and raw talent. It also features Jenny You, a Britney-Avril hybrid who's shooting straight for the top. But fame always comes at a price—and their path to stardom is full of speed bumps and roadblocks. But no matter what happens, they keep on rockin'—and so does this manga!

~Julie Taylor, Sr. Editor

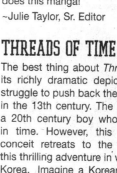

## THREADS OF TIME

The best thing about *Threads of Time* is its richly dramatic depiction of Korea's struggle to push back the Mongol Hordes in the 13th century. The plot focuses on a 20th century boy who ends up back in time. However, this science fiction conceit retreats to the background of this thrilling adventure in war-torn ancient Korea. Imagine a Korean general riding into battle with a battery of twelve men against two hundred Mongol warriors! Imagine back-stabbing politicians murdered in the clear of night. Imagine an entire village raped and slaughtered by Mongol hounds only to be avenged by a boy who just failed his high school science test.

~Luis Reyes, Editor

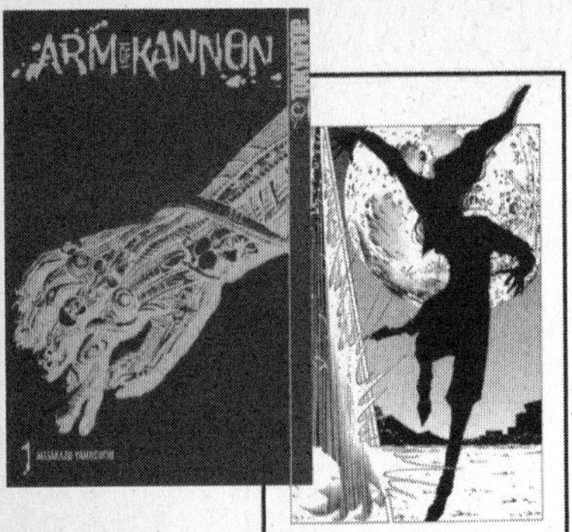
ARM OF KANNON

BY MASAKAZU YAMAGUCHI

## ARM OF KANNON

Good and evil race to find the mysterious Arm of Kannon—an ancient Buddhist relic that has the power to bring about the end of humanity. The relic has been locked in a sacred temple for thousands of years. However, it is released and its demonic form soon takes over the will of a young boy, Mao, who must now flee from the evil forces that hunt the arm for control of its awesome power. This sexually charged action/horror story, traversing a vast landscape of demons, swordsmen, magicians, street gangs and government super-soldiers, will make the hairs on the back of your neck stand on edge.

~Rob Valois, Editor

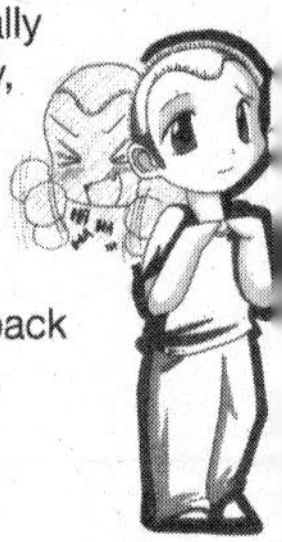

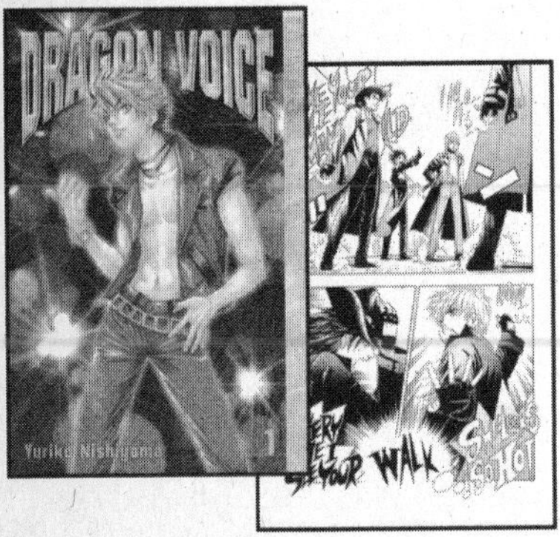
DRAGON VOICE
Yuriko Nishiyama
1

BY YURIKO NISHIYAMA

## DRAGON VOICE

I have to admit that Yuriko Nishiyama's *Dragon Voice* was not at all what I was expecting. As more a fan of action/adventure stories like *Samurai Deeper Kyo*, the singing and dancing hijinks of a Japanese boy-band seemed hardly like my cup of tea. But upon proofreading Volume 3 for fellow editor Lillian Diaz-Przybyl, I found *Dragon Voice* to be one of my favorites! Rin and his fellow Beatmen dazzle their way past all obstacles—rival boy-band Privee, theme-park prima donnas, or TV production pitfalls—and do it with style! This book is one of the most fun reads I've had in a long time!

~Aaron Suhr, Sr. Editor

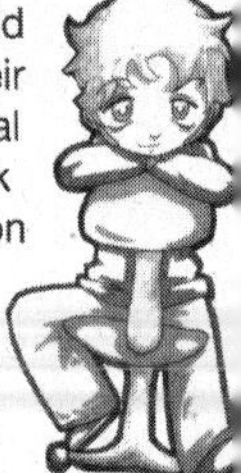

## SORCERER HUNTERS
### BY RAY OMISHI & SATORU AKAHORI

On the Spooner Continent, powerless commoners spend each day terrorized by merciless evil sorcérers. Big Mama has had enough, and she sends out an elite group of warriors—the Sorcerer Hunters: Carrot, Chocolat, Tira Misu, Gateau, and Marron.

The manga that inspired the hit anime!

**OT** OLDER TEEN AGE 16+

© Satoru Akahori/Ray Omishi

## iD_eNTITY
### BY HEE-JOON SON & YOON-KYUNG KIM

From Hee-Joon Son, creator of TOKYOPOP's *PhD: Phantasy Degree*!

Roto, Boromid and Ah-dol are a fellowship of friends who are terrific gamers. When Roto finds an ID card for the LostSaga online game with "Yureka" printed on it, he hacks into the game using "Yureka" as his identity. The trouble is, Yureka already has an identity all her own...

**T** TEEN AGE 13+

© Hee-Joon Son & Yoon-Kyung Kim, HAKSAN PUBLISHING CO., LTD.

From the creator of *Vampire Princess Miyu*!

## SHAOLIN SISTERS: REBORN
### BY TOSHIKI HIRANO & NARUMI KAKINOUCHI

Beginning with *Juline* and followed in *Shaolin Sisters*, *Shaolin Sisters: Reborn* gives the epic saga of Juline and her two sisters a modern spin. When an enigmatic masked man saves Julin Misumi from a mysterious bird woman, she learns her dreams of an age martial arts point to one thing...

**T** TEEN AGE 13+

© Narumi Kakinouchi

## The breakout manga that put CLAMP on the map!

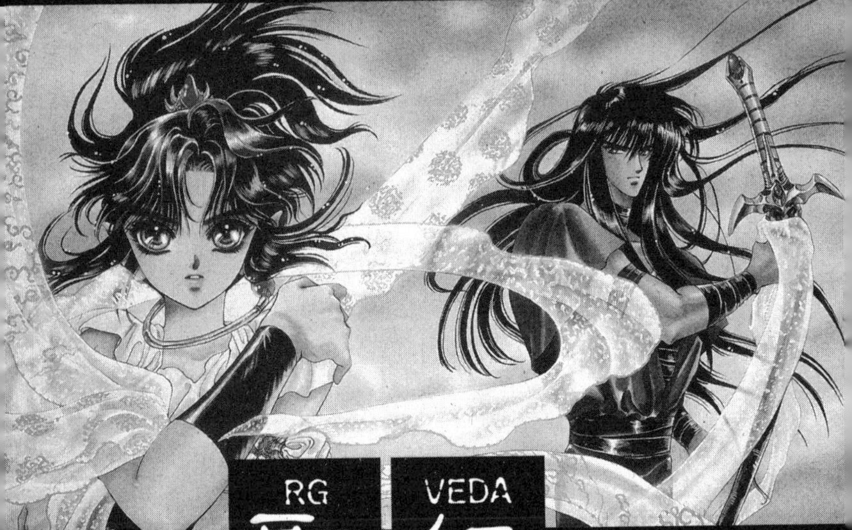

# RG VEDA 聖伝

At the dawn of creation, the world was a beautiful and tranquil place. When a powerful warlord rebelled against the king, a violent, chaotic age began.... Three hundred years later, a group of noble warriors embarks on a quest to find the prophesied Six Stars before the land is torn apart!

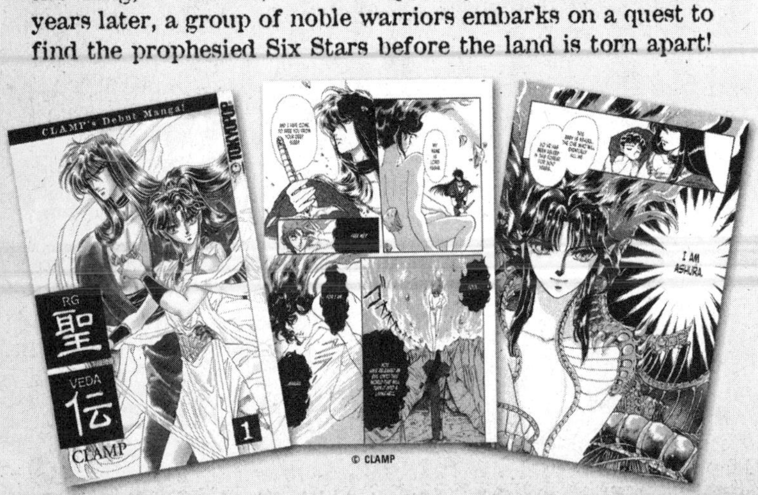
CLAMP's Debut Manga!
TOKYOPOP
RG
聖
VEDA
伝
1
CLAMP
I AM ASHURA.

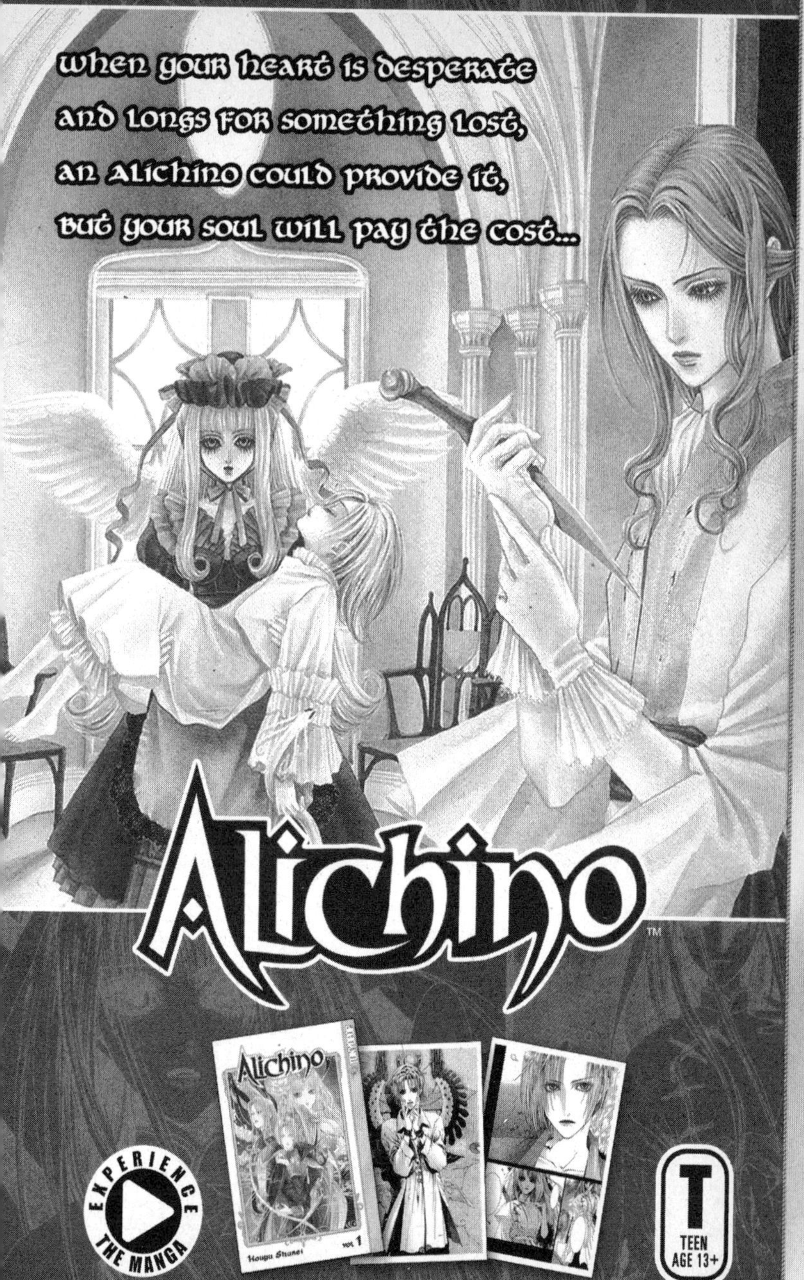
WHEN YOUR HEART IS DESPERATE
AND LONGS FOR SOMETHING LOST,
AN ALICHINO COULD PROVIDE IT,
BUT YOUR SOUL WILL PAY THE COST...
Alichino™
EXPERIENCE THE MANGA
T TEEN AGE 13+
www.TOKYOPOP.com/alichino
©1998 Kouyu Shurei. ©2005 TOKYOPOP Inc.
www.TOKYOPOP.com
TOKYOPOP

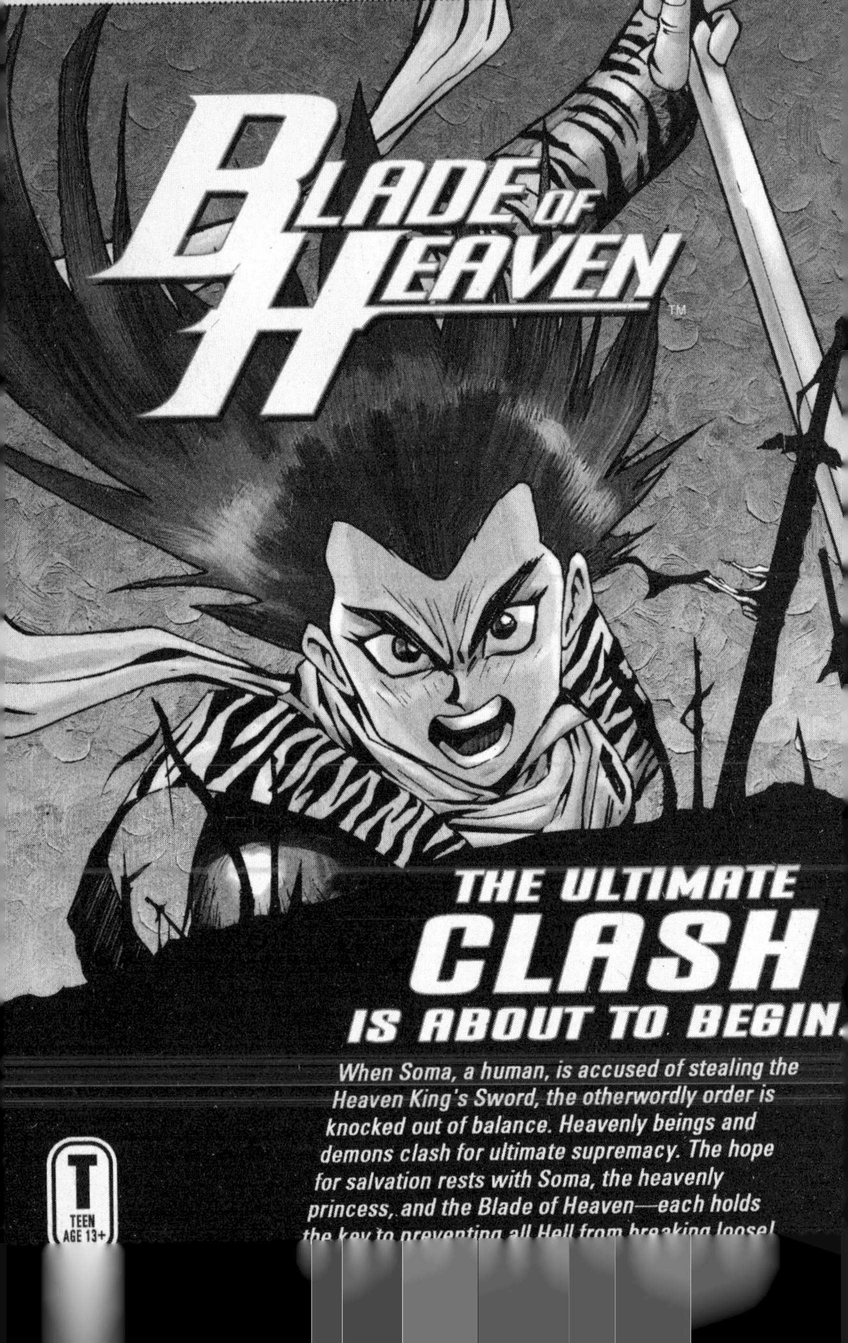
BLADE OF HEAVEN™
THE ULTIMATE CLASH IS ABOUT TO BEGIN.
When Soma, a human, is accused of stealing the Heaven King's Sword, the otherwordly order is knocked out of balance. Heavenly beings and demons clash for ultimate supremacy. The hope for salvation rests with Soma, the heavenly princess, and the Blade of Heaven—each holds the key to preventing all Hell from breaking loose!
T
TEEN AGE 13+